# Twin Star Exorcists

ONMYOJI

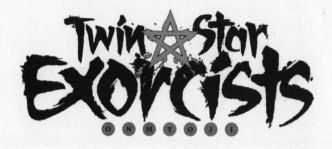

# Twin★Star Exorcists

ONMYOJI

5

STORY & ART
YOSHIAKI SUKENO

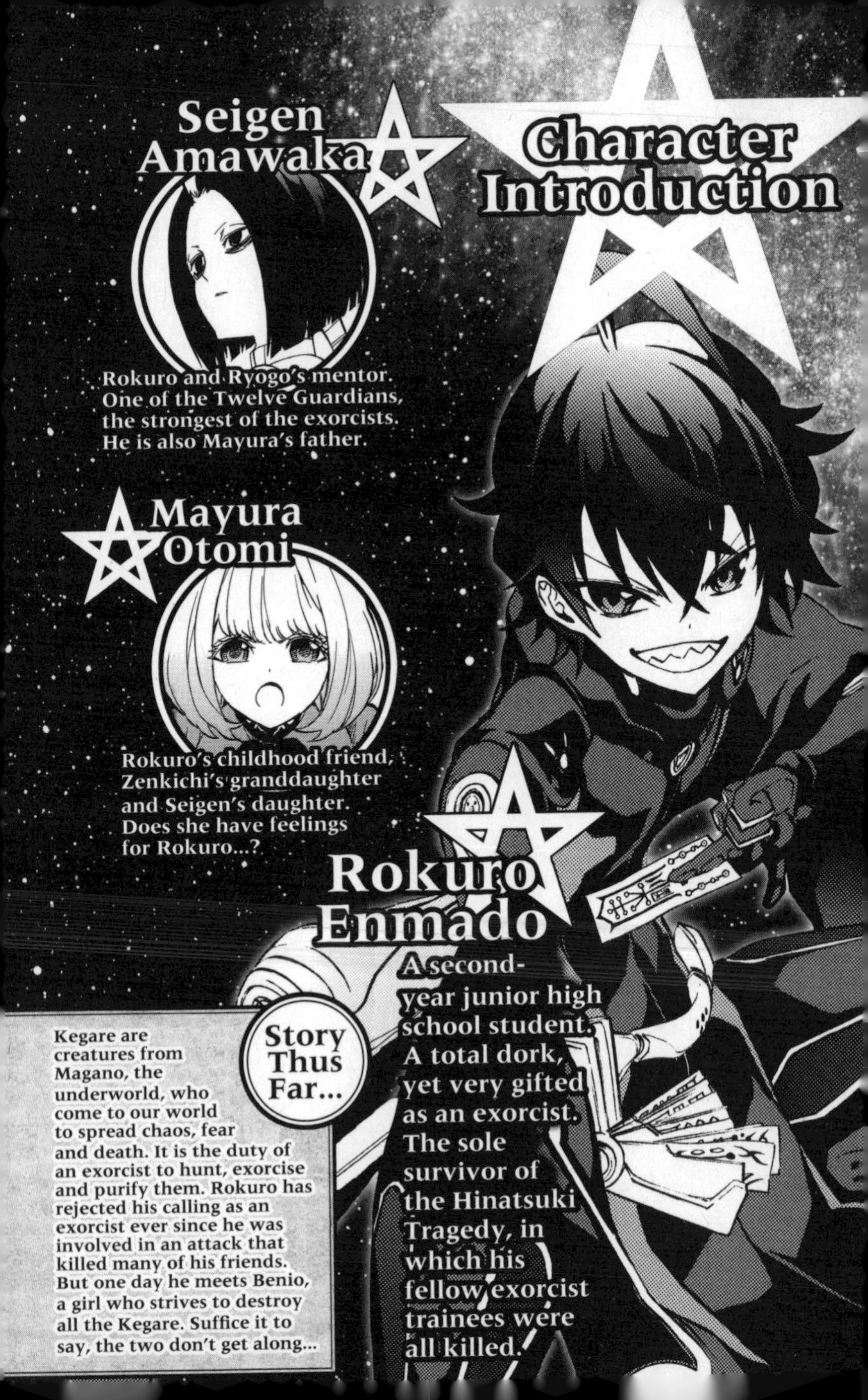
Character Introduction
Seigen Amawaka
Rokuro and Ryogo's mentor. One of the Twelve Guardians, the strongest of the exorcists. He is also Mayura's father.
Mayura Otomi
Rokuro's childhood friend, Zenkichi's granddaughter and Seigen's daughter. Does she have feelings for Rokuro...?
Rokuro Enmado
A second-year junior high school student. A total dork, yet very gifted as an exorcist. The sole survivor of the Hinatsuki Tragedy, in which his fellow exorcist trainees were all killed.
Story Thus Far...
Kegare are creatures from Magano, the underworld, who come to our world to spread chaos, fear and death. It is the duty of an exorcist to hunt, exorcise and purify them. Rokuro has rejected his calling as an exorcist ever since he was involved in an attack that killed many of his friends. But one day he meets Benio, a girl who strives to destroy all the Kegare. Suffice it to say, the two don't get along...

## Ryogo Nagitsuji

Ryogo grew up with Rokuro and is like a big brother to him. He has great faith in Rokuro's exorcism talent.

## Yuto Ijika

Benio's twin brother, who was thought to have died in the Hinatsuki Tragedy. In fact, he was the mastermind behind it, and has learned to use the Kegare Curse for his own sinister purposes.

## Kamui

A high-ranking Kegare, called a Basara, who has the ability to communicate in the human tongue. Kamui killed Benio's parents.

## Arima Tsuchimikado

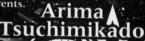

The chief exorcist of the Association of Unified Exorcists, which presides over all exorcists.

## Benio Adashino

The daughter of a prestigious family of skilled exorcists. She is an excellent exorcist, especially excelling in speed. Her favorite food is ohagi dumplings.

Chief Exorcist Arima tells Rokuro and Benio that they are prophesied to become the Twin Star Exorcists, marry each other and produce the Prophesied Child, the strongest exorcist of all. The two teenagers are not at all keen on getting together, but they grudgingly grow to respect each other's exorcism skills as they fight together against the Kegare.

Now Benio's twin brother Yuto has reappeared in Magano, the world of the Kegare. When Rokuro and Benio confront him there, Yuto destroys Benio's legs. Kamui, the Basara who killed their parents, offers to replace Benio's legs using the Kegare Curse. Benio accepts. And now the Twin Stars continue their deadly battle...

# Twin ★ Star Exorcists

O N M Y O J I

## EXORCISMS

**5**

**ONMYOJI** have worked for the Imperial Court since the Heian era. In addition to exorcising evil spirits, as civil servants they performed a variety of roles, including advising nobles by foretelling the future, creating the calendar, observing the movements of the stars, measuring time…

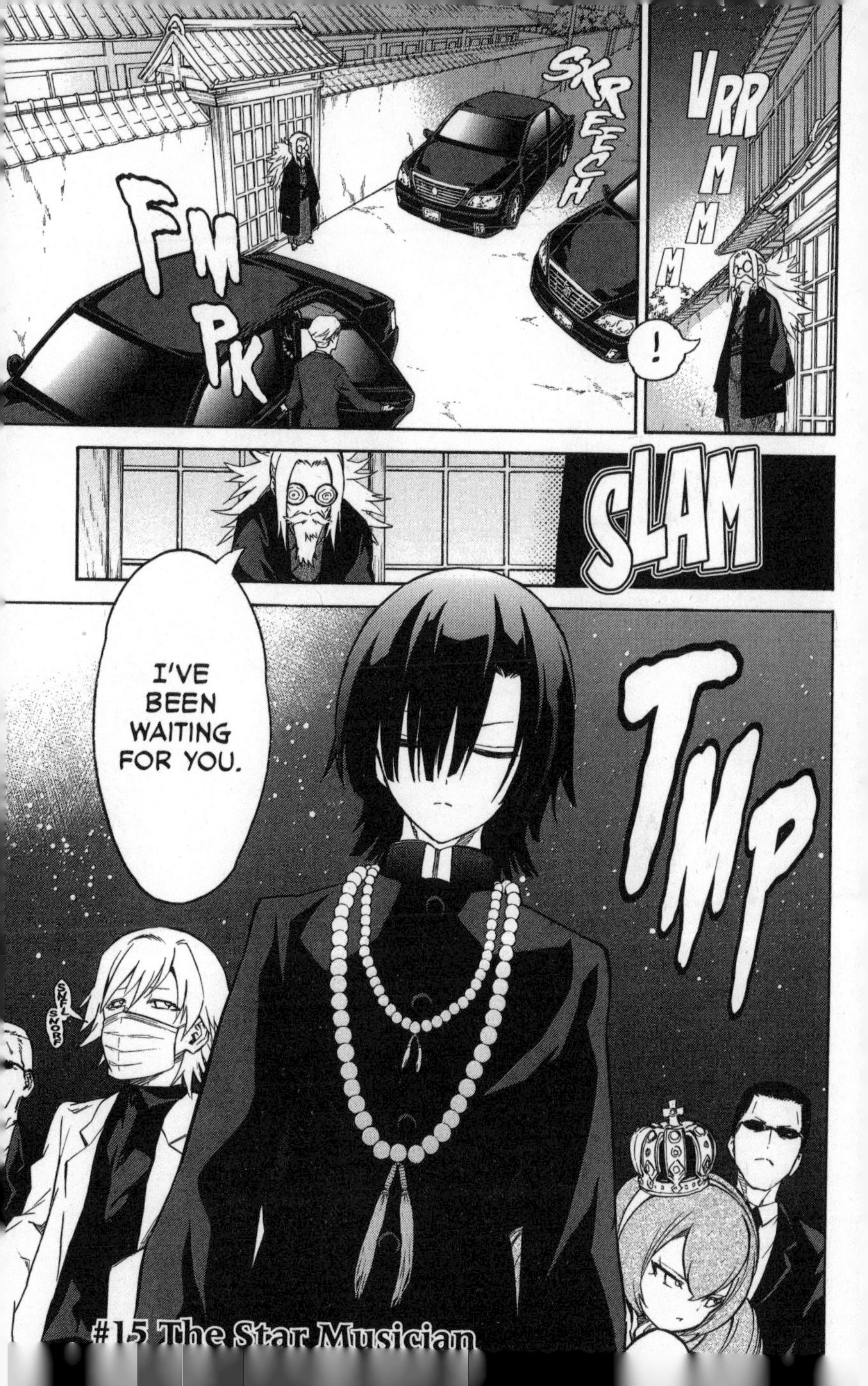
VRRMMMM
!
SKREECH
FMPK
SLAM
TMP
I'VE BEEN WAITING FOR YOU.
SNFL SNORF

# #15 The Star Musician

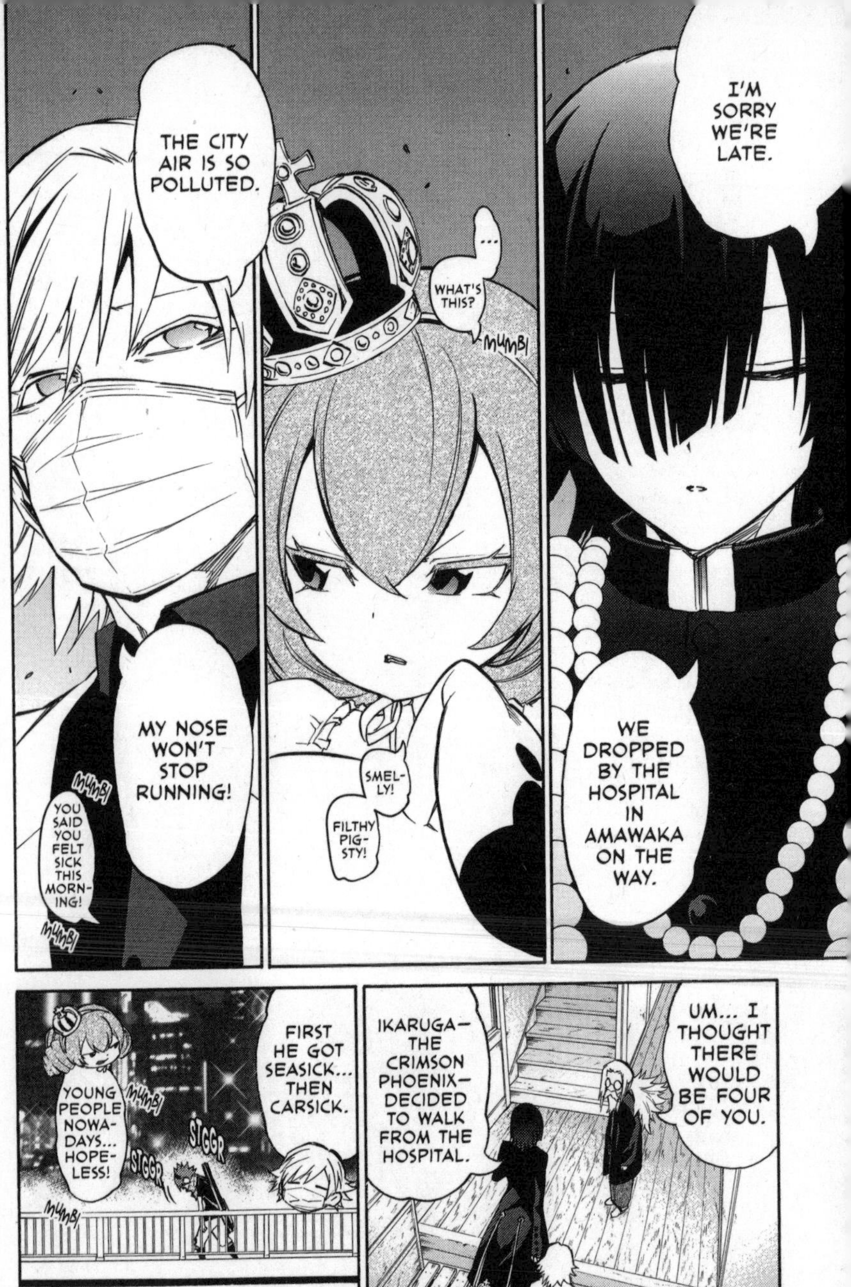
I'M SORRY WE'RE LATE.
WE DROPPED BY THE HOSPITAL IN AMAWAKA ON THE WAY.
...
WHAT'S THIS?
MUMBL
SMELLY!
FILTHY PIGSTY!
THE CITY AIR IS SO POLLUTED.
MY NOSE WON'T STOP RUNNING!
MUMBL
YOU SAID YOU FELT SICK THIS MORNING!
MUMBL
UM... I THOUGHT THERE WOULD BE FOUR OF YOU.
IKARUGA—THE CRIMSON PHOENIX—DECIDED TO WALK FROM THE HOSPITAL.
FIRST HE GOT SEASICK... THEN CARSICK.
MUMBL
YOUNG PEOPLE NOWADAYS... HOPELESS!
SIGGR
SIGGR
MUMBL

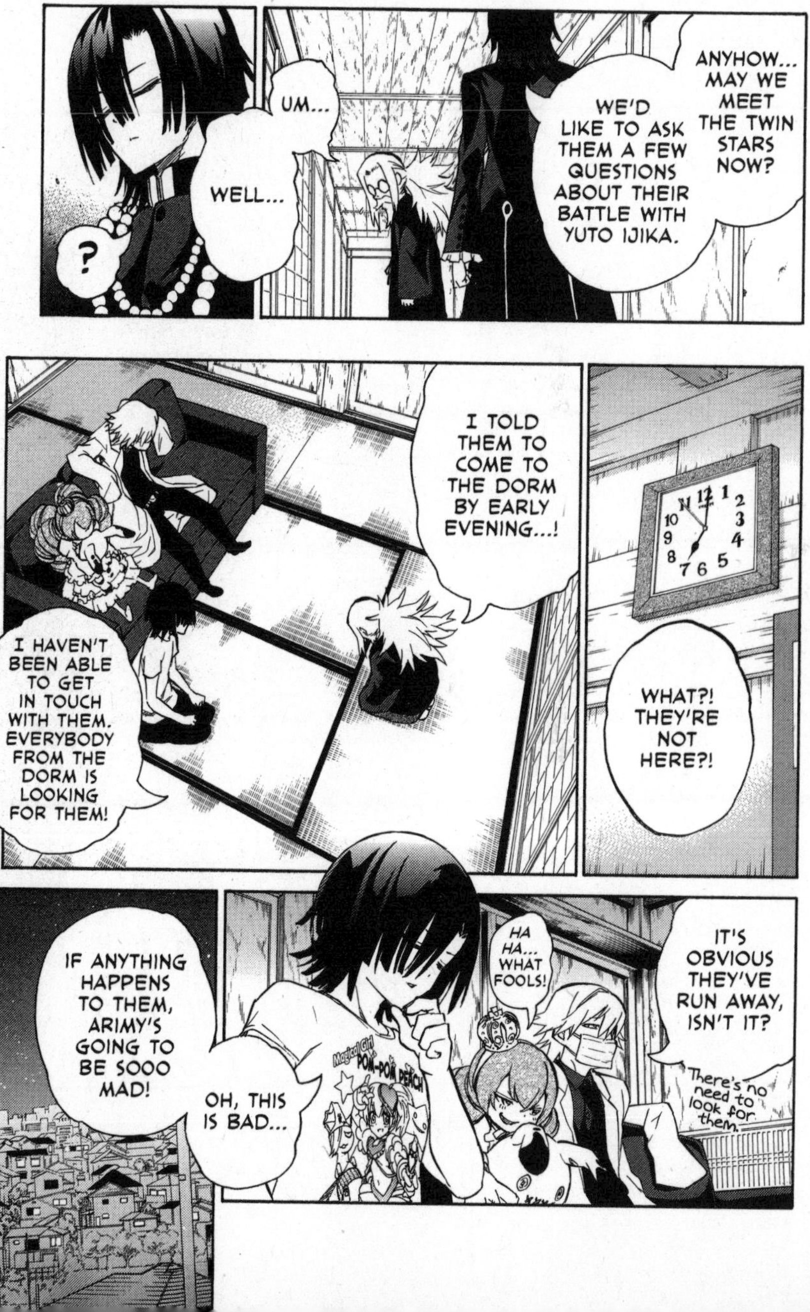
ANYHOW... MAY WE MEET THE TWIN STARS NOW?
WE'D LIKE TO ASK THEM A FEW QUESTIONS ABOUT THEIR BATTLE WITH YUTO IJIKA.
UM...
WELL...
?
WHAT?! THEY'RE NOT HERE?!
I TOLD THEM TO COME TO THE DORM BY EARLY EVENING...!
I HAVEN'T BEEN ABLE TO GET IN TOUCH WITH THEM. EVERYBODY FROM THE DORM IS LOOKING FOR THEM!
IT'S OBVIOUS THEY'VE RUN AWAY, ISN'T IT?
There's no need to look for them.
HA HA... WHAT FOOLS!
Magical Girl POM-POM PEACH
OH, THIS IS BAD...
IF ANYTHING HAPPENS TO THEM, ARIMY'S GOING TO BE SOOO MAD!

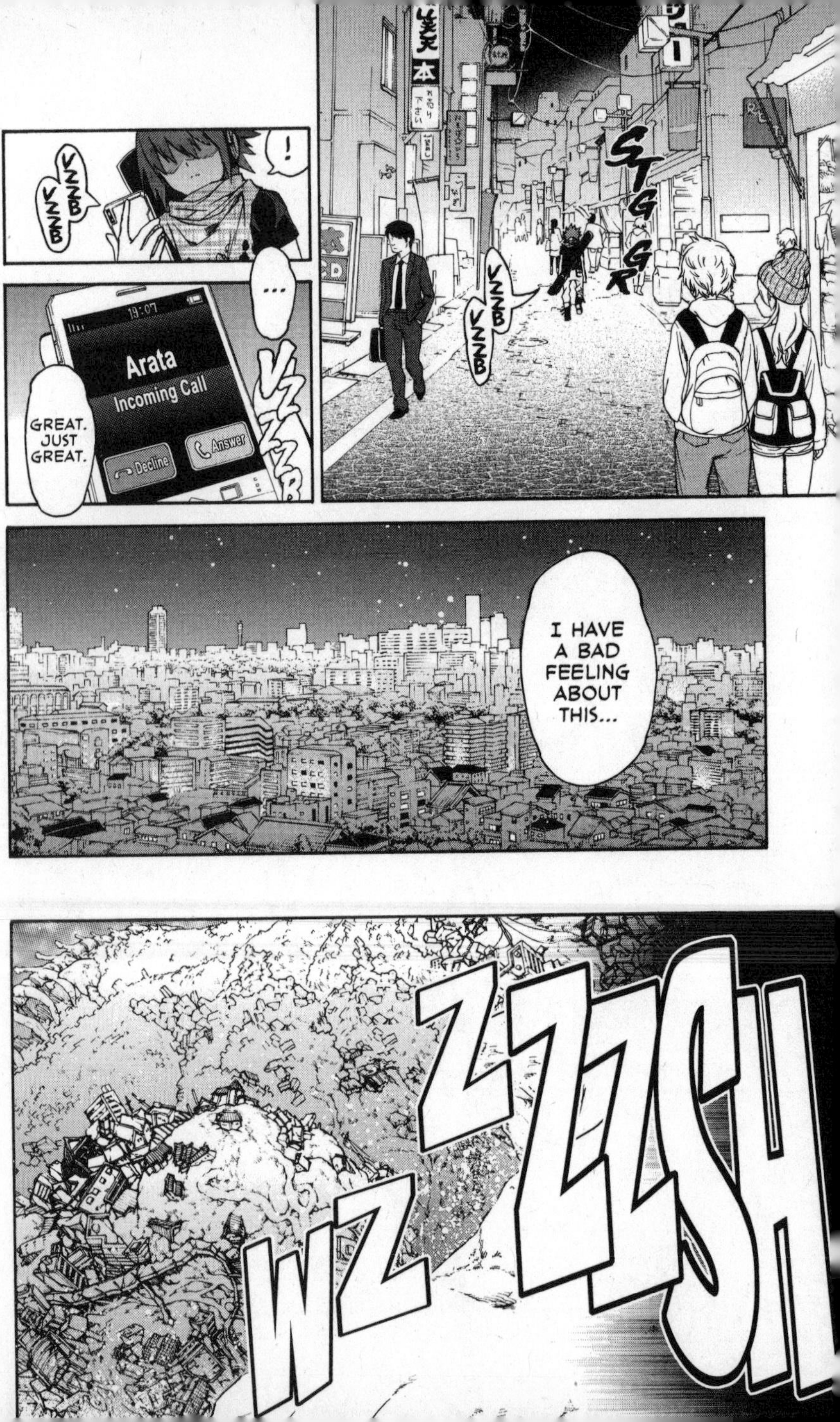
STGGR
VZZZB VZZZB
!
VZZZB VZZZB
...
VZZZB
19:07
Arata
Incoming Call
Answer
Decline
GREAT. JUST GREAT.
I HAVE A BAD FEELING ABOUT THIS...
WZZZSH

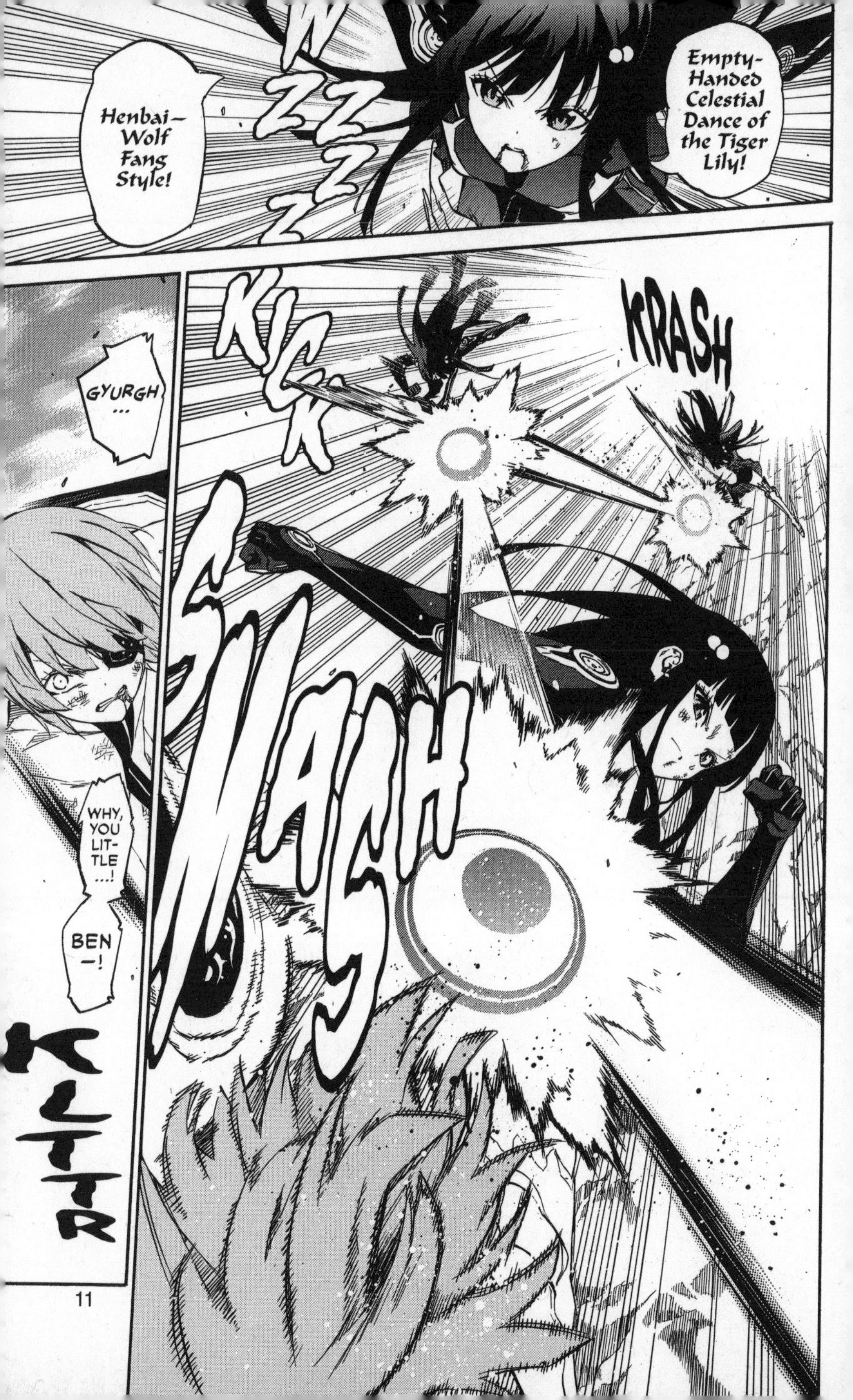

Empty-Handed Celestial Dance of the Tiger Lily!
WZZZZ
Henbai—Wolf Fang Style!
KRASH
KICK
GYURGH...
WHY, YOU LIT-TLE...!
BEN—!
KLTTR

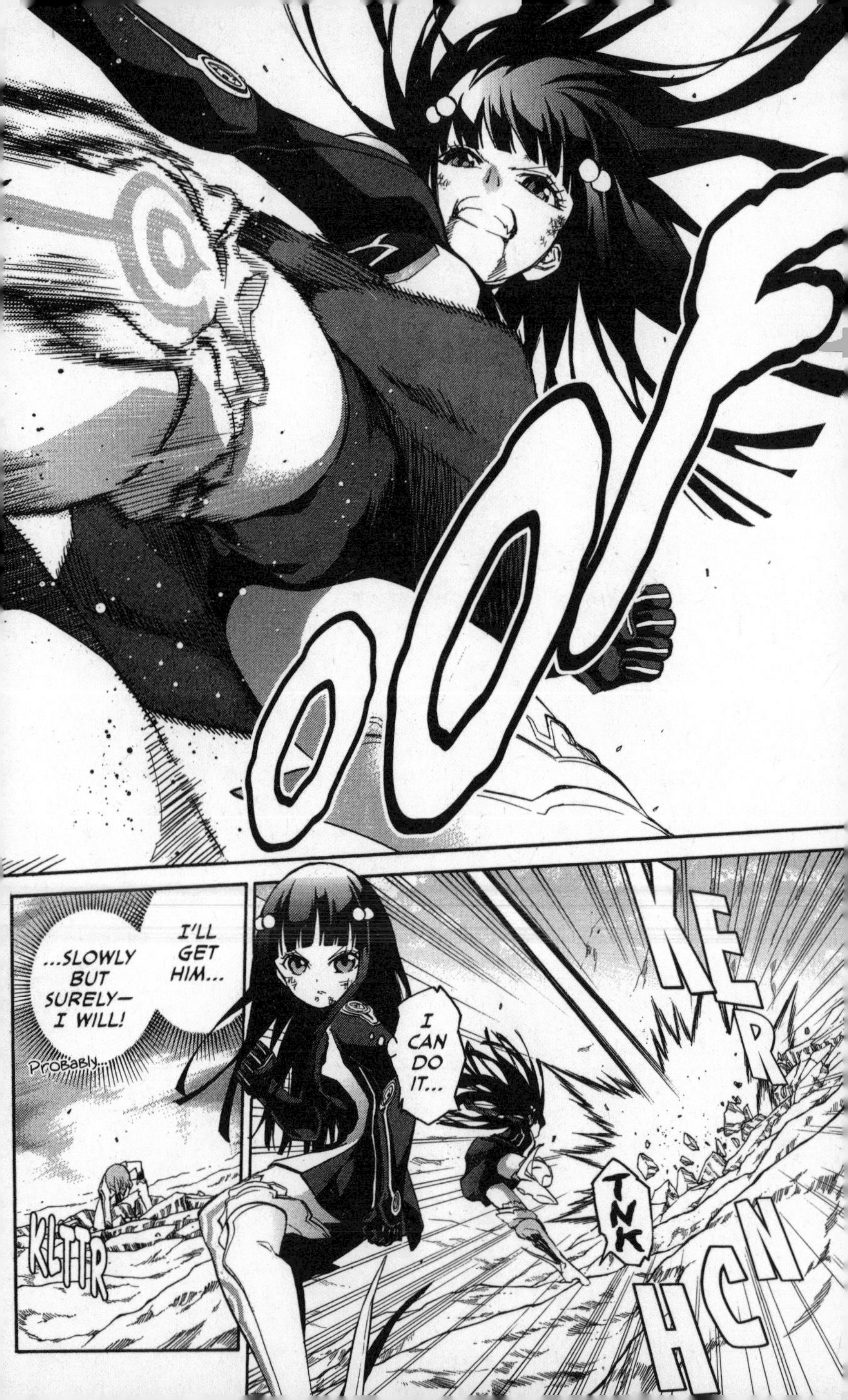
I CAN DO IT...
TNK
I'LL GET HIM...
...SLOWLY BUT SURELY— I WILL!
Probably...
KLTTR

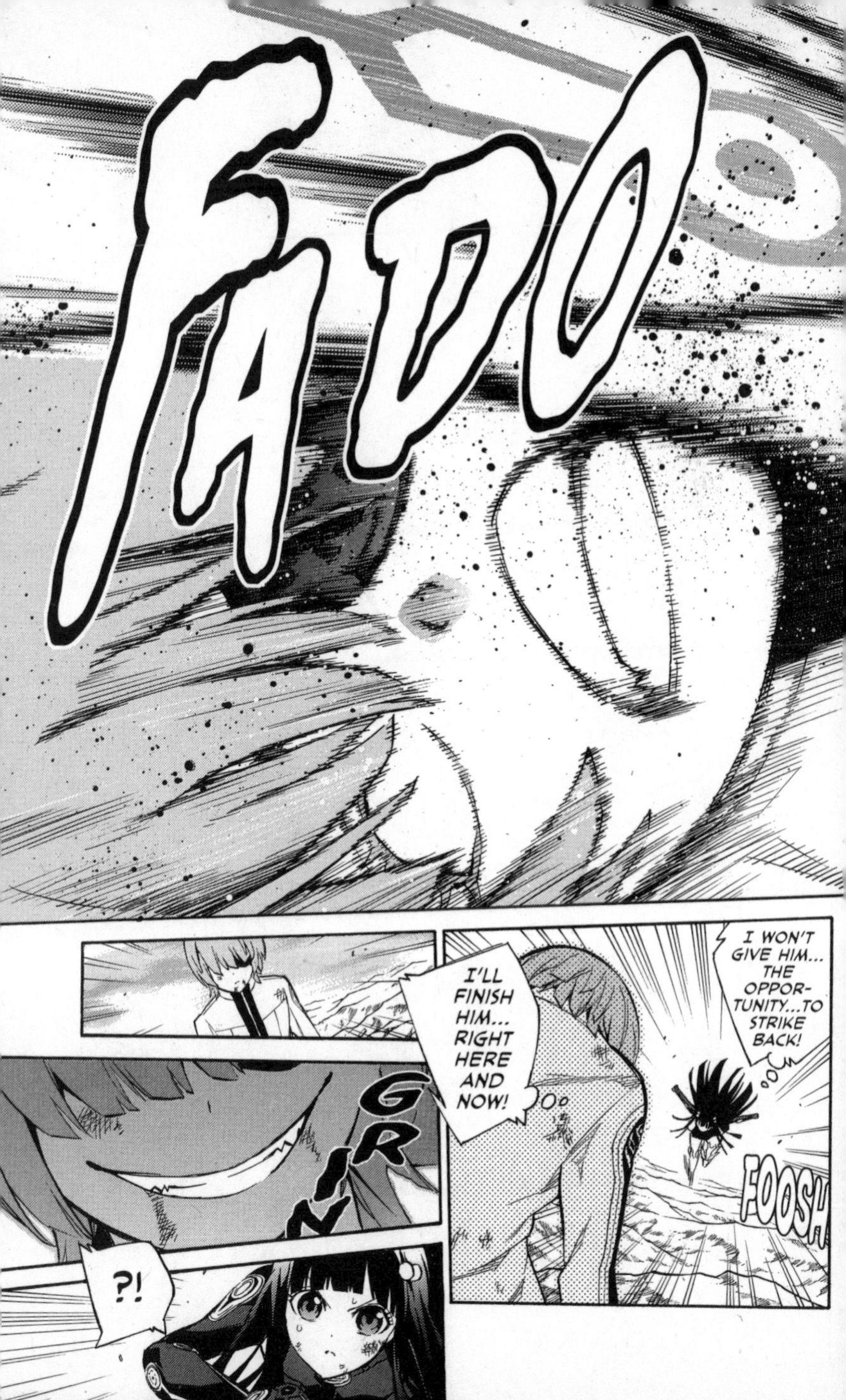
FADO
I WON'T GIVE HIM... THE OPPORTUNITY...TO STRIKE BACK!
I'LL FINISH HIM... RIGHT HERE AND NOW!
FOOSH
GRIN
?!

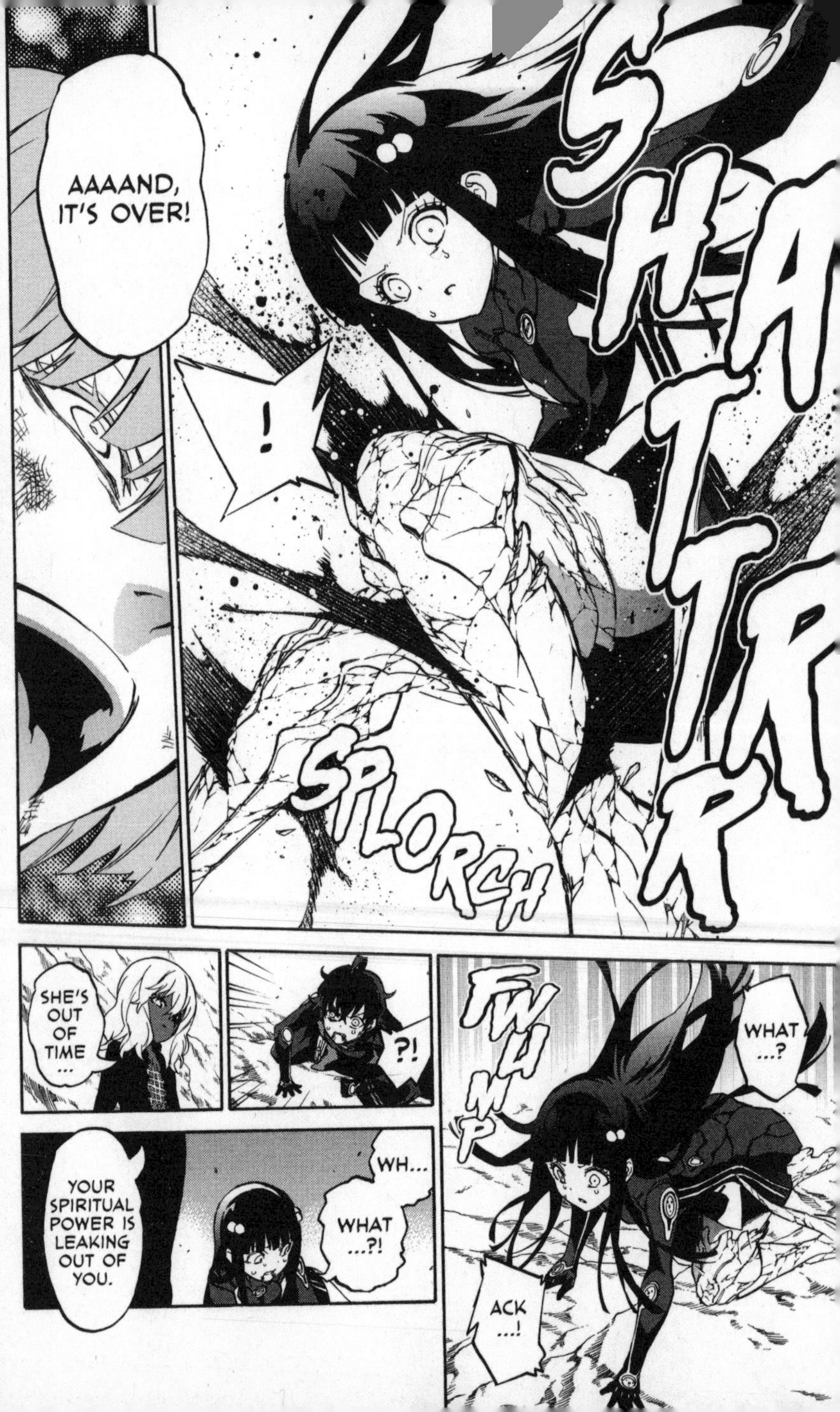
SHATTRR
!
SPLORCH
AAAAND, IT'S OVER!
FWUMP
WHAT ...?
ACK ...!
?!
SHE'S OUT OF TIME ...
WH...
WHAT ...?!
YOUR SPIRITUAL POWER IS LEAKING OUT OF YOU.

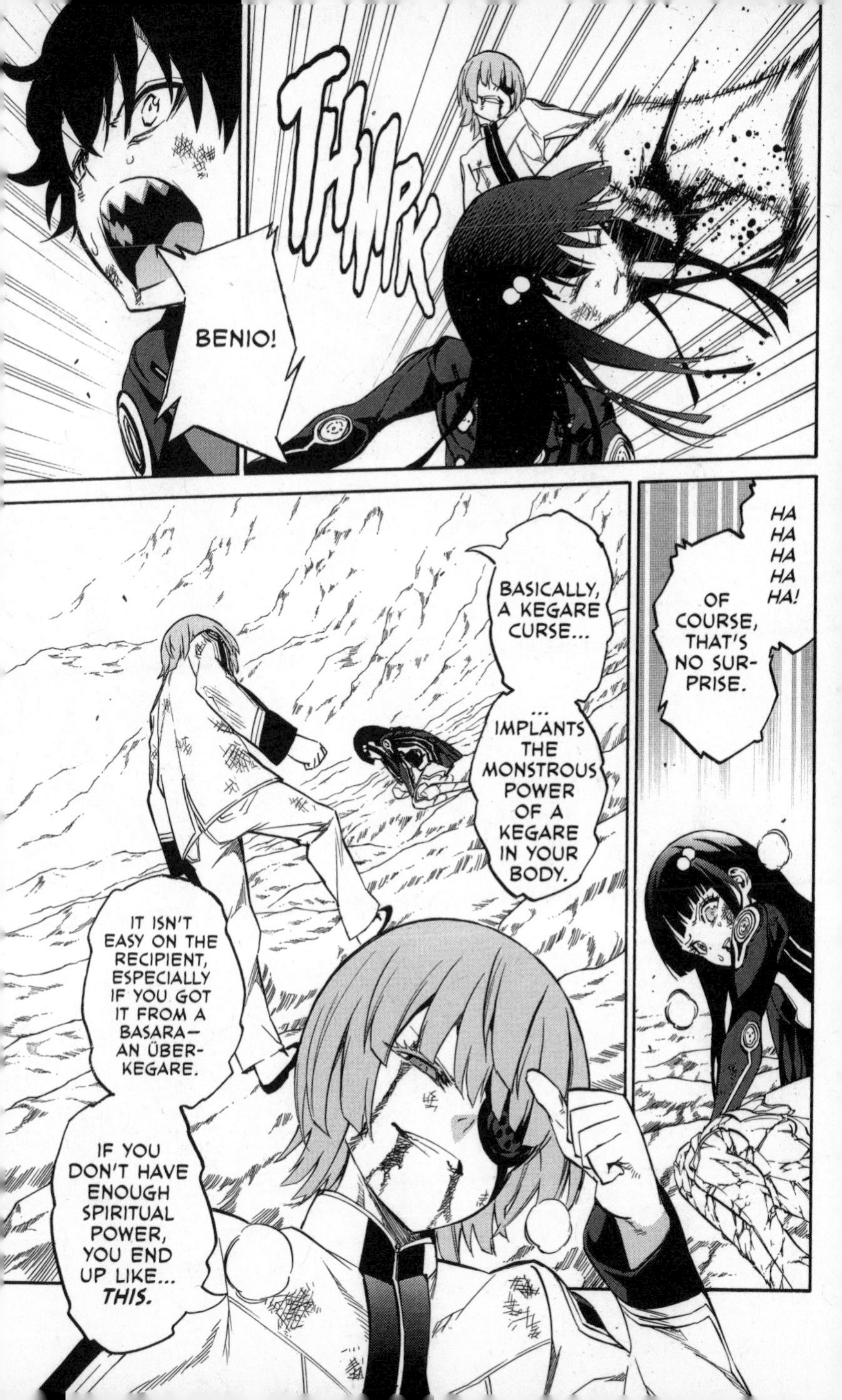
THMPK
BENIO!
HA HA HA HA HA!
OF COURSE, THAT'S NO SUR-PRISE.
BASICALLY, A KEGARE CURSE...
... IMPLANTS THE MONSTROUS POWER OF A KEGARE IN YOUR BODY.
IT ISN'T EASY ON THE RECIPIENT, ESPECIALLY IF YOU GOT IT FROM A BASARA—AN ÜBER-KEGARE.
IF YOU DON'T HAVE ENOUGH SPIRITUAL POWER, YOU END UP LIKE... ***THIS.***

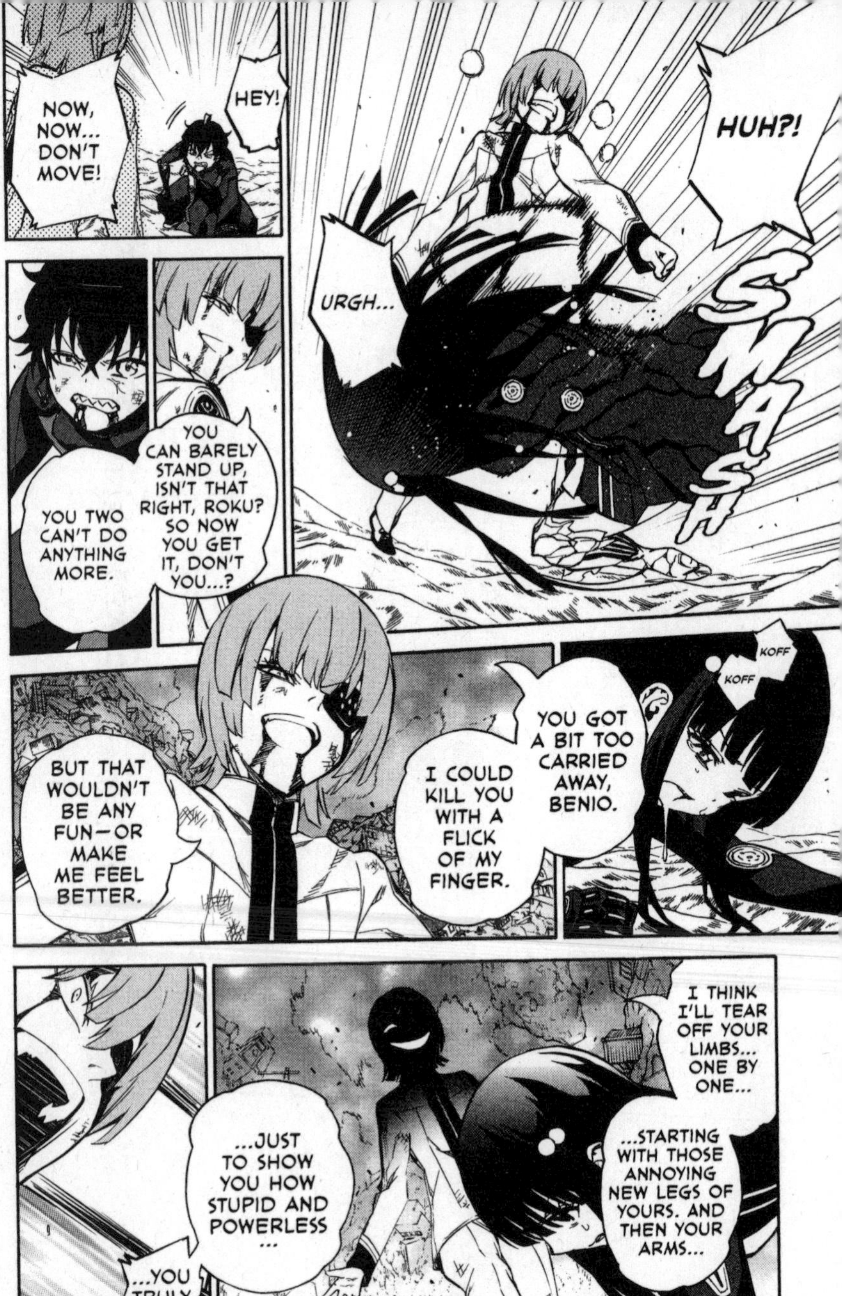
HUH?!
SMASH
URGH...
HEY!
NOW, NOW... DON'T MOVE!
YOU CAN BARELY STAND UP, ISN'T THAT RIGHT, ROKU? SO NOW YOU GET IT, DON'T YOU...?
YOU TWO CAN'T DO ANYTHING MORE.
KOFF
KOFF
YOU GOT A BIT TOO CARRIED AWAY, BENIO.
I COULD KILL YOU WITH A FLICK OF MY FINGER.
BUT THAT WOULDN'T BE ANY FUN—OR MAKE ME FEEL BETTER.
I THINK I'LL TEAR OFF YOUR LIMBS... ONE BY ONE...
...STARTING WITH THOSE ANNOYING NEW LEGS OF YOURS. AND THEN YOUR ARMS...
...JUST TO SHOW YOU HOW STUPID AND POWERLESS ...
...YOU TRULY ARE!

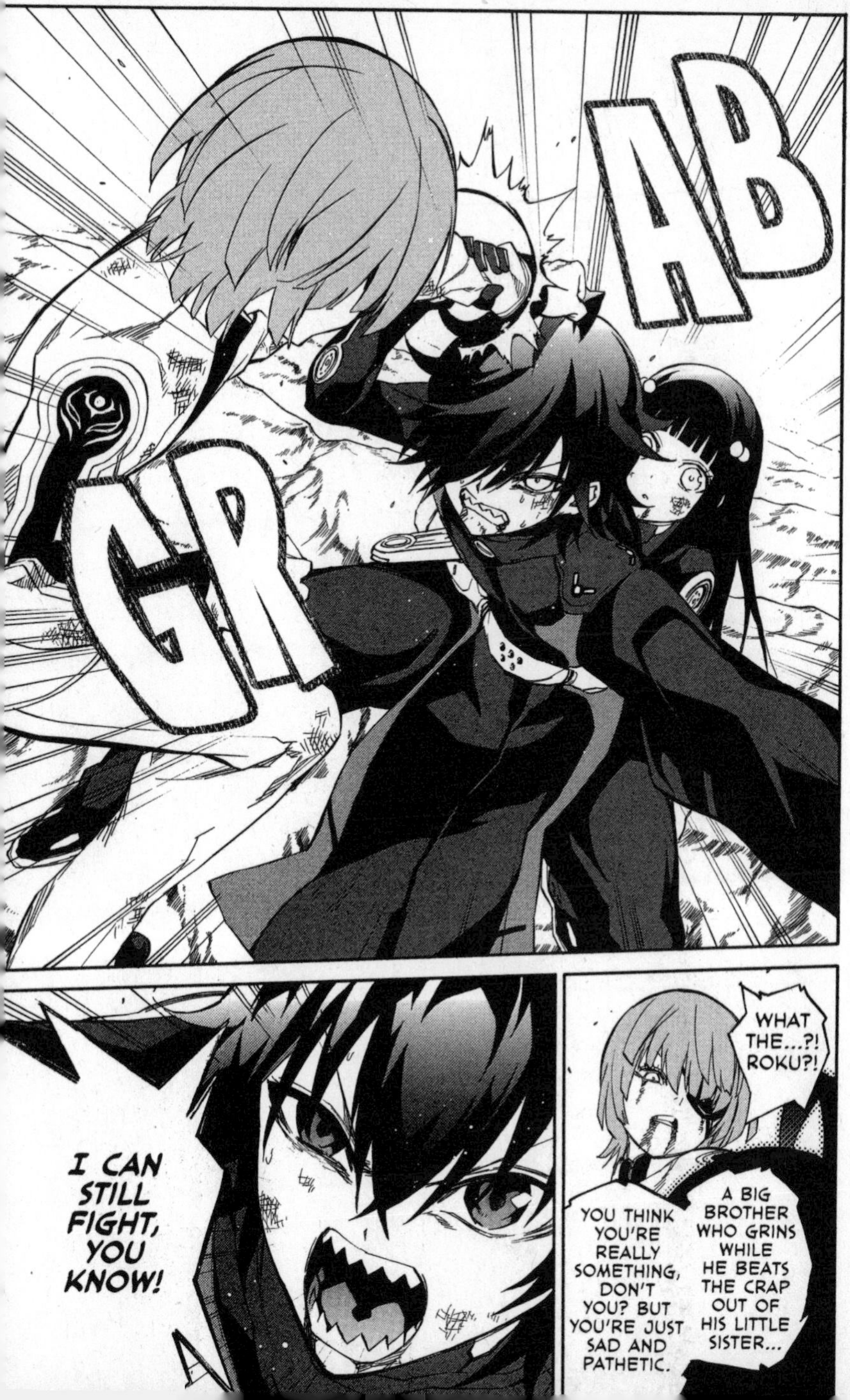
AB
GR
WHAT THE...?! ROKU?!
A BIG BROTHER WHO GRINS WHILE HE BEATS THE CRAP OUT OF HIS LITTLE SISTER...
YOU THINK YOU'RE REALLY SOMETHING, DON'T YOU? BUT YOU'RE JUST SAD AND PATHETIC.
I CAN STILL FIGHT, YOU KNOW!

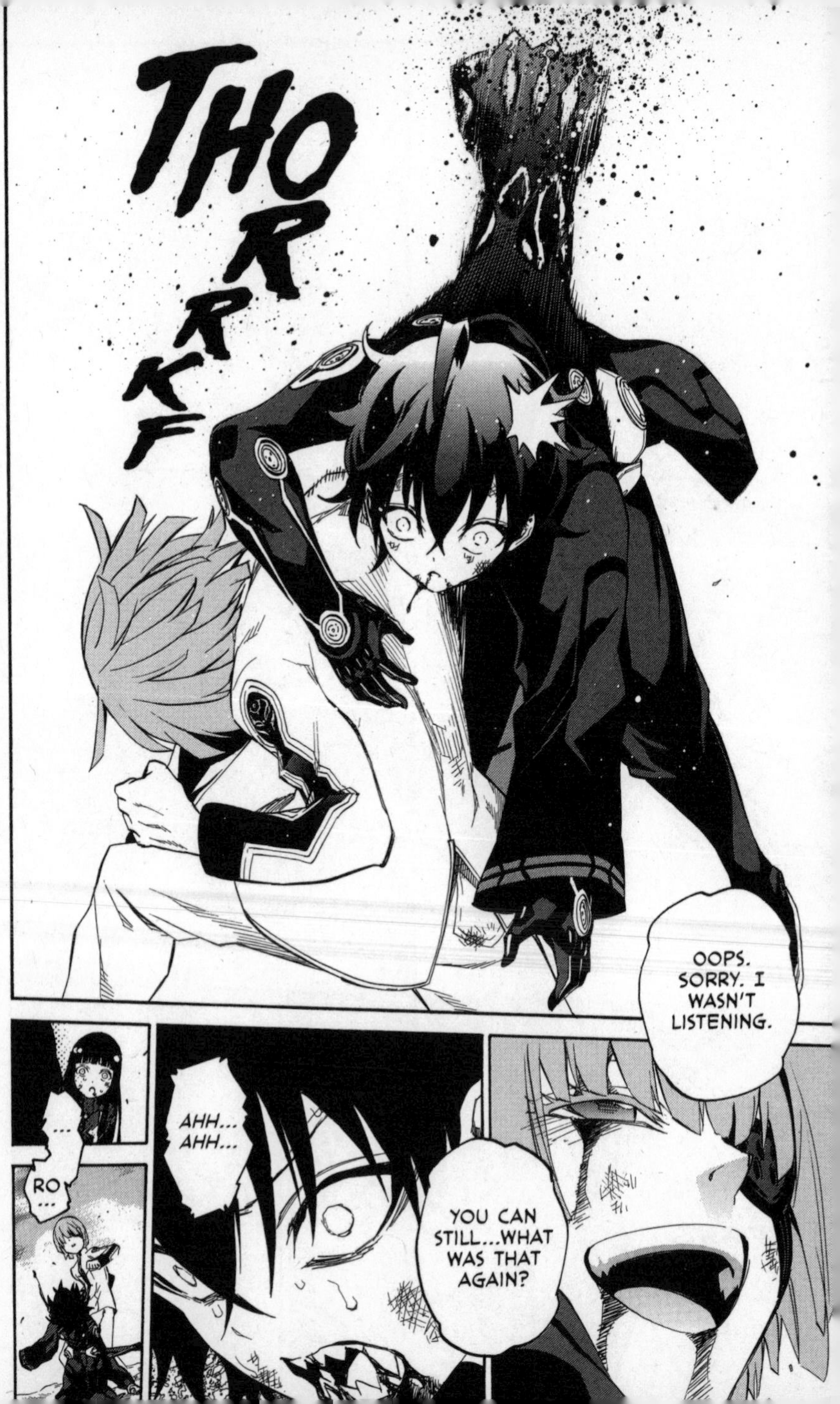
THORRKF
OOPS. SORRY. I WASN'T LISTENING.
YOU CAN STILL...WHAT WAS THAT AGAIN?
AHH... AHH...
...
RO...

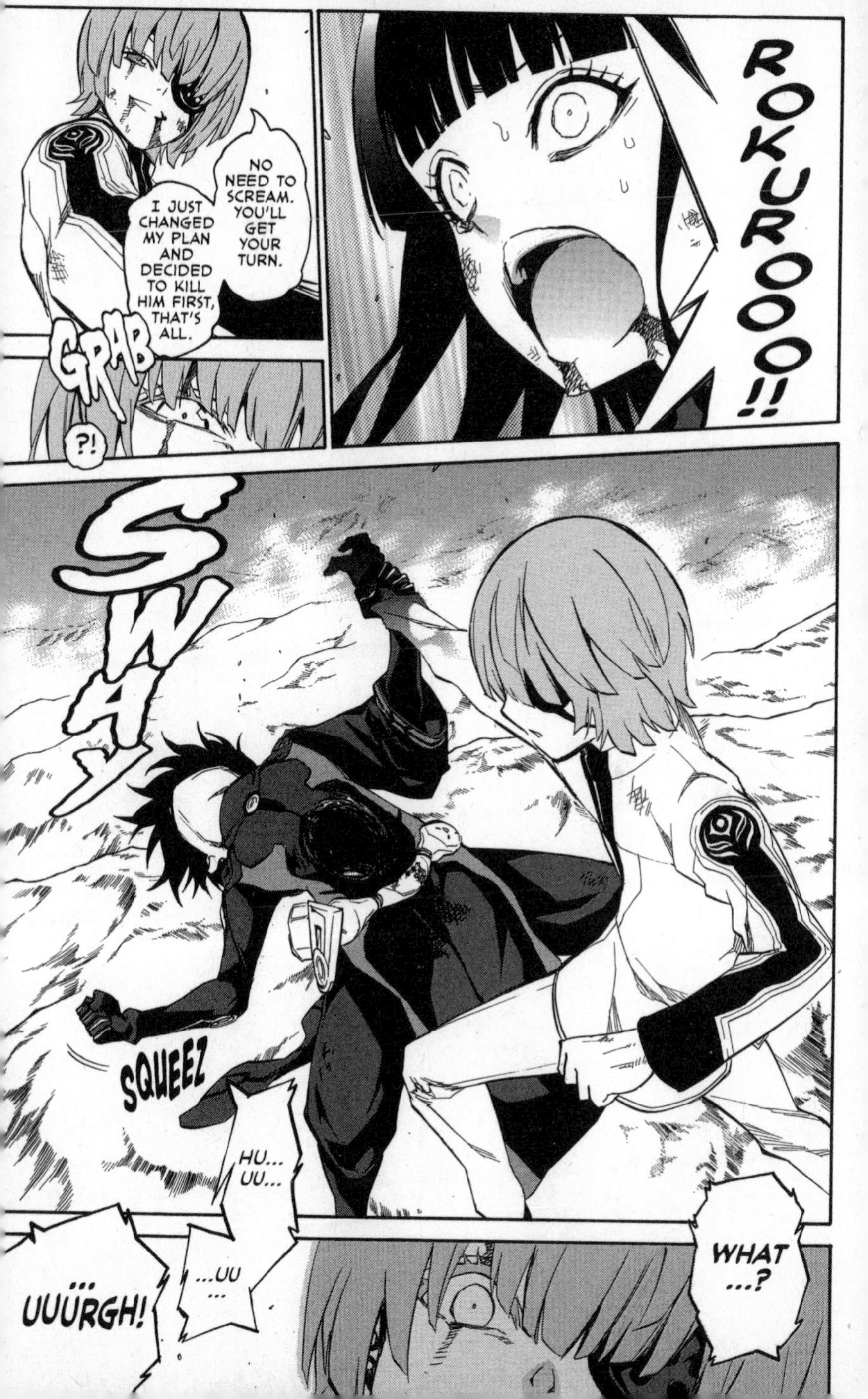
ROKUROOO!!
NO NEED TO SCREAM. YOU'LL GET YOUR TURN.
I JUST CHANGED MY PLAN AND DECIDED TO KILL HIM FIRST, THAT'S ALL.
GRAB
?!
SWAY
SQUEEZ
HU... UU...
WHAT ...?
...UU ...
... UUÜRGH!

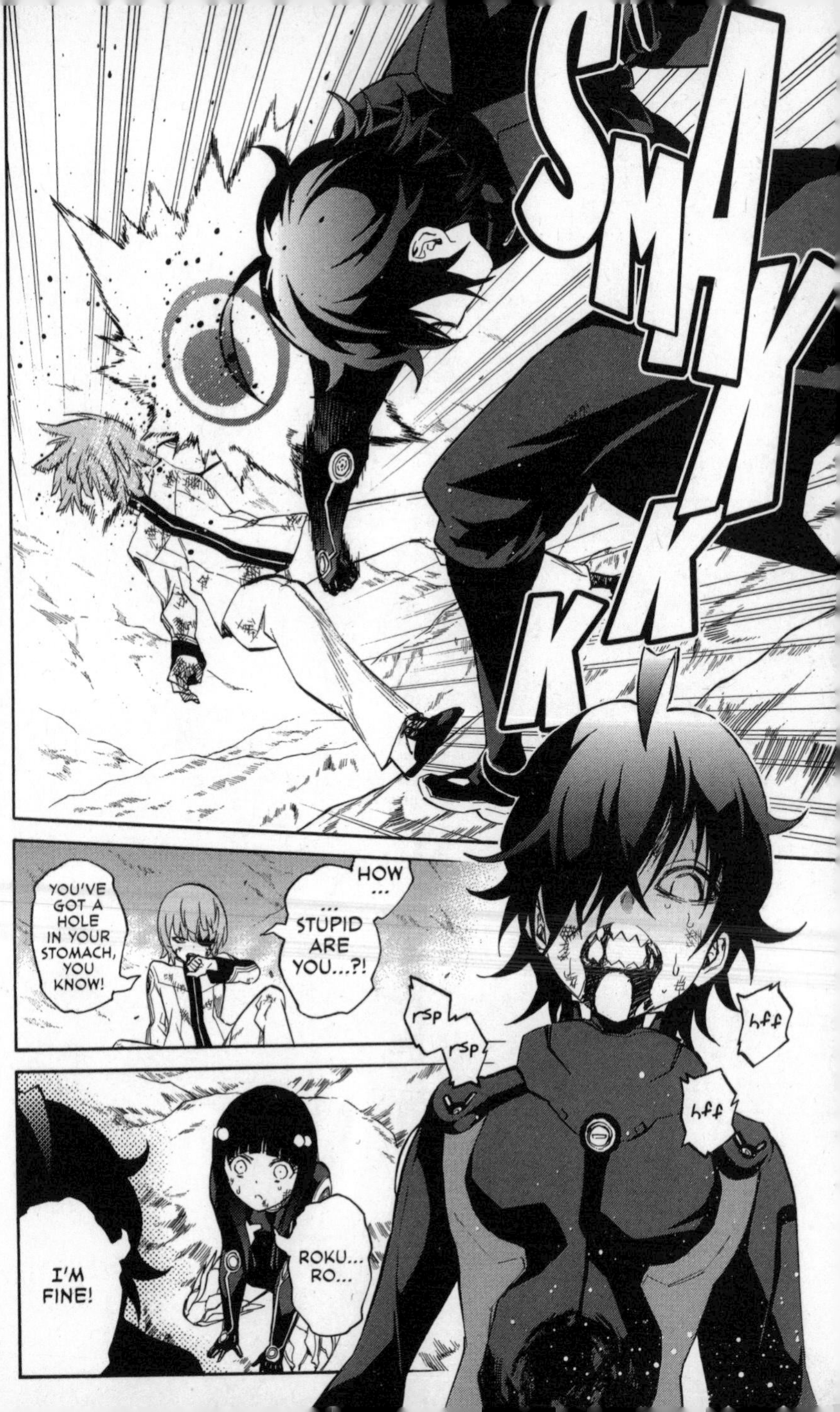
SMAKKK
rsp
rsp
hff
hff
HOW ... ... STUPID ARE YOU...?!
YOU'VE GOT A HOLE IN YOUR STOMACH, YOU KNOW!
ROKU... RO...
I'M FINE!

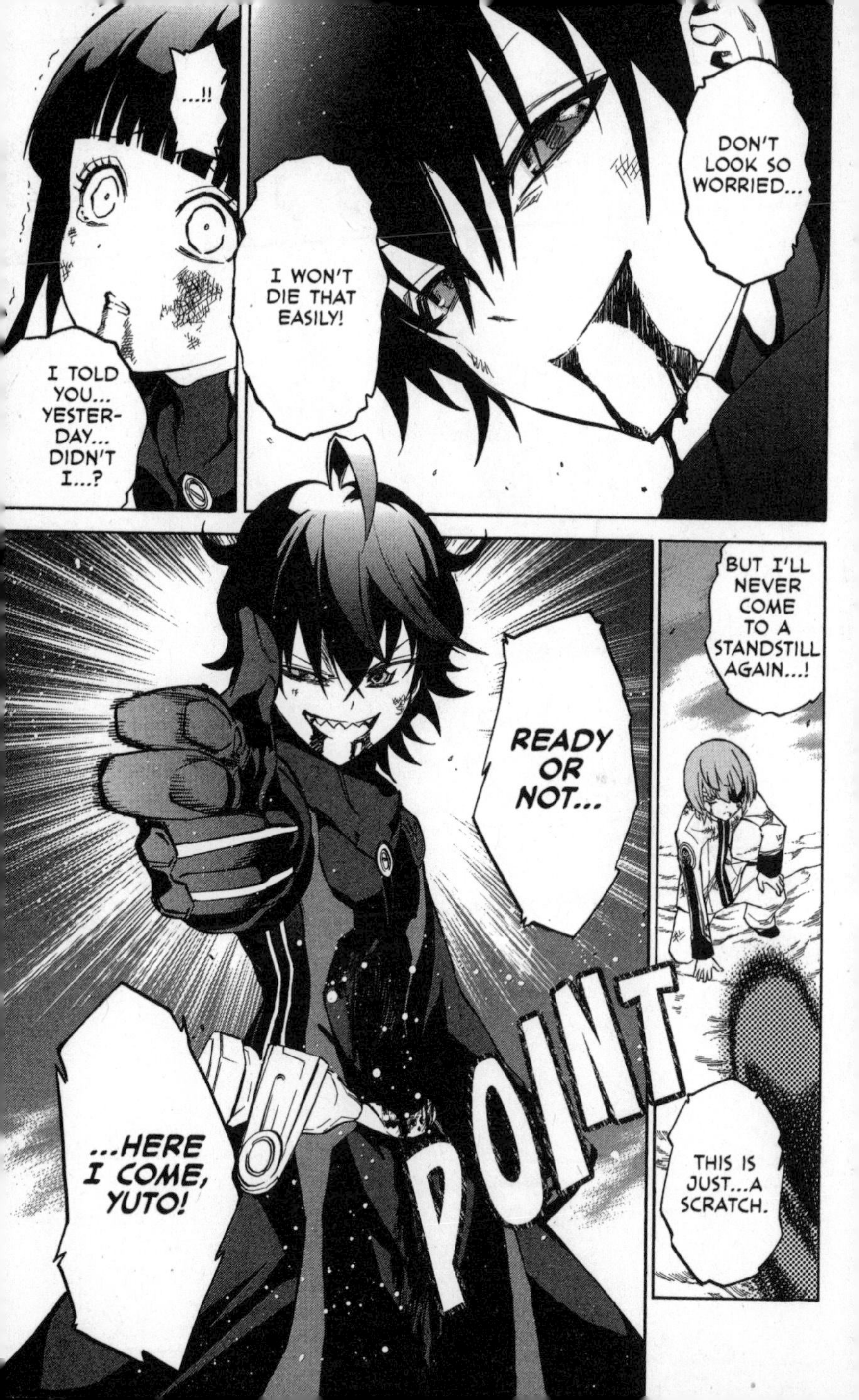
DON'T LOOK SO WORRIED...
I WON'T DIE THAT EASILY!
...!!
I TOLD YOU... YESTER-DAY... DIDN'T I...?
BUT I'LL NEVER COME TO A STANDSTILL AGAIN...!
THIS IS JUST...A SCRATCH.
READY OR NOT...
POINT
...HERE I COME, YUTO!

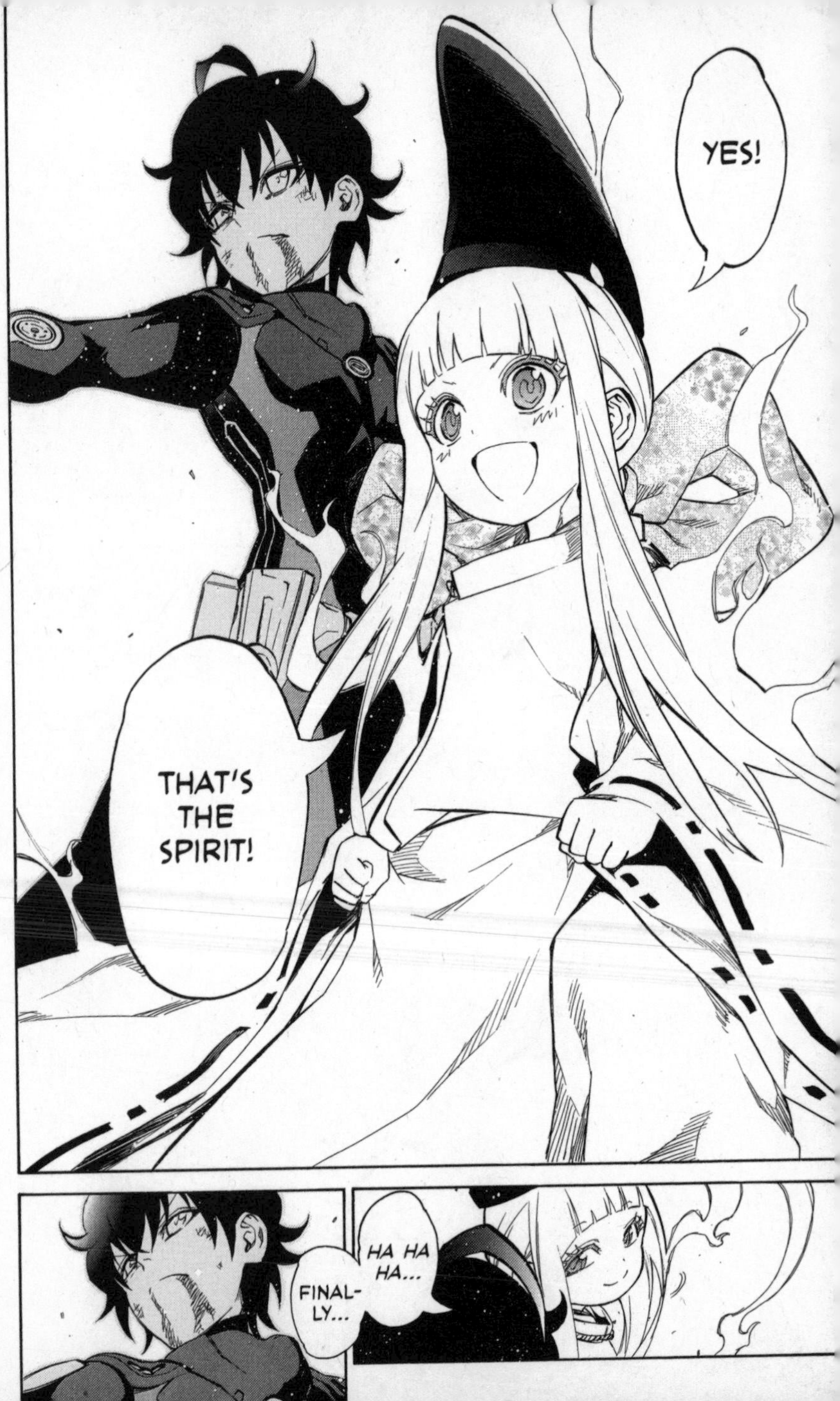
YES!
THAT'S THE SPIRIT!
HA HA HA...
FINAL-LY...

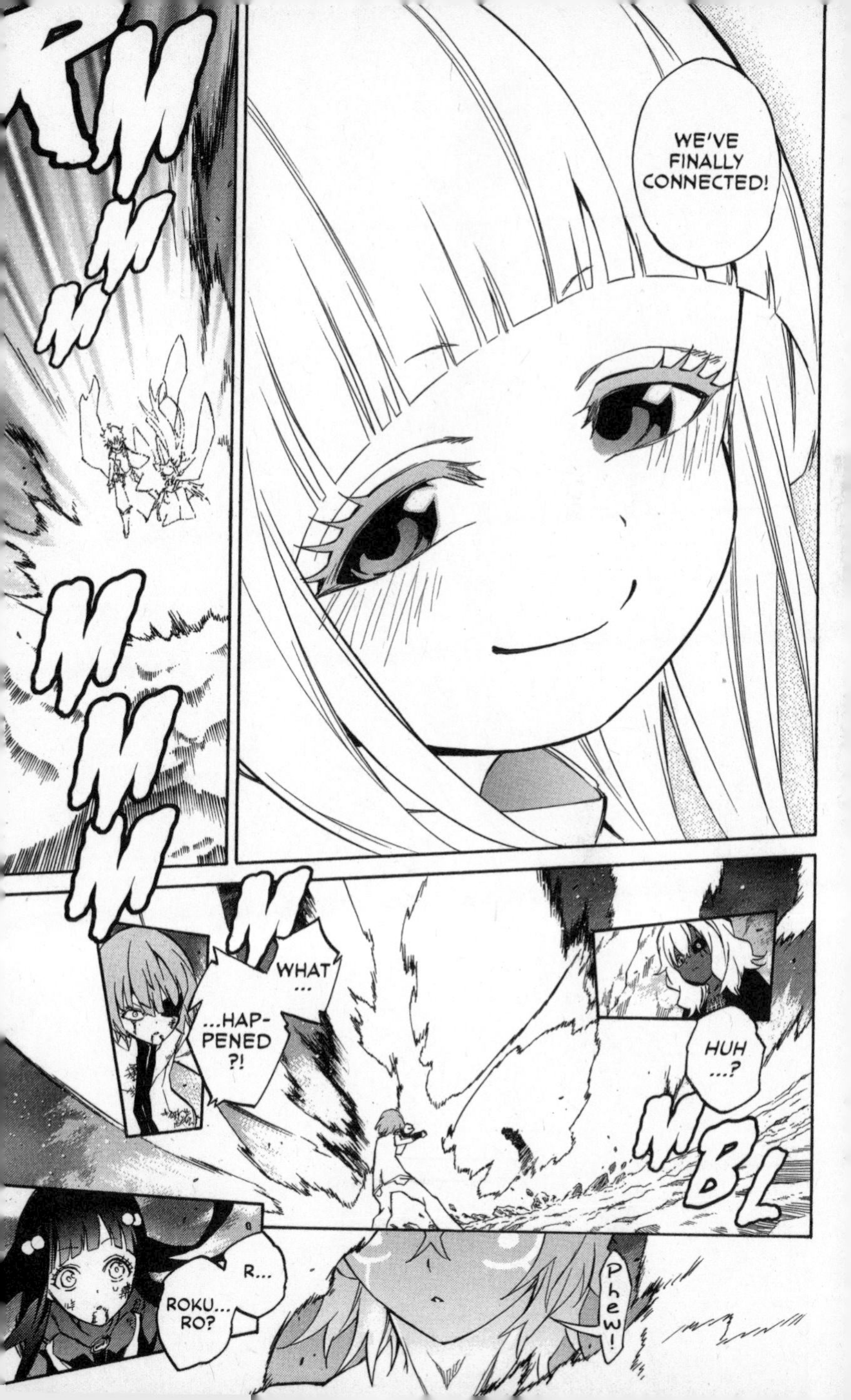
WE'VE FINALLY CONNECTED!
RMMMMMMMM
HUH ...?
MBL
WHAT ...
...HAP-PENED ?!
Phew!
R...
ROKU... RO?

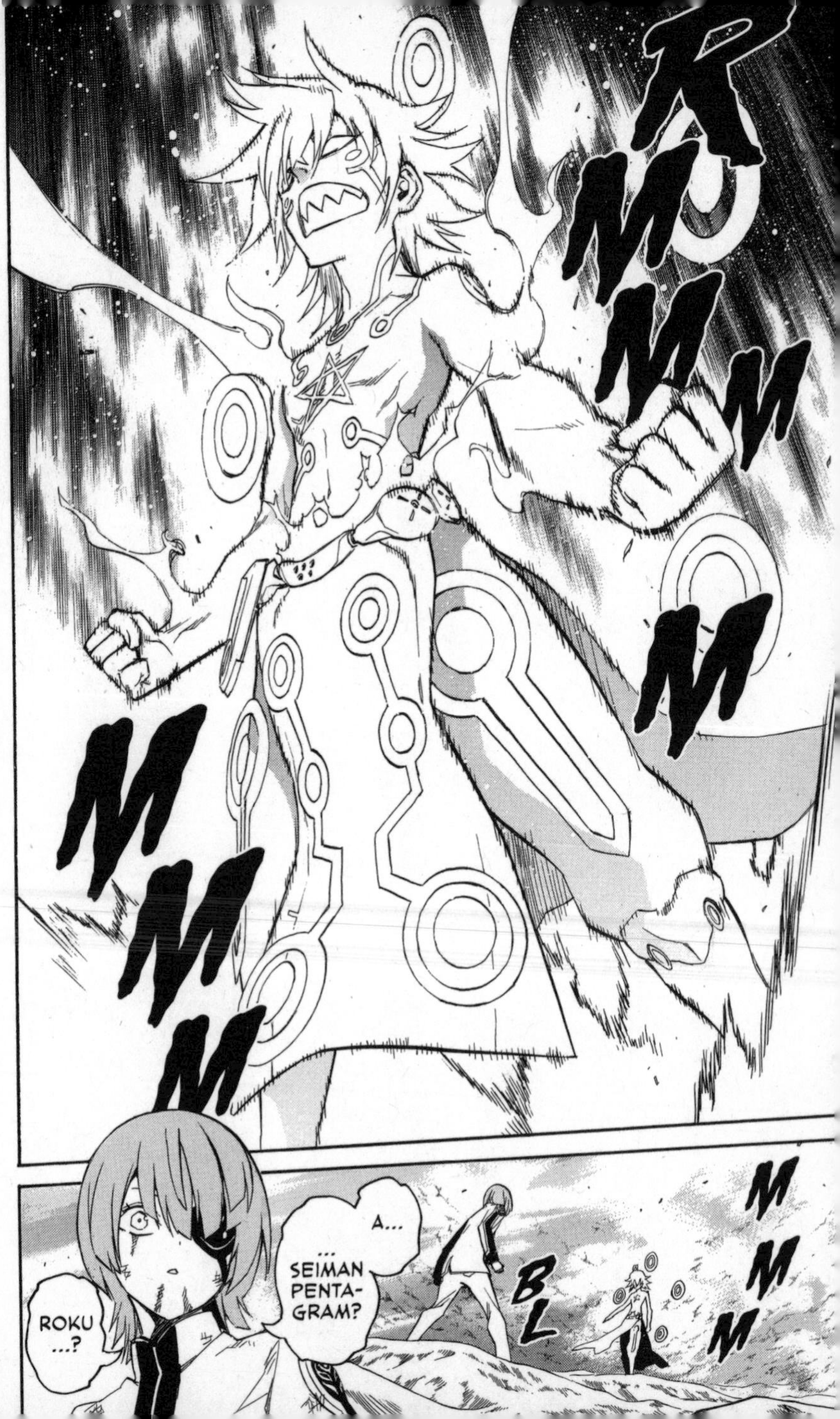
RUMMMM
MM
MMM
MMMM
BL
A...
... SEIMAN PENTA-GRAM?
ROKU ...?

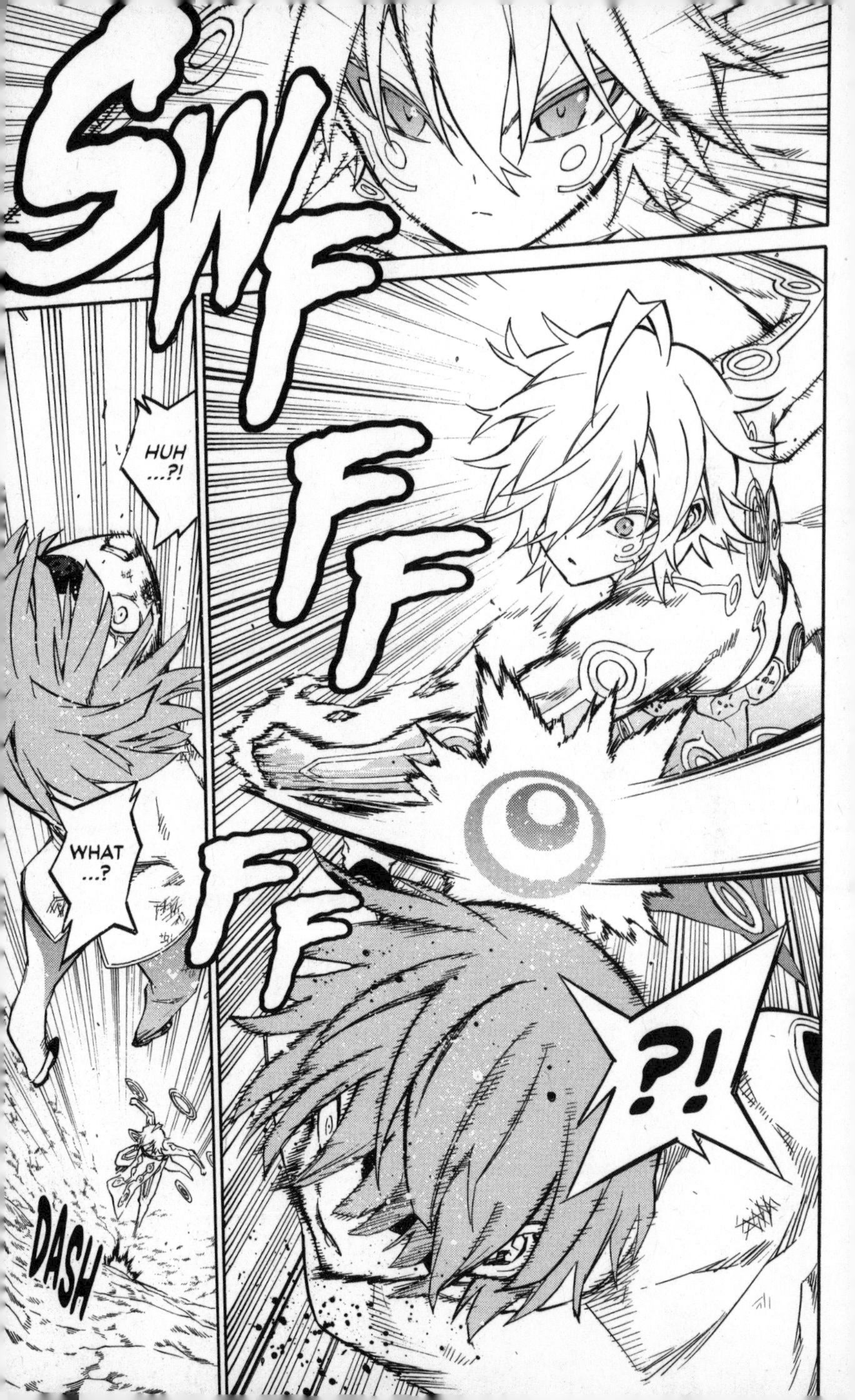
SHFFFFF
?!
HUH ...?!
WHAT ...?
DASH

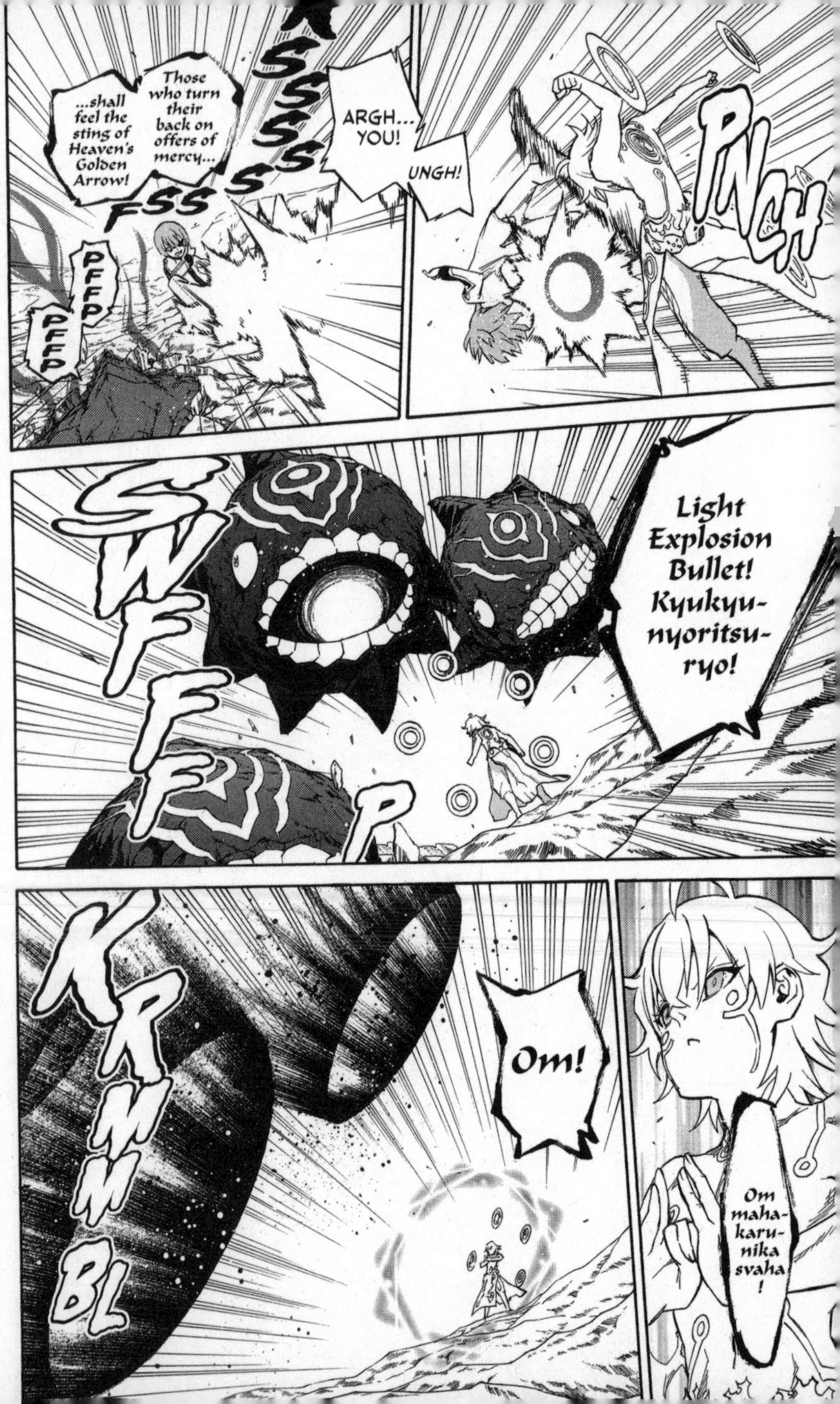
UNGH!
PINCH
ARGH... YOU!
KSSSSS
Those who turn their back on offers of mercy...
...shall feel the sting of Heaven's Golden Arrow!
FSS
PFFP
PFFP
Light Explosion Bullet! Kyukyu-nyoritsu-ryo!
SWFFFP
Om maha-karu-nika svaha!
Om!
KRMMMBL

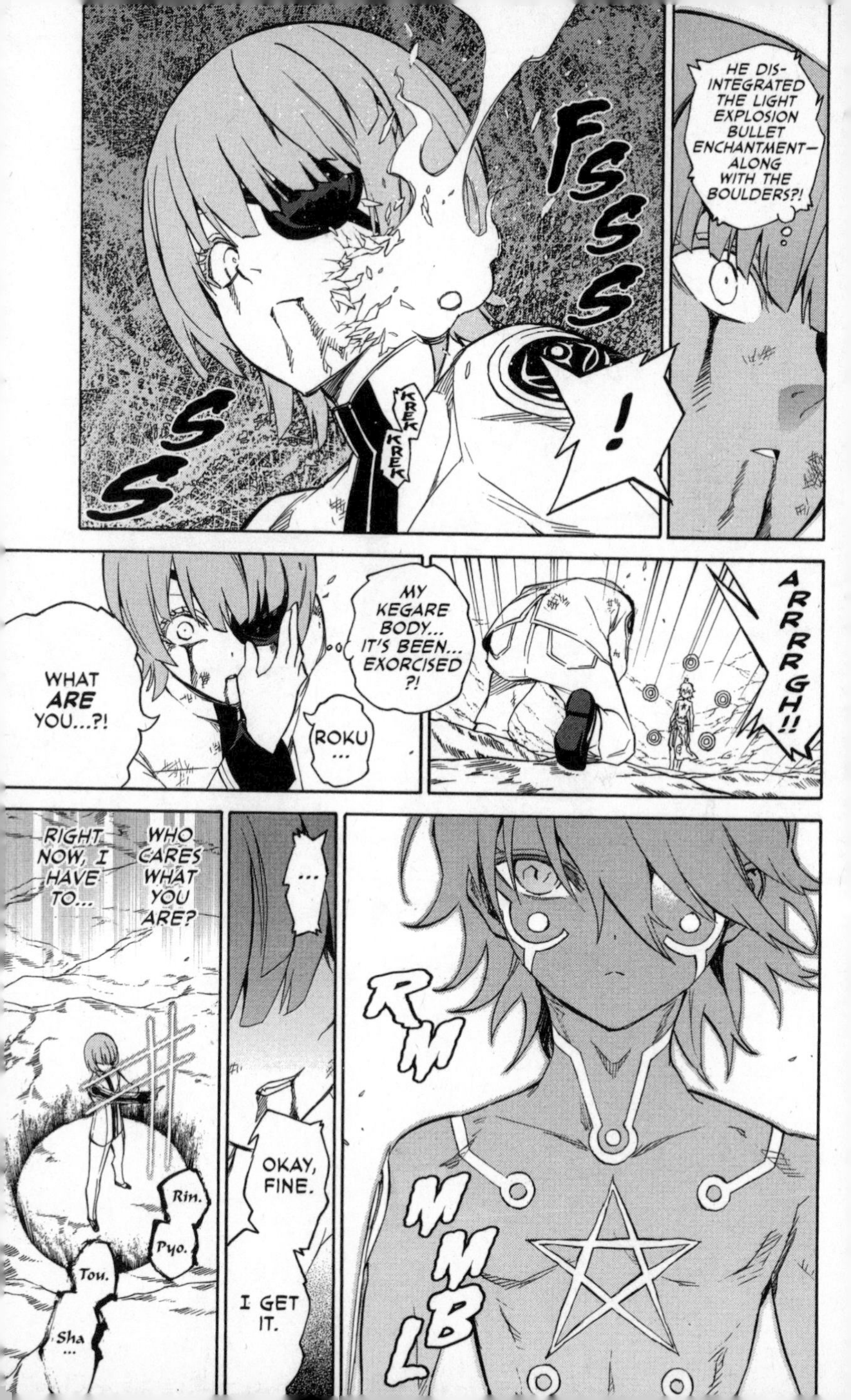
HE DIS-INTEGRATED THE LIGHT EXPLOSION BULLET ENCHANTMENT—ALONG WITH THE BOULDERS?!
FSSS
!
KREK KREK
SSS
ARRRRGH!!
MY KEGARE BODY... IT'S BEEN... EXORCISED?!
ROKU...
WHAT ARE YOU...?!
RMMMBL
...
OKAY, FINE.
I GET IT.
WHO CARES WHAT YOU ARE?
RIGHT NOW, I HAVE TO...
Rin.
Pyo.
Tou.
Sha...

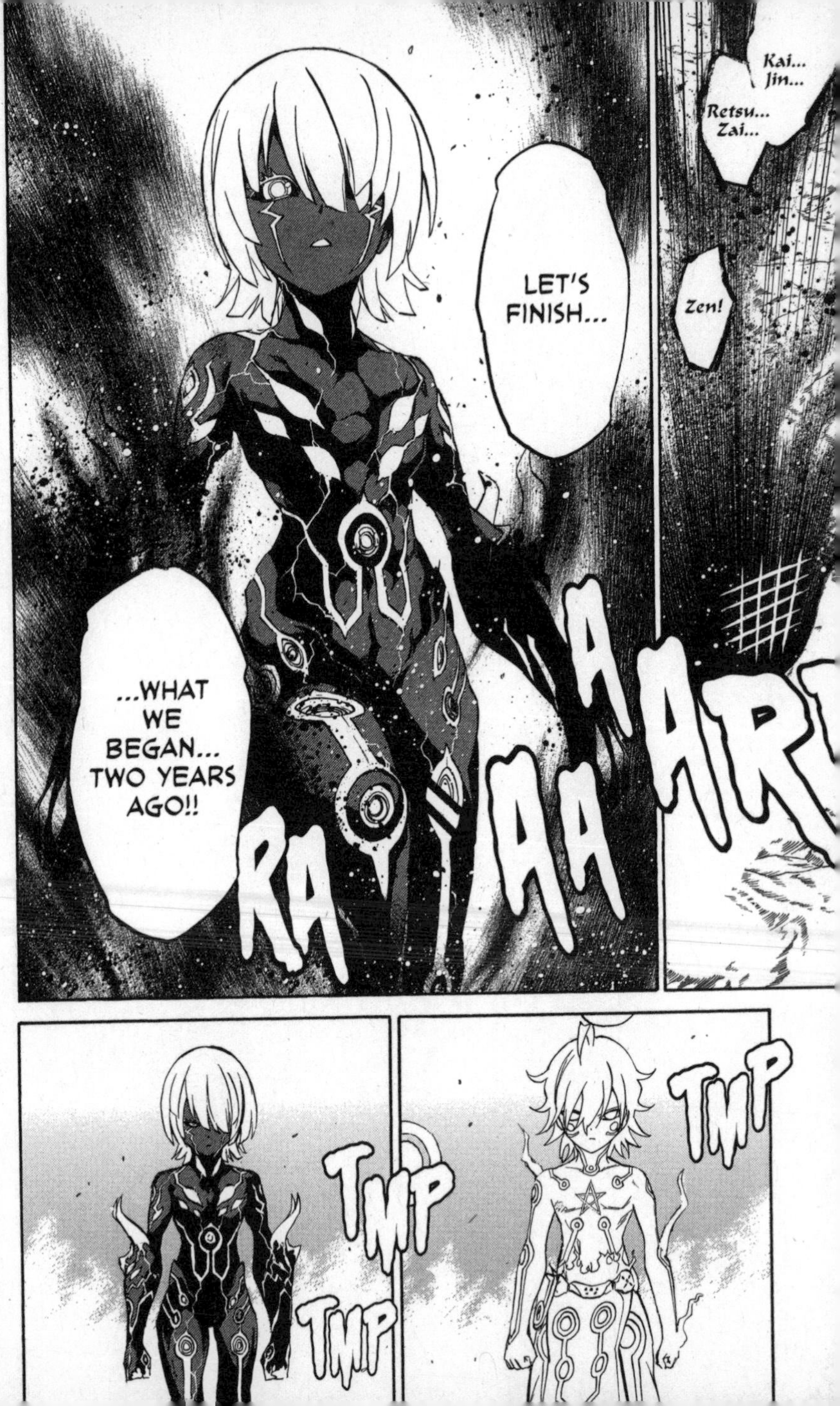
Kai... Jin...
Retsu... Zai...
Zen!
LET'S FINISH...
...WHAT WE BEGAN... TWO YEARS AGO!!
RAAAA
AR
TMP
TMP
TMP

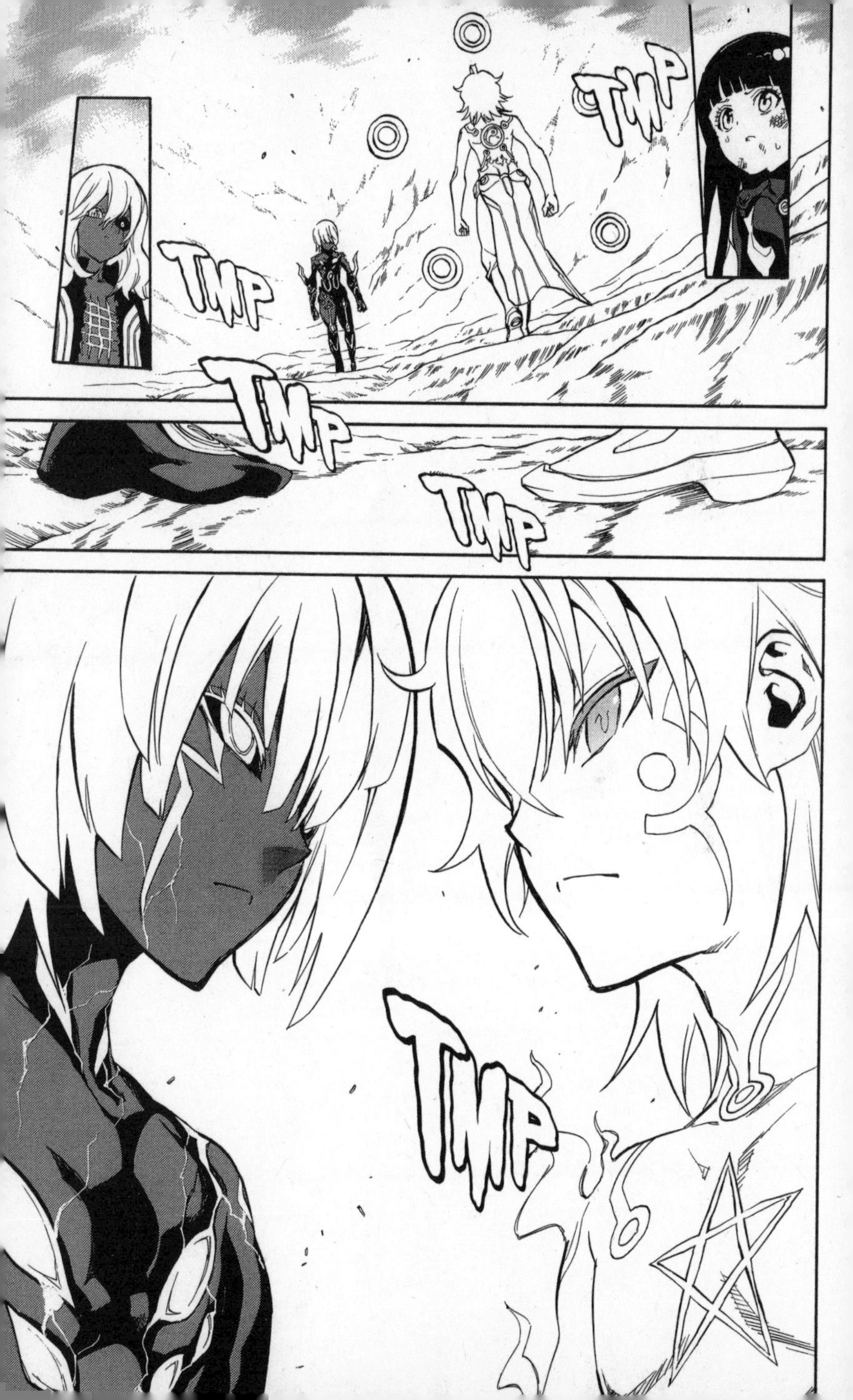
TMP
TMP
TMP
TMP
TMP

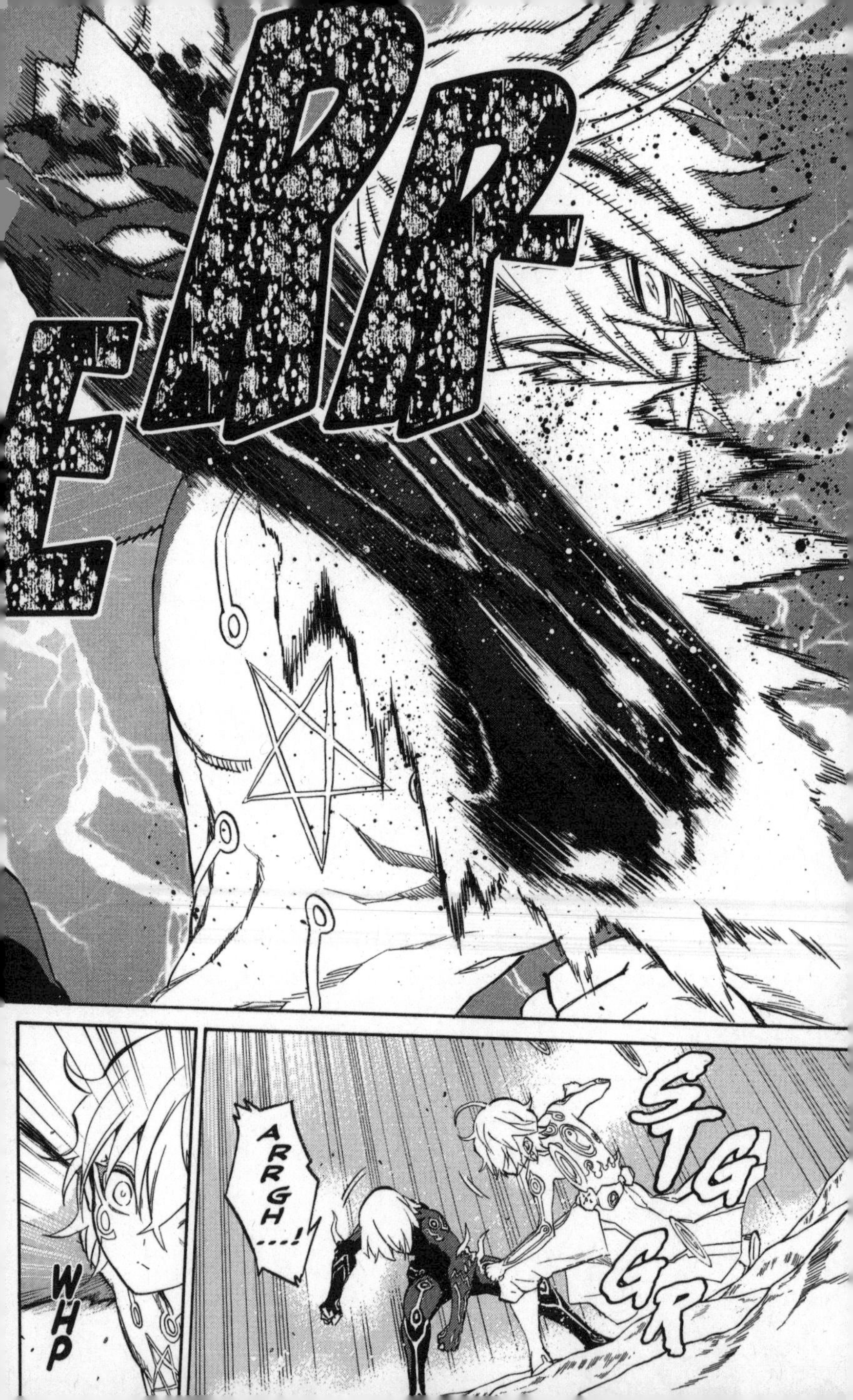
FRR-
ARRGH...!
STGGGR
WHP

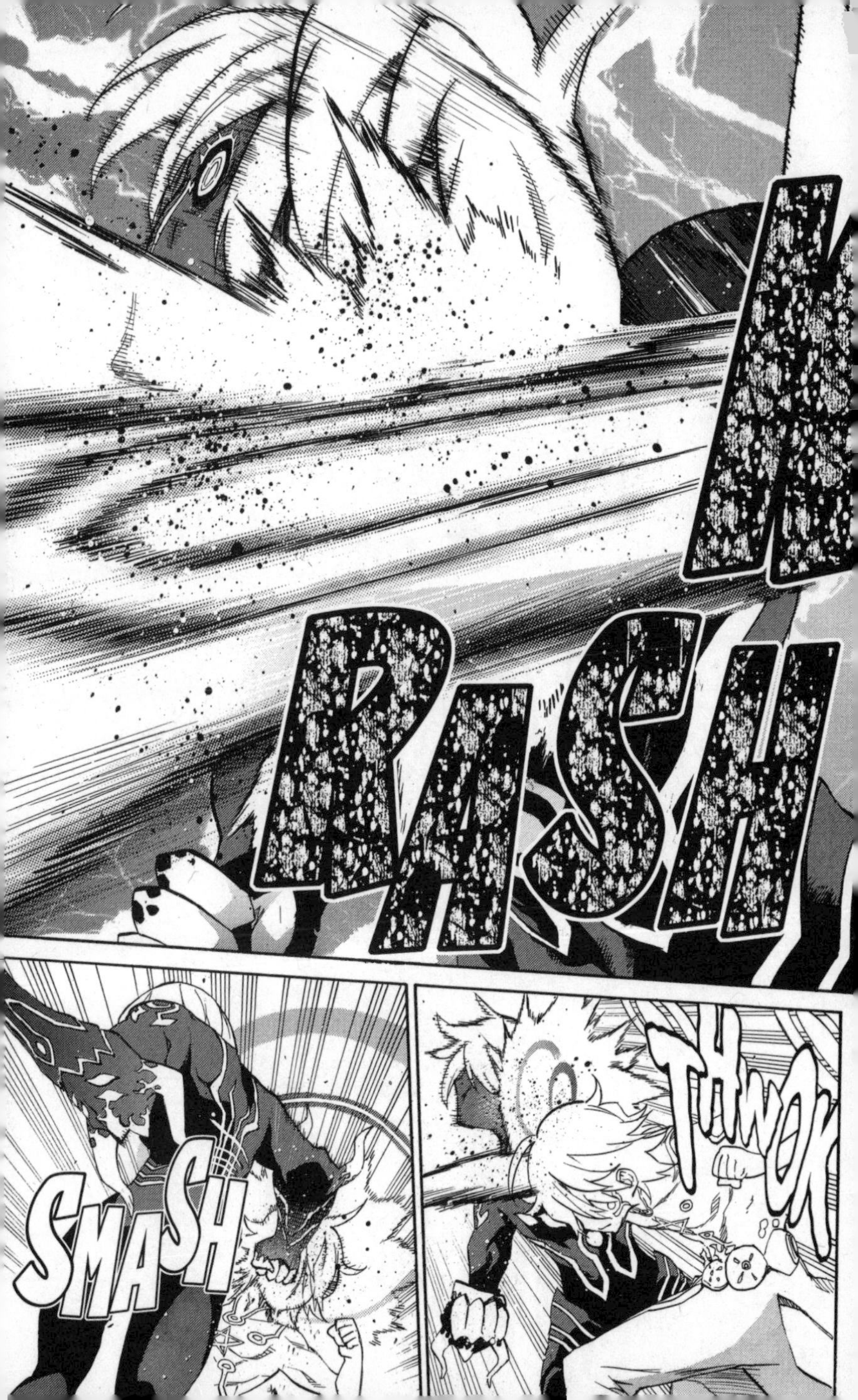
KRASH
THWOK
SMASH

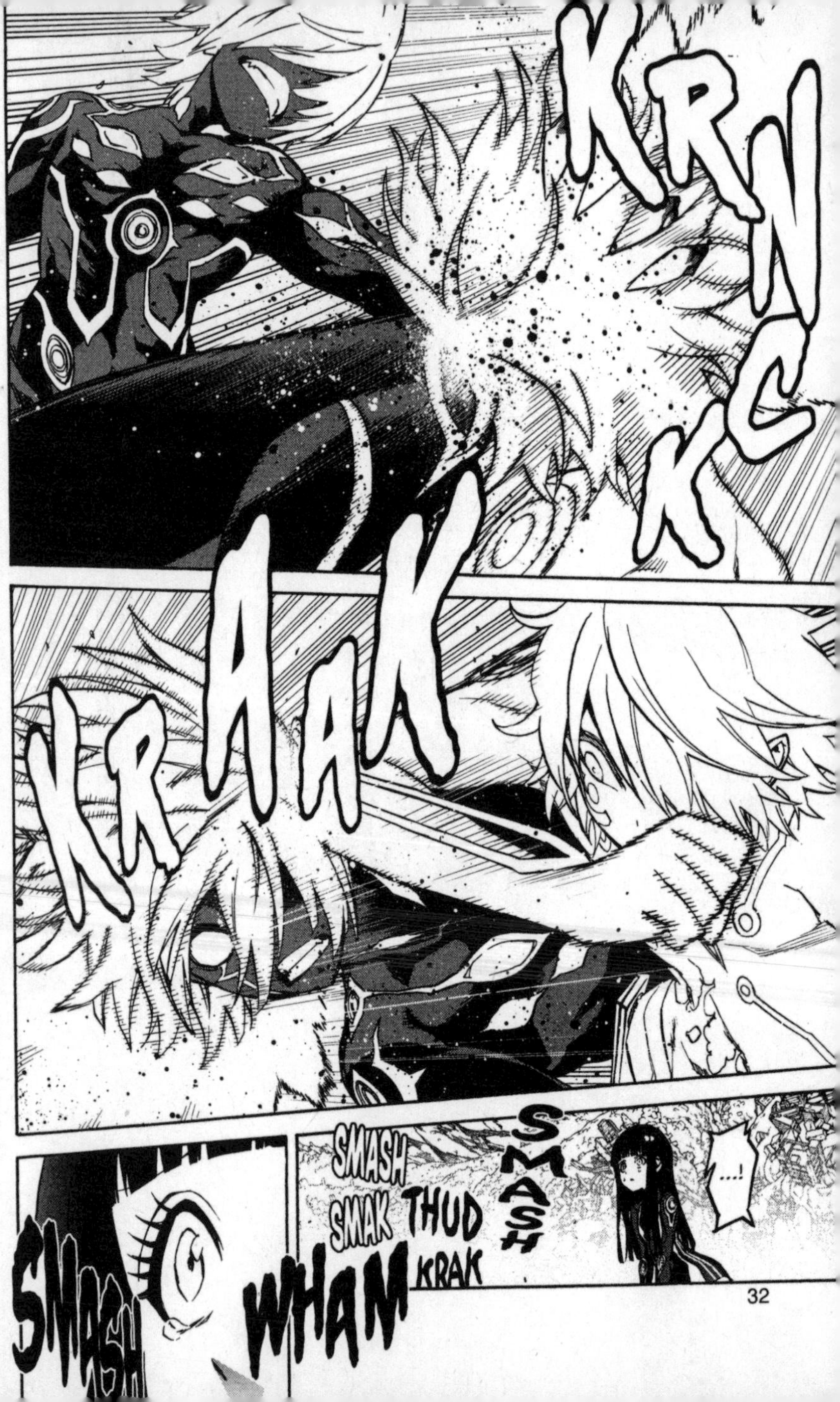
KRNCK
KRAAK
...!
SMASH
SMASH
SMAK
THUD
KRAK
SMASH
WHAM

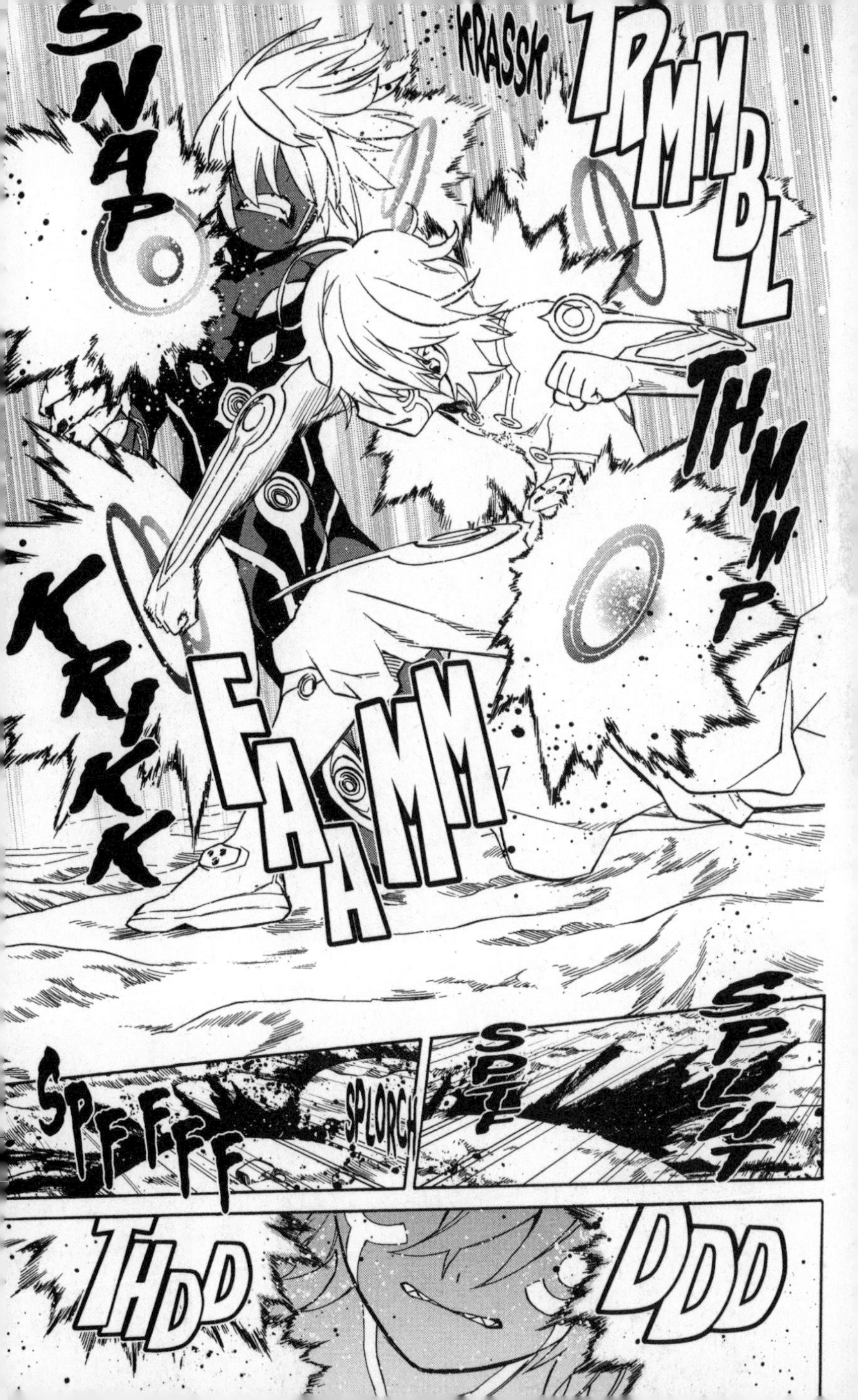
TRMMBL
KRASSK
SNAP
THMMP
FAAMM
KRIKK
SPLIT
SPIT
SPLORCH
SPFFFF
THDD
DDD

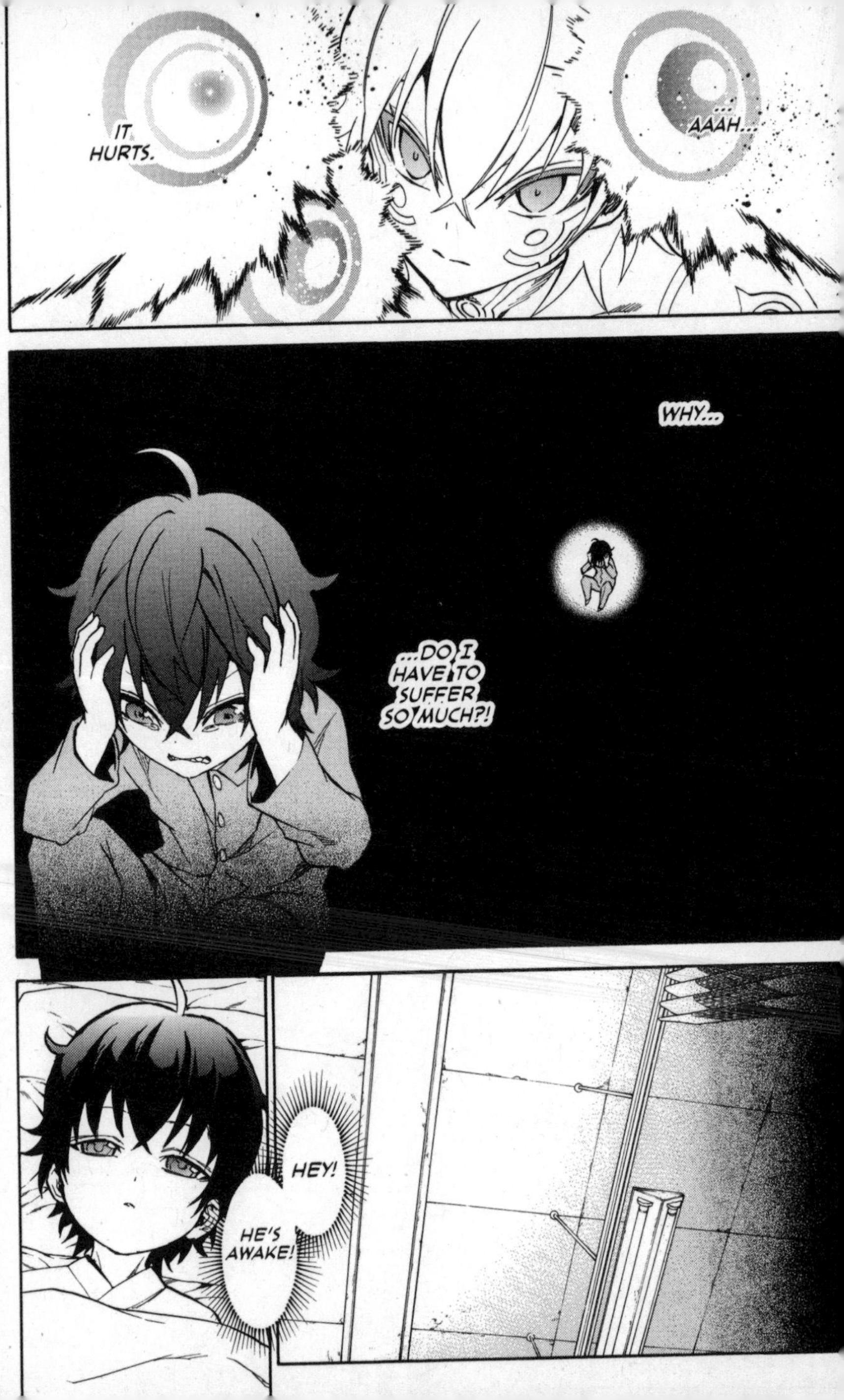
...AAAH...
IT HURTS.
WHY...
...DO I HAVE TO SUFFER SO MUCH?!
HEY!
HE'S AWAKE!

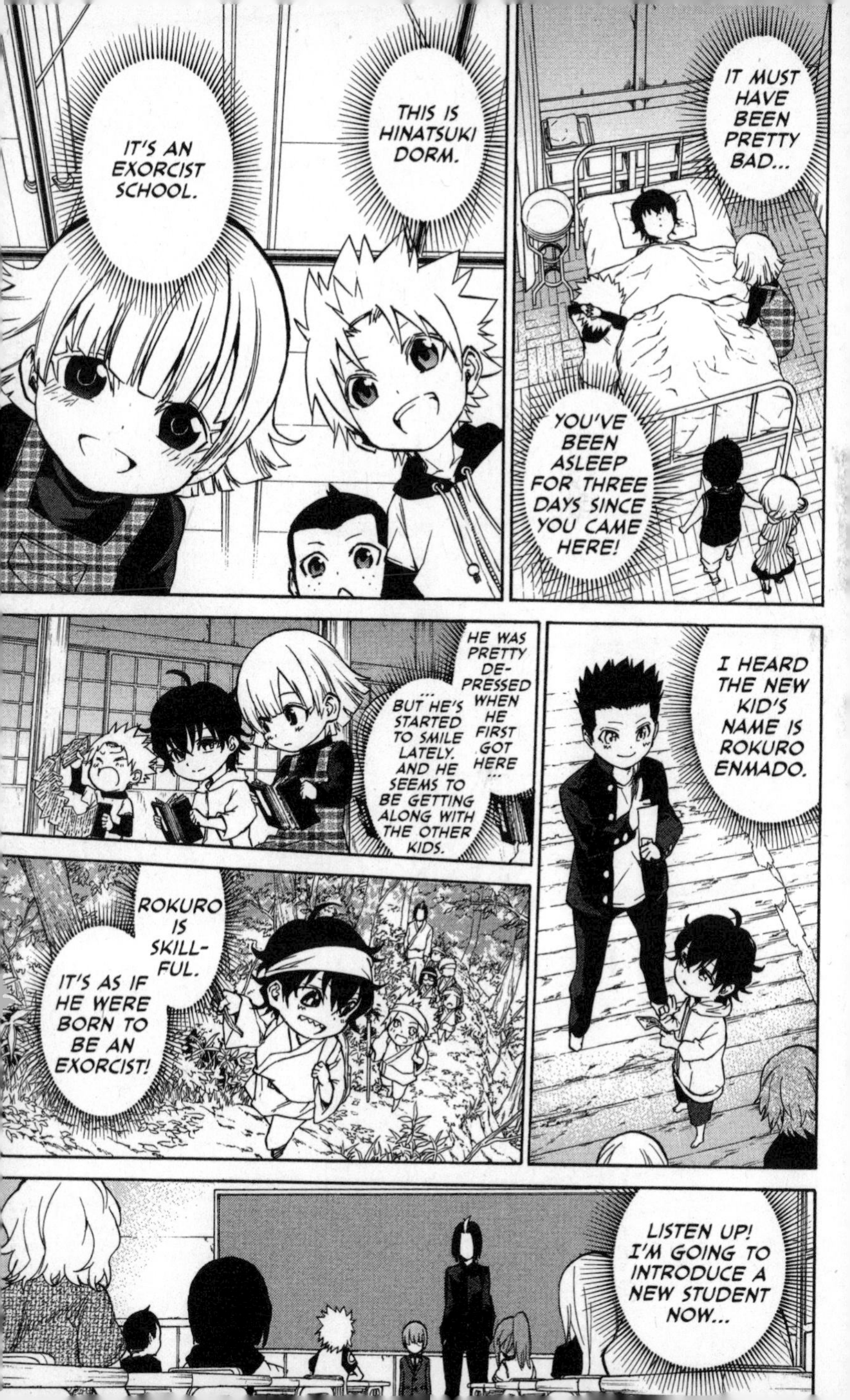
IT MUST HAVE BEEN PRETTY BAD...
YOU'VE BEEN ASLEEP FOR THREE DAYS SINCE YOU CAME HERE!
THIS IS HINATSUKI DORM.
IT'S AN EXORCIST SCHOOL.
I HEARD THE NEW KID'S NAME IS ROKURO ENMADO.
HE WAS PRETTY DEPRESSED WHEN HE FIRST GOT HERE...
...BUT HE'S STARTED TO SMILE LATELY. AND HE SEEMS TO BE GETTING ALONG WITH THE OTHER KIDS.
ROKURO IS SKILLFUL.
IT'S AS IF HE WERE BORN TO BE AN EXORCIST!
LISTEN UP! I'M GOING TO INTRODUCE A NEW STUDENT NOW...

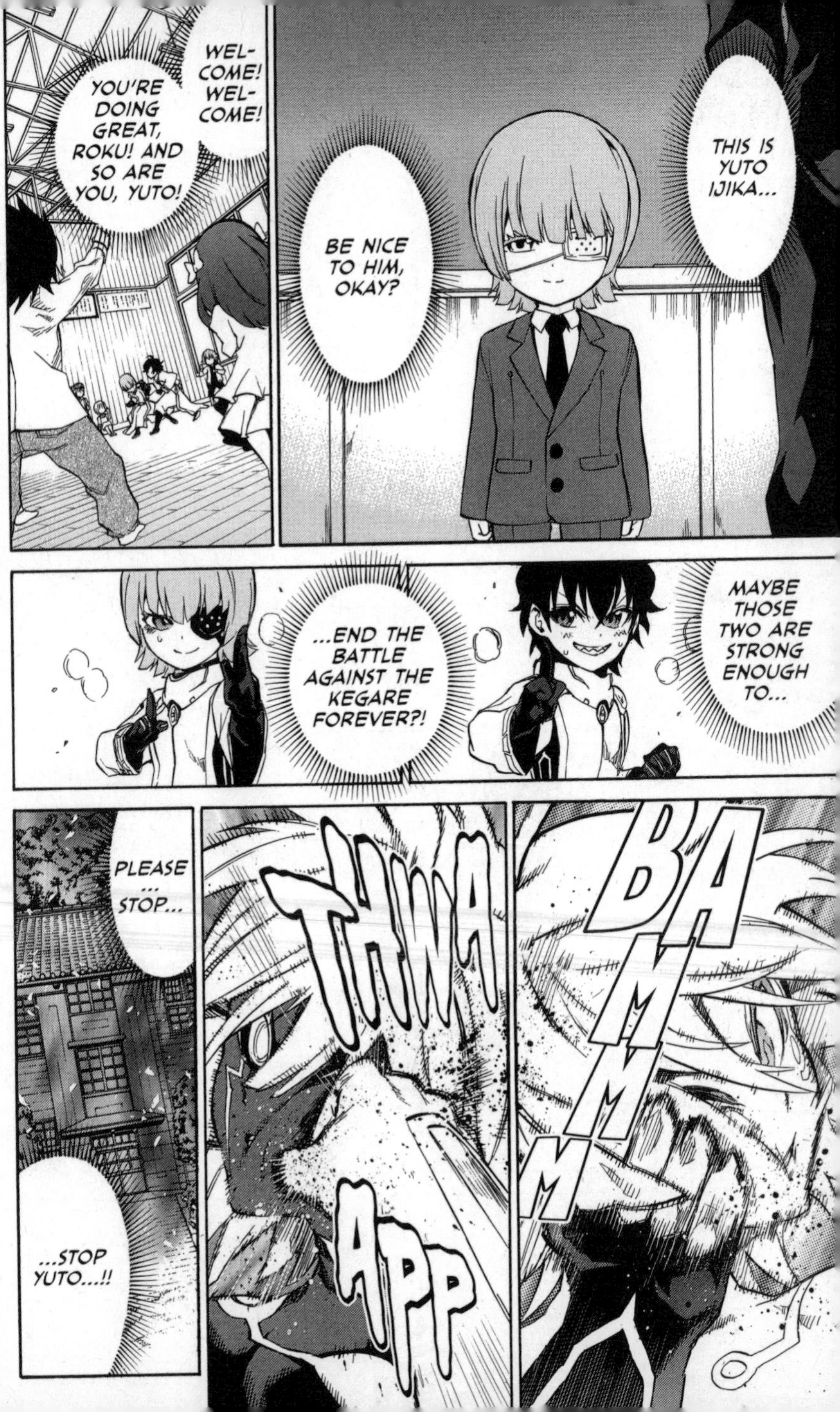
THIS IS YUTO IJIKA...
BE NICE TO HIM, OKAY?
WEL-COME! WEL-COME!
YOU'RE DOING GREAT, ROKU! AND SO ARE YOU, YUTO!
MAYBE THOSE TWO ARE STRONG ENOUGH TO...
...END THE BATTLE AGAINST THE KEGARE FOREVER?!
BAMMM
THWA
APP
PLEASE... STOP...
...STOP YUTO...!!

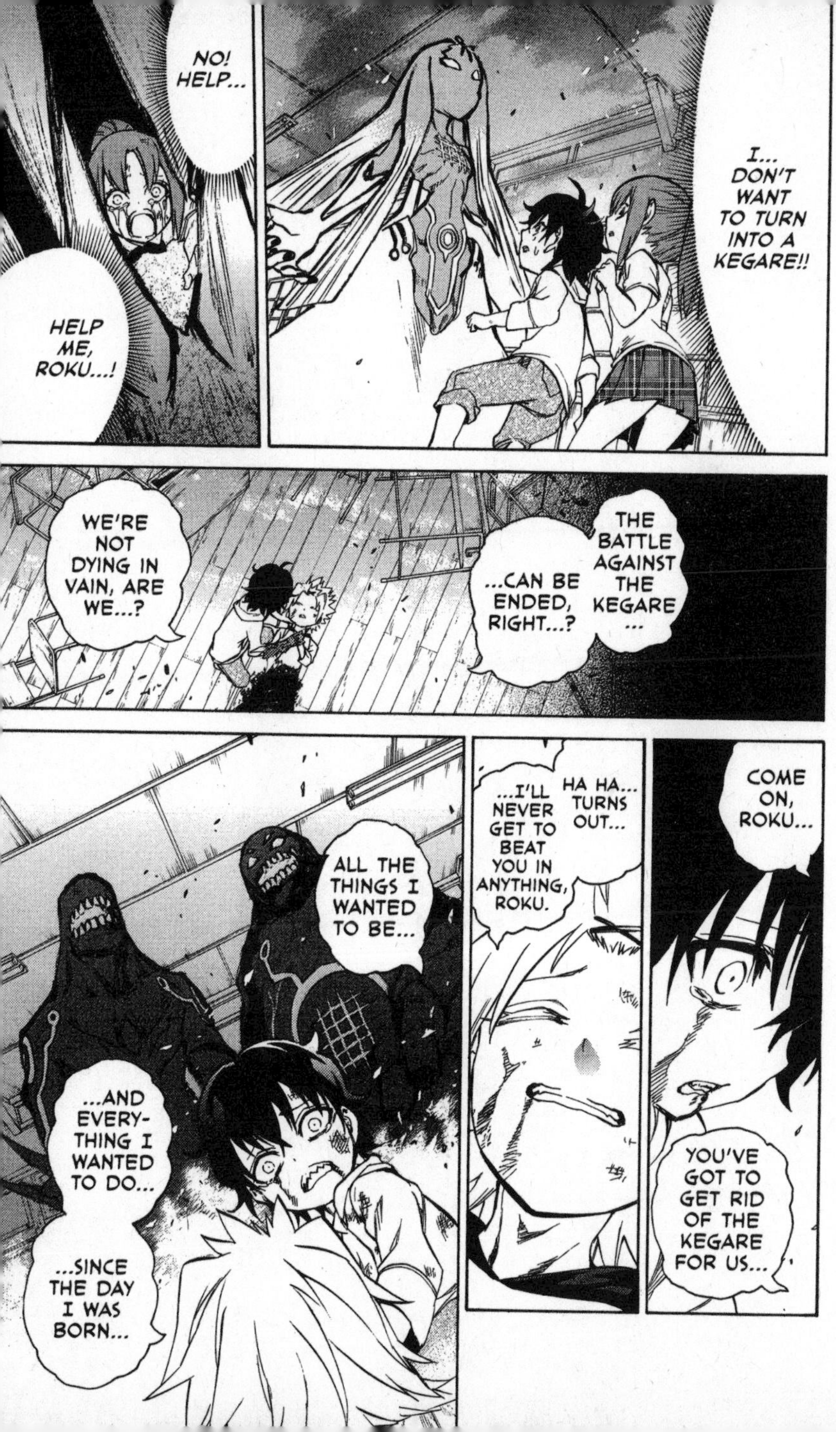
I... DON'T WANT TO TURN INTO A KEGARE!!
NO! HELP...
HELP ME, ROKU...!
THE BATTLE AGAINST THE KEGARE ...
...CAN BE ENDED, RIGHT...?
WE'RE NOT DYING IN VAIN, ARE WE...?
COME ON, ROKU...
YOU'VE GOT TO GET RID OF THE KEGARE FOR US...
HA HA... TURNS OUT...
...I'LL NEVER GET TO BEAT YOU IN ANYTHING, ROKU.
ALL THE THINGS I WANTED TO BE...
...AND EVERY-THING I WANTED TO DO...
...SINCE THE DAY I WAS BORN...

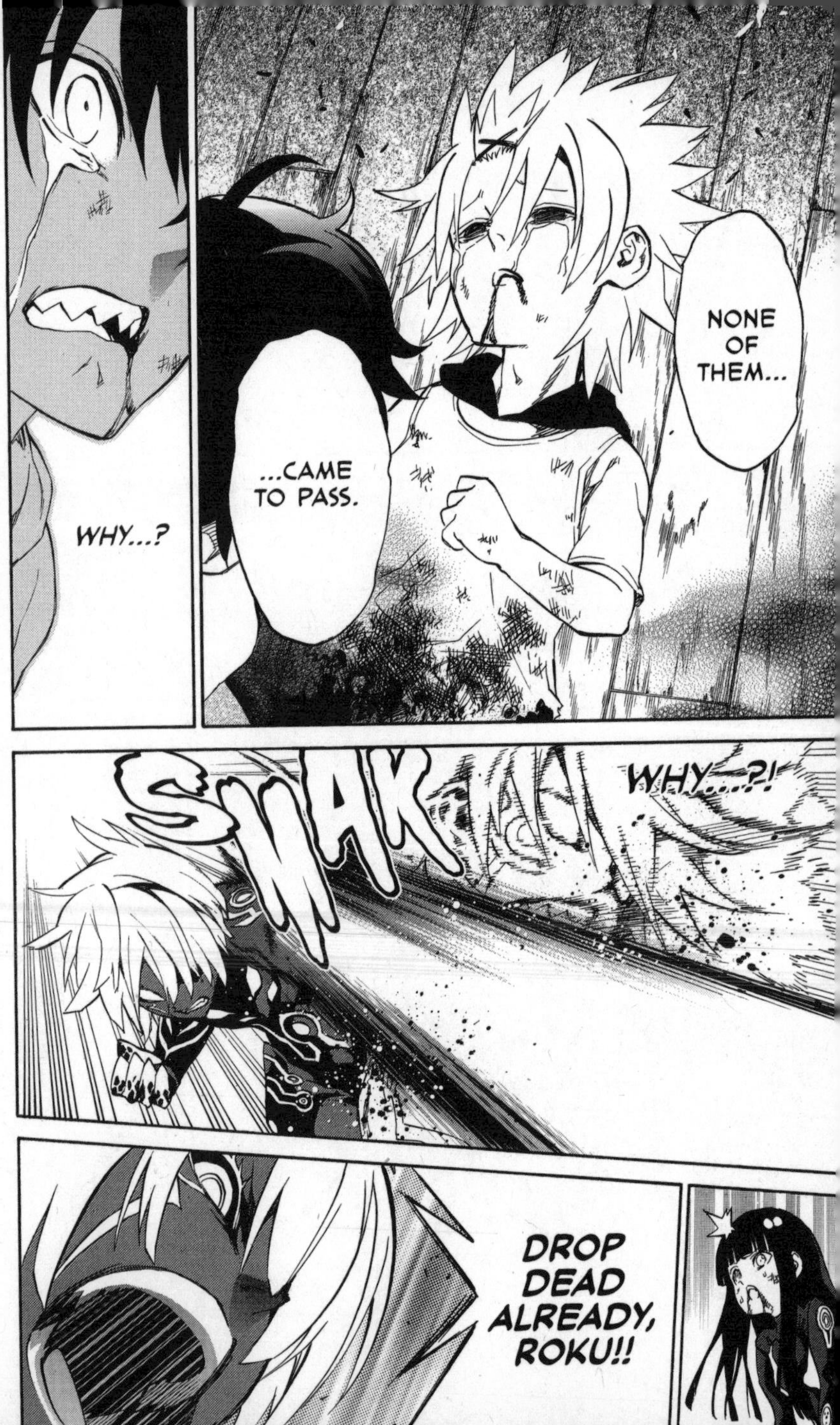
NONE OF THEM...
...CAME TO PASS.
WHY...?
WHY...?!
SNAK
DROP DEAD ALREADY, ROKU!!

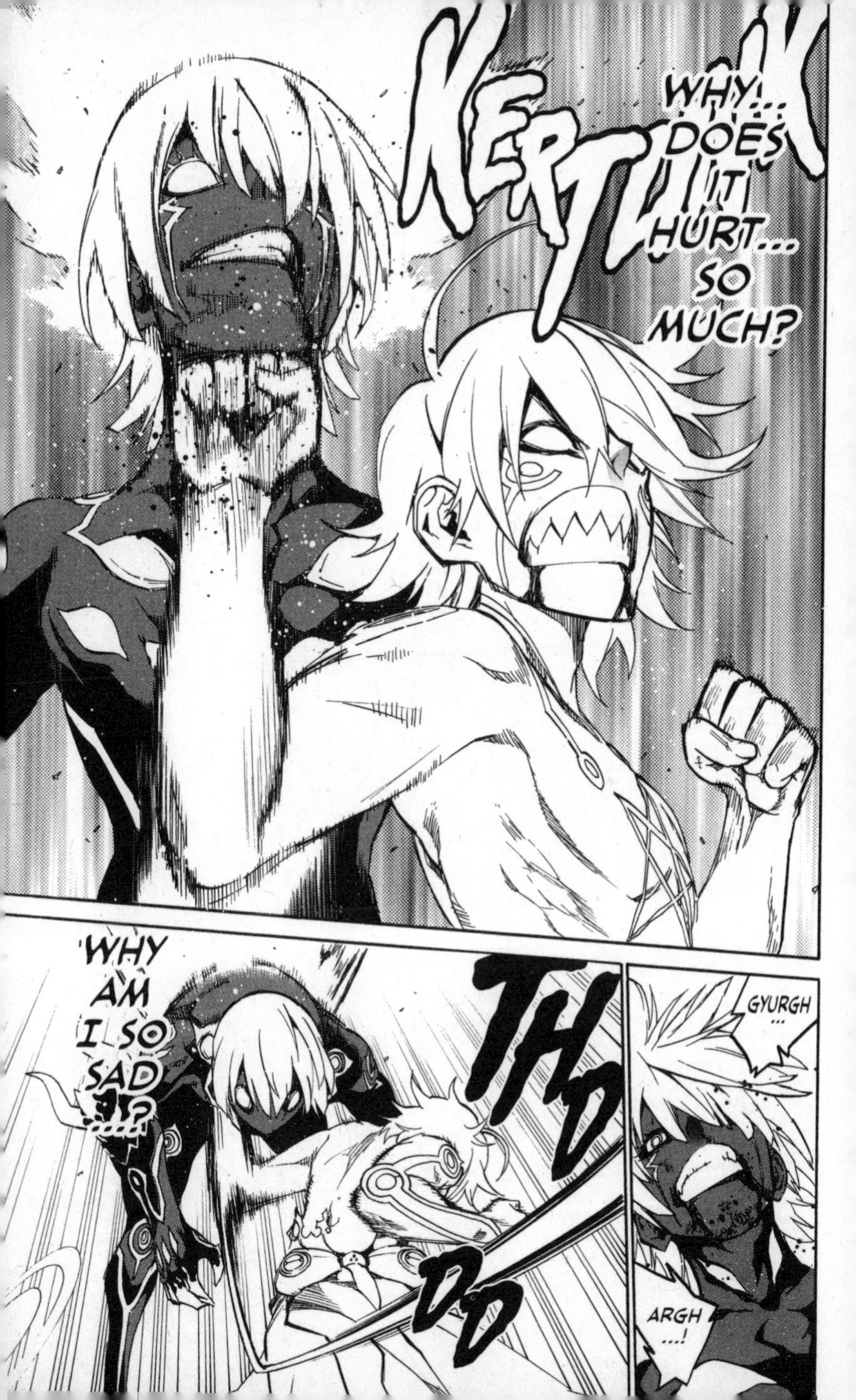
WHY... DOES IT HURT... SO MUCH?
GYURGH...
ARGH...!
WHY AM I SO SAD...?

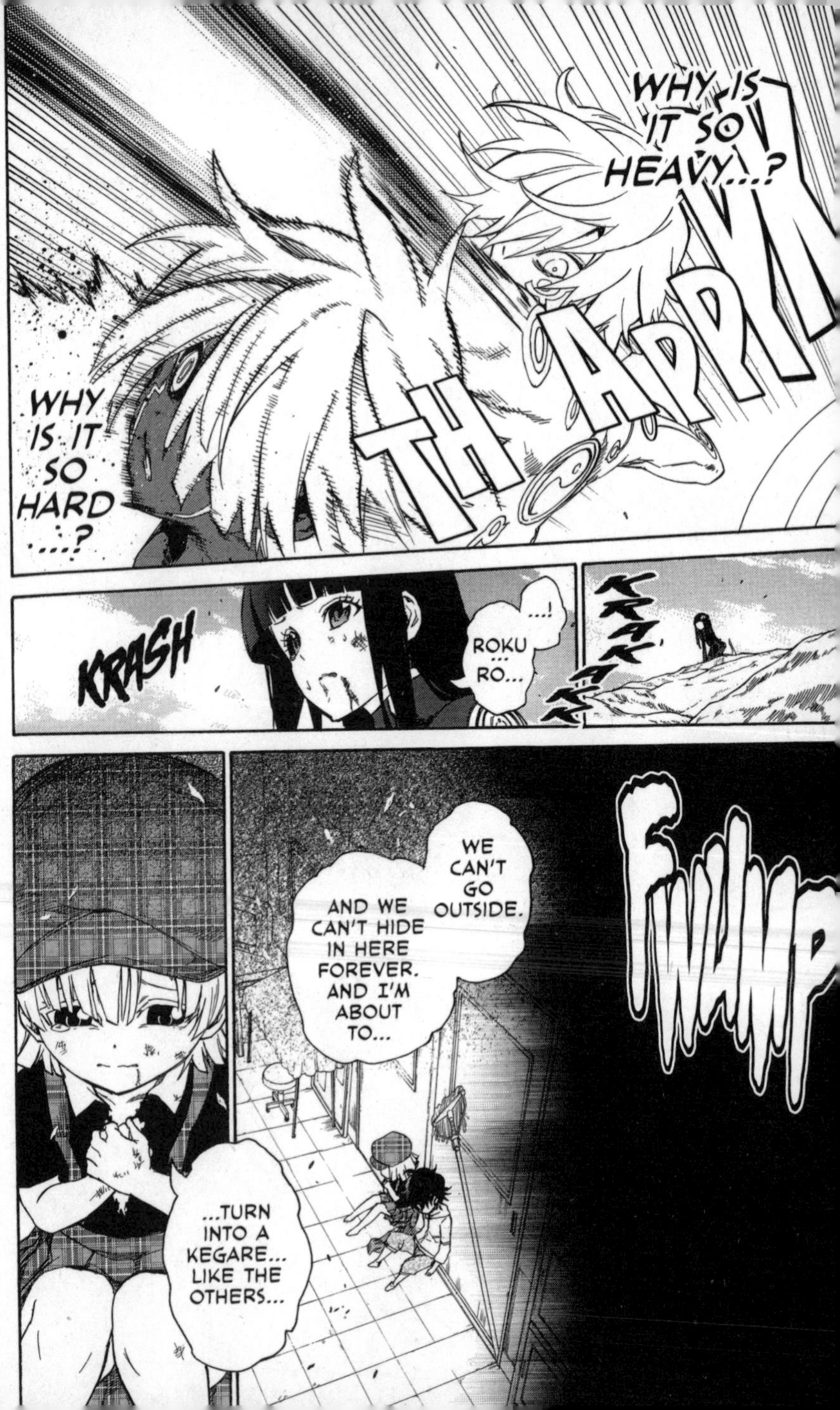
WHY IS IT SO HEAVY...?
THAPP
WHY IS IT SO HARD...?
KRAKAKAK
...!
ROKU... RO...
KRASH
FWUMP
WE CAN'T GO OUTSIDE.
AND WE CAN'T HIDE IN HERE FOREVER. AND I'M ABOUT TO...
...TURN INTO A KEGARE... LIKE THE OTHERS...

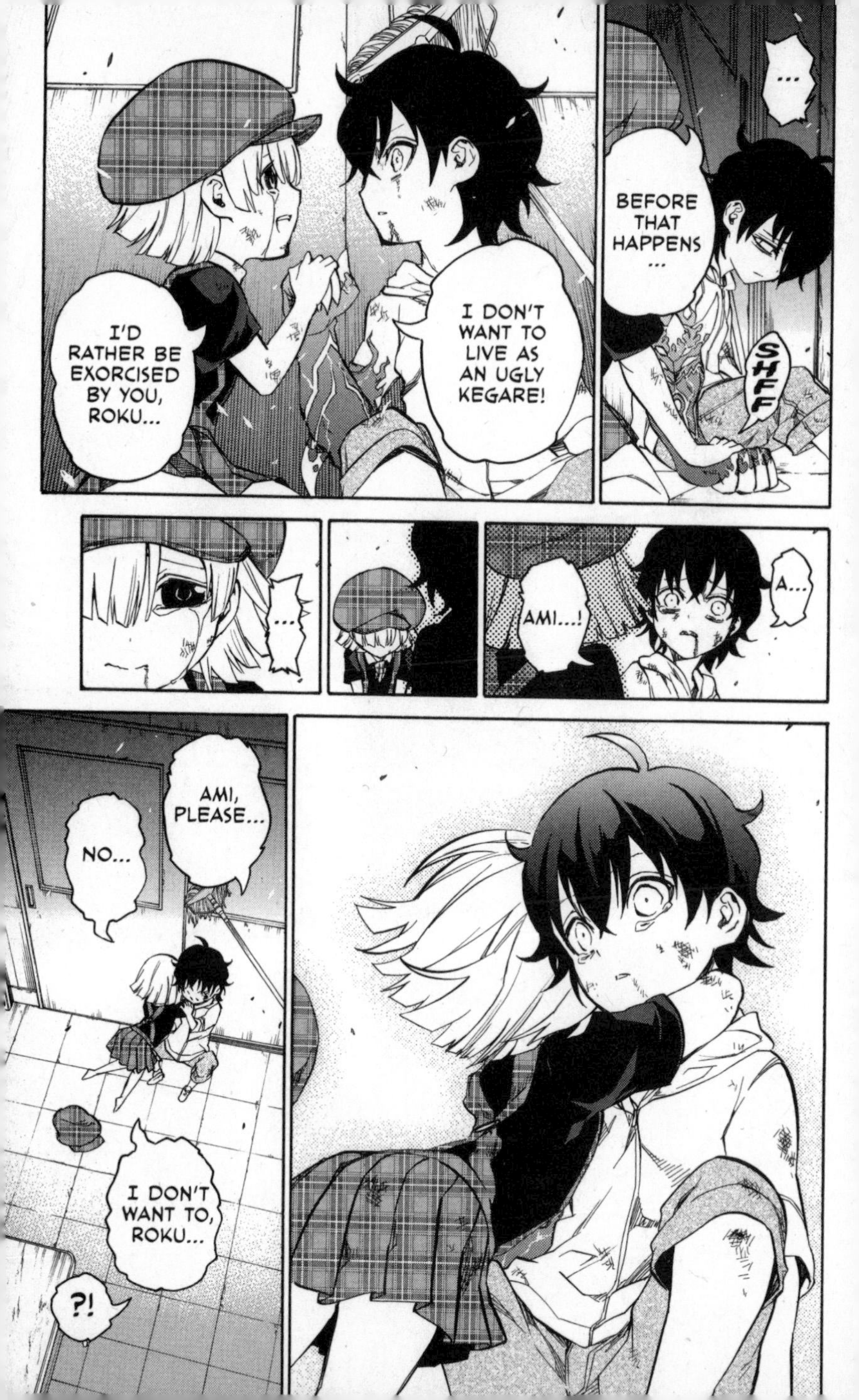
...
BEFORE THAT HAPPENS ...
SHFF
I DON'T WANT TO LIVE AS AN UGLY KEGARE!
I'D RATHER BE EXORCISED BY YOU, ROKU...
A...
AMI...!
...
AMI, PLEASE...
NO...
I DON'T WANT TO, ROKU...
?!

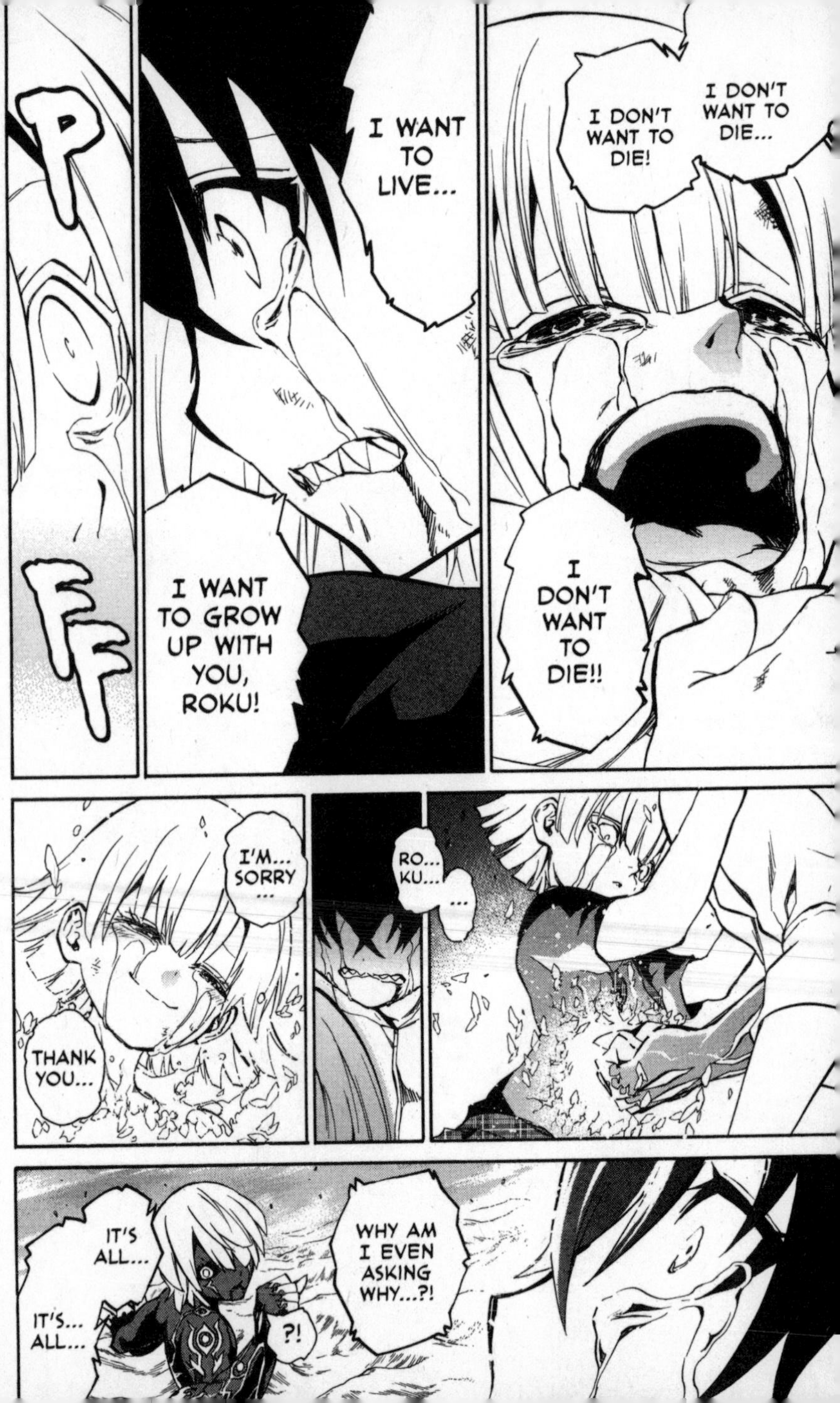
I DON'T WANT TO DIE...
I DON'T WANT TO DIE!
I DON'T WANT TO DIE!!
I WANT TO LIVE...
I WANT TO GROW UP WITH YOU, ROKU!
PFF
RO... KU... ...
I'M... SORRY ...
THANK YOU...
WHY AM I EVEN ASKING WHY...?!
?!
IT'S ALL...
IT'S... ALL...

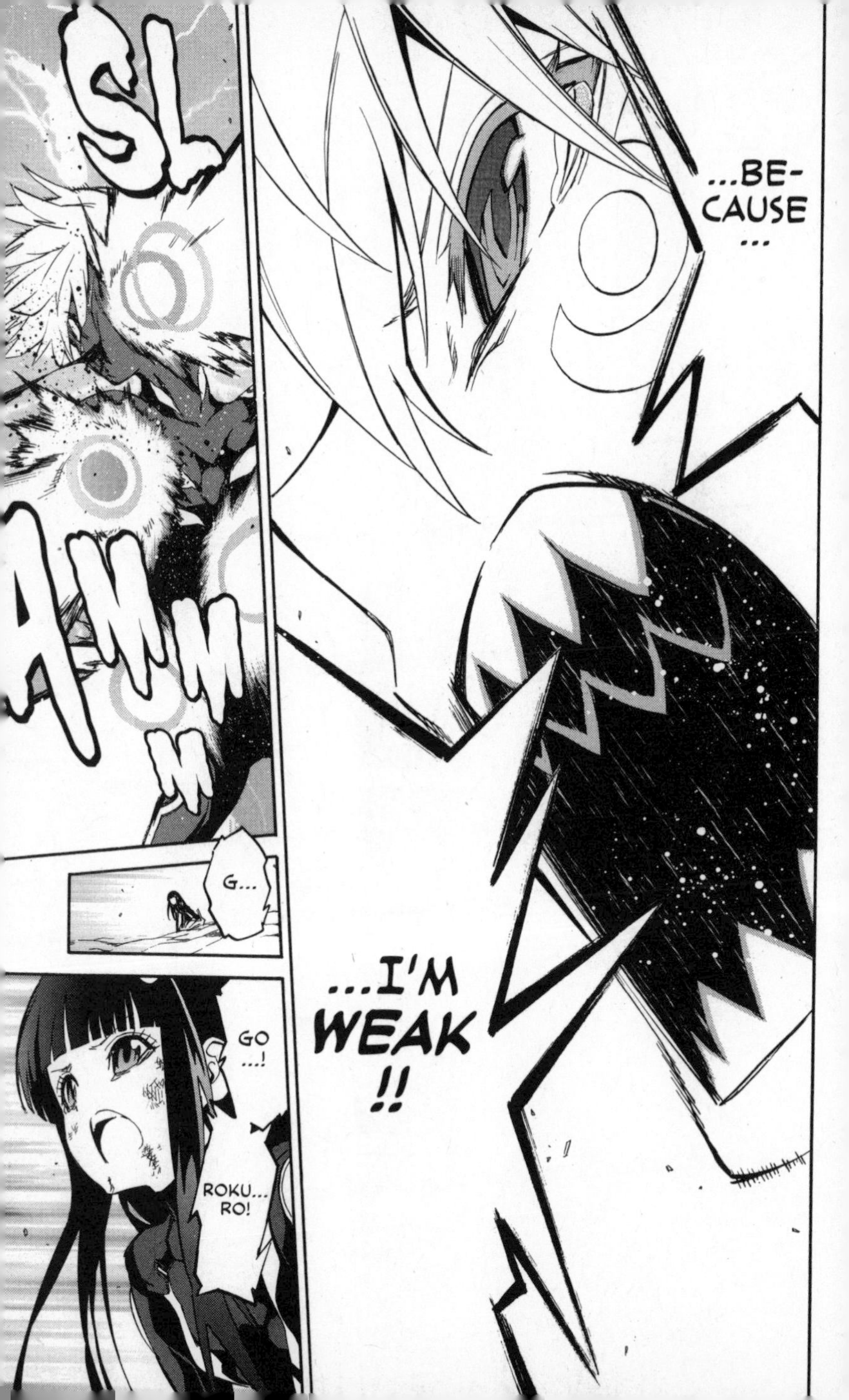
...BE-
CAUSE
...
...I'M
WEAK
!!
SL
AMM
M
G...
GO
...!
ROKU...
RO!

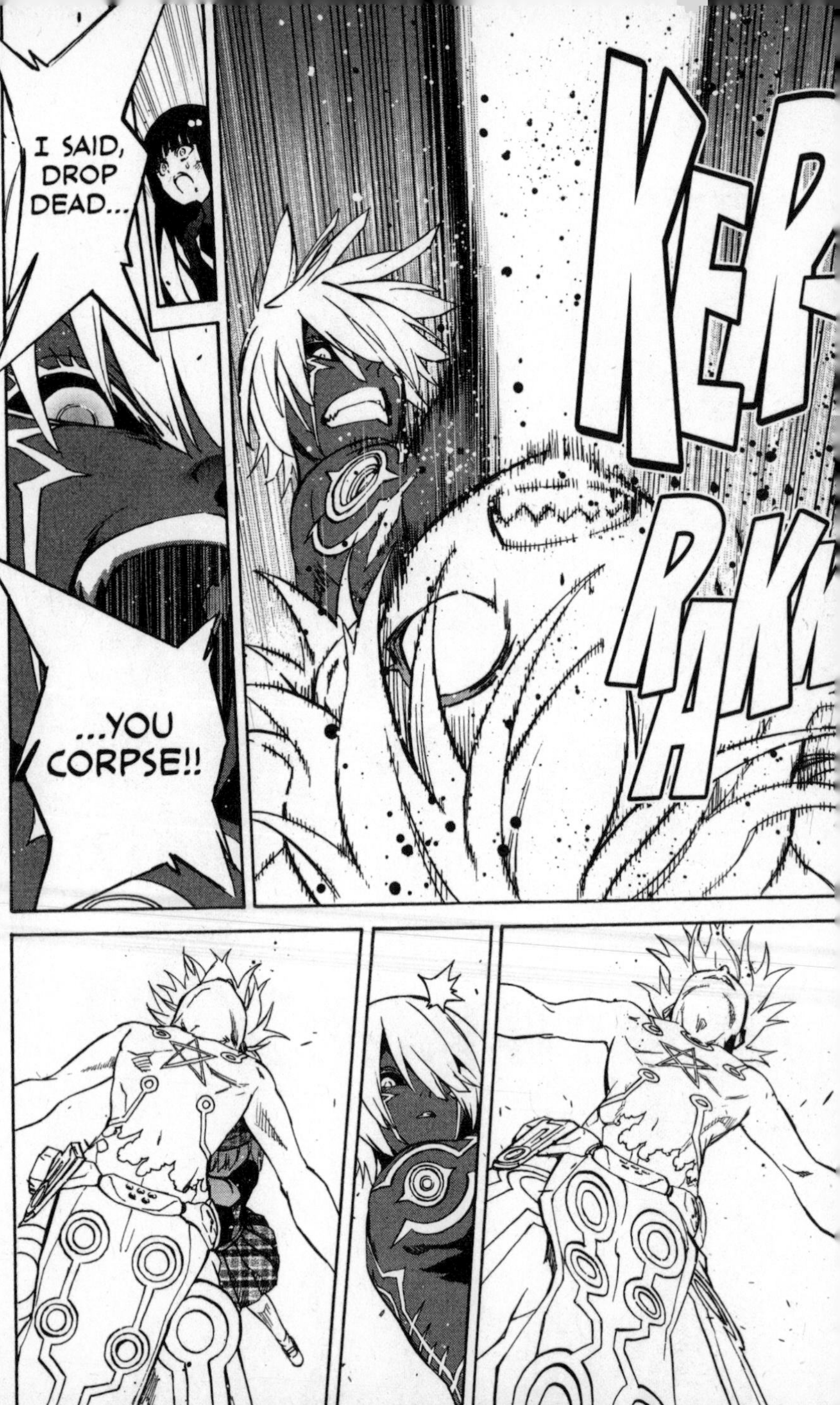
I SAID, DROP DEAD...
...YOU CORPSE!!

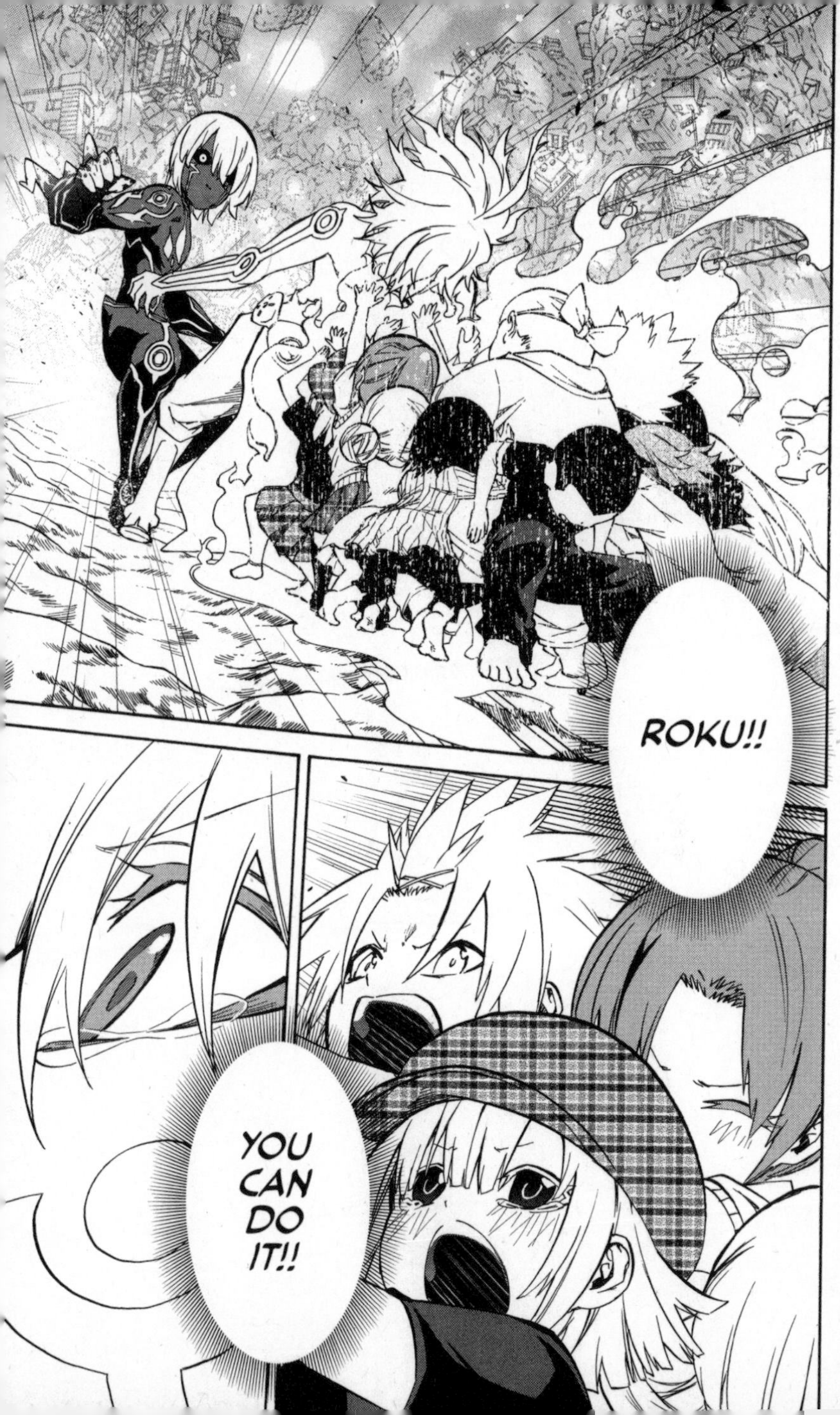
ROKU!!
YOU CAN DO IT!!

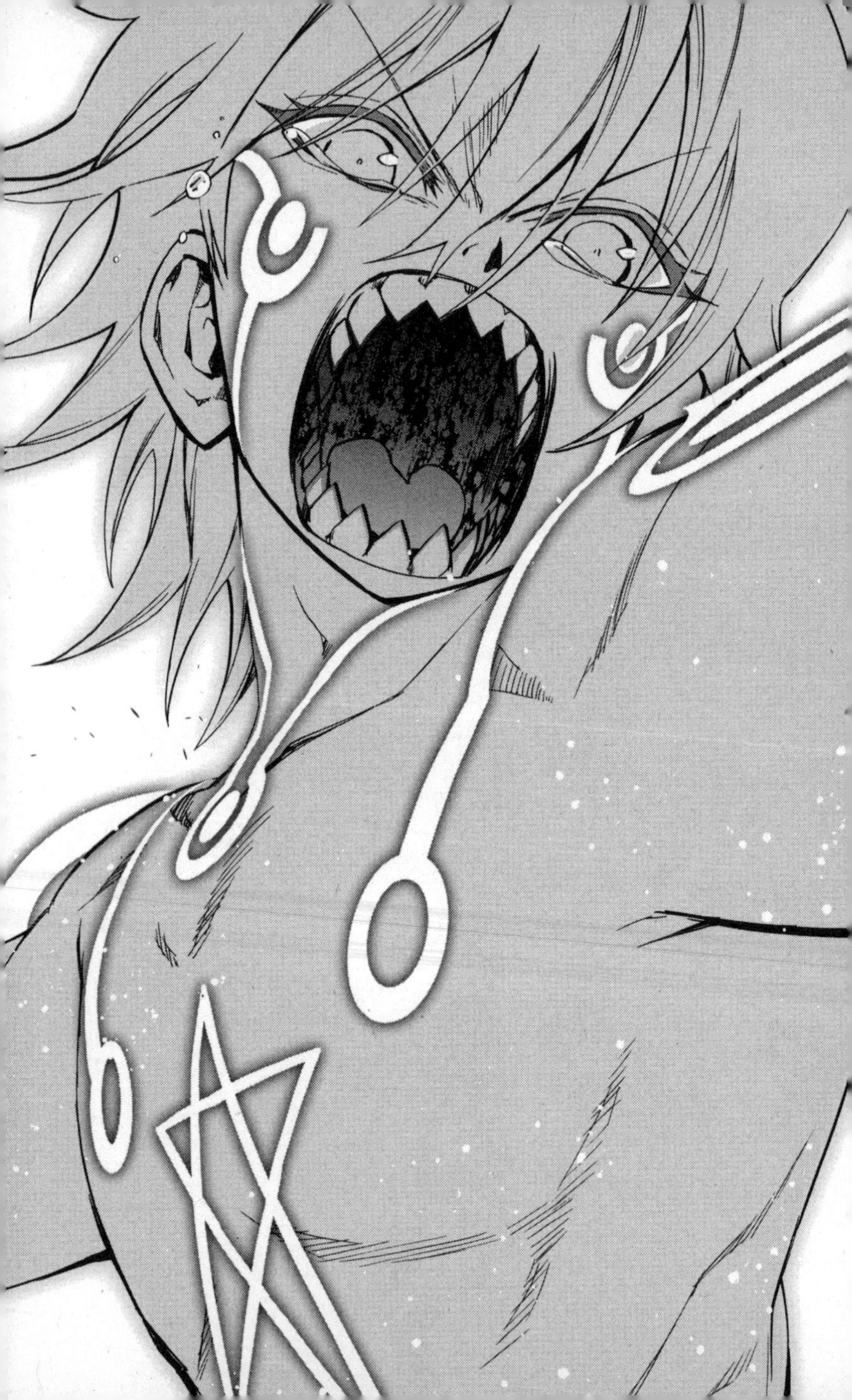

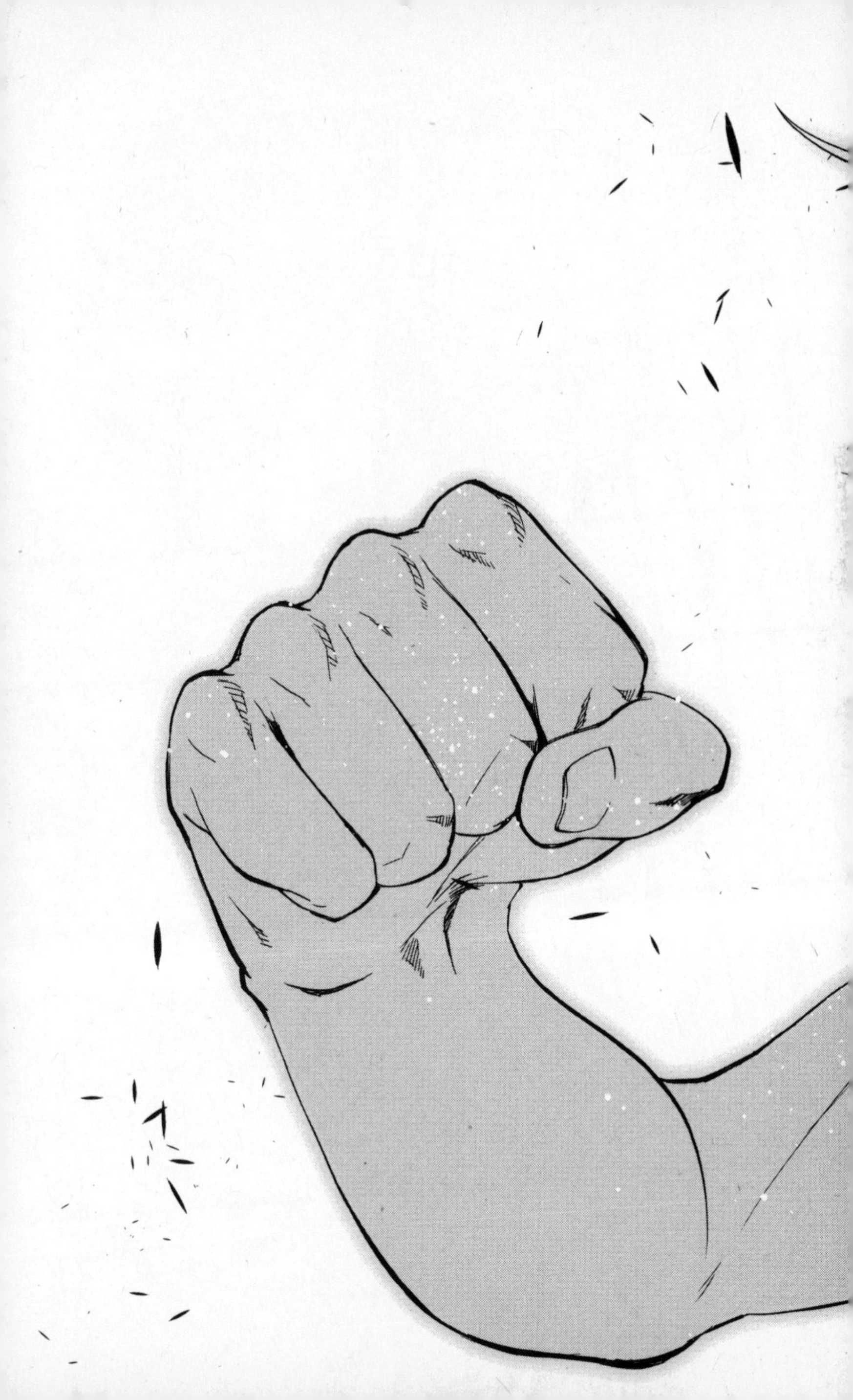

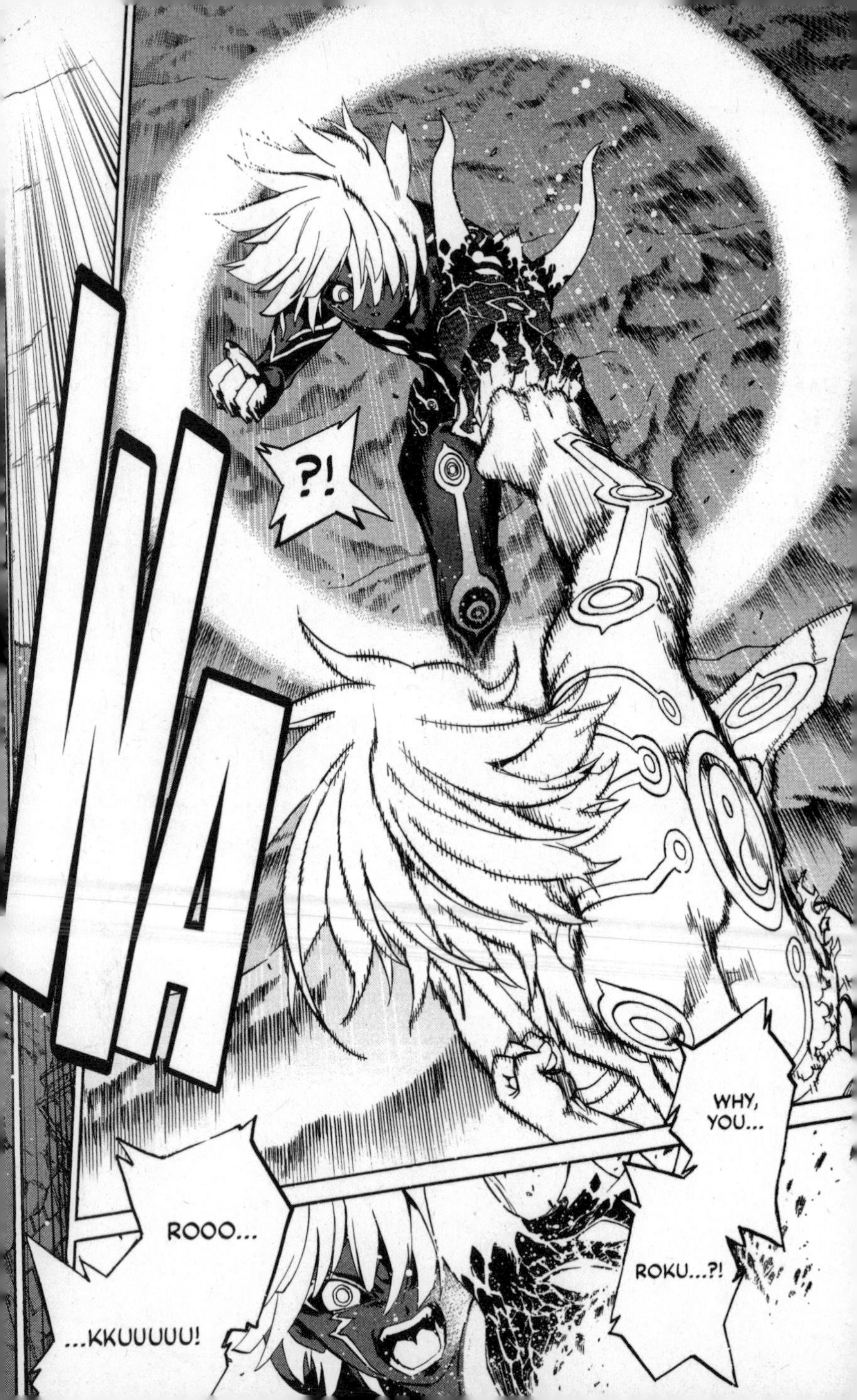
?!
WHY, YOU... ROKU...?!
ROOO... ...KKUUUUU!

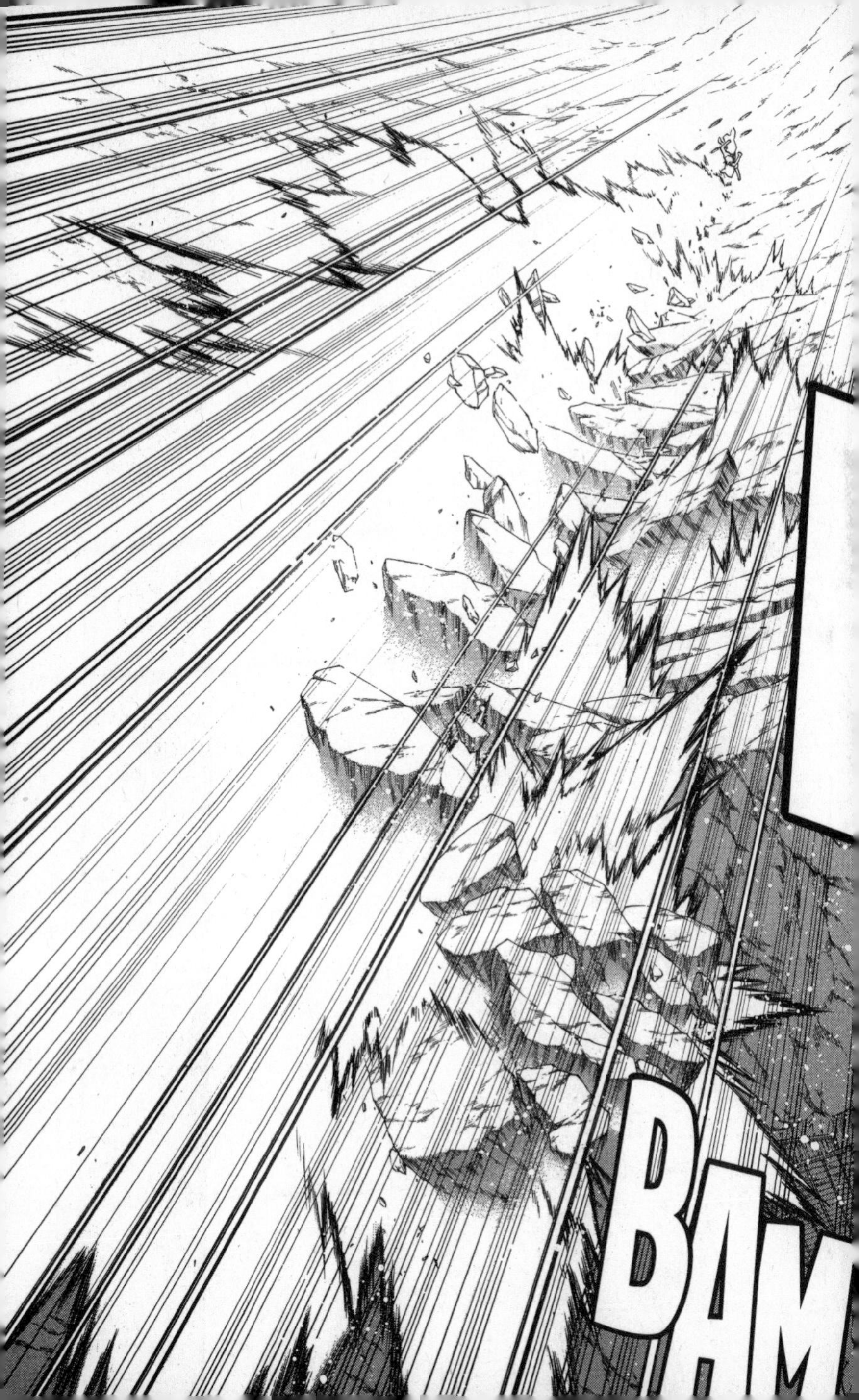
BAM

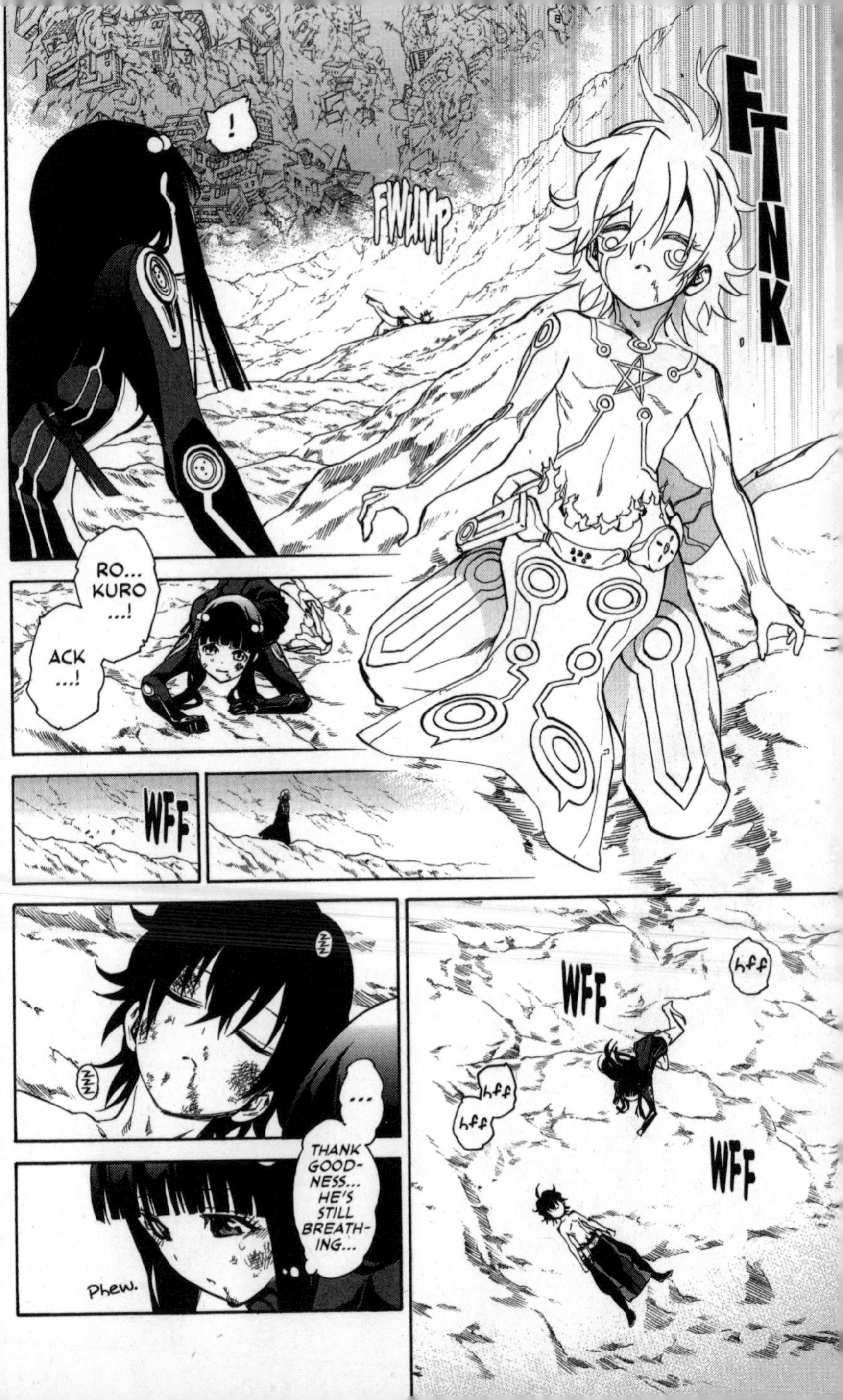

FTNK
FWUMP
!
RO... KURO ...!
ACK ...!
WFF
hff
WFF
hff
hff
WFF
ZZZ
ZZZ
...
THANK GOOD-NESS... HE'S STILL BREATH-ING...
Phew.

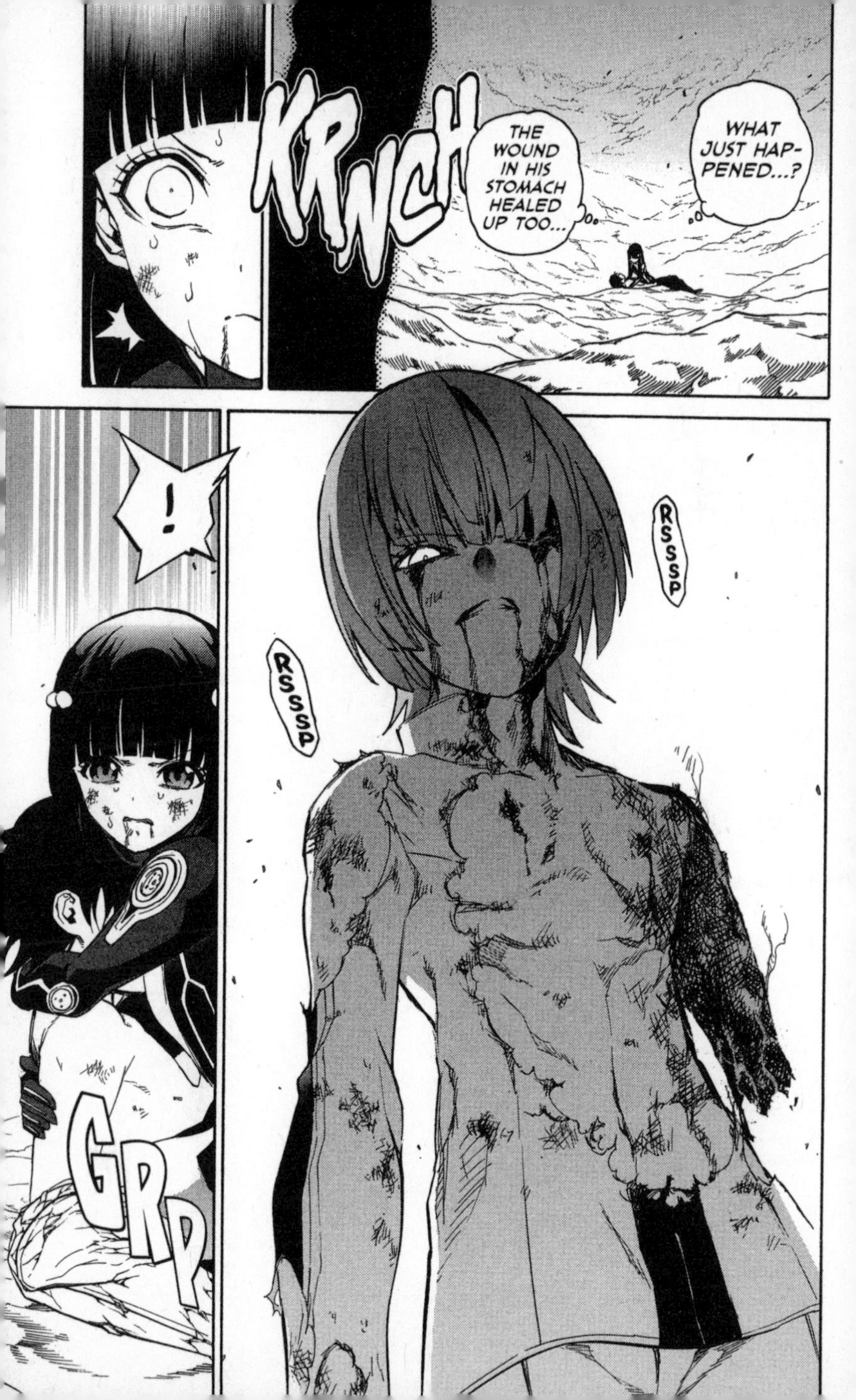
WHAT JUST HAP-PENED...?
THE WOUND IN HIS STOMACH HEALED UP TOO...
KRNCH
RSSSP
RSSSP
!
GRP

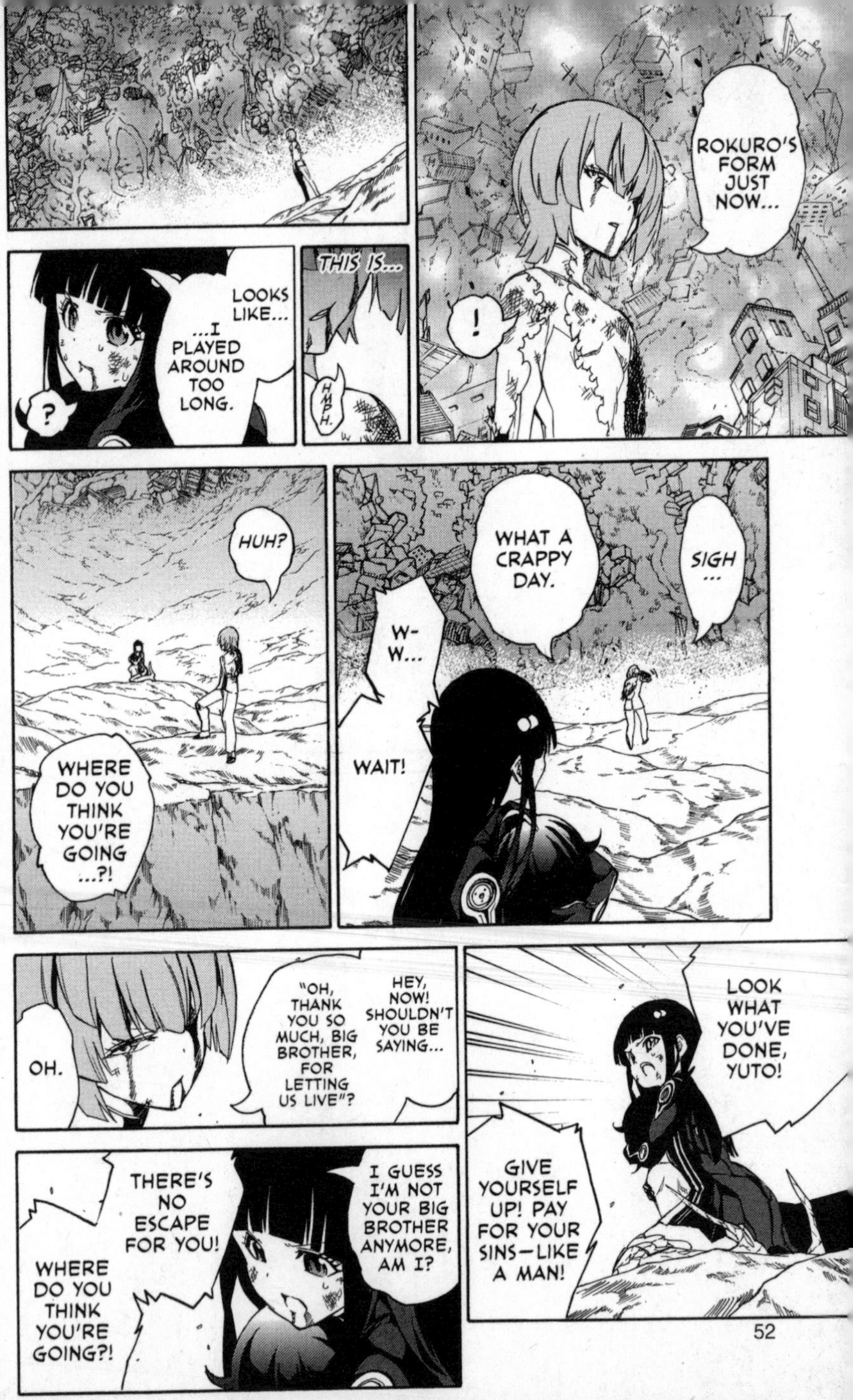
ROKURO'S FORM JUST NOW...
!
THIS IS...
HMPH.
LOOKS LIKE... ...I PLAYED AROUND TOO LONG.
?
SIGH...
WHAT A CRAPPY DAY.
W-W...
WAIT!
HUH?
WHERE DO YOU THINK YOU'RE GOING...?!
LOOK WHAT YOU'VE DONE, YUTO!
GIVE YOURSELF UP! PAY FOR YOUR SINS—LIKE A MAN!
HEY, NOW! SHOULDN'T YOU BE SAYING...
"OH, THANK YOU SO MUCH, BIG BROTHER, FOR LETTING US LIVE"?
OH.
I GUESS I'M NOT YOUR BIG BROTHER ANYMORE, AM I?
THERE'S NO ESCAPE FOR YOU!
WHERE DO YOU THINK YOU'RE GOING?!

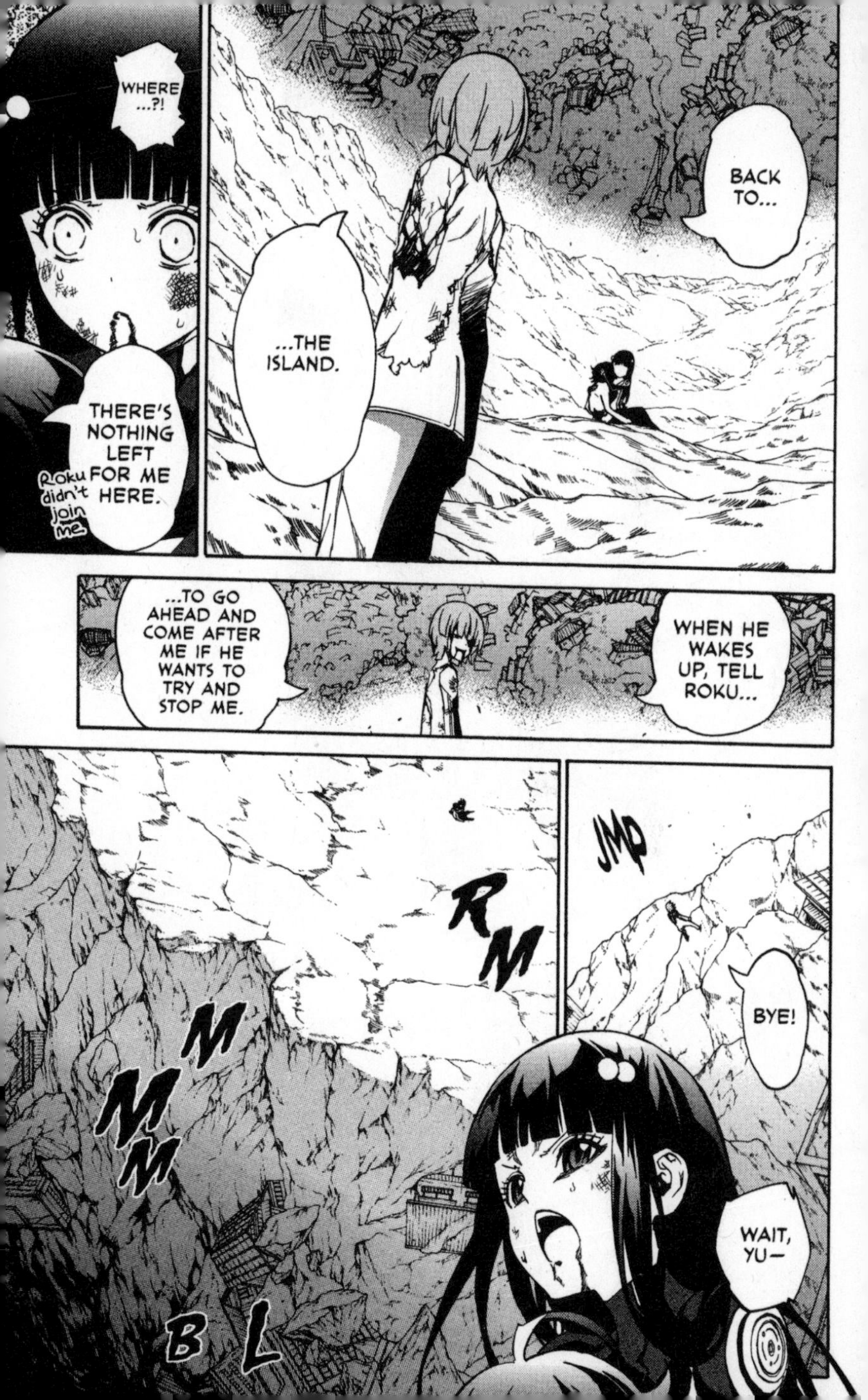
BACK TO...
...THE ISLAND.
WHERE ...?!
THERE'S NOTHING LEFT FOR ME HERE.
Roku didn't join me.
WHEN HE WAKES UP, TELL ROKU...
...TO GO AHEAD AND COME AFTER ME IF HE WANTS TO TRY AND STOP ME.
JMP
BYE!
WAIT, YU—
RM
MMM
BL

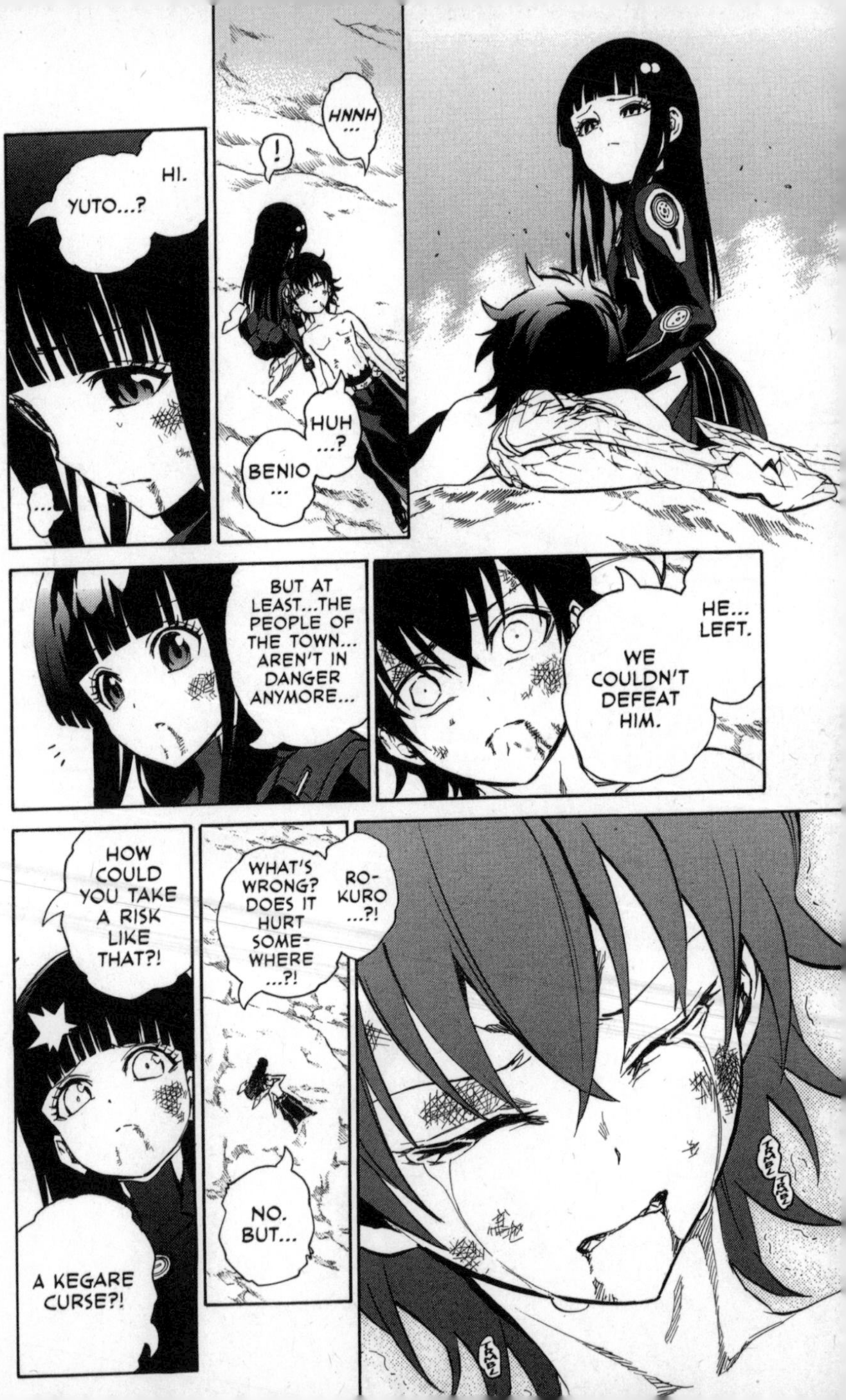
HNNH ...
!
HUH ...?
BENIO ...
HI.
YUTO...?
...
HE... LEFT.
WE COULDN'T DEFEAT HIM.
BUT AT LEAST...THE PEOPLE OF THE TOWN... AREN'T IN DANGER ANYMORE...
RO-KURO ...?!
WHAT'S WRONG? DOES IT HURT SOME-WHERE ...?!
NO. BUT...
HOW COULD YOU TAKE A RISK LIKE THAT?!
A KEGARE CURSE?!

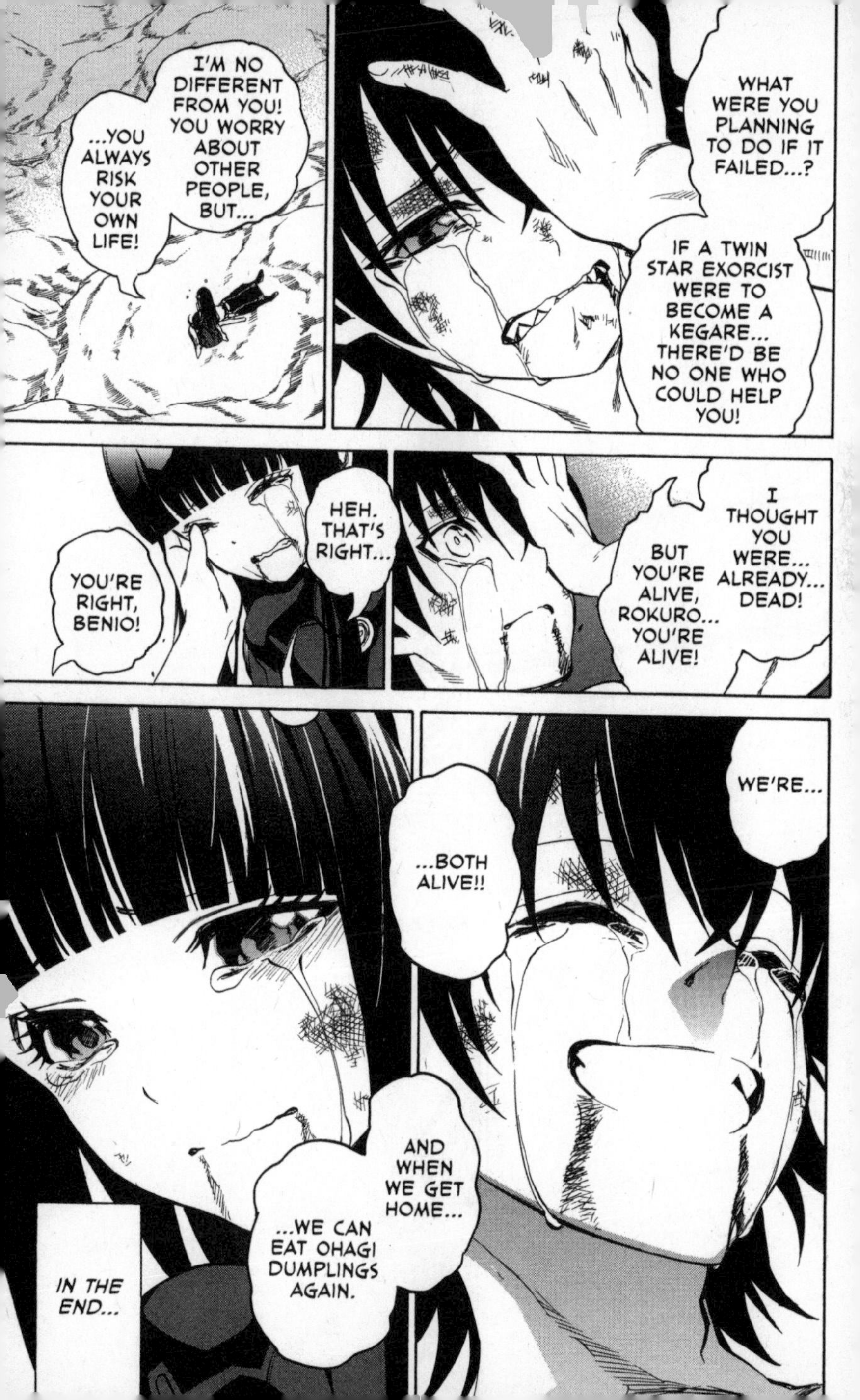
WHAT WERE YOU PLANNING TO DO IF IT FAILED...?
IF A TWIN STAR EXORCIST WERE TO BECOME A KEGARE... THERE'D BE NO ONE WHO COULD HELP YOU!
I'M NO DIFFERENT FROM YOU! YOU WORRY ABOUT OTHER PEOPLE, BUT...
...YOU ALWAYS RISK YOUR OWN LIFE!
I THOUGHT YOU WERE... ALREADY... DEAD!
BUT YOU'RE ALIVE, ROKURO... YOU'RE ALIVE!
HEH. THAT'S RIGHT...
YOU'RE RIGHT, BENIO!
WE'RE...
...BOTH ALIVE!!
AND WHEN WE GET HOME...
...WE CAN EAT OHAGI DUMPLINGS AGAIN.
IN THE END...

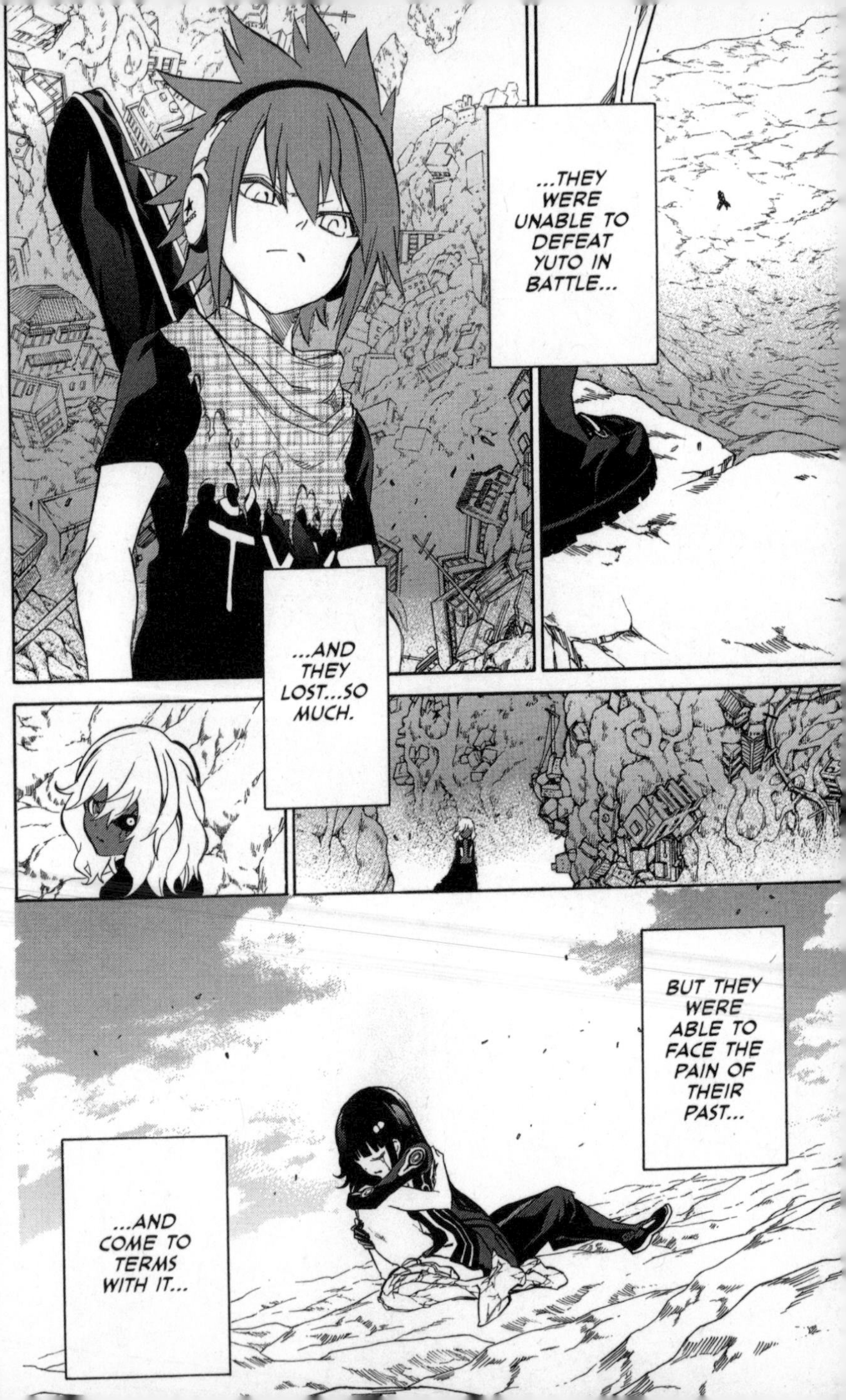
...THEY WERE UNABLE TO DEFEAT YUTO IN BATTLE...
...AND THEY LOST...SO MUCH.
BUT THEY WERE ABLE TO FACE THE PAIN OF THEIR PAST...
...AND COME TO TERMS WITH IT...

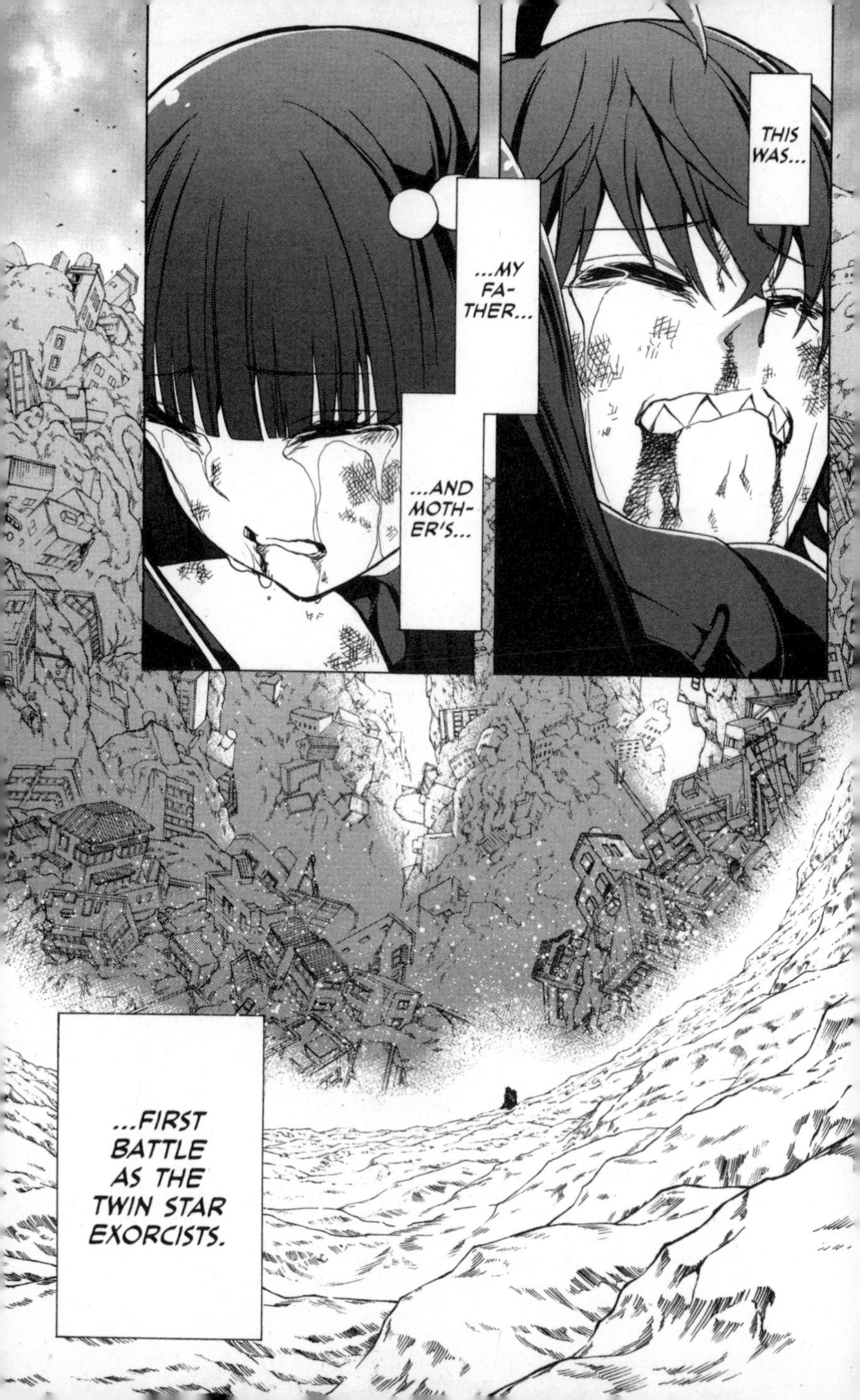
THIS WAS...
...MY FA- THER...
...AND MOTH- ER'S...
...FIRST BATTLE AS THE TWIN STAR EXORCISTS.

## Column ⑩ Seiman

A pentagram, also known as the Seimei bellflower symbol. This symbol wards off evil. It is said to have been created by Abeno Seimei. In this manga, you can see the symbol when the Kegare are exorcised as well as on Rokuro's chest when he's powered up. When casting a spell, modern-day exorcists usually use the Seiman by drawing it in midair or writing it on a piece of paper with a brush or some such instrument. The reason this Seimei bellflower symbol wards off evil is that its shape symbolizes the yin and yang and the Five Elements. I'll explain the yin and yang and Five Elements in the next column.

# #16 The Day Rokuro Arrived

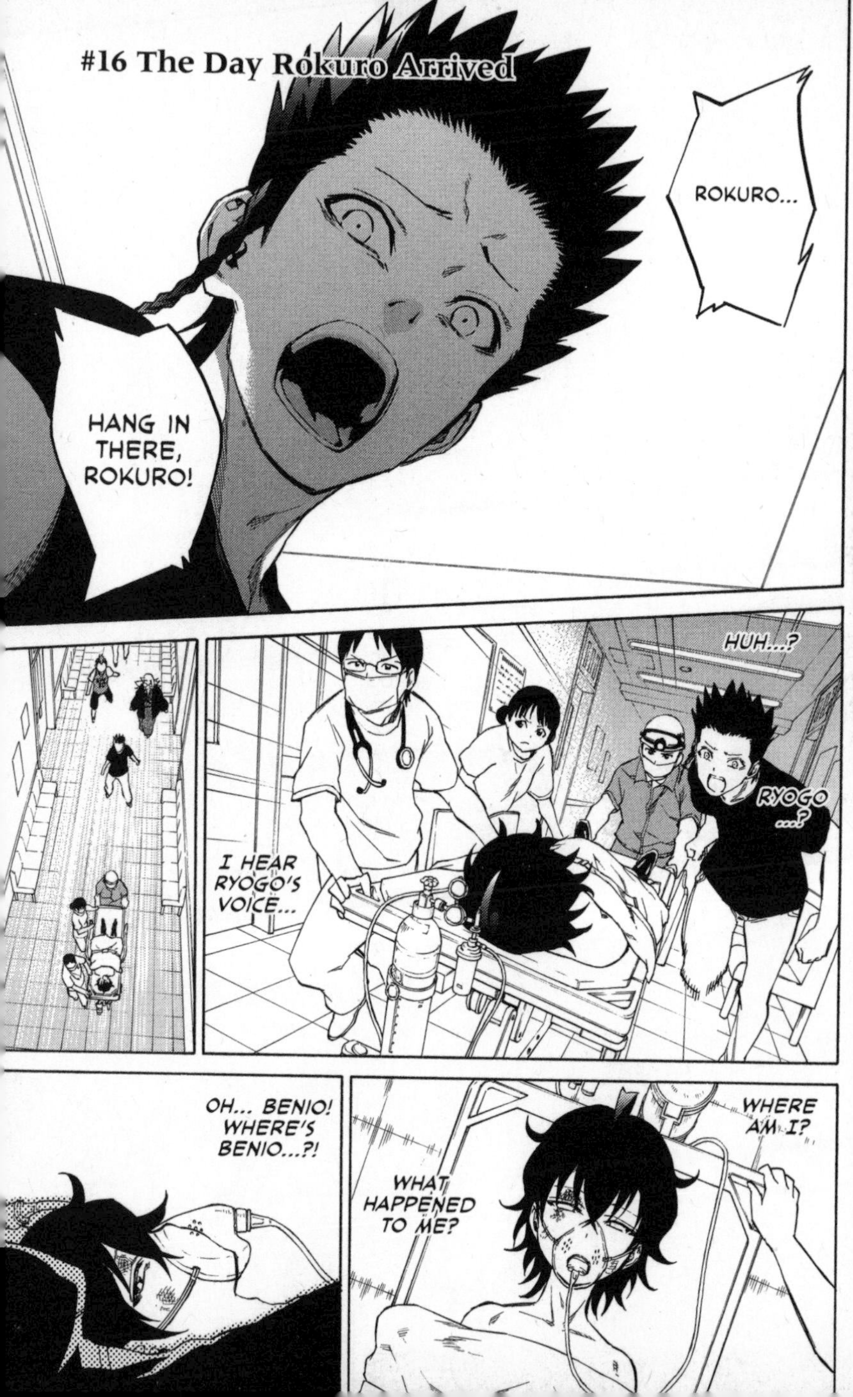
ROKURO...
HANG IN THERE, ROKURO!
HUH...?
RYOGO...?
I HEAR RYOGO'S VOICE...
WHERE AM I?
WHAT HAPPENED TO ME?
OH... BENIO! WHERE'S BENIO...?!

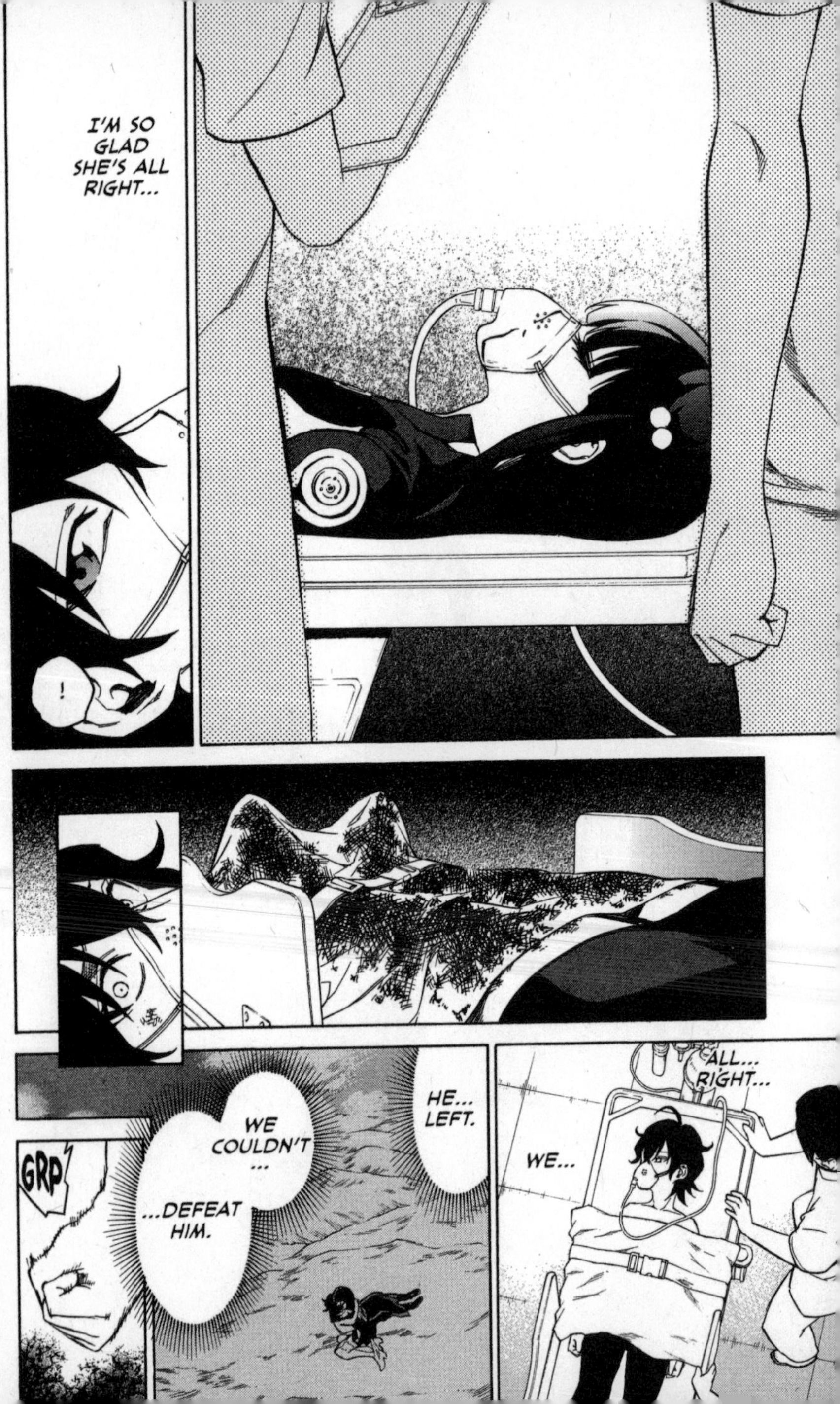
I'M SO GLAD SHE'S ALL RIGHT...
!
ALL... RIGHT...
WE...
HE... LEFT.
WE COULDN'T ...
...DEFEAT HIM.
GRP

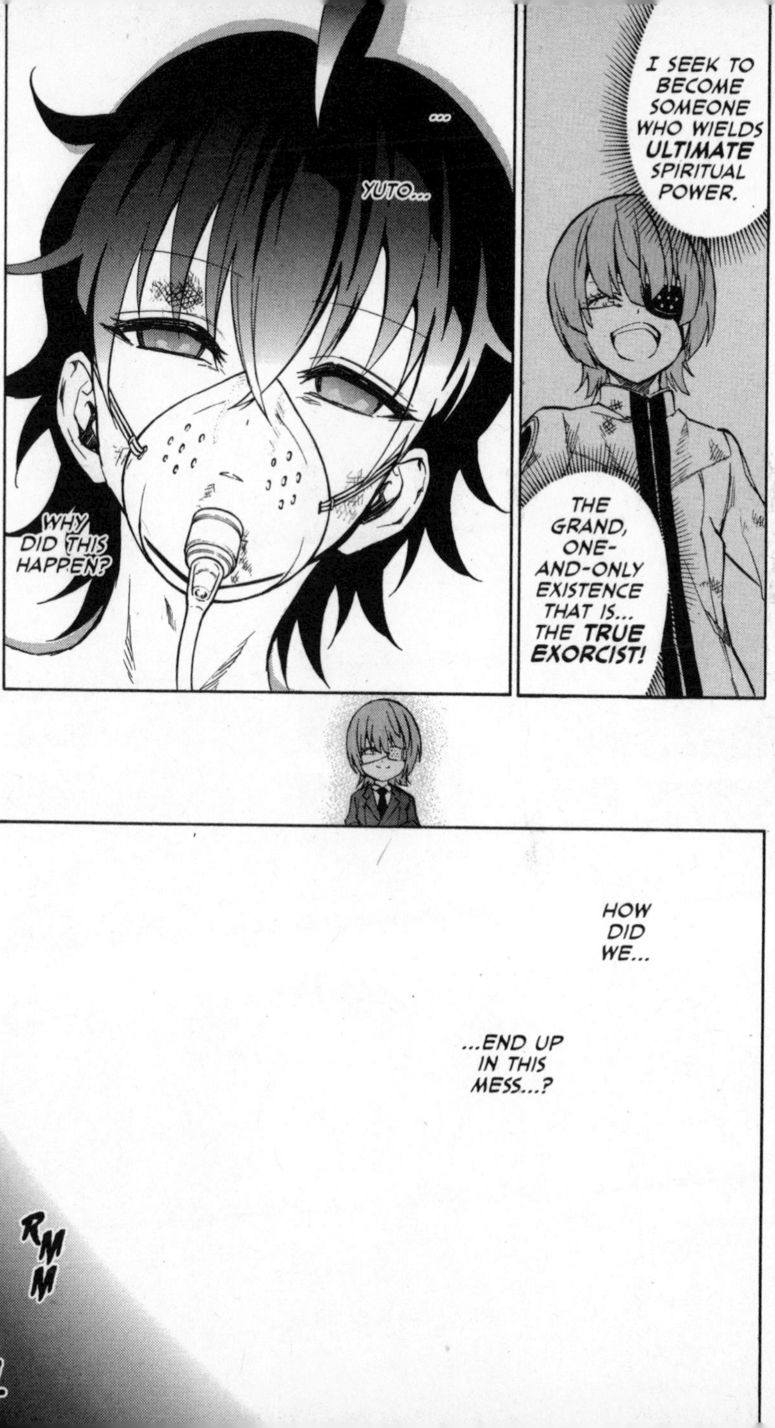
I SEEK TO BECOME SOMEONE WHO WIELDS ULTIMATE SPIRITUAL POWER.
THE GRAND, ONE-AND-ONLY EXISTENCE THAT IS... THE TRUE EXORCIST!
...
YUTO...
WHY DID THIS HAPPEN?
HOW DID WE...
...END UP IN THIS MESS...?
RMM
MBL

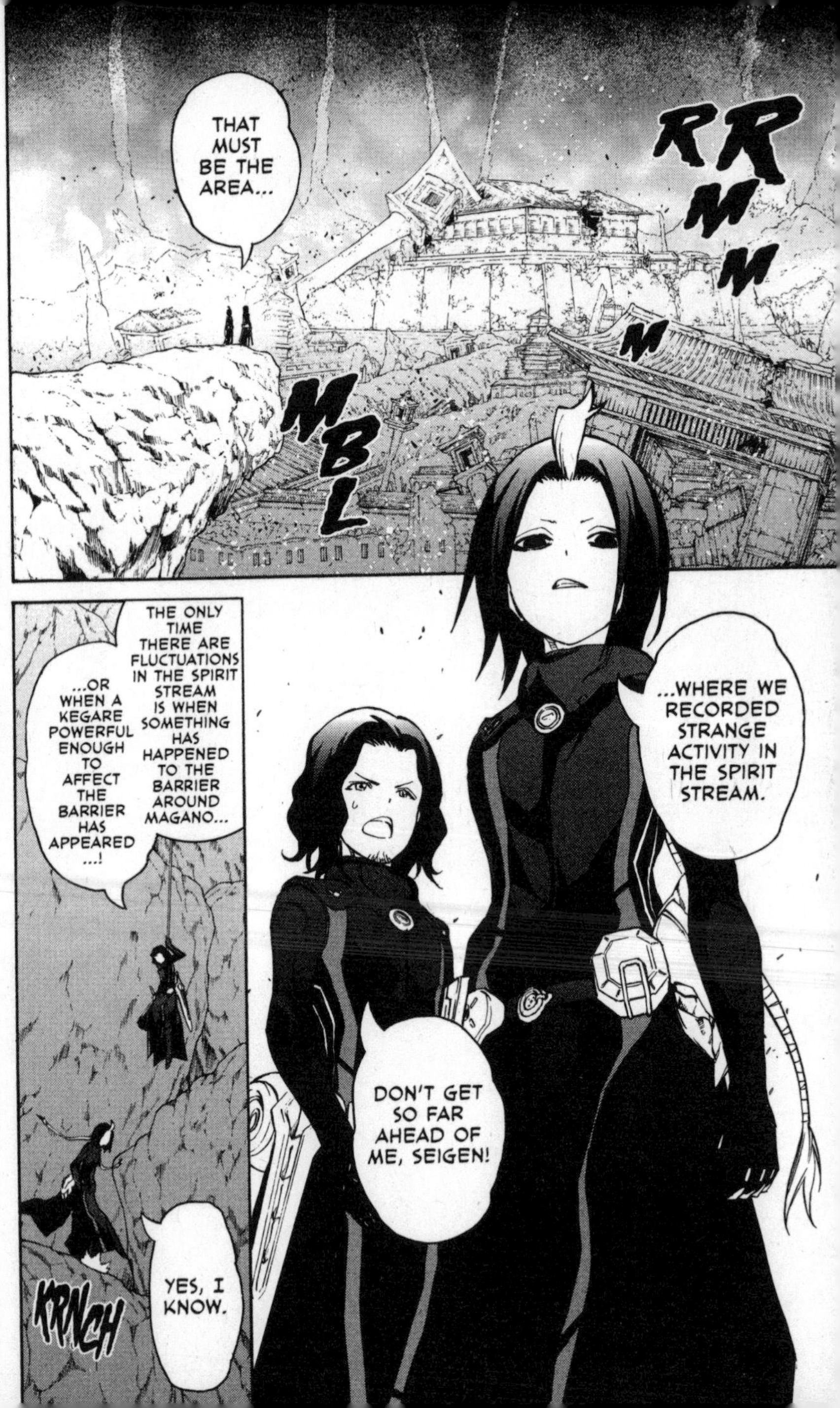
RRMMMMBL
THAT MUST BE THE AREA...
...WHERE WE RECORDED STRANGE ACTIVITY IN THE SPIRIT STREAM.
THE ONLY TIME THERE ARE FLUCTUATIONS IN THE SPIRIT STREAM IS WHEN SOMETHING HAS HAPPENED TO THE BARRIER AROUND MAGANO...
...OR WHEN A KEGARE POWERFUL ENOUGH TO AFFECT THE BARRIER HAS APPEARED...!
DON'T GET SO FAR AHEAD OF ME, SEIGEN!
YES, I KNOW.
KRNCH

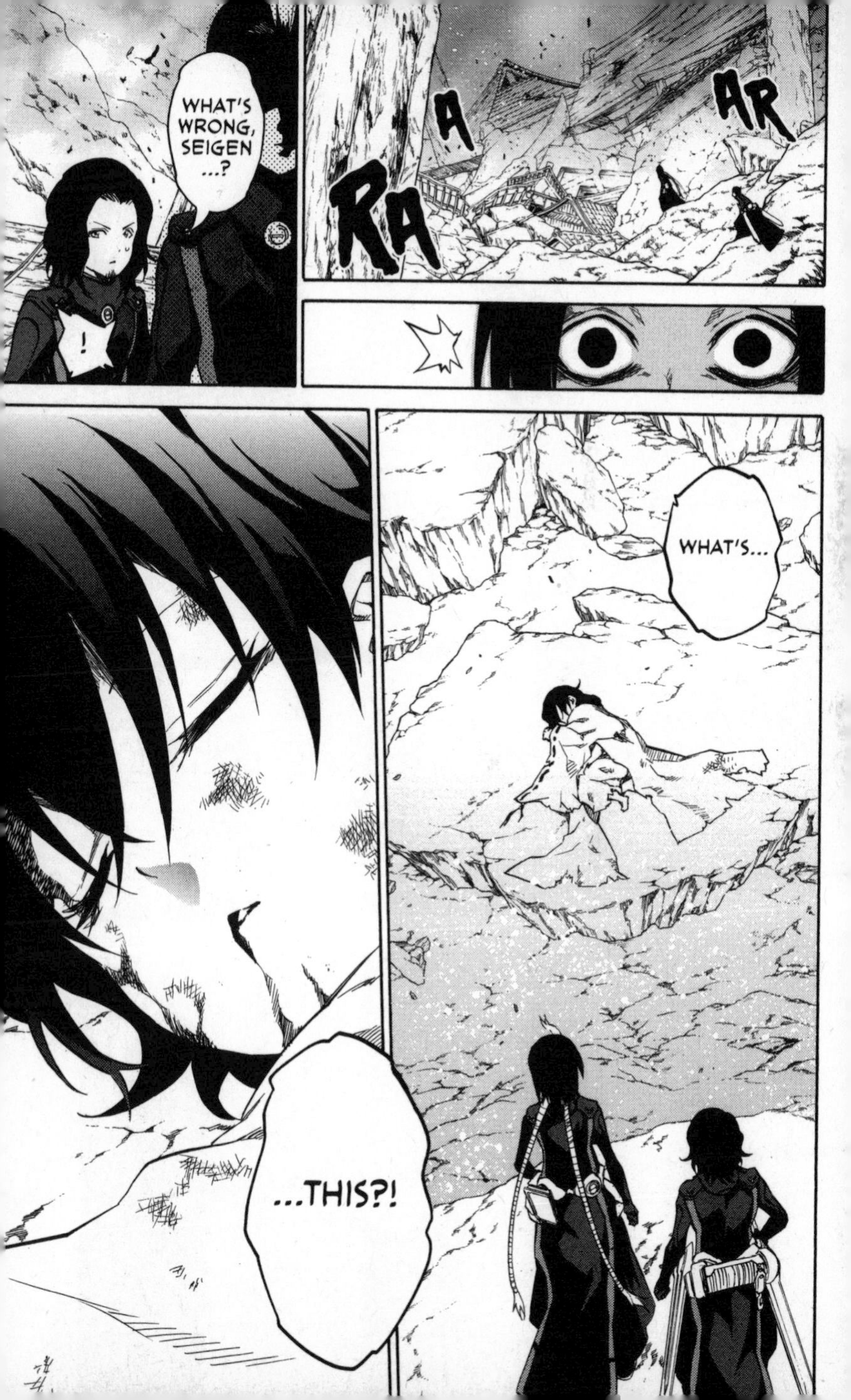
RA A AR
WHAT'S WRONG, SEIGEN ...?
!
WHAT'S...
...THIS?!

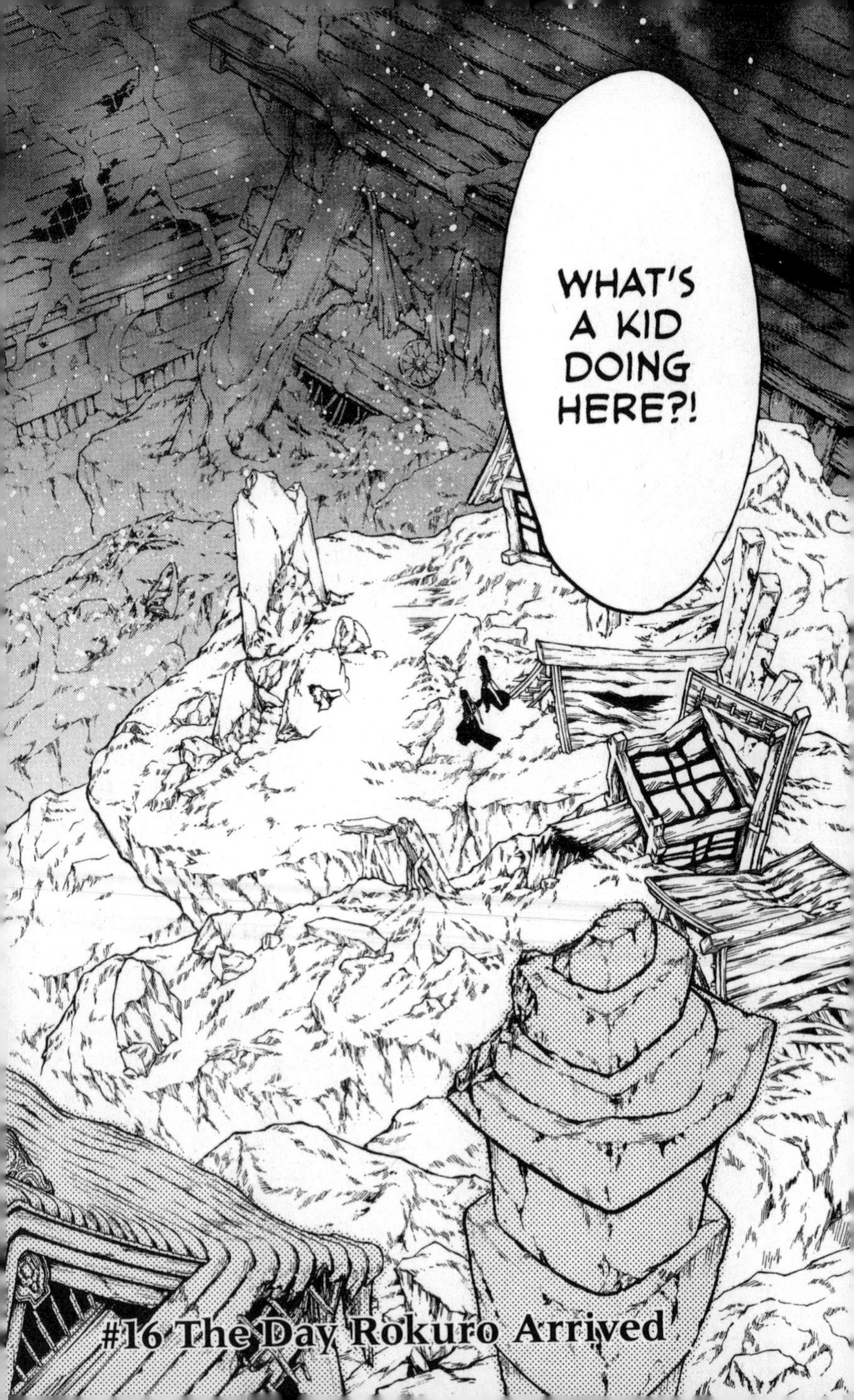
WHAT'S A KID DOING HERE?!

# #16 The Day Rokuro Arrived

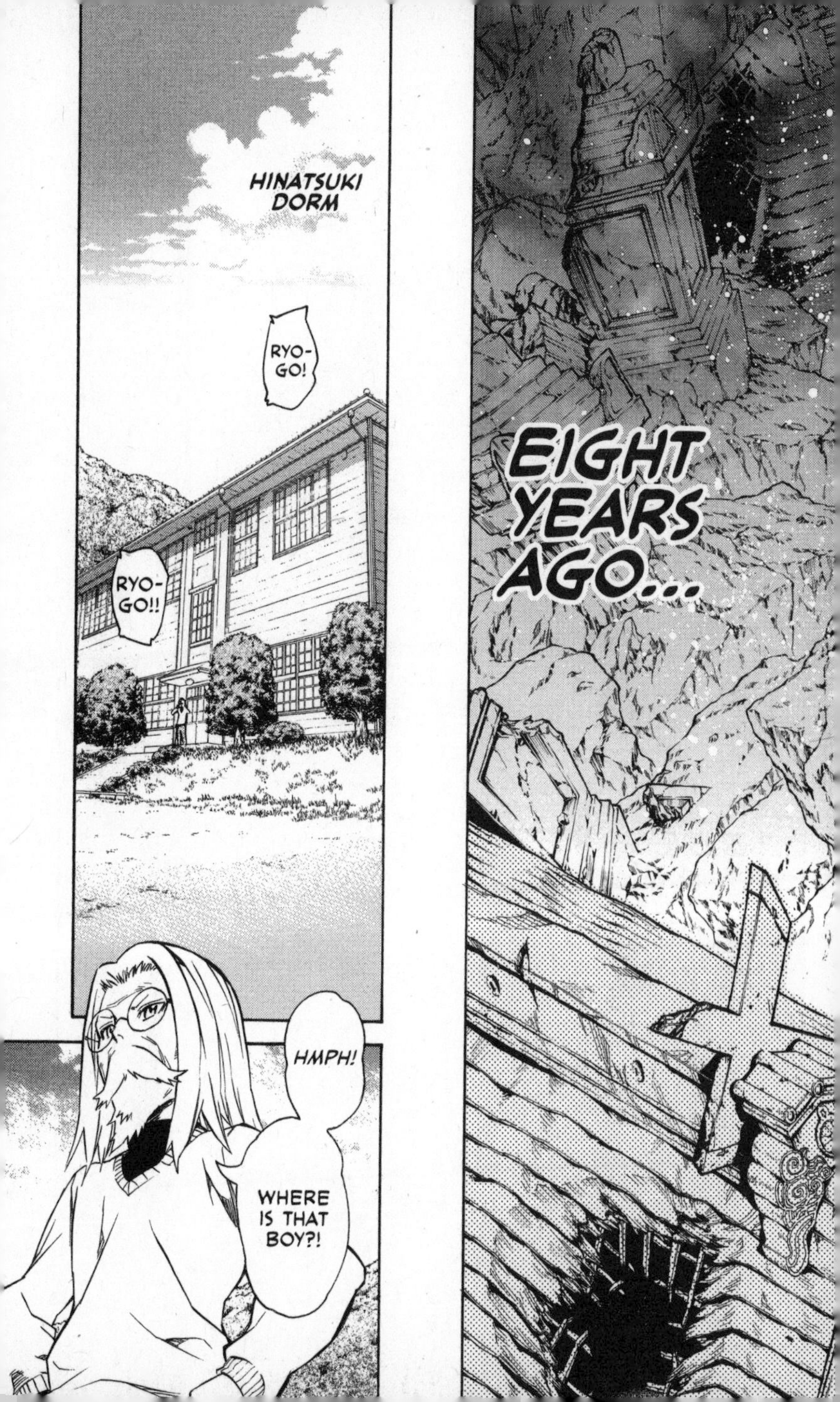
EIGHT YEARS AGO...
HINATSUKI DORM
RYO-GO!
RYO-GO!!
HMPH!
WHERE IS THAT BOY?!

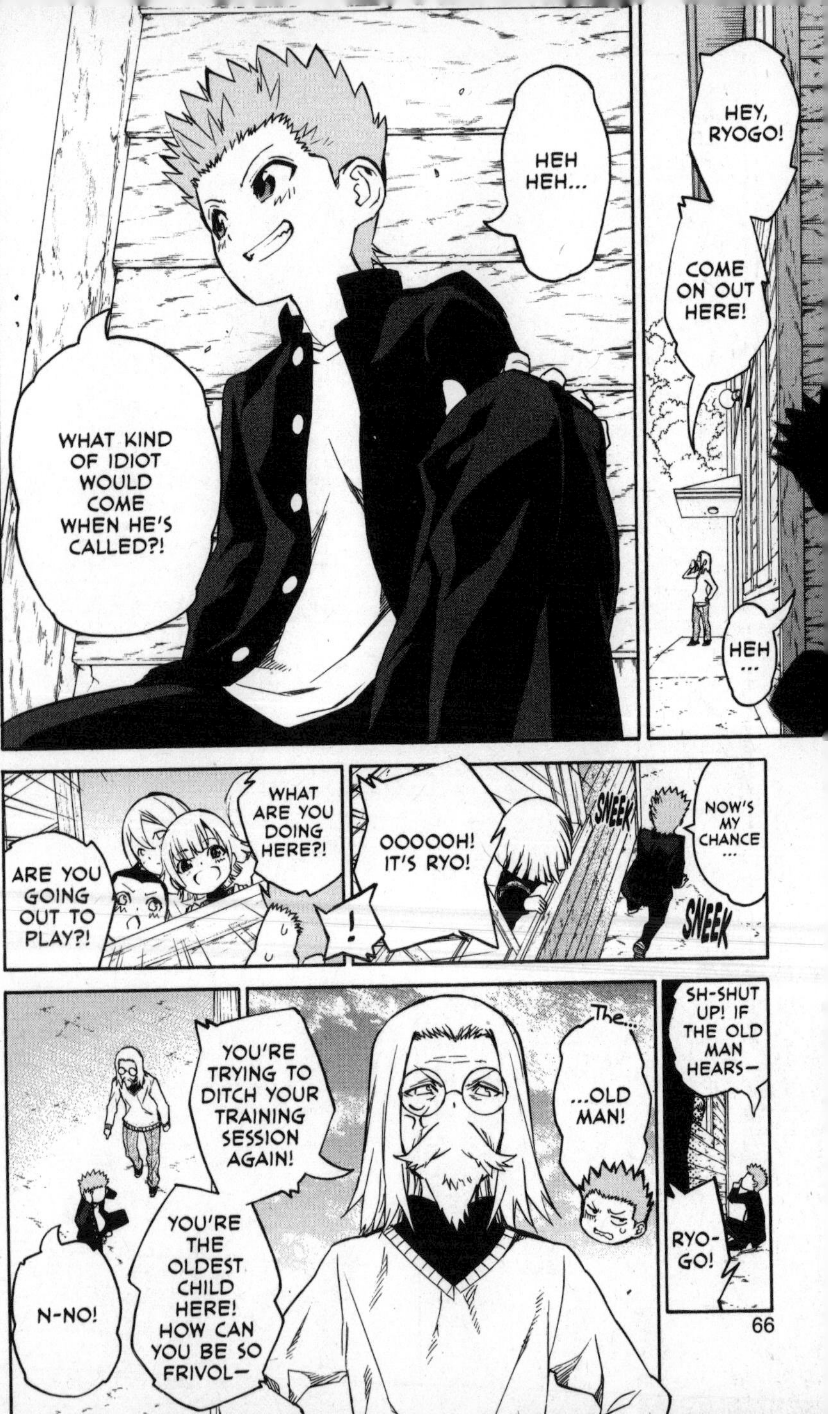
HEY, RYOGO!
COME ON OUT HERE!
HEH ...
HEH HEH...
WHAT KIND OF IDIOT WOULD COME WHEN HE'S CALLED?!
NOW'S MY CHANCE ...
SNEEK
SNEEK
OOOOOH! IT'S RYO!
!
WHAT ARE YOU DOING HERE?!
ARE YOU GOING OUT TO PLAY?!
SH-SHUT UP! IF THE OLD MAN HEARS—
RYO-GO!
The...
...OLD MAN!
YOU'RE TRYING TO DITCH YOUR TRAINING SESSION AGAIN!
YOU'RE THE OLDEST CHILD HERE! HOW CAN YOU BE SO FRIVOL—
N-NO!

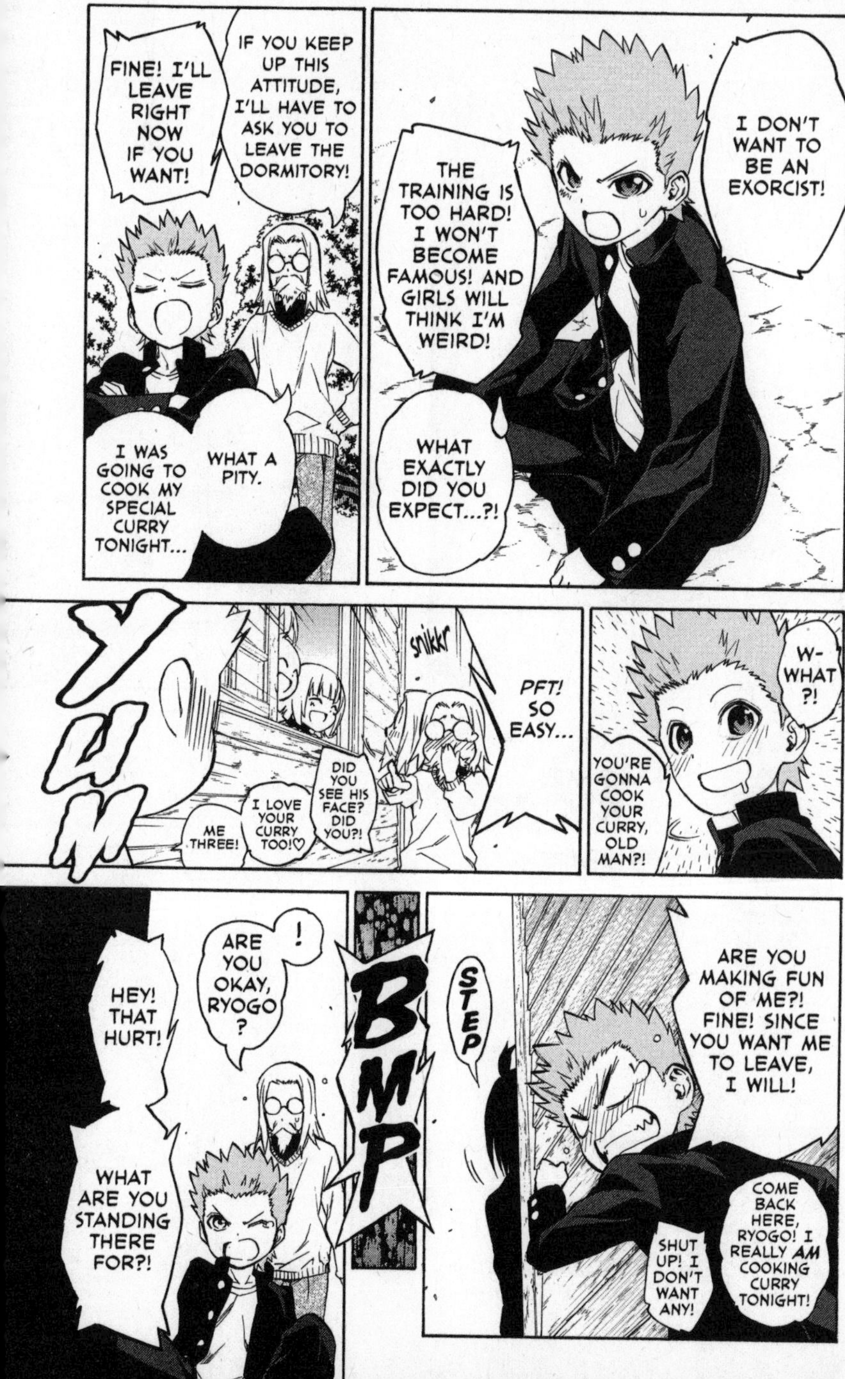
I DON'T WANT TO BE AN EXORCIST!
THE TRAINING IS TOO HARD! I WON'T BECOME FAMOUS! AND GIRLS WILL THINK I'M WEIRD!
WHAT EXACTLY DID YOU EXPECT...?!
IF YOU KEEP UP THIS ATTITUDE, I'LL HAVE TO ASK YOU TO LEAVE THE DORMITORY!
FINE! I'LL LEAVE RIGHT NOW IF YOU WANT!
WHAT A PITY.
I WAS GOING TO COOK MY SPECIAL CURRY TONIGHT...
W-WHAT?!
YOU'RE GONNA COOK YOUR CURRY, OLD MAN?!
snikkr
PFT! SO EASY...
DID YOU SEE HIS FACE? DID YOU?!
I LOVE YOUR CURRY TOO!♡
ME THREE!
YUM
ARE YOU MAKING FUN OF ME?! FINE! SINCE YOU WANT ME TO LEAVE, I WILL!
COME BACK HERE, RYOGO! I REALLY AM COOKING CURRY TONIGHT!
SHUT UP! I DON'T WANT ANY!
STEP
BMP
!
ARE YOU OKAY, RYOGO?
HEY! THAT HURT!
WHAT ARE YOU STANDING THERE FOR?!

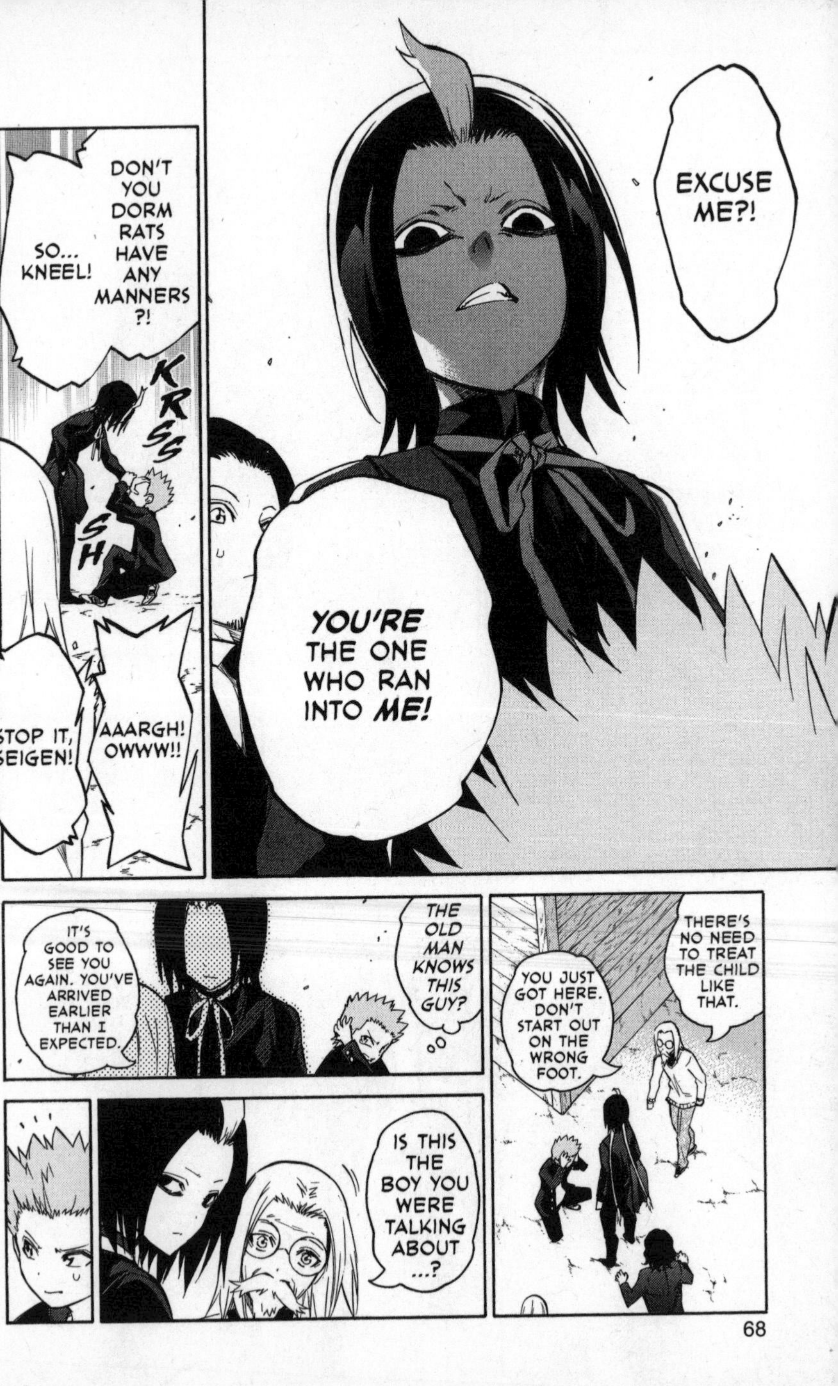
EXCUSE ME?!
YOU'RE THE ONE WHO RAN INTO ME!
DON'T YOU DORM RATS HAVE ANY MANNERS ?!
SO... KNEEL!
KRSSSH
AAARGH! OWWW!!
STOP IT, SEIGEN!
THERE'S NO NEED TO TREAT THE CHILD LIKE THAT.
YOU JUST GOT HERE. DON'T START OUT ON THE WRONG FOOT.
THE OLD MAN KNOWS THIS GUY?
IT'S GOOD TO SEE YOU AGAIN. YOU'VE ARRIVED EARLIER THAN I EXPECTED.
IS THIS THE BOY YOU WERE TALKING ABOUT ...?

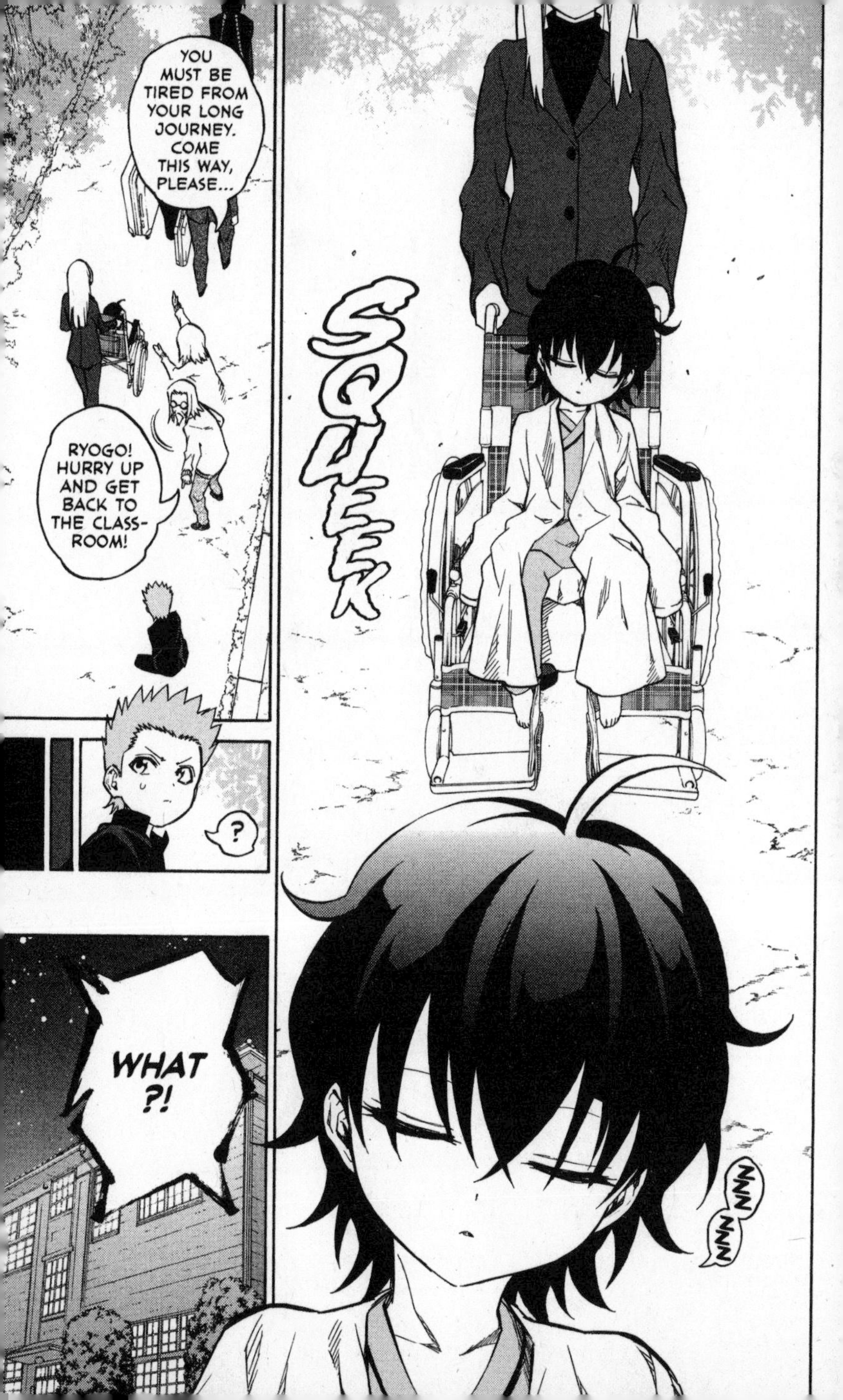
SQUEEK
NNN NNN
YOU MUST BE TIRED FROM YOUR LONG JOURNEY. COME THIS WAY, PLEASE...
RYOGO! HURRY UP AND GET BACK TO THE CLASS-ROOM!
?
WHAT ?!

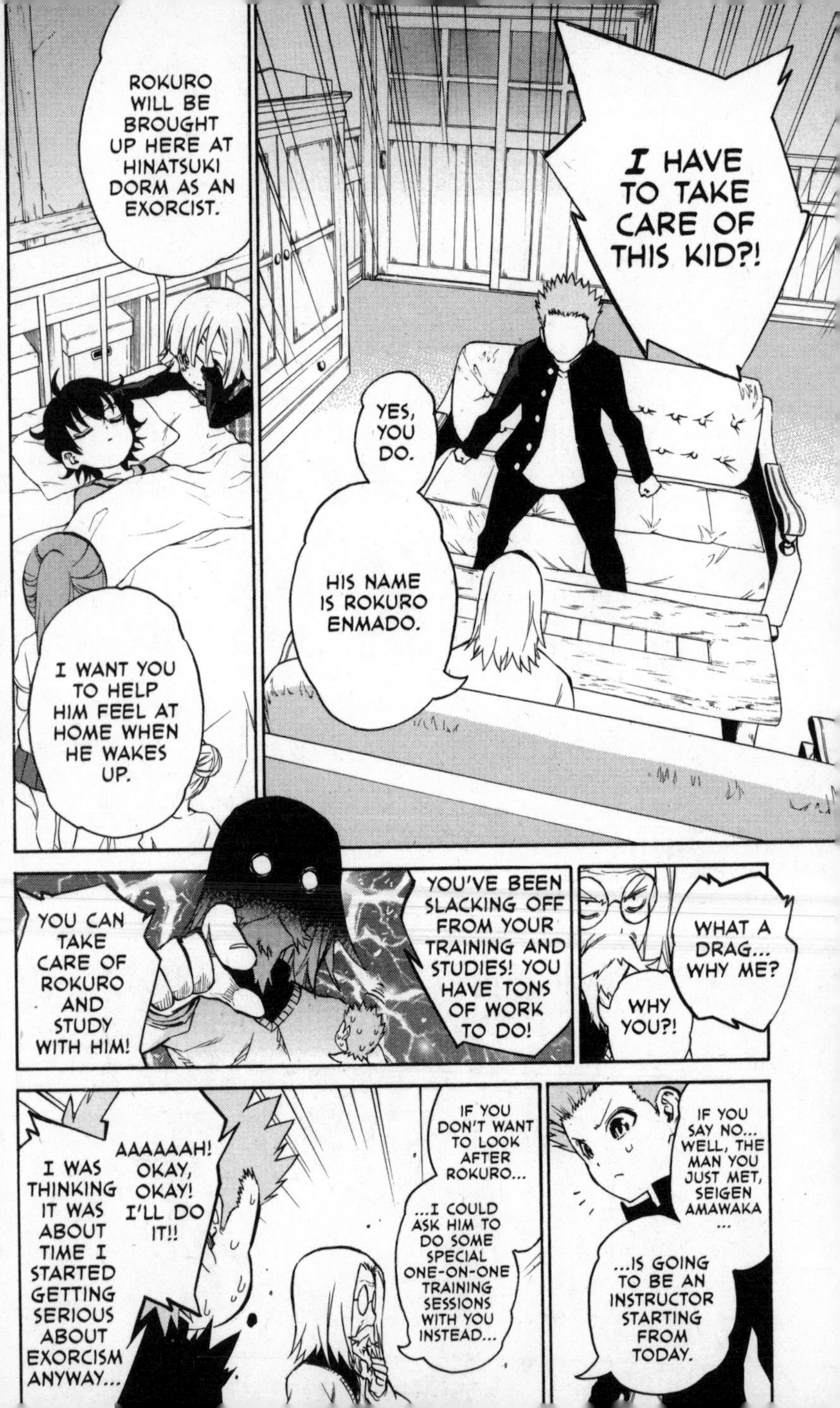
I HAVE TO TAKE CARE OF THIS KID?!
YES, YOU DO.
HIS NAME IS ROKURO ENMADO.
ROKURO WILL BE BROUGHT UP HERE AT HINATSUKI DORM AS AN EXORCIST.
I WANT YOU TO HELP HIM FEEL AT HOME WHEN HE WAKES UP.
WHAT A DRAG... WHY ME?
WHY YOU?!
YOU'VE BEEN SLACKING OFF FROM YOUR TRAINING AND STUDIES! YOU HAVE TONS OF WORK TO DO!
YOU CAN TAKE CARE OF ROKURO AND STUDY WITH HIM!
IF YOU SAY NO... WELL, THE MAN YOU JUST MET, SEIGEN AMAWAKA ...
...IS GOING TO BE AN INSTRUCTOR STARTING FROM TODAY.
IF YOU DON'T WANT TO LOOK AFTER ROKURO...
...I COULD ASK HIM TO DO SOME SPECIAL ONE-ON-ONE TRAINING SESSIONS WITH YOU INSTEAD...
AAAAAAH! OKAY, OKAY! I'LL DO IT!!
I WAS THINKING IT WAS ABOUT TIME I STARTED GETTING SERIOUS ABOUT EXORCISM ANYWAY...

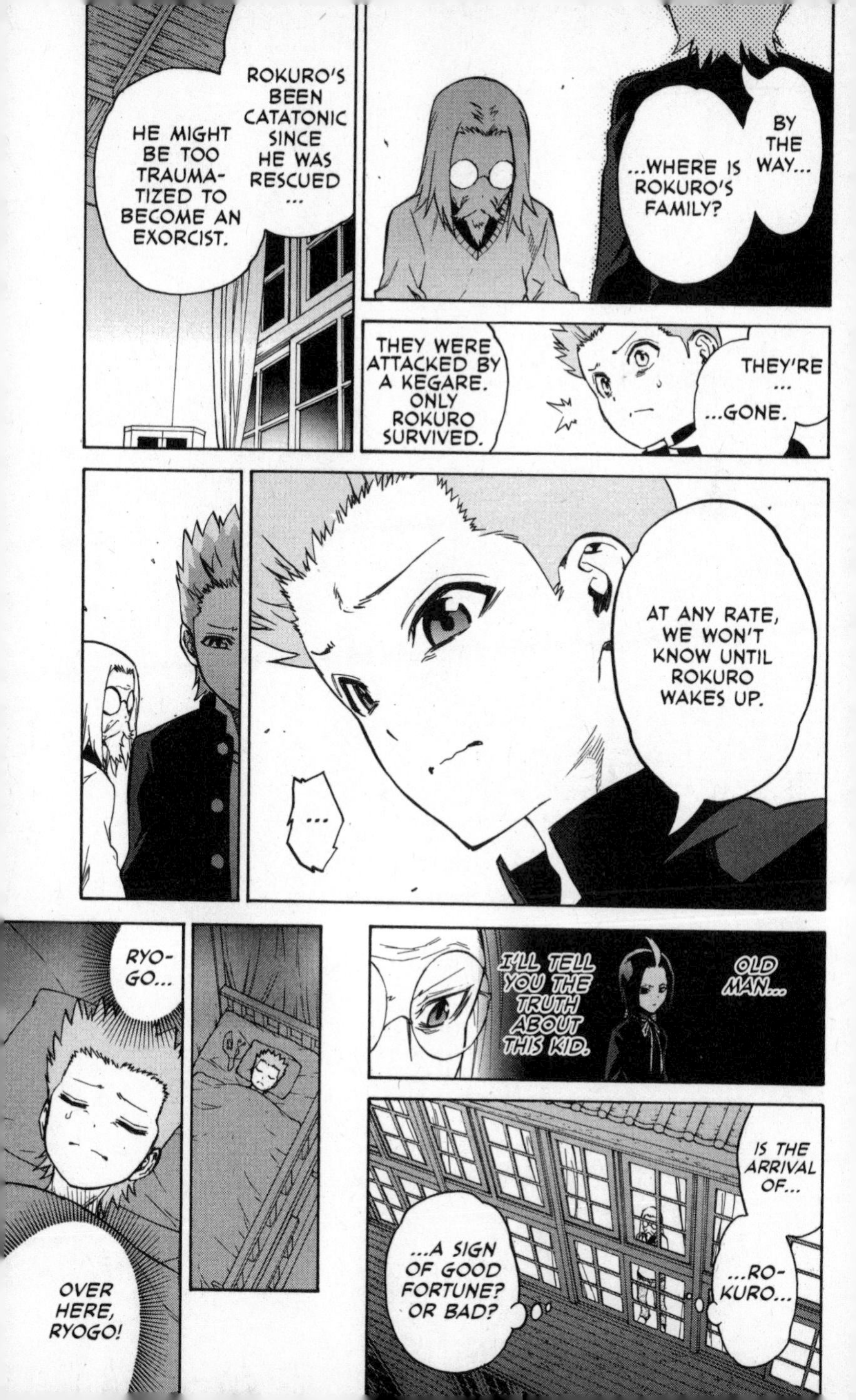
BY THE WAY...
...WHERE IS ROKURO'S FAMILY?
THEY'RE ... ...GONE.
THEY WERE ATTACKED BY A KEGARE. ONLY ROKURO SURVIVED.
ROKURO'S BEEN CATATONIC SINCE HE WAS RESCUED ...
HE MIGHT BE TOO TRAUMA-TIZED TO BECOME AN EXORCIST.
AT ANY RATE, WE WON'T KNOW UNTIL ROKURO WAKES UP.
...
OLD MAN...
I'LL TELL YOU THE TRUTH ABOUT THIS KID.
IS THE ARRIVAL OF...
...RO-KURO...
...A SIGN OF GOOD FORTUNE? OR BAD?
RYO-GO...
OVER HERE, RYOGO!

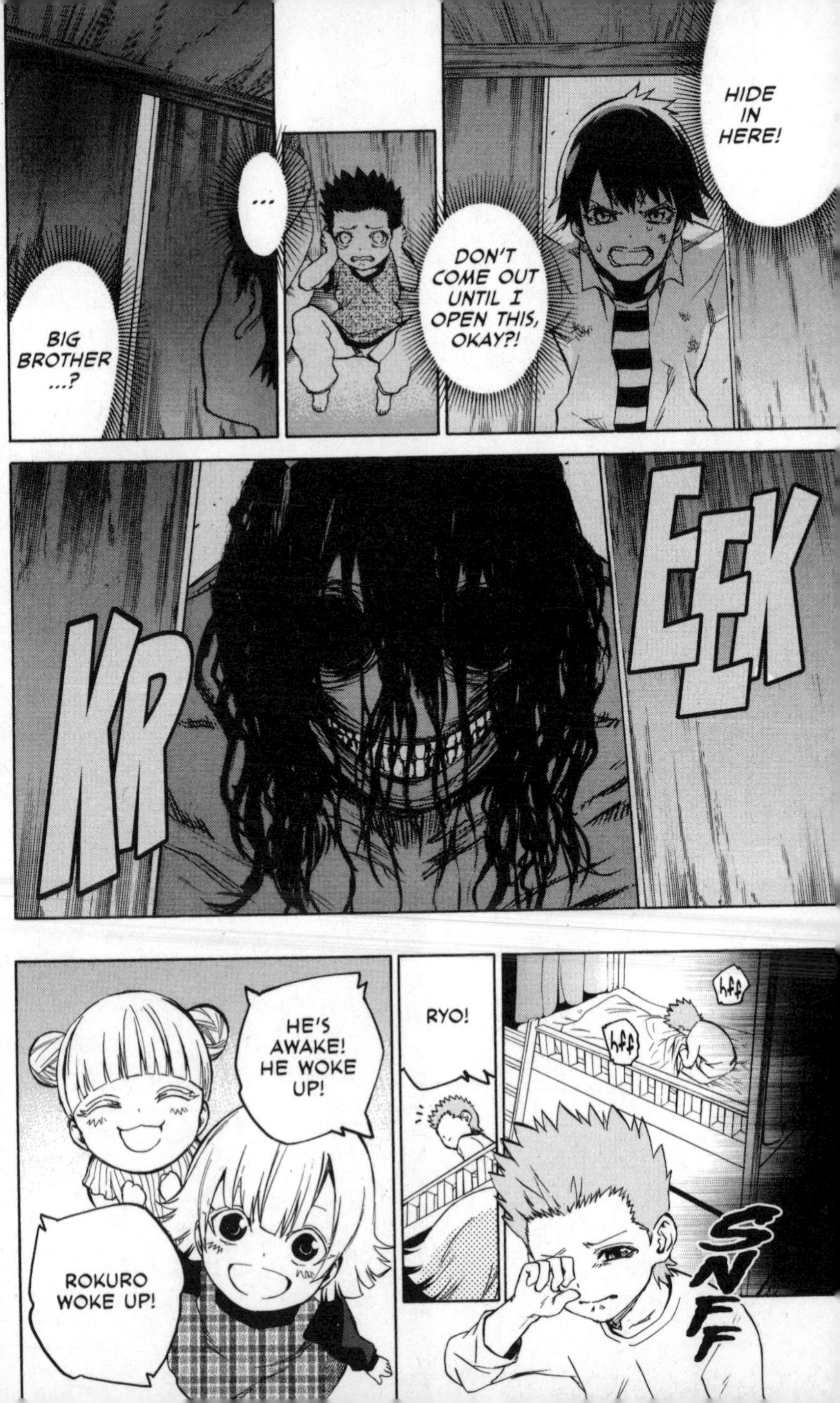
HIDE IN HERE!
DON'T COME OUT UNTIL I OPEN THIS, OKAY?!
...
BIG BROTHER ...?
EEK
KR
hff
hff
SNFF
RYO!
HE'S AWAKE! HE WOKE UP!
ROKURO WOKE UP!

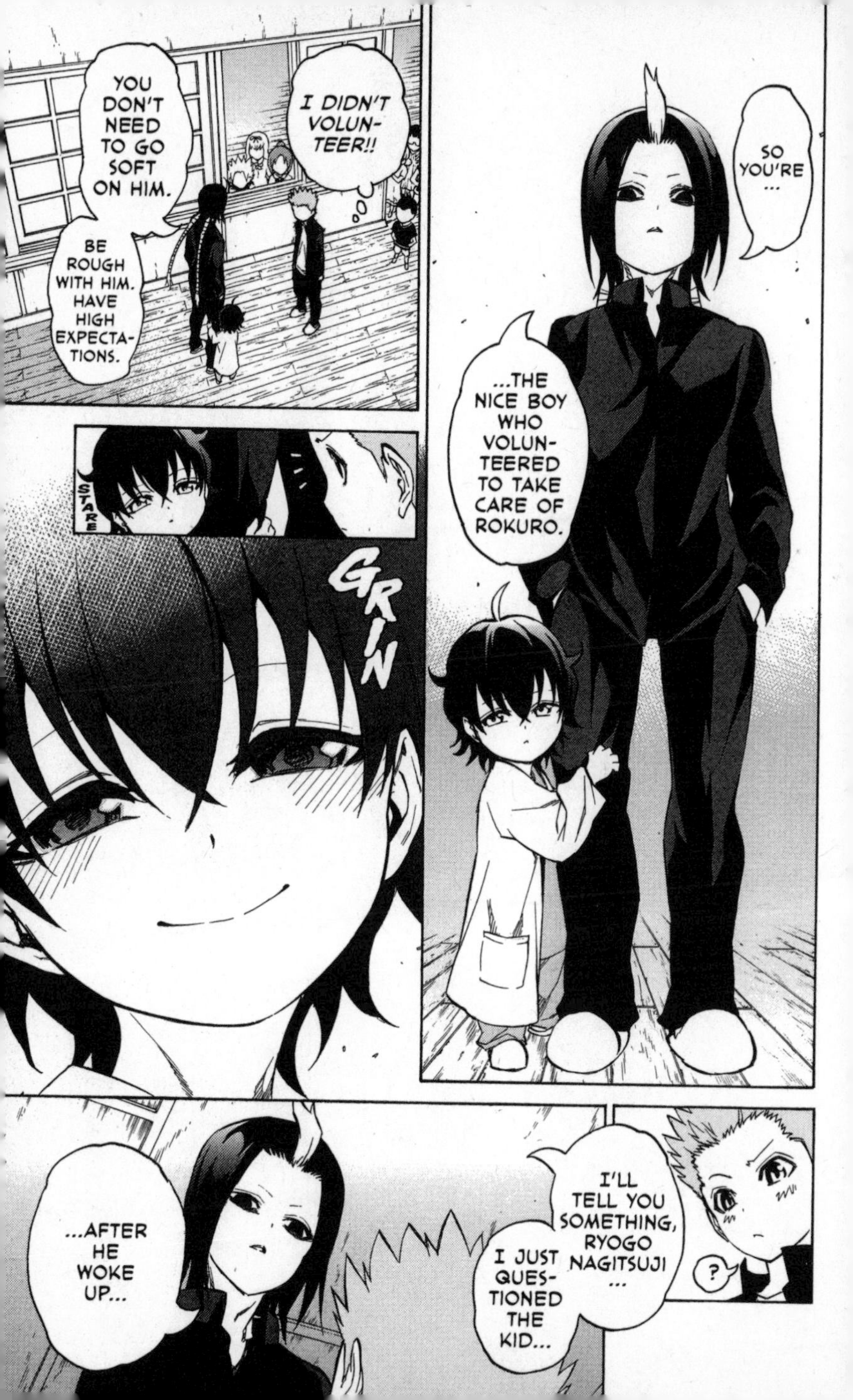
SO YOU'RE ...
...THE NICE BOY WHO VOLUNTEERED TO TAKE CARE OF ROKURO.
I DIDN'T VOLUNTEER!!
YOU DON'T NEED TO GO SOFT ON HIM.
BE ROUGH WITH HIM. HAVE HIGH EXPECTATIONS.
STARE
GRIN
I'LL TELL YOU SOMETHING, RYOGO NAGITSUJI ...
?
I JUST QUESTIONED THE KID...
...AFTER HE WOKE UP...

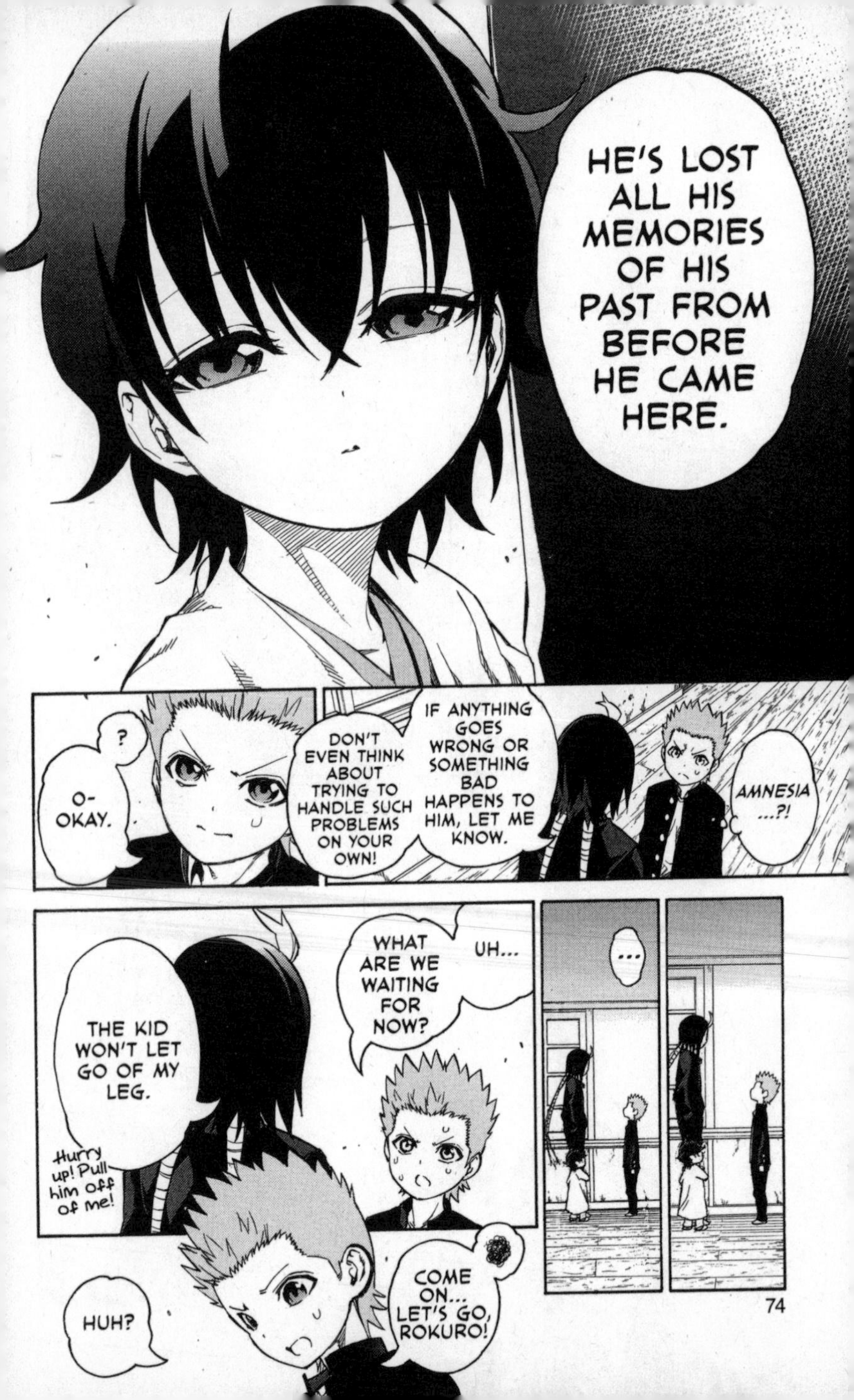
HE'S LOST ALL HIS MEMORIES OF HIS PAST FROM BEFORE HE CAME HERE.
AMNESIA ...?!
IF ANYTHING GOES WRONG OR SOMETHING BAD HAPPENS TO HIM, LET ME KNOW.
DON'T EVEN THINK ABOUT TRYING TO HANDLE SUCH PROBLEMS ON YOUR OWN!
?
O-OKAY.
...
UH...
WHAT ARE WE WAITING FOR NOW?
THE KID WON'T LET GO OF MY LEG.
Hurry up! Pull him off of me!
COME ON... LET'S GO, ROKURO!
HUH?

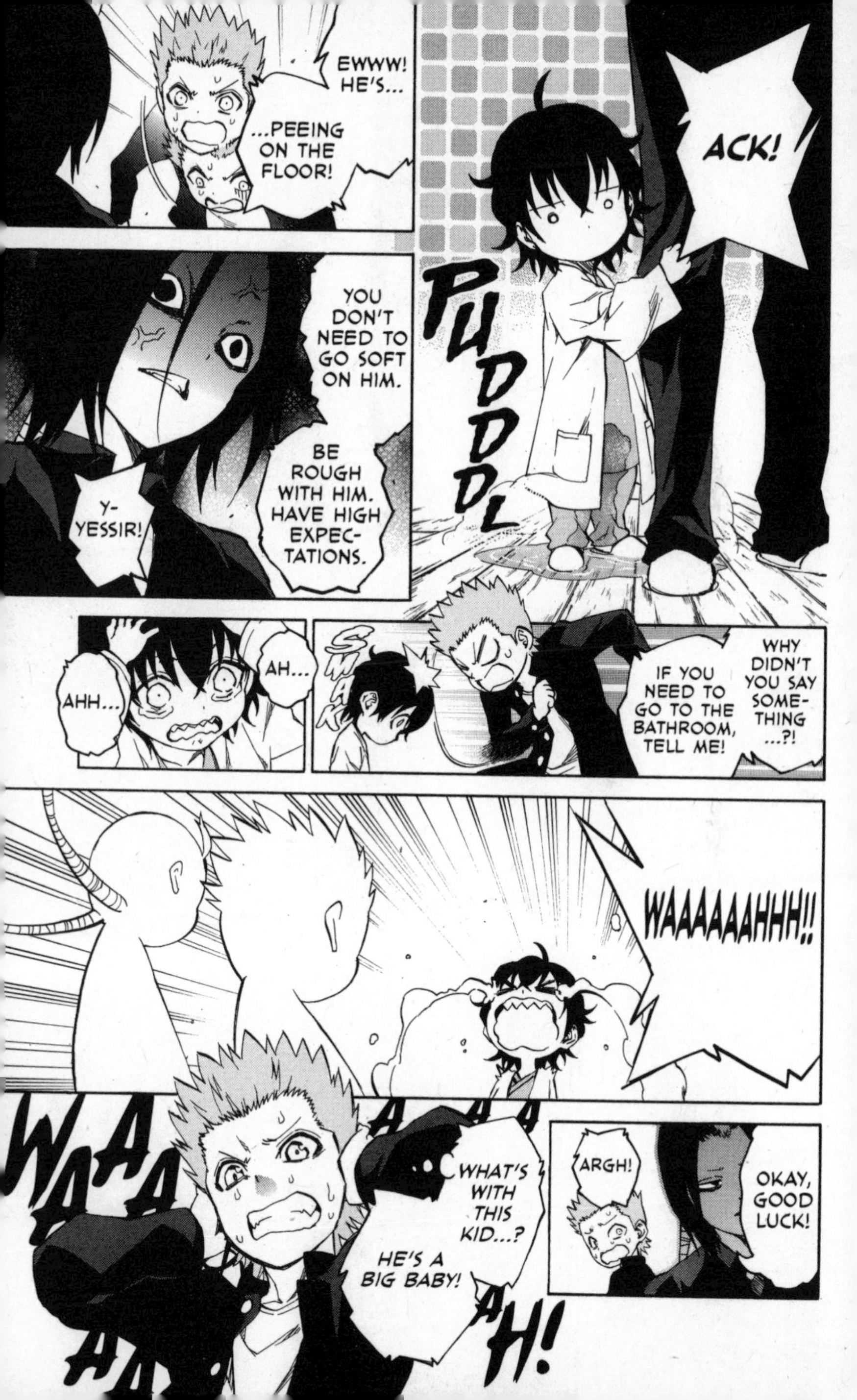
ACK!
PUDDL
EWWW! HE'S...
...PEEING ON THE FLOOR!
YOU DON'T NEED TO GO SOFT ON HIM.
BE ROUGH WITH HIM. HAVE HIGH EXPECTATIONS.
Y-YESSIR!
WHY DIDN'T YOU SAY SOMETHING...?!
IF YOU NEED TO GO TO THE BATHROOM, TELL ME!
AH...
AHH...
WAAAAAAHHH!!
OKAY, GOOD LUCK!
ARGH!
WHAT'S WITH THIS KID...?
HE'S A BIG BABY!
WAAAAAAAAAH!

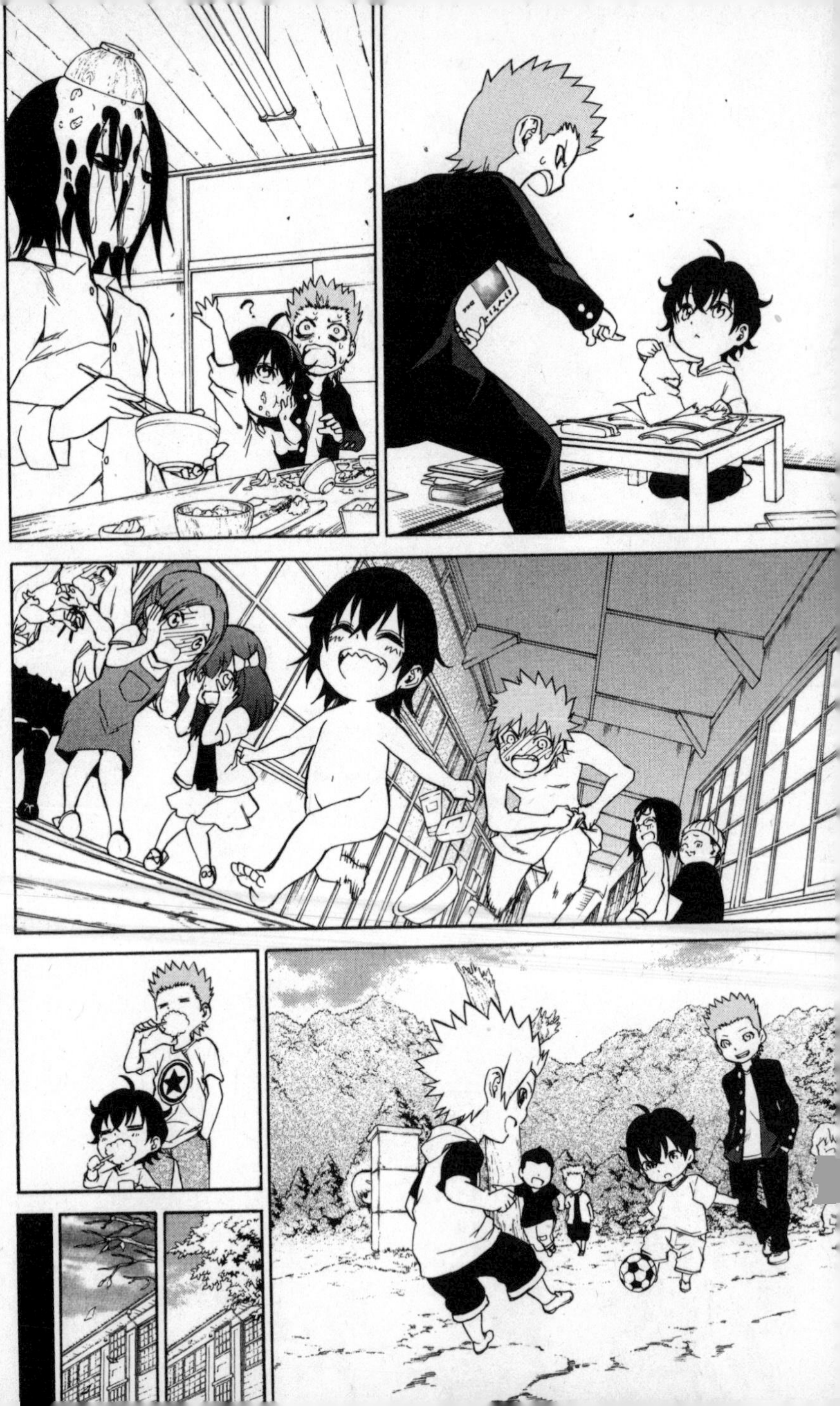

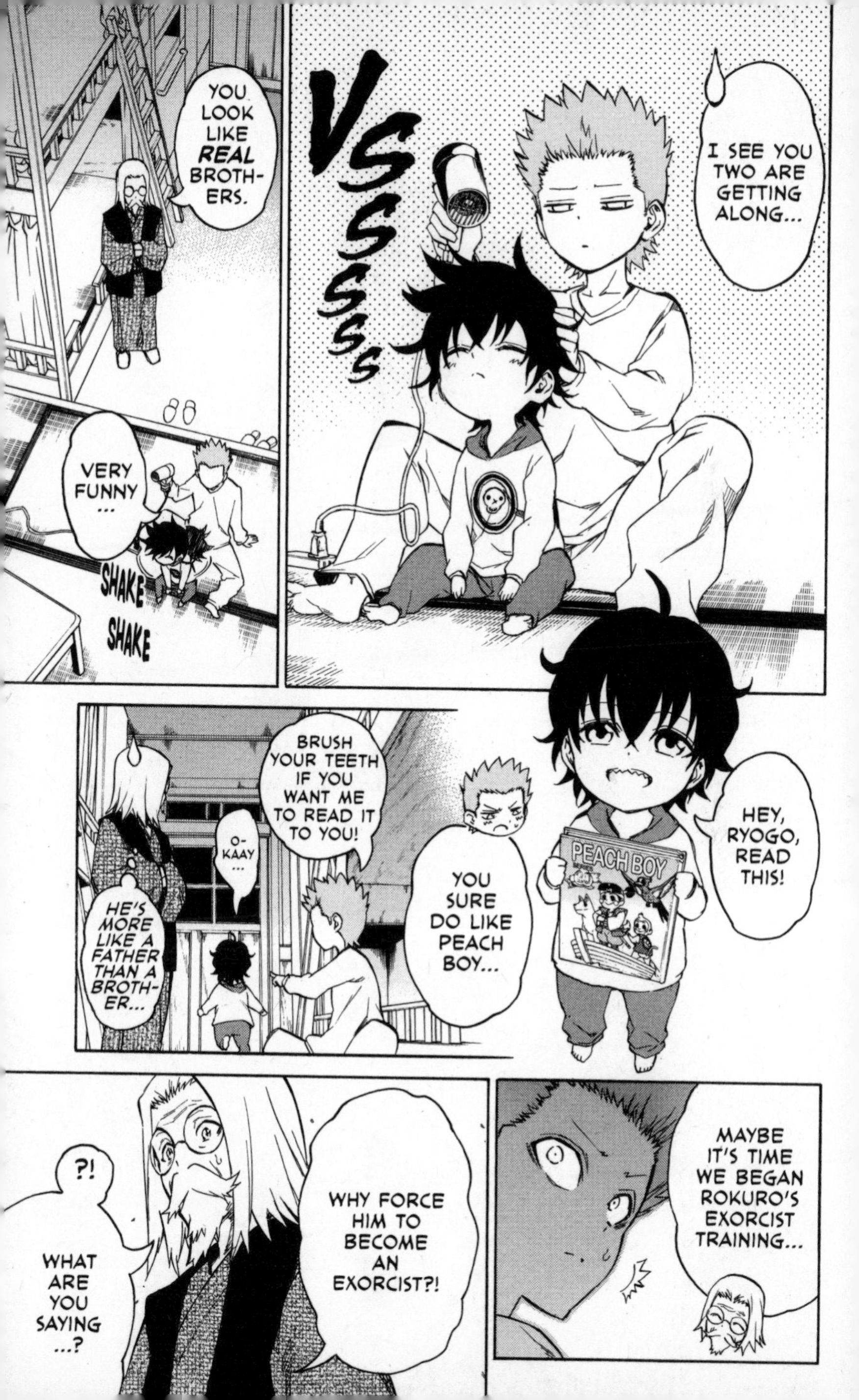
I SEE YOU TWO ARE GETTING ALONG...
VSSSSSS
YOU LOOK LIKE REAL BROTHERS.
VERY FUNNY...
SHAKE SHAKE
HEY, RYOGO, READ THIS!
PEACH BOY
YOU SURE DO LIKE PEACH BOY...
BRUSH YOUR TEETH IF YOU WANT ME TO READ IT TO YOU!
O-KAAY...
HE'S MORE LIKE A FATHER THAN A BROTHER...
MAYBE IT'S TIME WE BEGAN ROKURO'S EXORCIST TRAINING...
WHY FORCE HIM TO BECOME AN EXORCIST?!
?!
WHAT ARE YOU SAYING...?

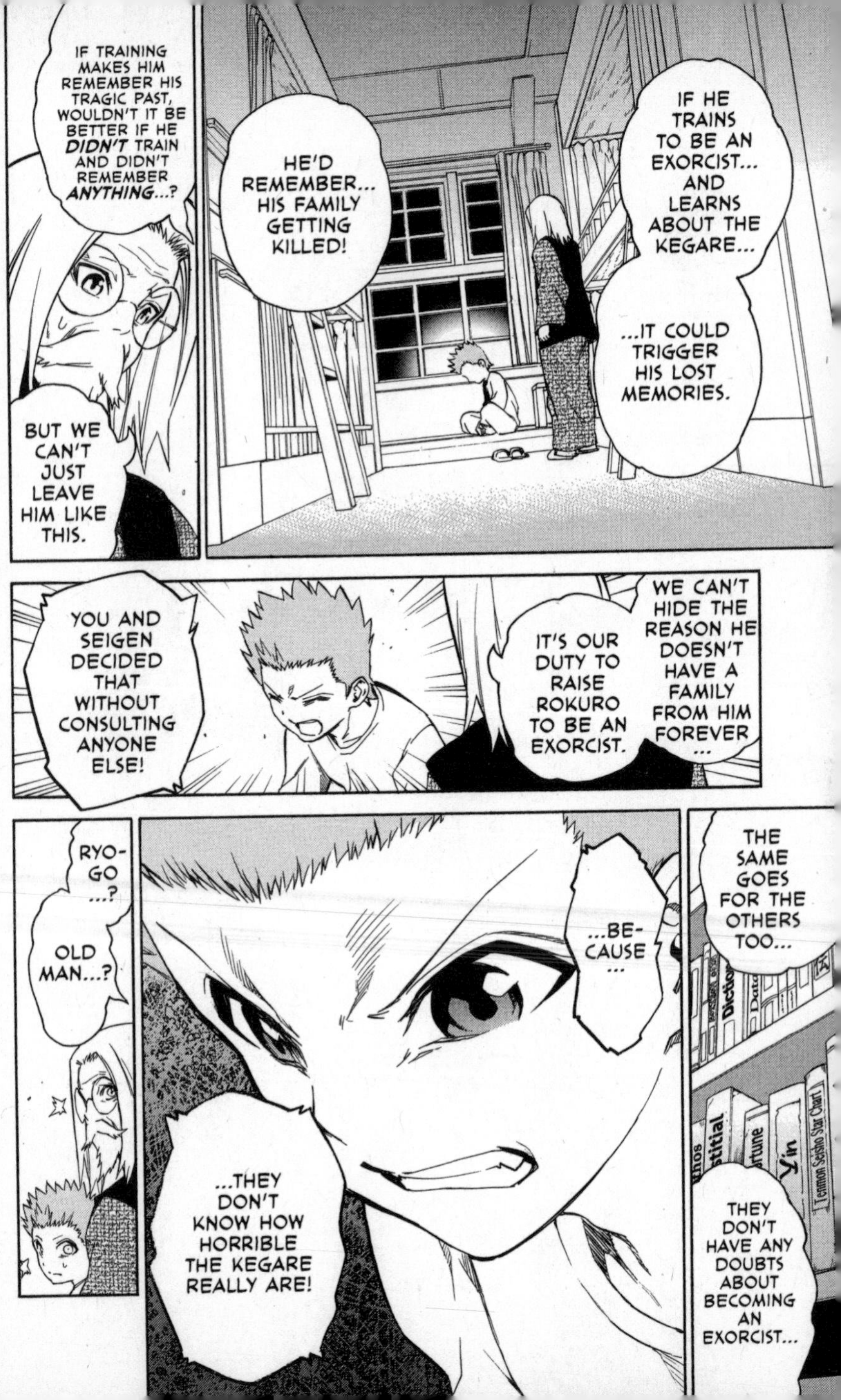
IF HE TRAINS TO BE AN EXORCIST... AND LEARNS ABOUT THE KEGARE...
...IT COULD TRIGGER HIS LOST MEMORIES.
HE'D REMEMBER... HIS FAMILY GETTING KILLED!
IF TRAINING MAKES HIM REMEMBER HIS TRAGIC PAST, WOULDN'T IT BE BETTER IF HE *DIDN'T* TRAIN AND DIDN'T REMEMBER *ANYTHING*...?
BUT WE CAN'T JUST LEAVE HIM LIKE THIS.
WE CAN'T HIDE THE REASON HE DOESN'T HAVE A FAMILY FROM HIM FOREVER...
IT'S OUR DUTY TO RAISE ROKURO TO BE AN EXORCIST.
YOU AND SEIGEN DECIDED THAT WITHOUT CONSULTING ANYONE ELSE!
THE SAME GOES FOR THE OTHERS TOO...
THEY DON'T HAVE ANY DOUBTS ABOUT BECOMING AN EXORCIST...
...BE-CAUSE...
...THEY DON'T KNOW HOW HORRIBLE THE KEGARE REALLY ARE!
RYO-GO...?
OLD MAN...?

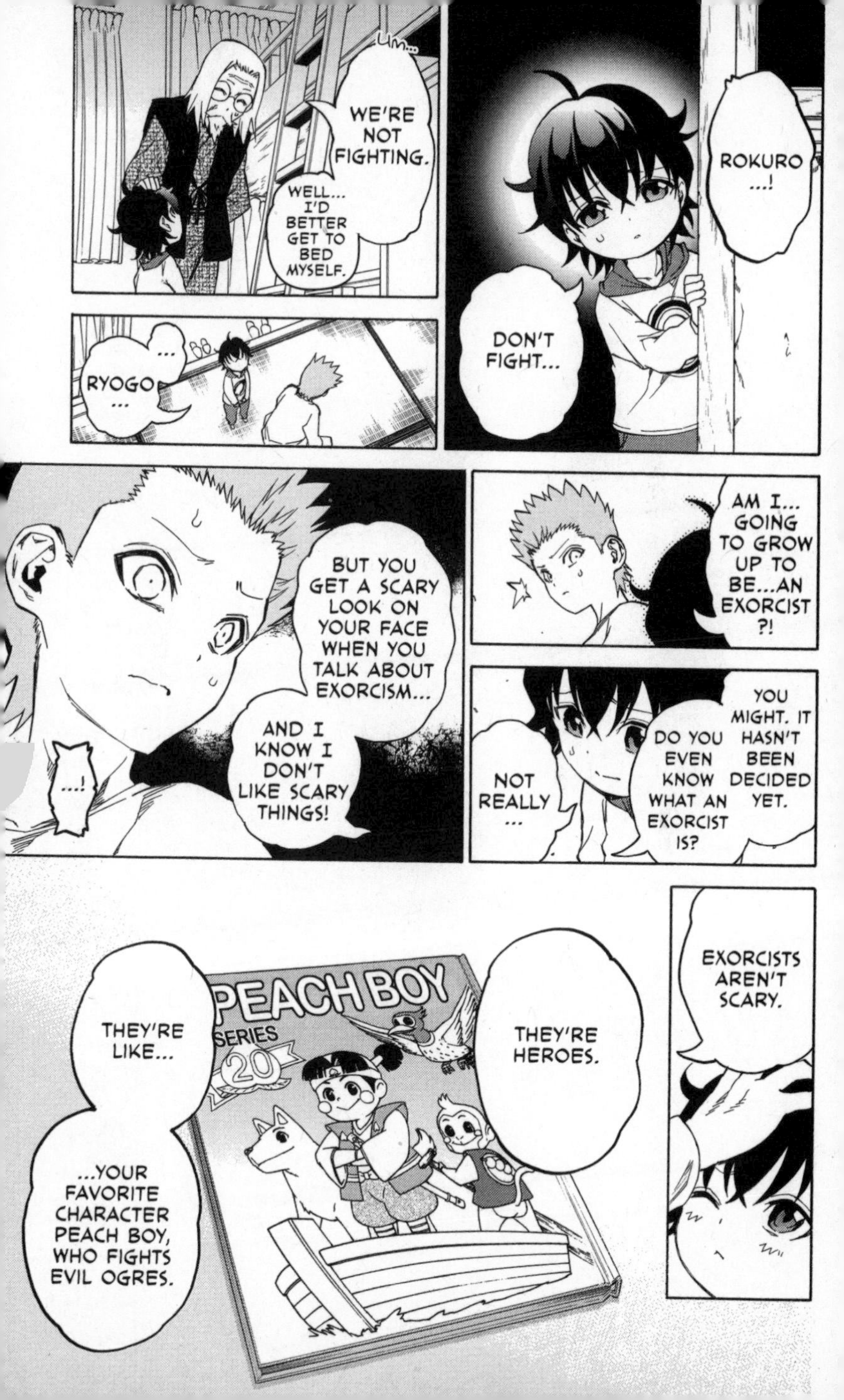
ROKURO ...!
DON'T FIGHT...
Um...
WE'RE NOT FIGHTING.
WELL... I'D BETTER GET TO BED MYSELF.
... RYOGO ...
AM I... GOING TO GROW UP TO BE...AN EXORCIST ?!
YOU MIGHT. IT HASN'T BEEN DECIDED YET.
DO YOU EVEN KNOW WHAT AN EXORCIST IS?
NOT REALLY ...
BUT YOU GET A SCARY LOOK ON YOUR FACE WHEN YOU TALK ABOUT EXORCISM...
AND I KNOW I DON'T LIKE SCARY THINGS!
...!
EXORCISTS AREN'T SCARY.
THEY'RE HEROES.
THEY'RE LIKE...
PEACH BOY
SERIES
20
...YOUR FAVORITE CHARACTER PEACH BOY, WHO FIGHTS EVIL OGRES.

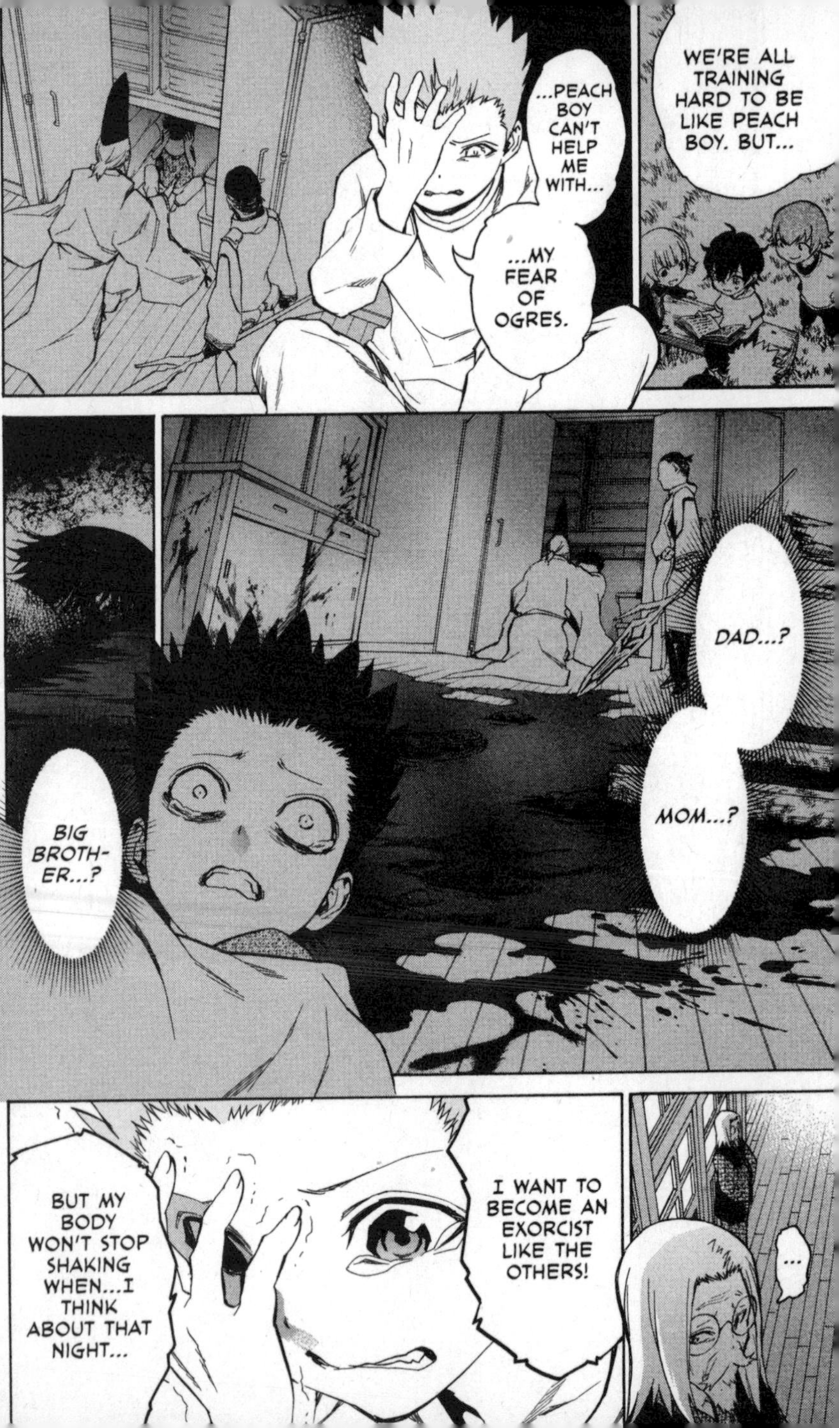
WE'RE ALL TRAINING HARD TO BE LIKE PEACH BOY. BUT...
...PEACH BOY CAN'T HELP ME WITH...
...MY FEAR OF OGRES.
DAD...?
MOM...?
BIG BROTHER-ER...?
...
I WANT TO BECOME AN EXORCIST LIKE THE OTHERS!
BUT MY BODY WON'T STOP SHAKING WHEN...I THINK ABOUT THAT NIGHT...

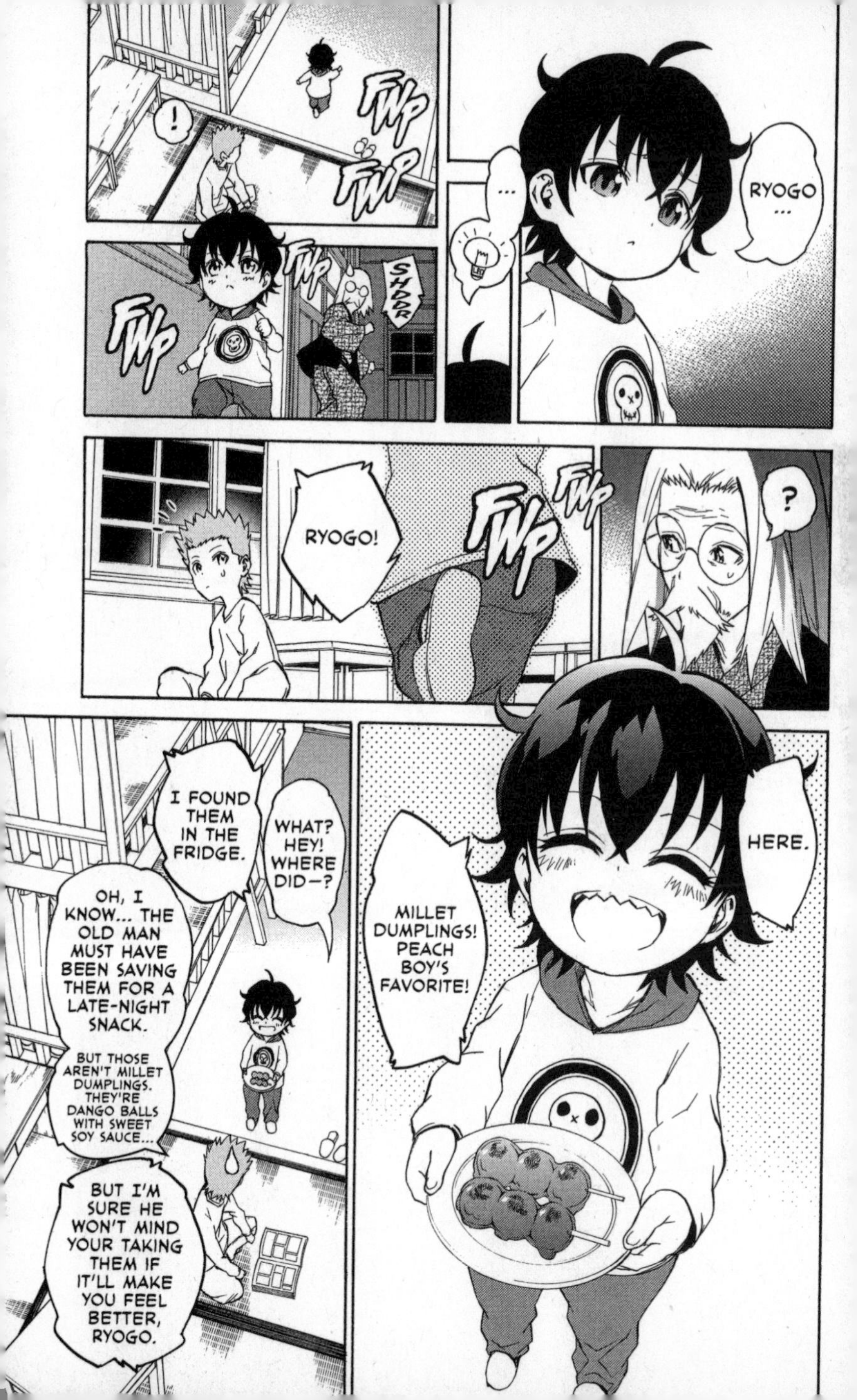
RYOGO ...
...
FWP
FWP
!
FWP
SHDDR
FWP
?
FWP
FWP
RYOGO!
HERE.
MILLET DUMPLINGS! PEACH BOY'S FAVORITE!
WHAT? HEY! WHERE DID—?
I FOUND THEM IN THE FRIDGE.
OH, I KNOW... THE OLD MAN MUST HAVE BEEN SAVING THEM FOR A LATE-NIGHT SNACK.
BUT THOSE AREN'T MILLET DUMPLINGS. THEY'RE DANGO BALLS WITH SWEET SOY SAUCE...
BUT I'M SURE HE WON'T MIND YOUR TAKING THEM IF IT'LL MAKE YOU FEEL BETTER, RYOGO.

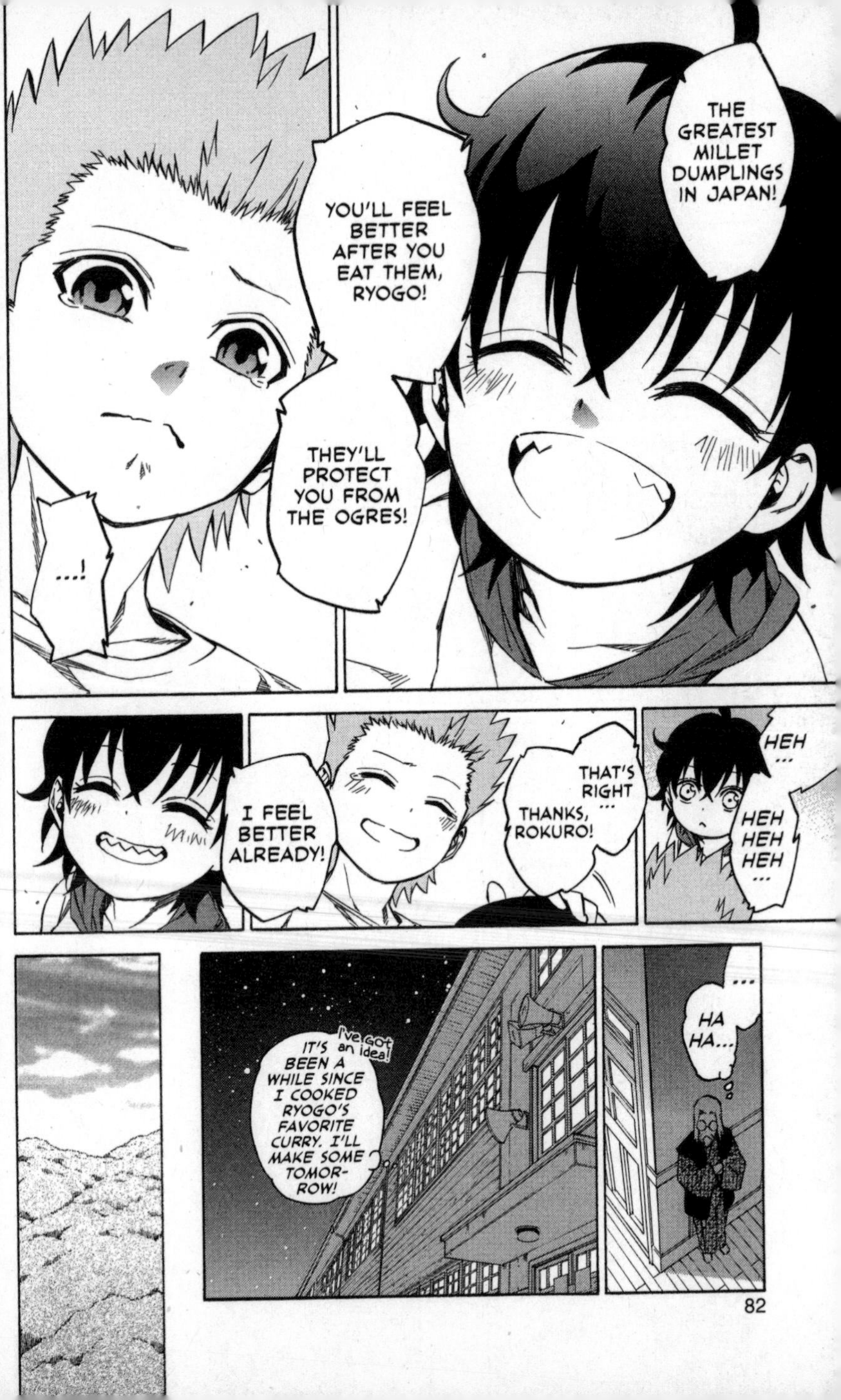
THE GREATEST MILLET DUMPLINGS IN JAPAN!
YOU'LL FEEL BETTER AFTER YOU EAT THEM, RYOGO!
THEY'LL PROTECT YOU FROM THE OGRES!
...!
HEH...
HEH HEH HEH...
THAT'S RIGHT...
THANKS, ROKURO!
I FEEL BETTER ALREADY!
...
HA HA...
I've got an idea!
IT'S BEEN A WHILE SINCE I COOKED RYOGO'S FAVORITE CURRY. I'LL MAKE SOME TOMOR-ROW!

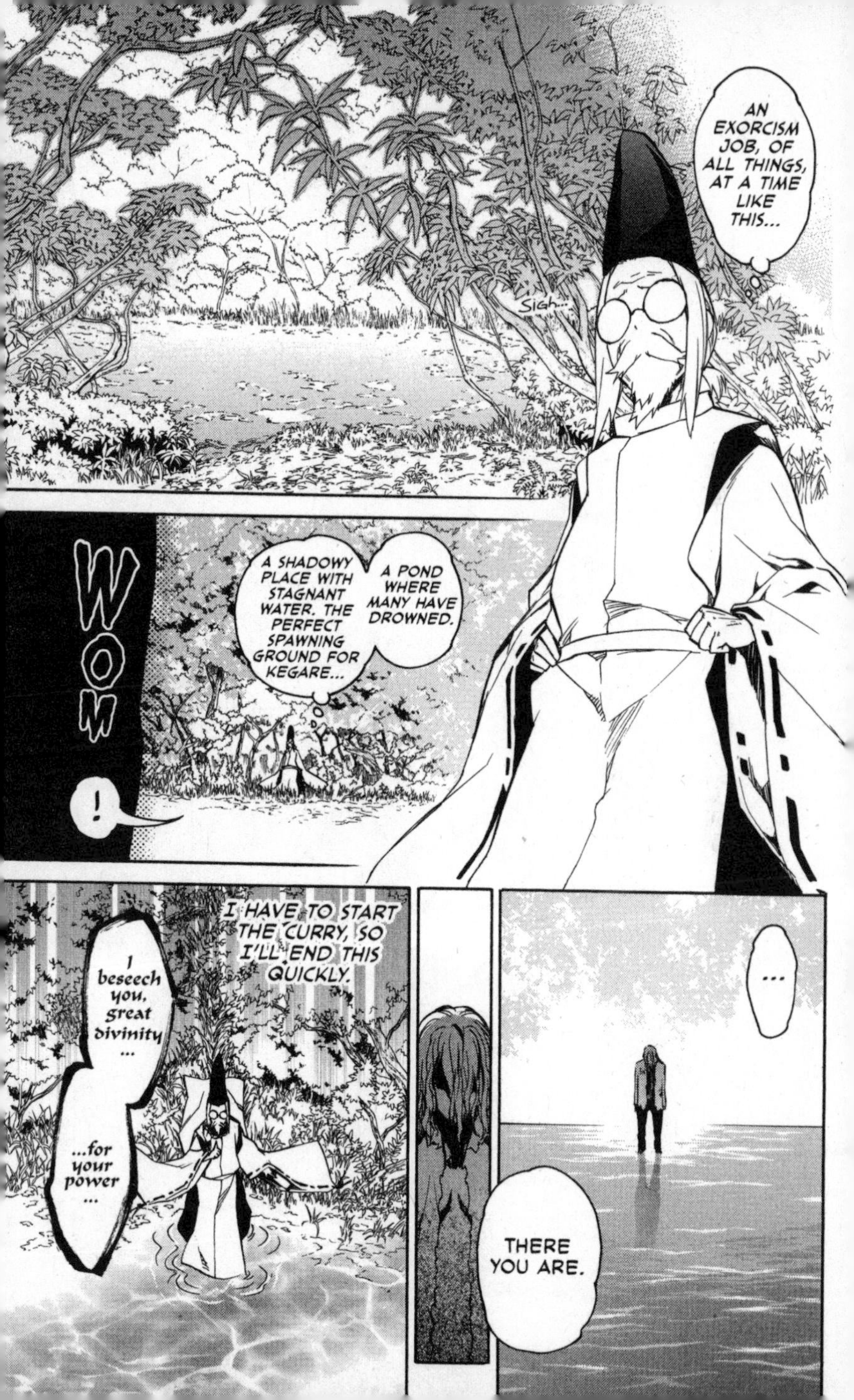
AN EXORCISM JOB, OF ALL THINGS, AT A TIME LIKE THIS...
Sigh...
A POND WHERE MANY HAVE DROWNED.
A SHADOWY PLACE WITH STAGNANT WATER. THE PERFECT SPAWNING GROUND FOR KEGARE...
WOM
!
...
THERE YOU ARE.
I HAVE TO START THE CURRY, SO I'LL END THIS QUICKLY.
I beseech you, great divinity...
...for your power...

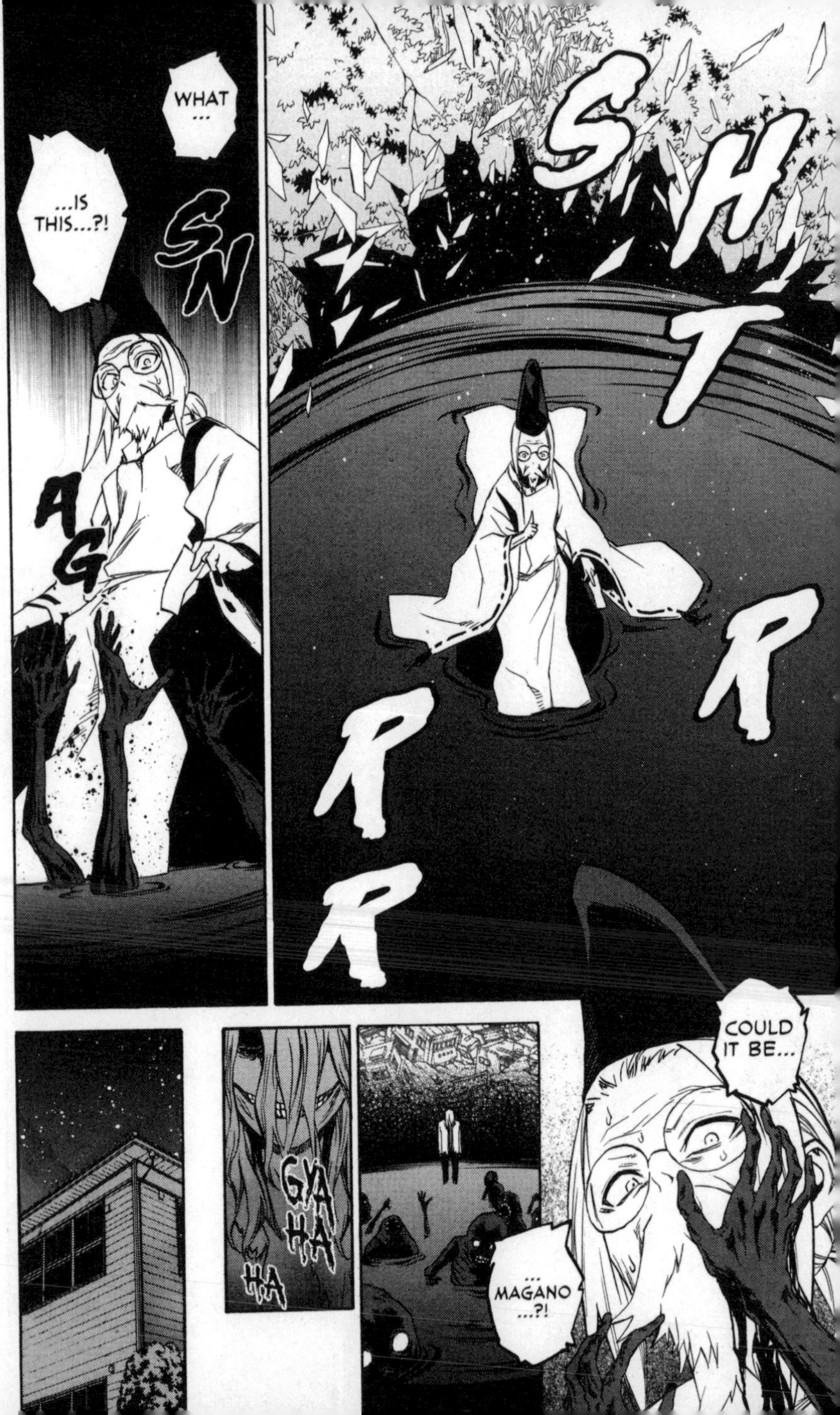
SHT
RRR
WHAT...
...IS THIS...?!
SN
AG
COULD IT BE...
...MAGANO...?!
GYA HA
HA

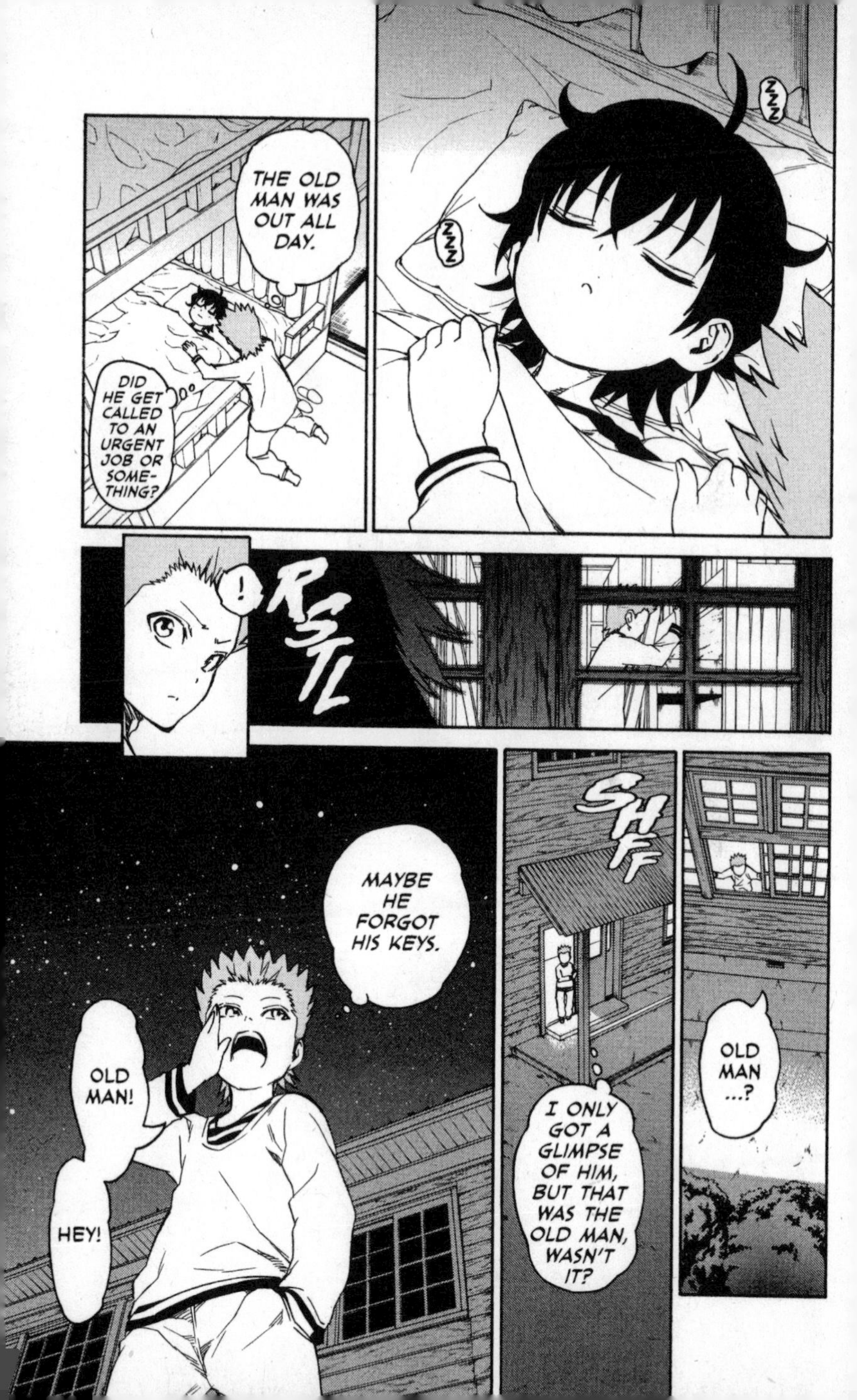
ZZZ
ZZZ
THE OLD MAN WAS OUT ALL DAY.
DID HE GET CALLED TO AN URGENT JOB OR SOME-THING?
RSTL
!
OLD MAN ...?
SHFF
I ONLY GOT A GLIMPSE OF HIM, BUT THAT WAS THE OLD MAN, WASN'T IT?
MAYBE HE FORGOT HIS KEYS.
OLD MAN!
HEY!

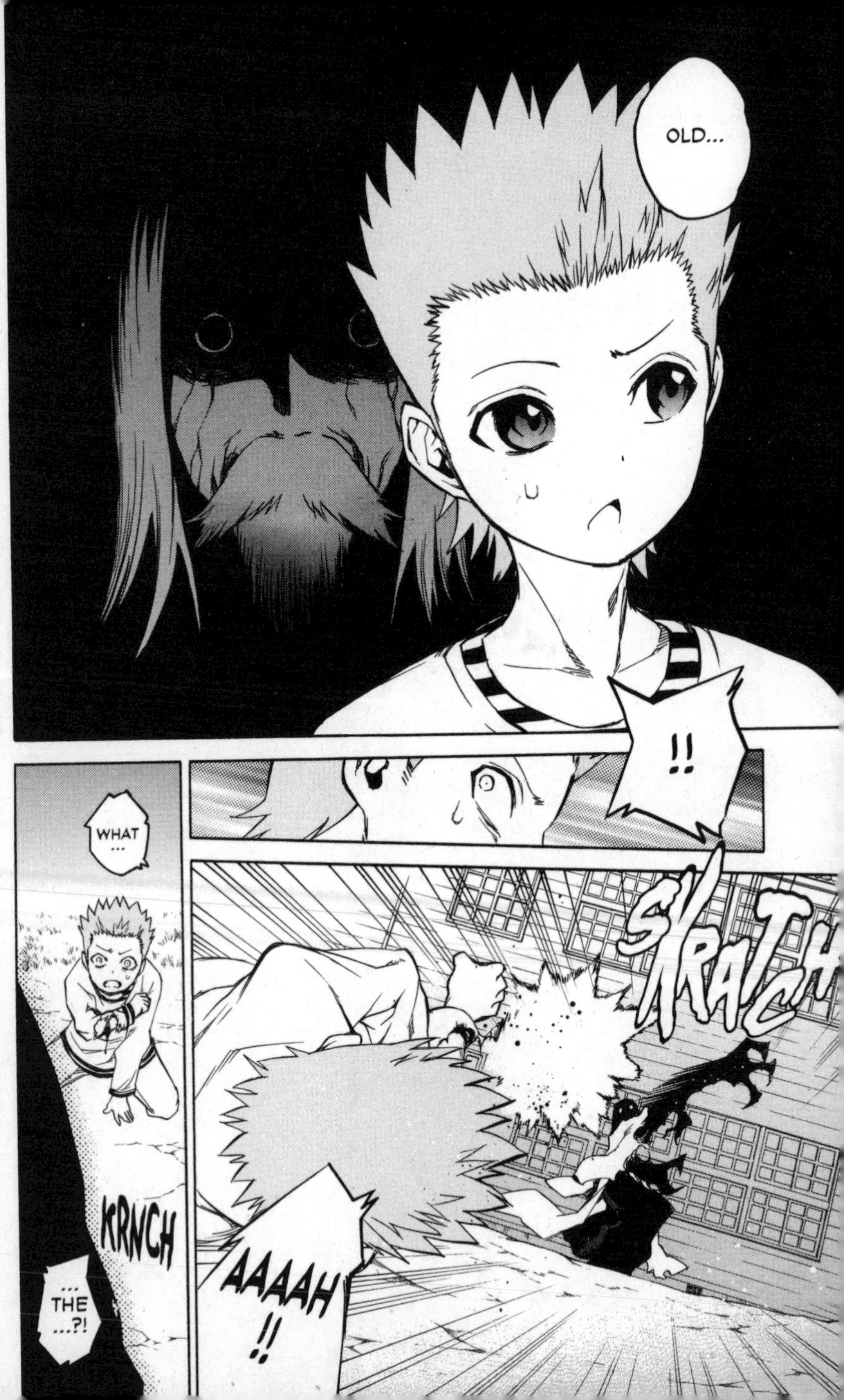

OLD...
!!
SKRATCH
AAAAH!!
WHAT...
KRNCH
...THE...?!

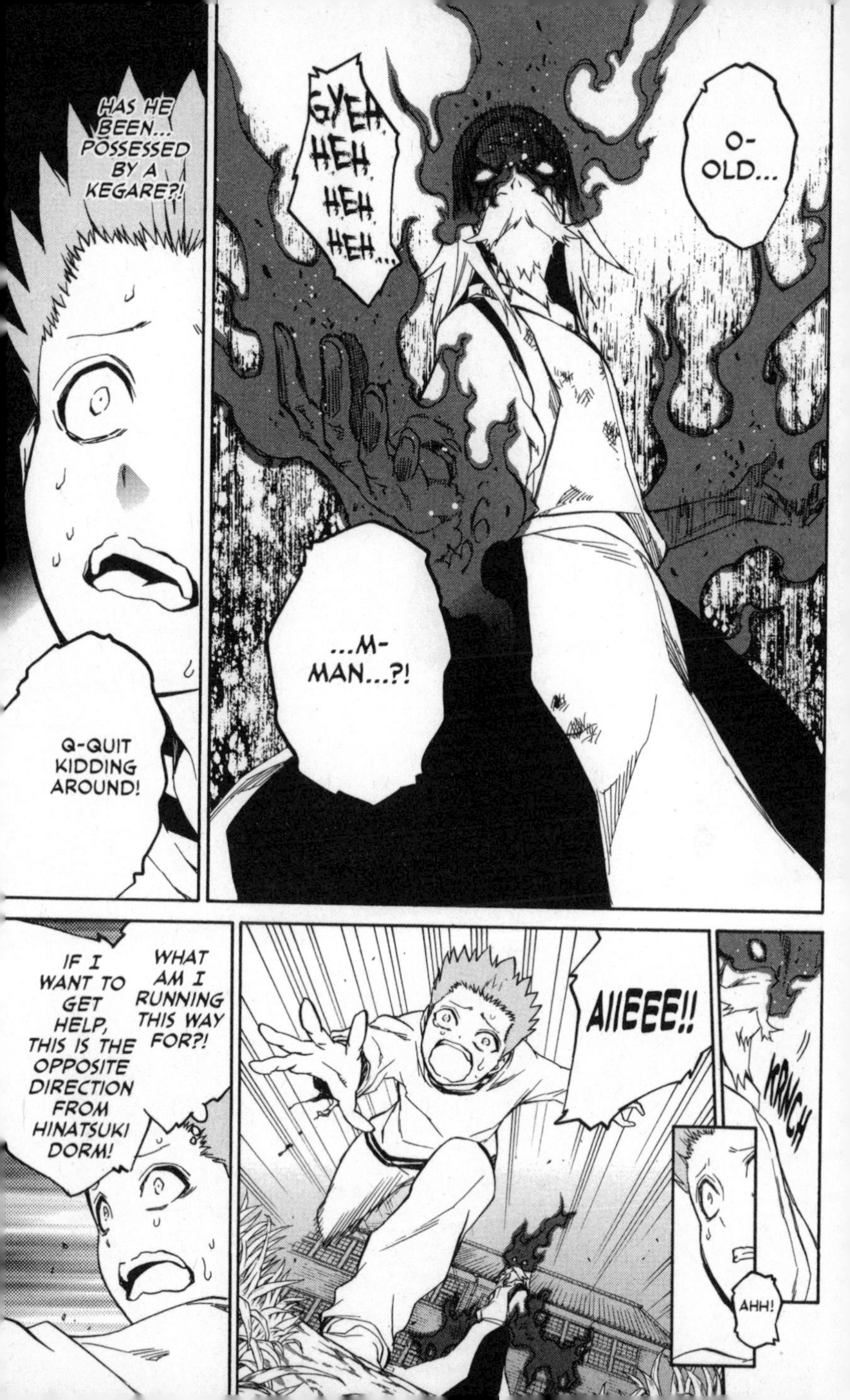
O-OLD...
GYEH HEH HEH HEH...
...M-MAN...?!
HAS HE BEEN... POSSESSED BY A KEGARE?!
Q-QUIT KIDDING AROUND!
KRNCH
AHH!
AIIEEE!!
WHAT AM I RUNNING THIS WAY FOR?!
IF I WANT TO GET HELP, THIS IS THE OPPOSITE DIRECTION FROM HINATSUKI DORM!

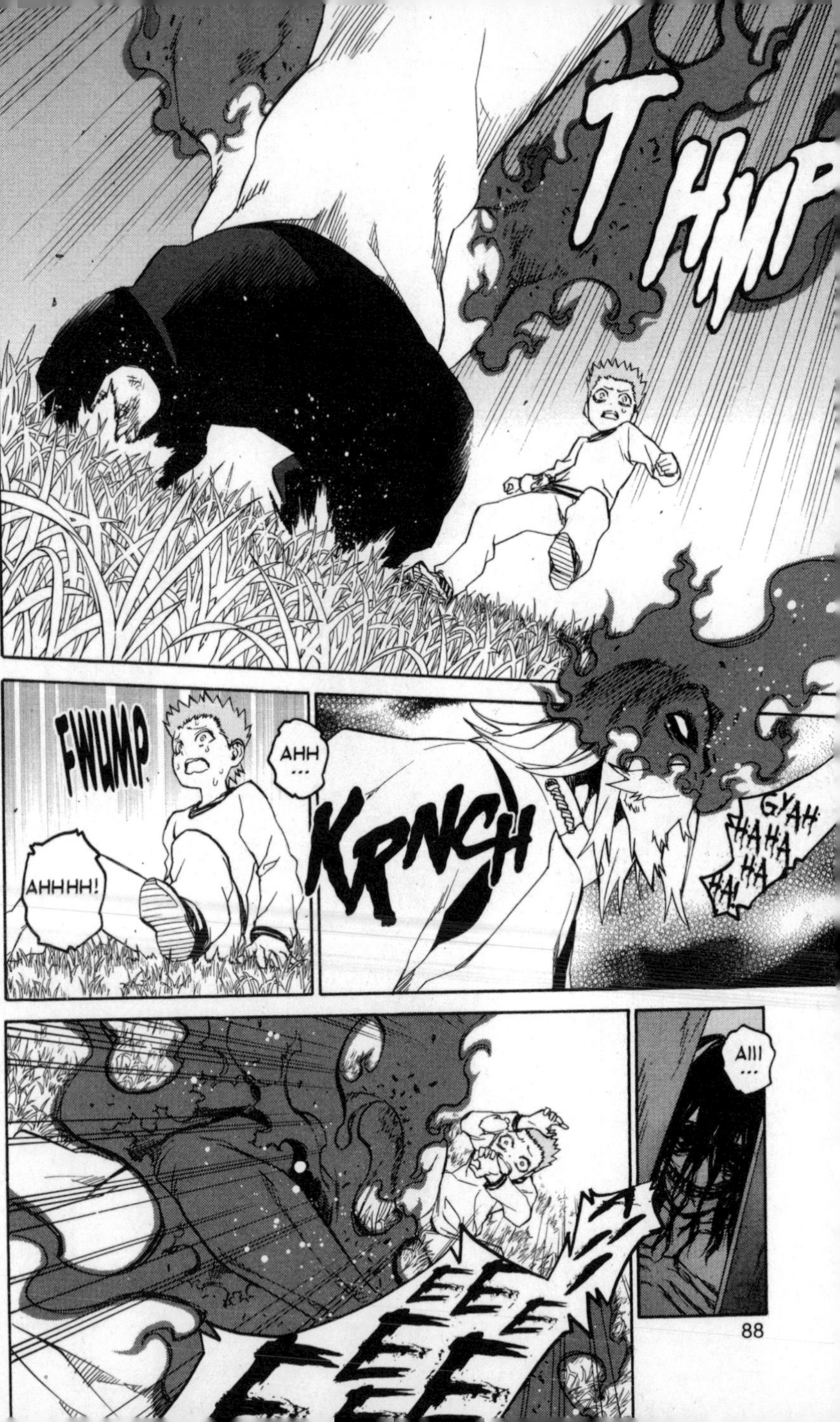
THMP
GYAH HA HA HA HA!
KRNCH
AHH ...
FWUMP
AHHHH!
AIII ...
EEEEEE

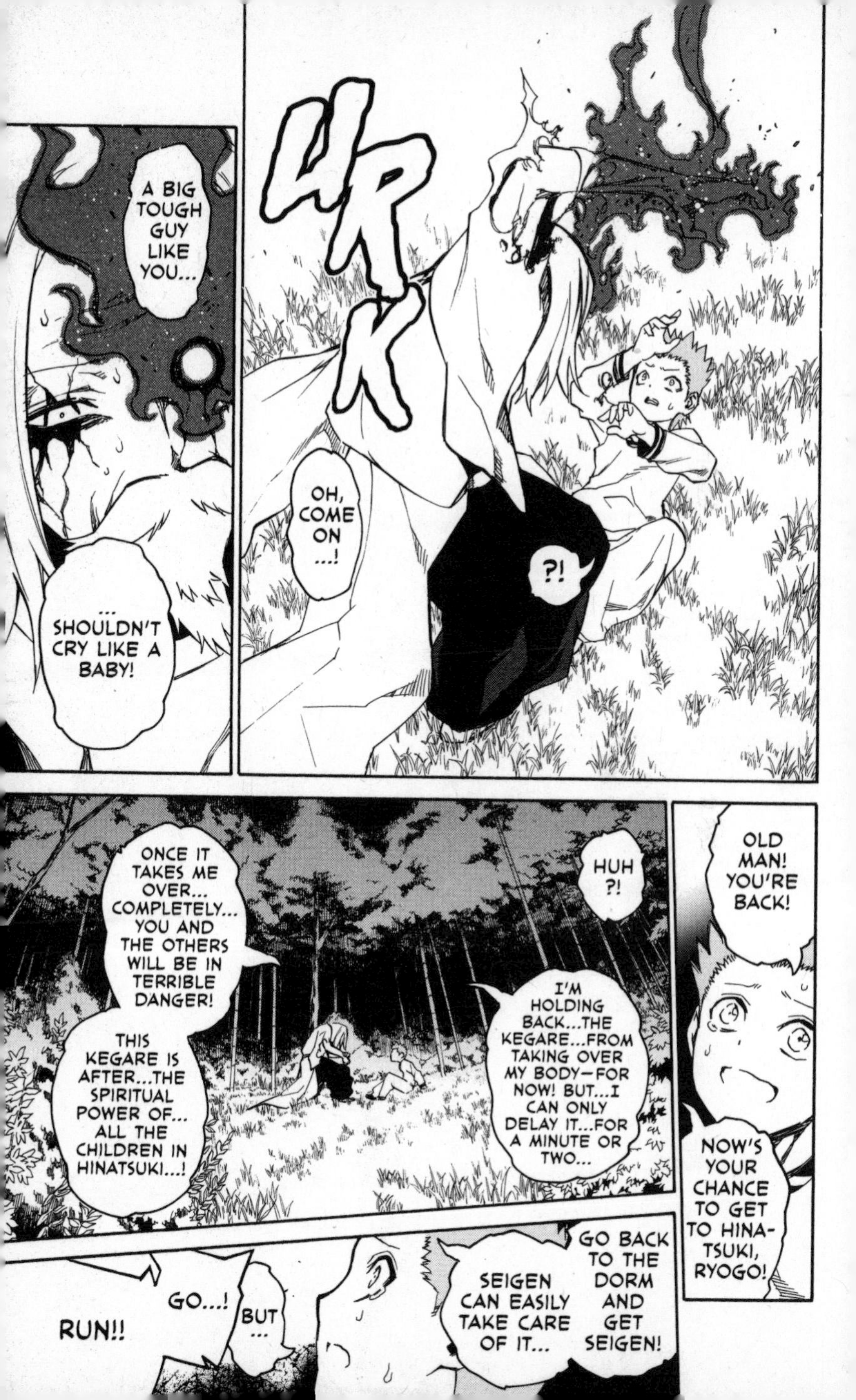
URK
OH, COME ON ...!
?!
A BIG TOUGH GUY LIKE YOU...
... SHOULDN'T CRY LIKE A BABY!
OLD MAN! YOU'RE BACK!
NOW'S YOUR CHANCE TO GET TO HINA-TSUKI, RYOGO!
HUH ?!
I'M HOLDING BACK...THE KEGARE...FROM TAKING OVER MY BODY—FOR NOW! BUT...I CAN ONLY DELAY IT...FOR A MINUTE OR TWO...
ONCE IT TAKES ME OVER... COMPLETELY... YOU AND THE OTHERS WILL BE IN TERRIBLE DANGER!
THIS KEGARE IS AFTER...THE SPIRITUAL POWER OF... ALL THE CHILDREN IN HINATSUKI...!
GO BACK TO THE DORM AND GET SEIGEN!
SEIGEN CAN EASILY TAKE CARE OF IT...
BUT ...
GO...!
RUN!!

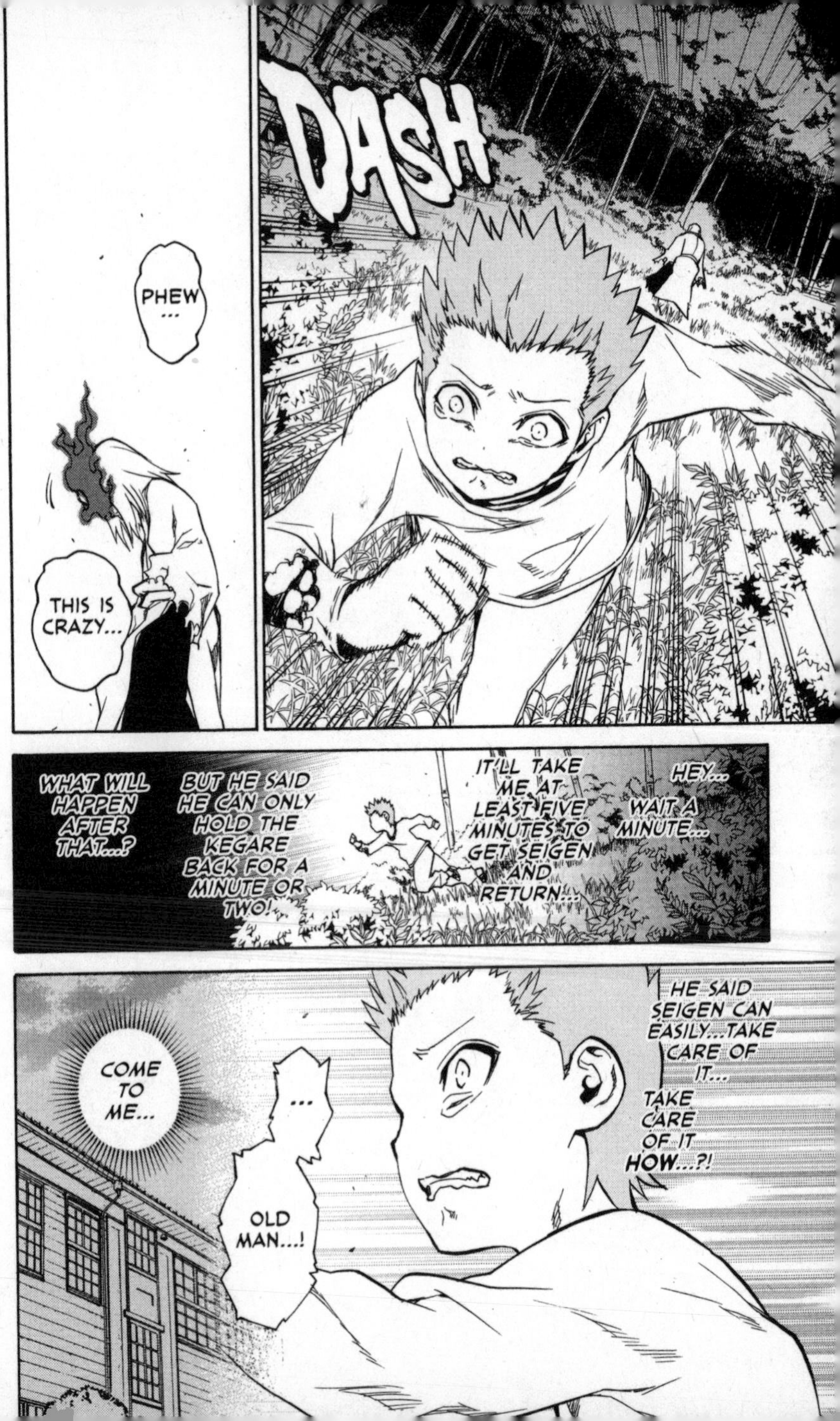
DASH
PHEW...
THIS IS CRAZY...
HEY... WAIT A MINUTE...
IT'LL TAKE ME AT LEAST FIVE MINUTES TO GET SEIGEN AND RETURN...
BUT HE SAID HE CAN ONLY HOLD THE KEGARE BACK FOR A MINUTE OR TWO!
WHAT WILL HAPPEN AFTER THAT...?
HE SAID SEIGEN CAN EASILY...TAKE CARE OF IT...
TAKE CARE OF IT HOW...?!
...
COME TO ME...
OLD MAN...!

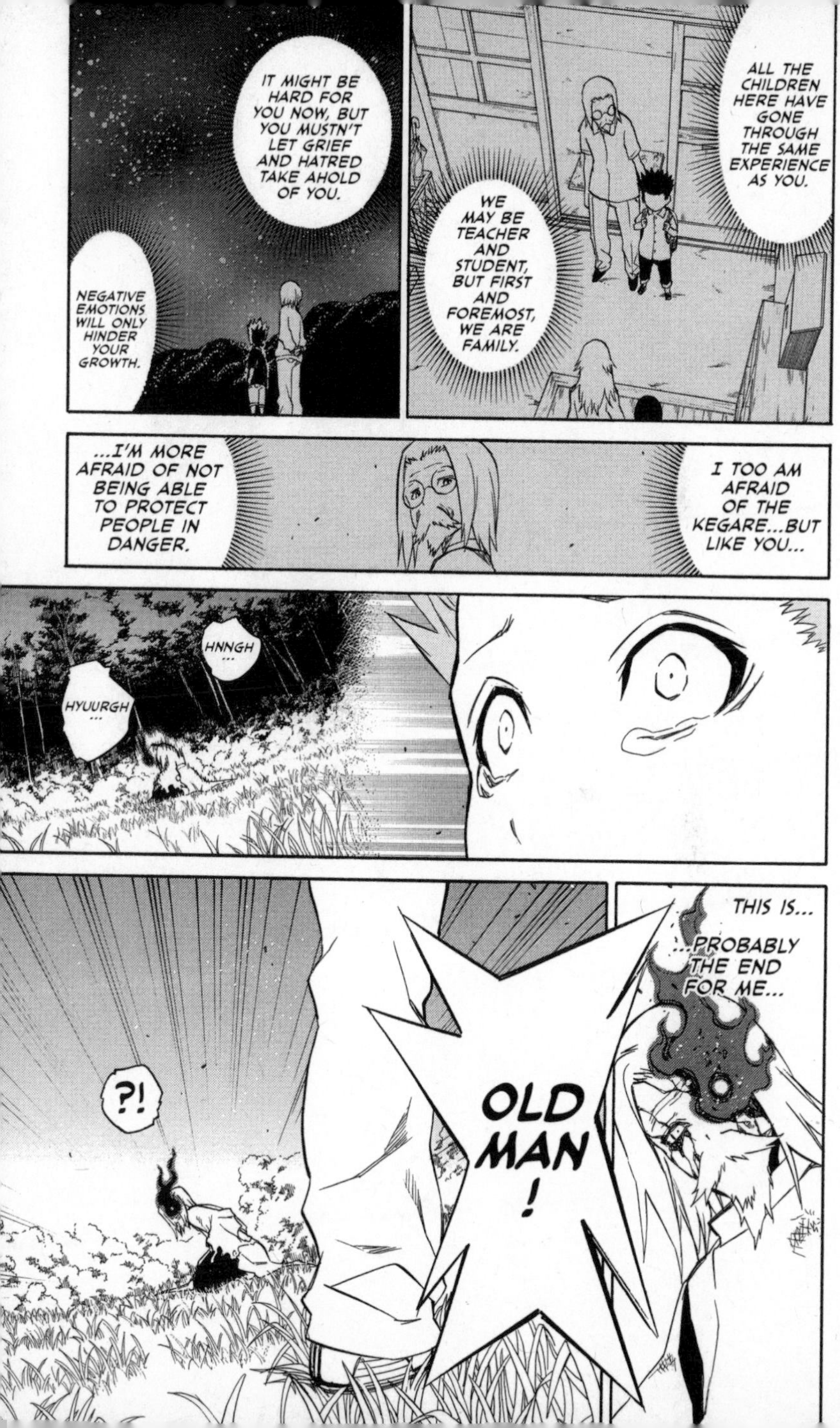
ALL THE CHILDREN HERE HAVE GONE THROUGH THE SAME EXPERIENCE AS YOU.
WE MAY BE TEACHER AND STUDENT, BUT FIRST AND FOREMOST, WE ARE FAMILY.
IT MIGHT BE HARD FOR YOU NOW, BUT YOU MUSTN'T LET GRIEF AND HATRED TAKE AHOLD OF YOU.
NEGATIVE EMOTIONS WILL ONLY HINDER YOUR GROWTH.
I TOO AM AFRAID OF THE KEGARE...BUT LIKE YOU...
...I'M MORE AFRAID OF NOT BEING ABLE TO PROTECT PEOPLE IN DANGER.
HNNGH...
HYUURGH...
THIS IS...
...PROBABLY THE END FOR ME...
OLD MAN!
?!

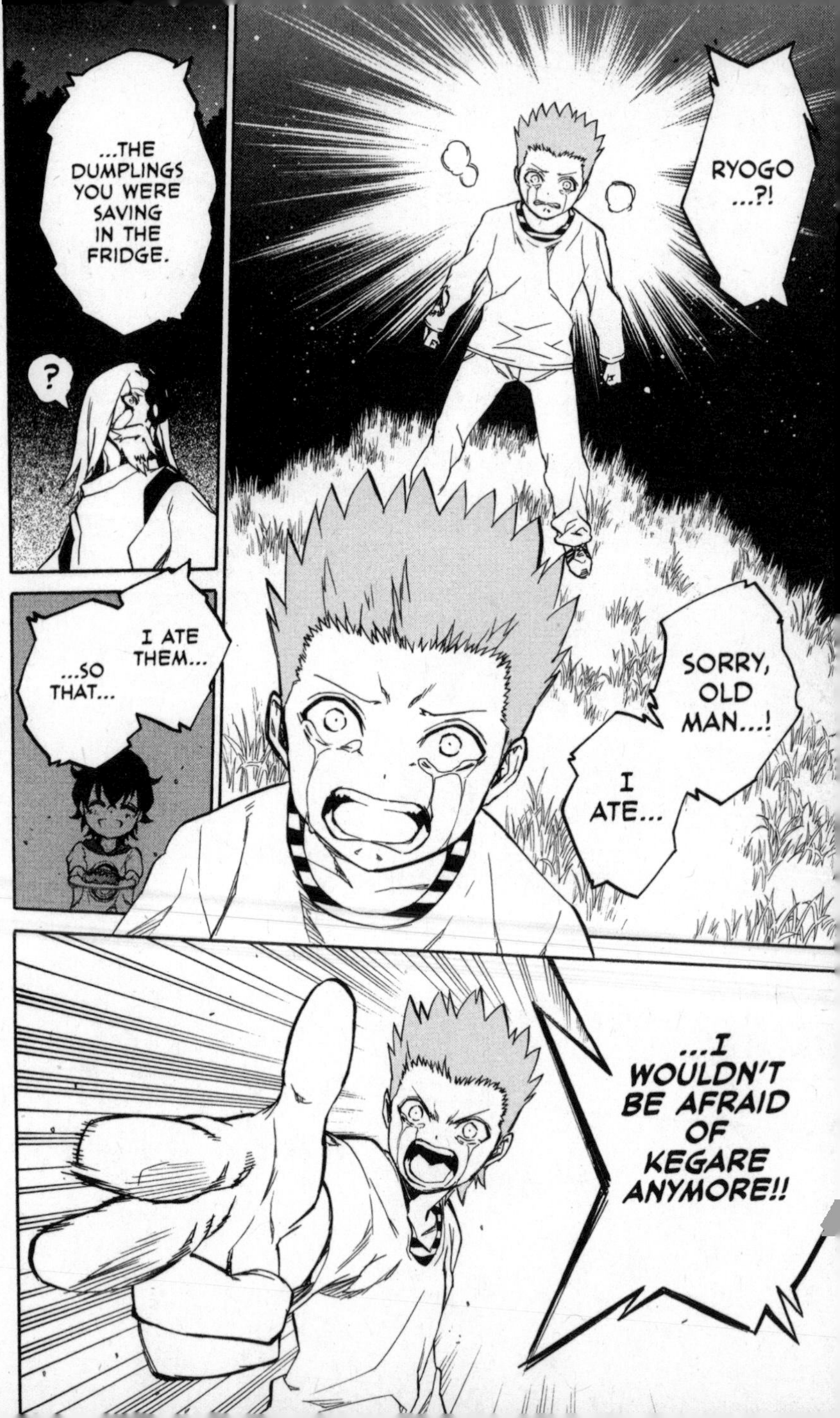
RYOGO ...?!
SORRY, OLD MAN...!
I ATE...
...THE DUMPLINGS YOU WERE SAVING IN THE FRIDGE.
?
I ATE THEM...
...SO THAT...
...I WOULDN'T BE AFRAID OF KEGARE ANYMORE!!

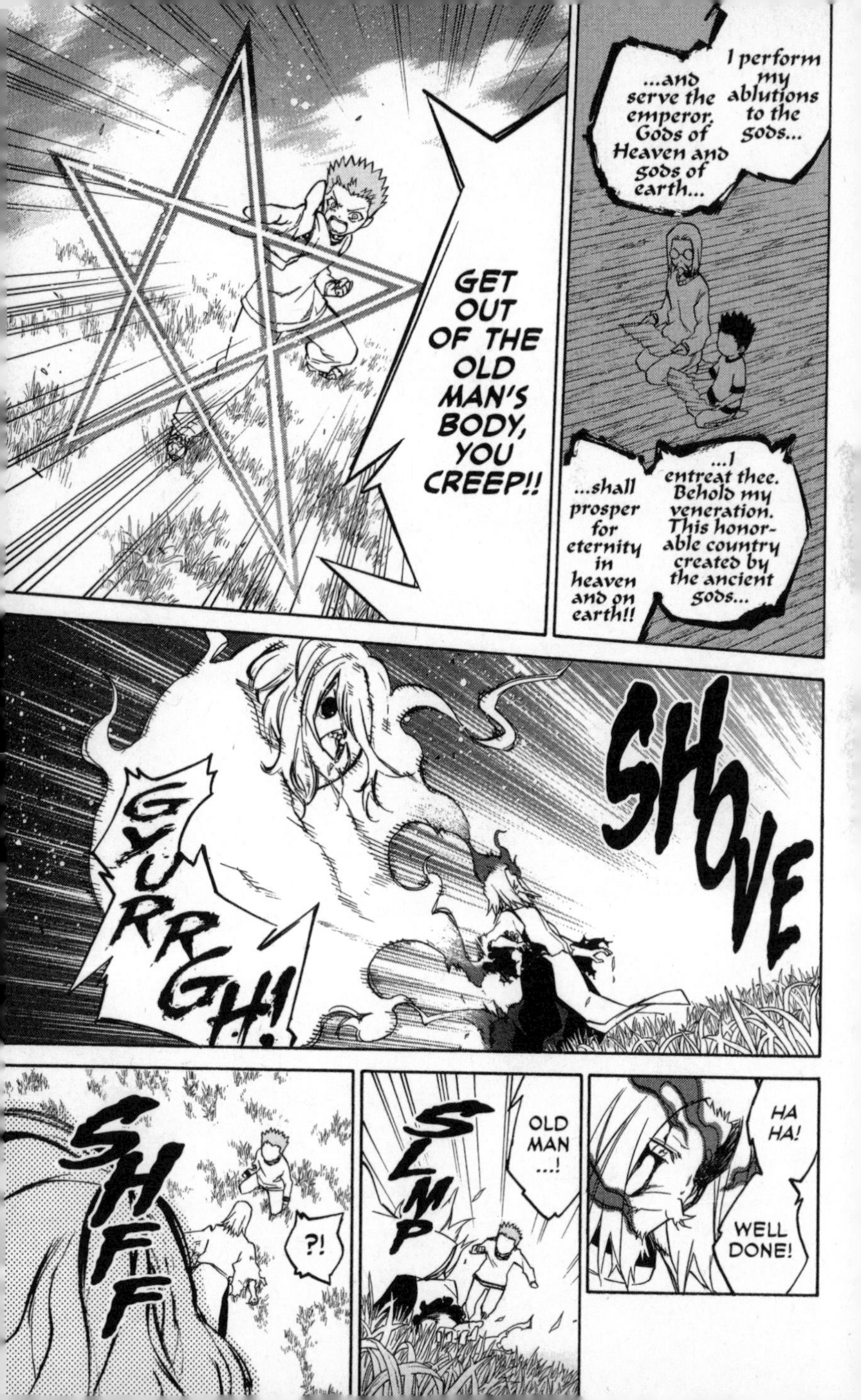
I perform my ablutions to the gods...
...and serve the emperor. Gods of Heaven and gods of earth...
...I entreat thee. Behold my veneration. This honorable country created by the ancient gods...
...shall prosper for eternity in heaven and on earth!!
GET OUT OF THE OLD MAN'S BODY, YOU CREEP!!
SHOVE
GYURRRGH!
HA HA!
WELL DONE!
OLD MAN ...!
SLMP
?!
SHFF

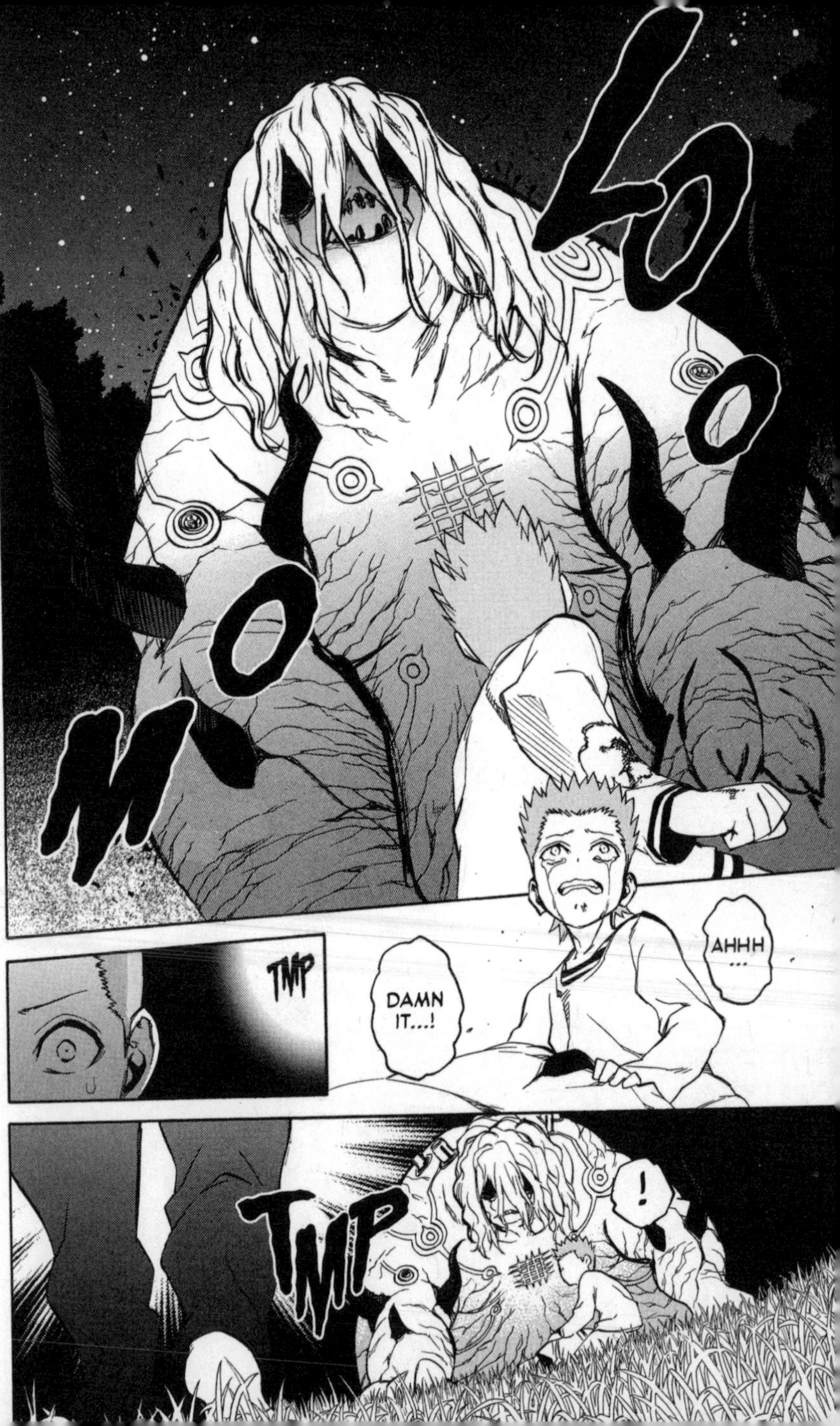
AHHH...
DAMN IT...!
TMP
!
TMP

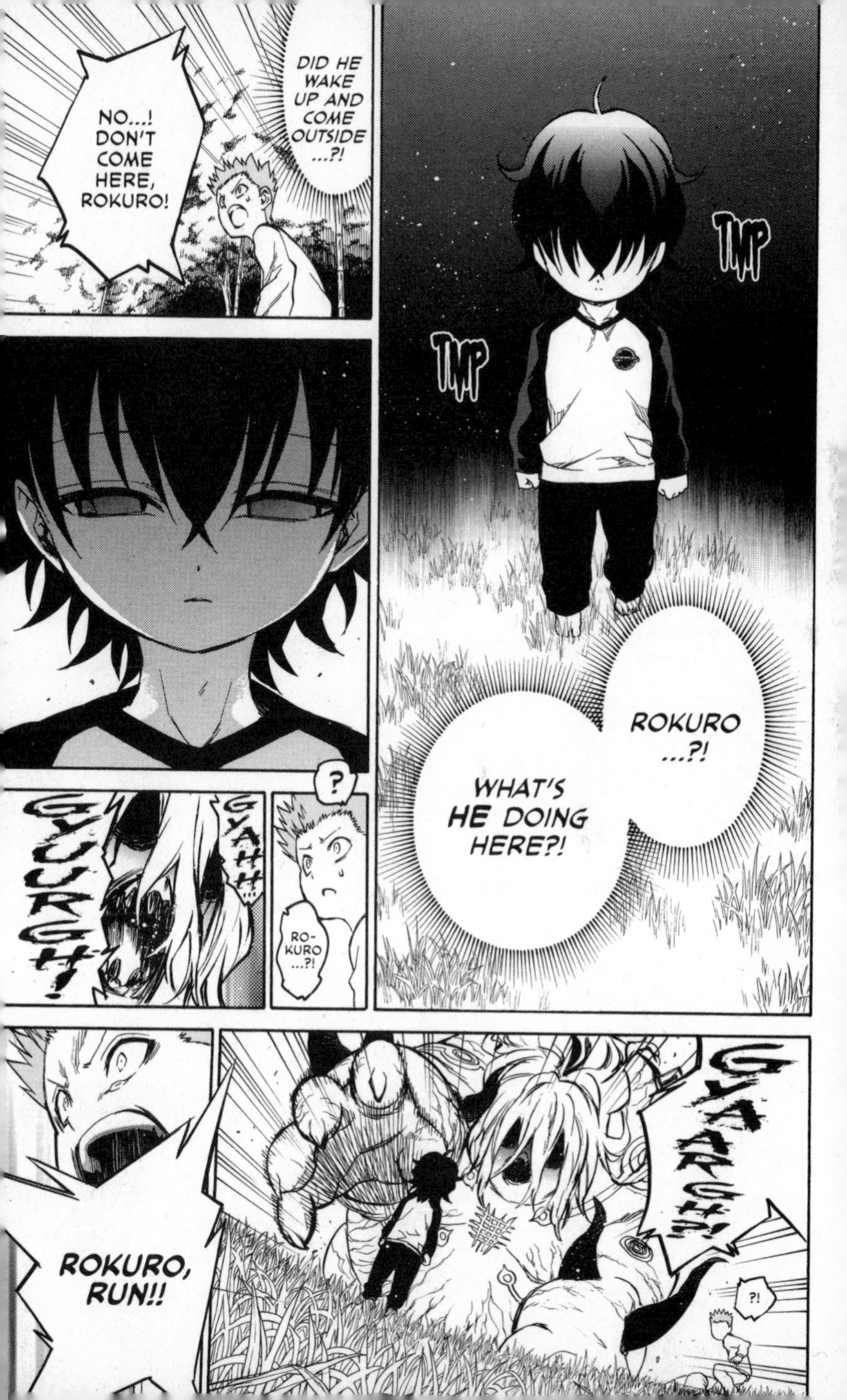
TMP
TMP
ROKURO ...?! WHAT'S HE DOING HERE?!
DID HE WAKE UP AND COME OUTSIDE ...?!
NO...! DON'T COME HERE, ROKURO!
?
RO-KURO ...?!
GYAHH...
GYUURGH!
GYAARGH!
?!
ROKURO, RUN!!

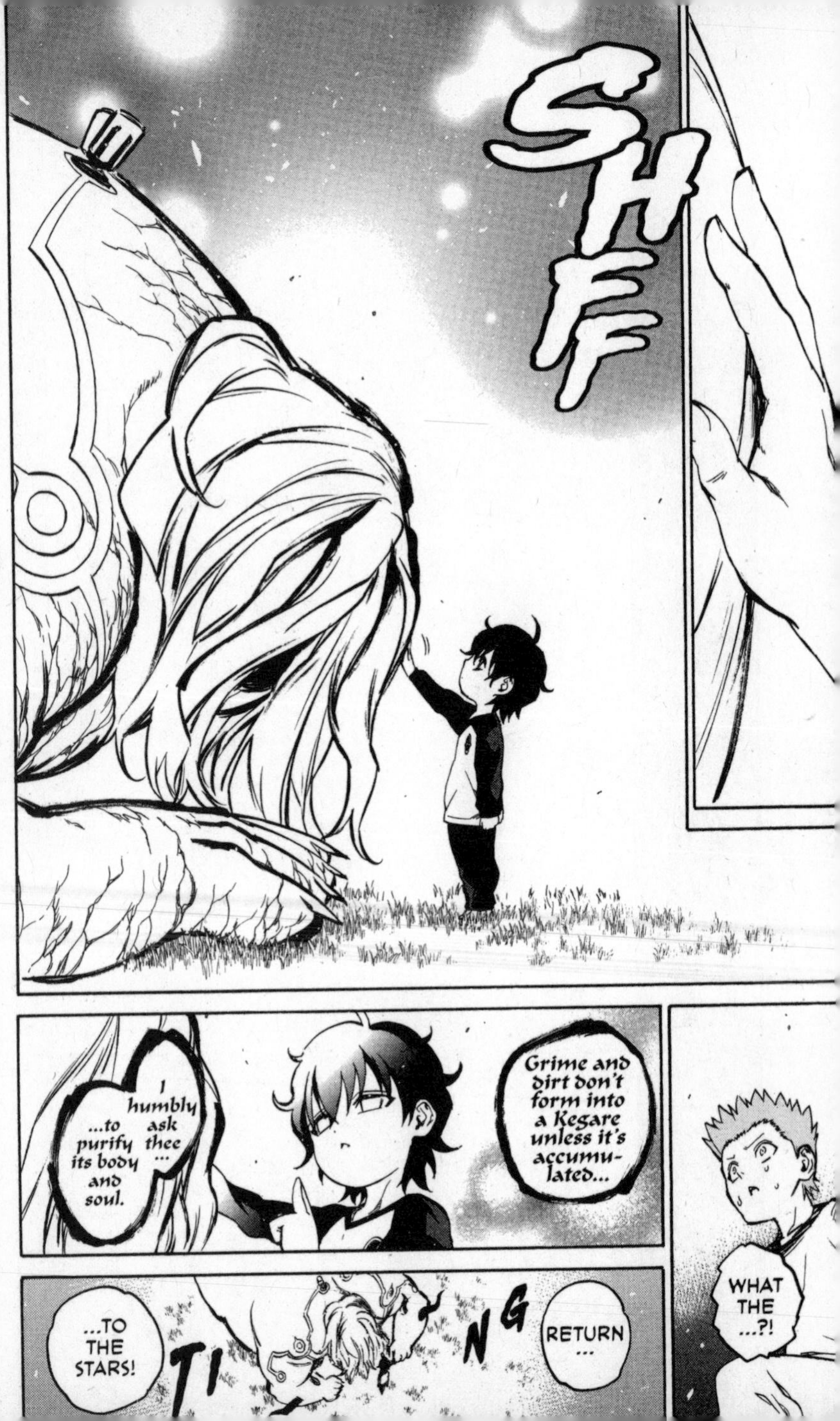
SHFF
WHAT THE ...?!
Grime and dirt don't form into a Kegare unless it's accumulated...
I humbly ask thee ...
...to purify its body and soul.
RETURN ...
TING
...TO THE STARS!

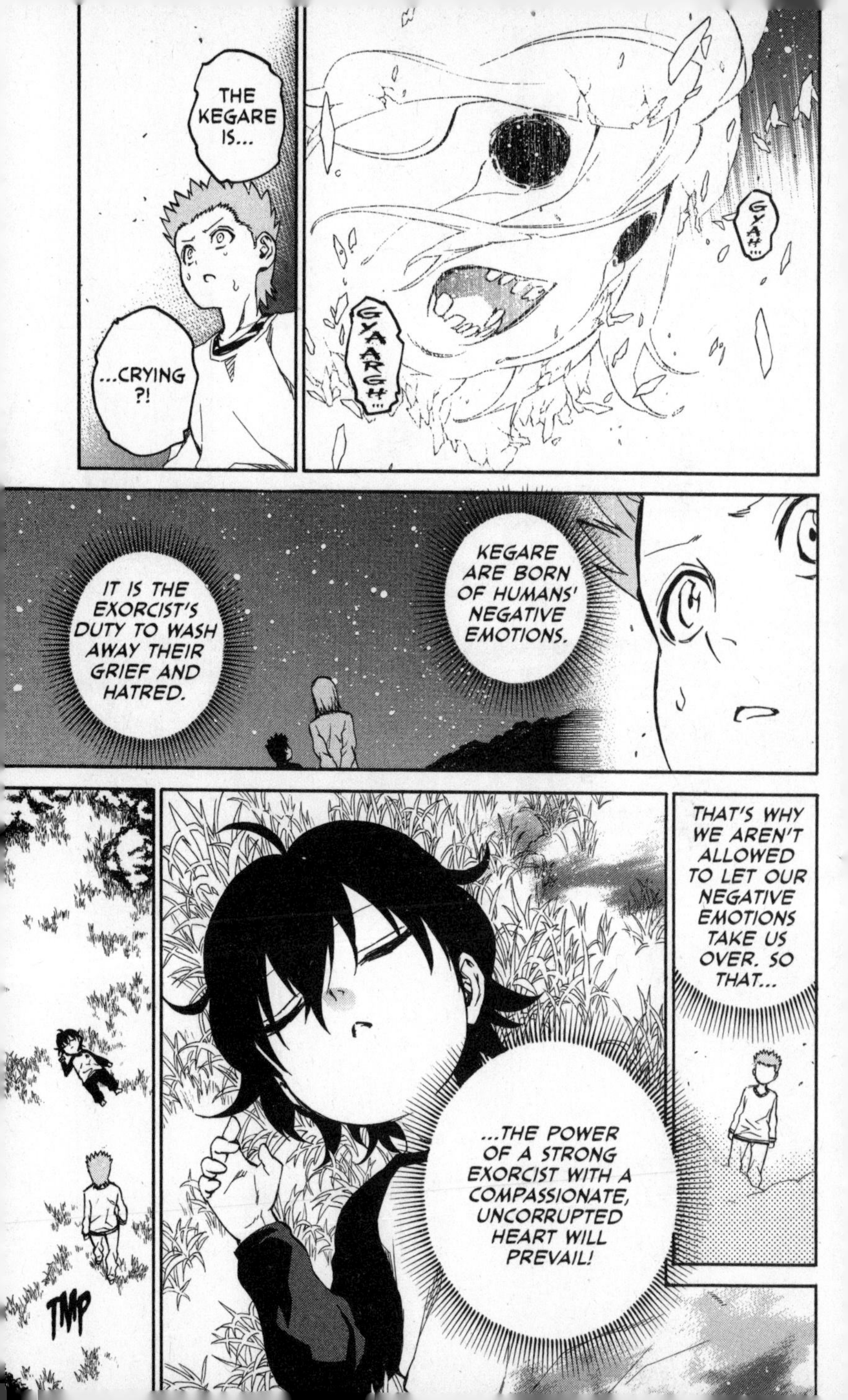
GYAH...
GYAARGH...
THE KEGARE IS...
...CRYING?!
KEGARE ARE BORN OF HUMANS' NEGATIVE EMOTIONS.
IT IS THE EXORCIST'S DUTY TO WASH AWAY THEIR GRIEF AND HATRED.
THAT'S WHY WE AREN'T ALLOWED TO LET OUR NEGATIVE EMOTIONS TAKE US OVER. SO THAT...
...THE POWER OF A STRONG EXORCIST WITH A COMPASSIONATE, UNCORRUPTED HEART WILL PREVAIL!
TMP

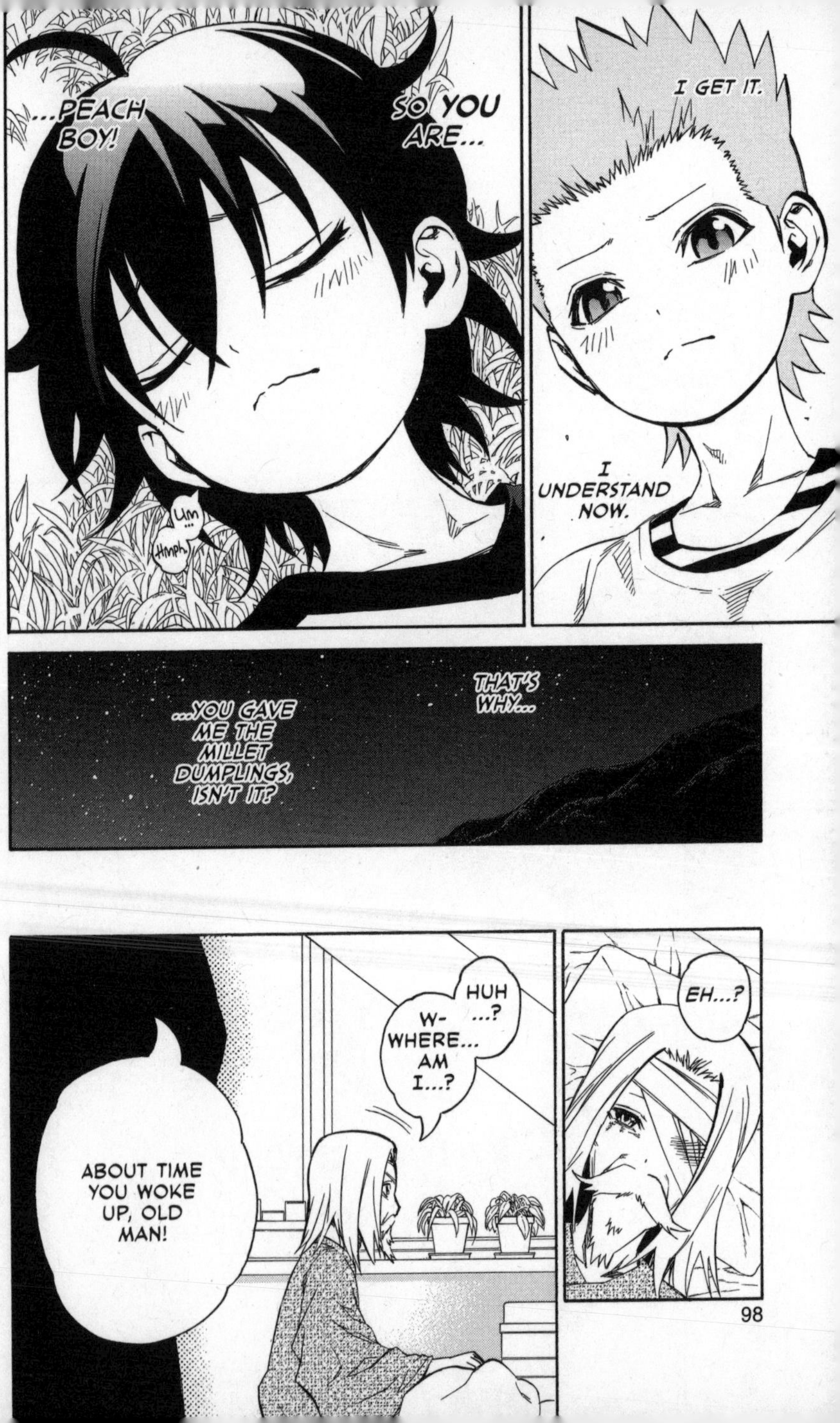
I GET IT.
I UNDERSTAND NOW.
SO YOU ARE...
...PEACH BOY!
Um...
Hmph.
THAT'S WHY...
...YOU GAVE ME THE MILLET DUMPLINGS, ISN'T IT?
EH...?
HUH...?
W-WHERE... AM I...?
ABOUT TIME YOU WOKE UP, OLD MAN!

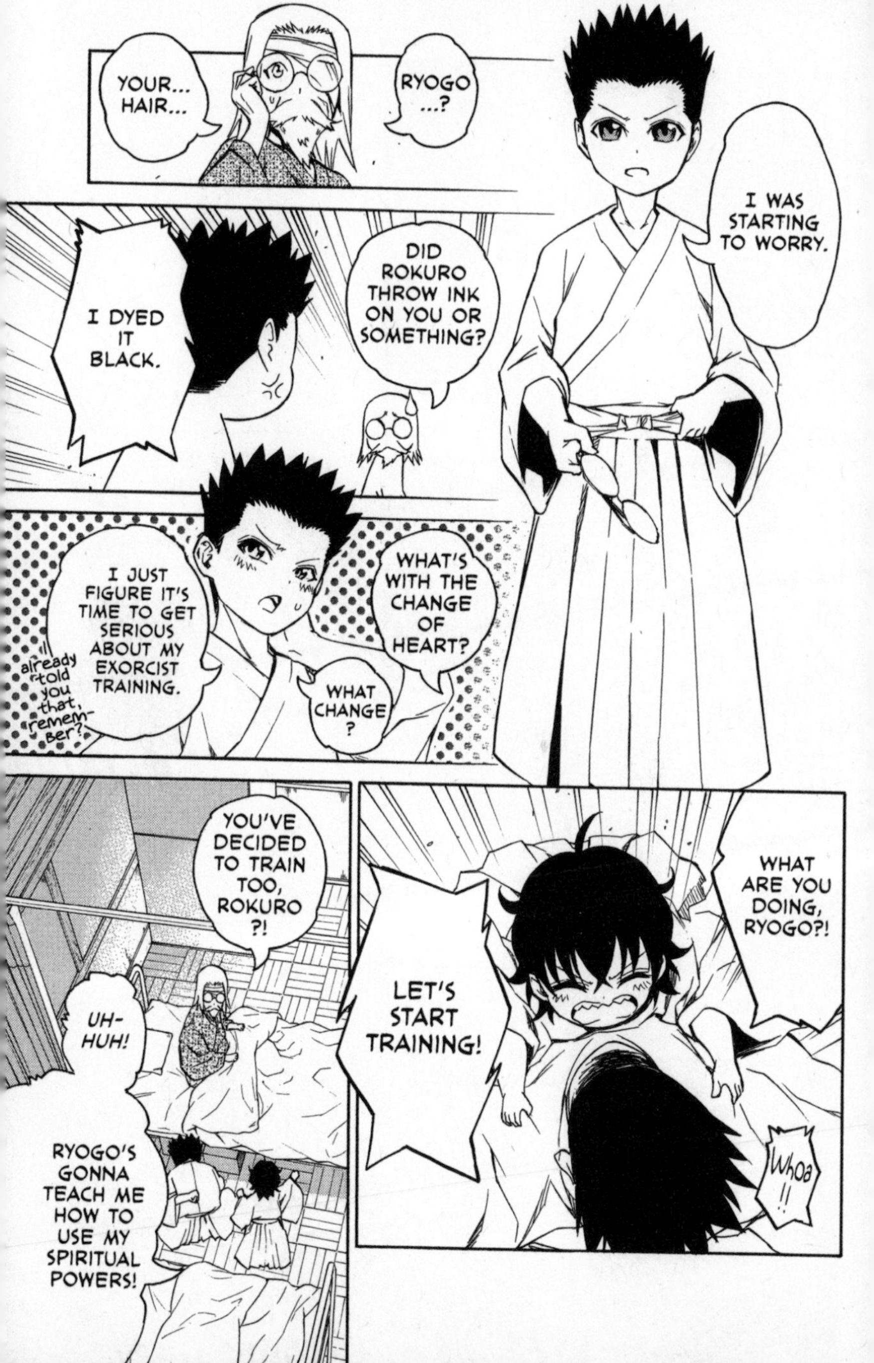
I WAS STARTING TO WORRY.
RYOGO ...?
YOUR... HAIR...
DID ROKURO THROW INK ON YOU OR SOMETHING?
I DYED IT BLACK.
WHAT'S WITH THE CHANGE OF HEART?
WHAT CHANGE?
I JUST FIGURE IT'S TIME TO GET SERIOUS ABOUT MY EXORCIST TRAINING.
I already told you that, remember?
WHAT ARE YOU DOING, RYOGO?!
LET'S START TRAINING!
Whoa!!
YOU'VE DECIDED TO TRAIN TOO, ROKURO?!
UH-HUH!
RYOGO'S GONNA TEACH ME HOW TO USE MY SPIRITUAL POWERS!

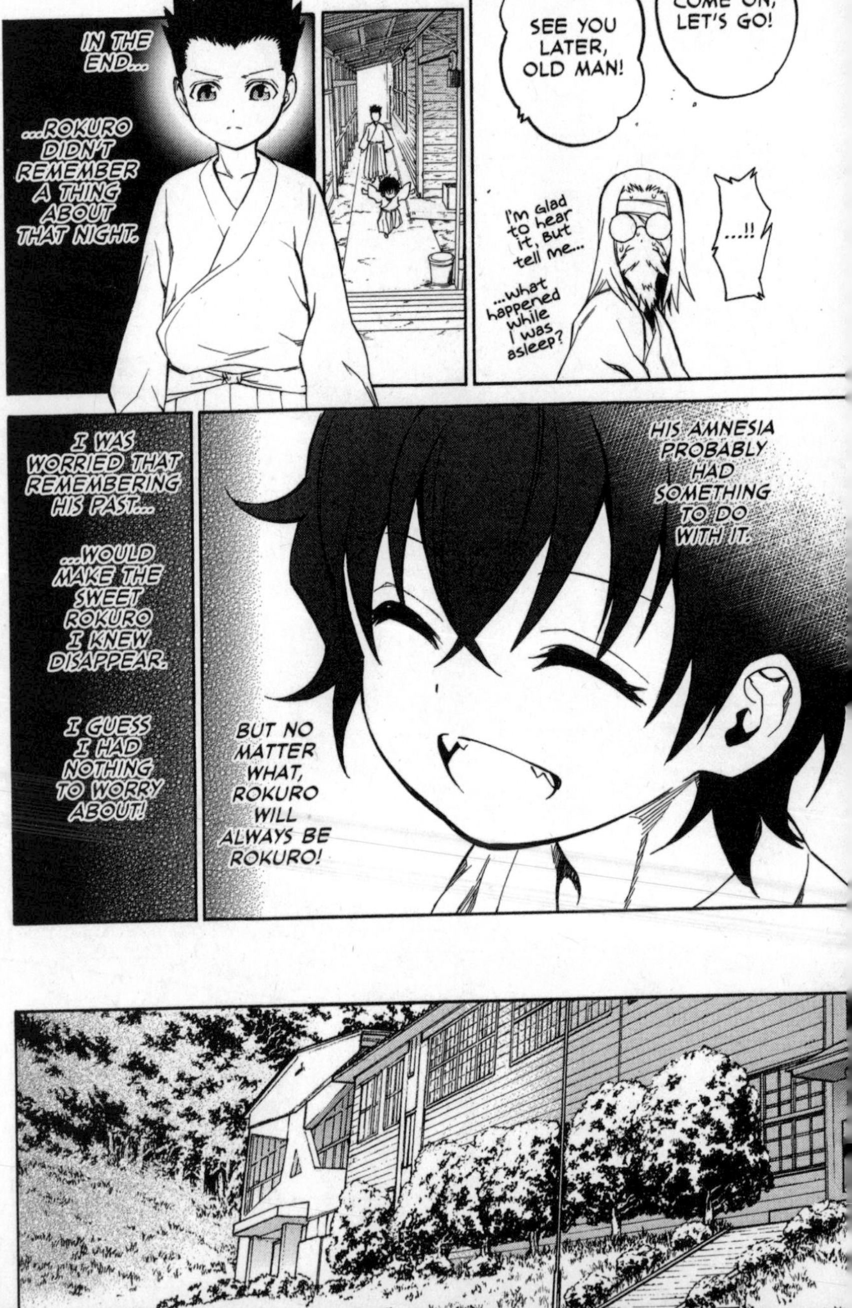
COME ON, LET'S GO!
SEE YOU LATER, OLD MAN!
...!!
I'm glad to hear it, but tell me...
...what happened while I was asleep?
IN THE END...
...ROKURO DIDN'T REMEMBER A THING ABOUT THAT NIGHT.
HIS AMNESIA PROBABLY HAD SOMETHING TO DO WITH IT.
BUT NO MATTER WHAT, ROKURO WILL ALWAYS BE ROKURO!
I WAS WORRIED THAT REMEMBERING HIS PAST...
...WOULD MAKE THE SWEET ROKURO I KNEW DISAPPEAR.
I GUESS I HAD NOTHING TO WORRY ABOUT!

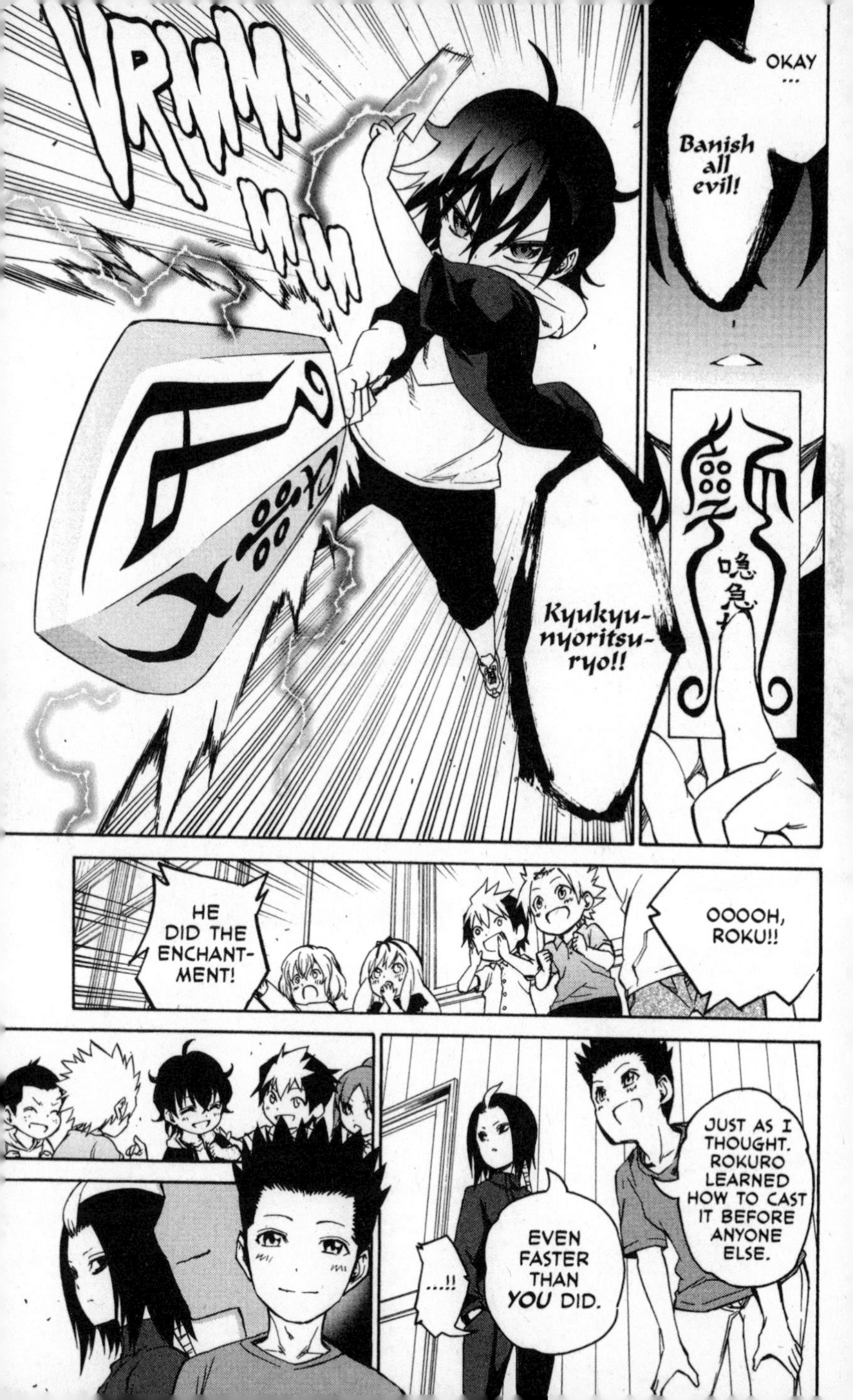
OKAY ...
Banish all evil!
Kyukyu-nyoritsu-ryo!!
VRMM MM
OOOOH, ROKU!!
HE DID THE ENCHANT-MENT!
JUST AS I THOUGHT. ROKURO LEARNED HOW TO CAST IT BEFORE ANYONE ELSE.
EVEN FASTER THAN YOU DID.
...!!

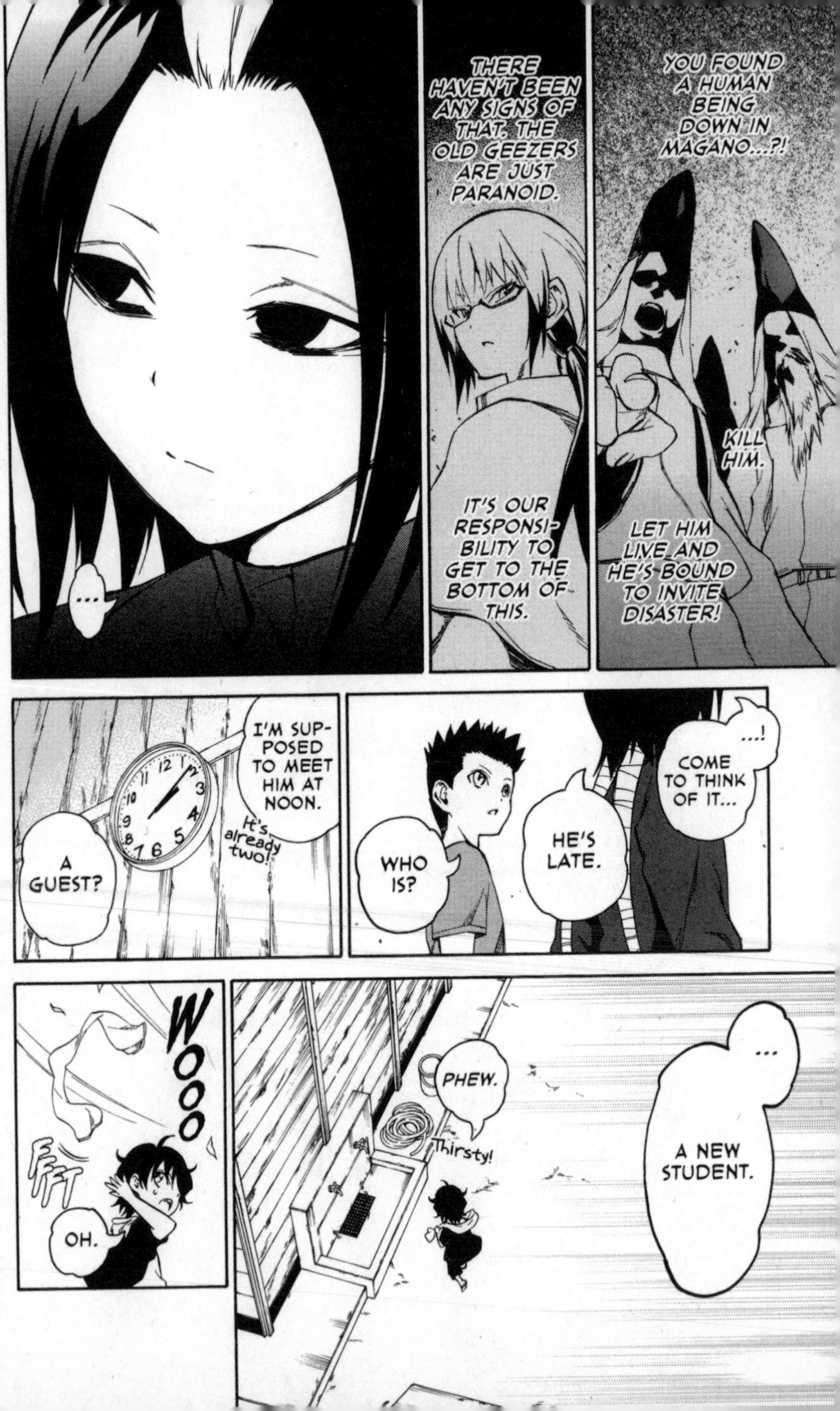
YOU FOUND A HUMAN BEING DOWN IN MAGANO...?!
KILL HIM.
LET HIM LIVE AND HE'S BOUND TO INVITE DISASTER!
THERE HAVEN'T BEEN ANY SIGNS OF THAT. THE OLD GEEZERS ARE JUST PARANOID.
IT'S OUR RESPONSI-BILITY TO GET TO THE BOTTOM OF THIS.
...
...!
COME TO THINK OF IT...
HE'S LATE.
WHO IS?
I'M SUP-POSED TO MEET HIM AT NOON.
It's already two!
A GUEST?
...
A NEW STUDENT.
PHEW.
Thirsty!
WOOOO
FFFT
OH.

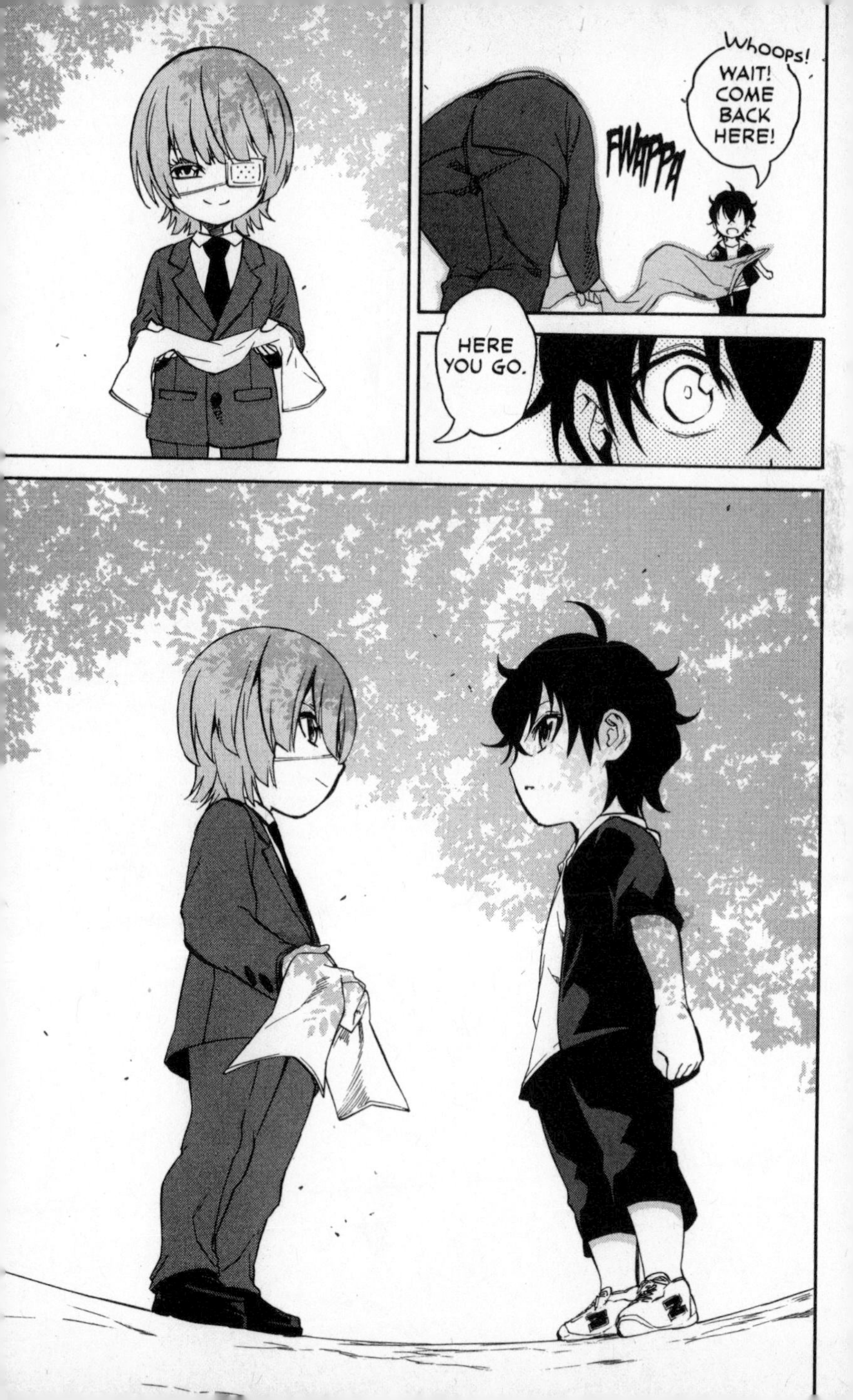
Whoops!
WAIT! COME BACK HERE!
FWAPPA
HERE YOU GO.

# Column ⑪

### The Theory of Yin, Yang and the Five Elements

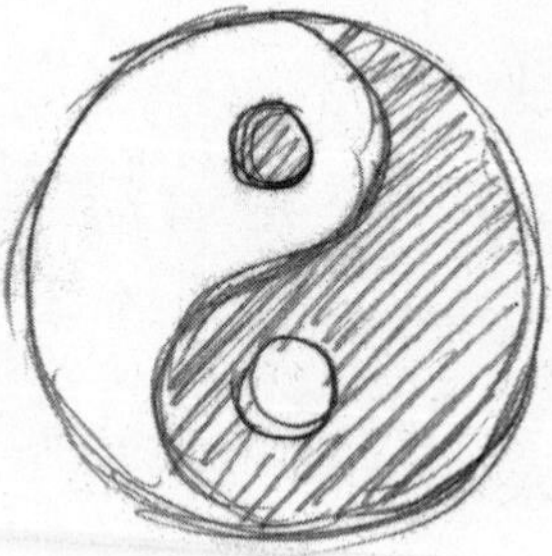

In ancient China, it was believed that every phenomenon in the world could be divided into yin, yang and the five elements of wood, fire, earth, metal and water (which form the basis of *onmyodo*). The cycle of each of these elements reacting to each other to create is called *sojo*, and the cycle of elements reacting to each other to destroy is called *sokoku*.

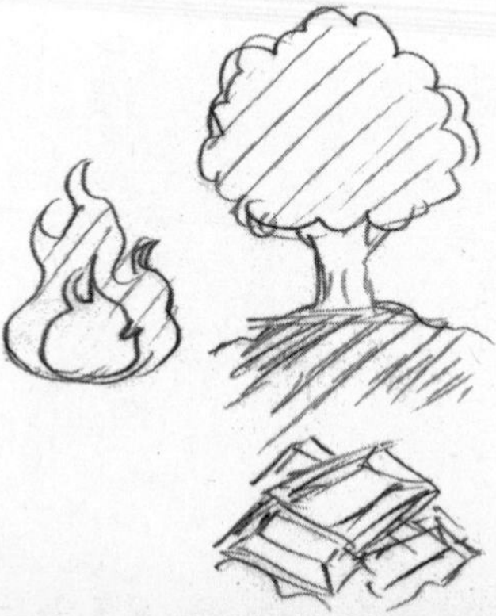

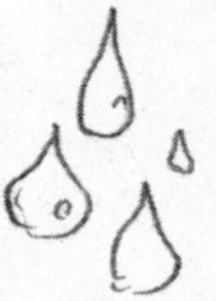

# #17 Two Paths, Their Paths

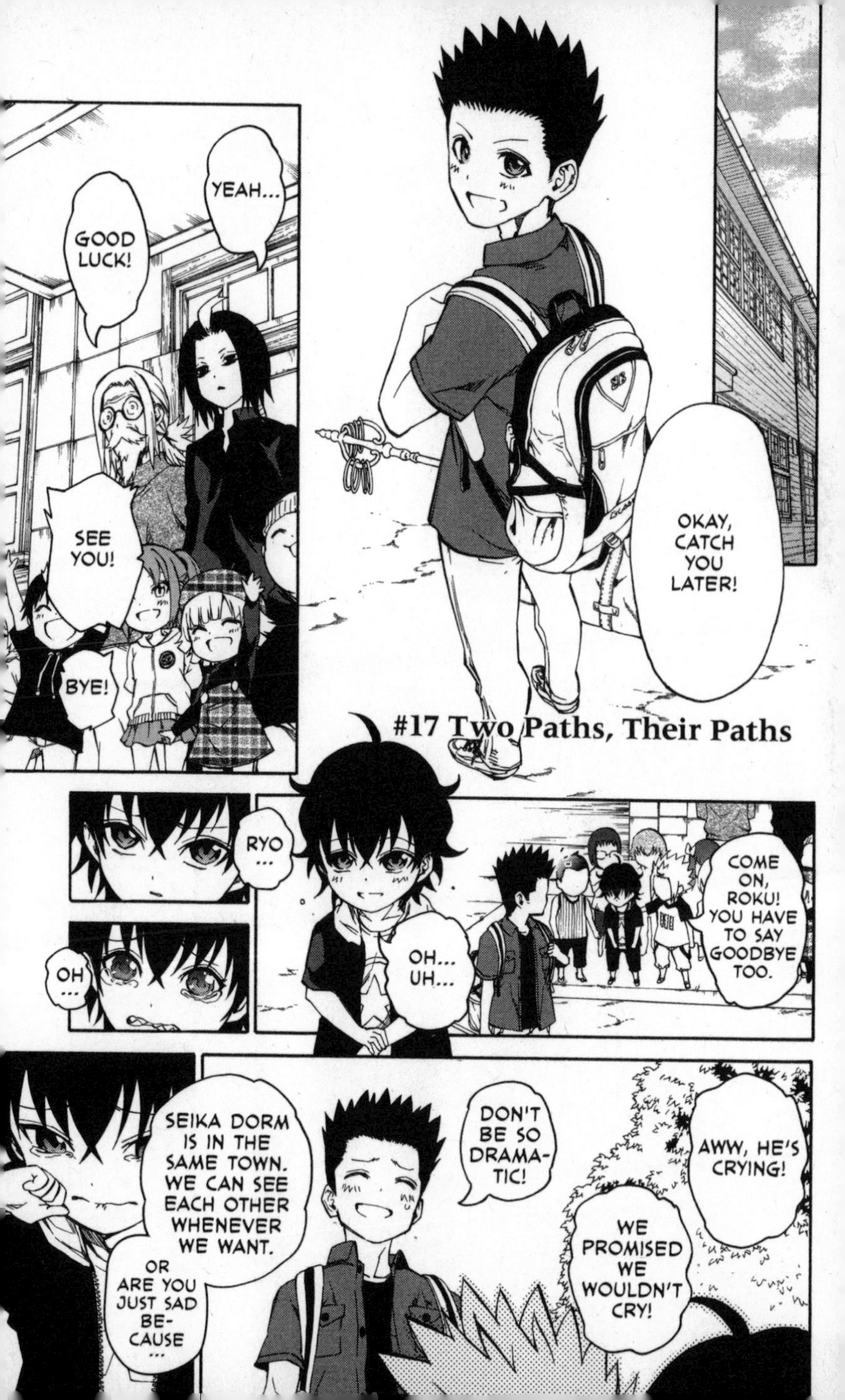
OKAY, CATCH YOU LATER!
YEAH...
GOOD LUCK!
SEE YOU!
BYE!
COME ON, ROKU! YOU HAVE TO SAY GOODBYE TOO.
OH... UH...
RYO ...
OH ...
AWW, HE'S CRYING!
WE PROMISED WE WOULDN'T CRY!
DON'T BE SO DRAMA-TIC!
SEIKA DORM IS IN THE SAME TOWN. WE CAN SEE EACH OTHER WHENEVER WE WANT.
OR ARE YOU JUST SAD BE-CAUSE ...

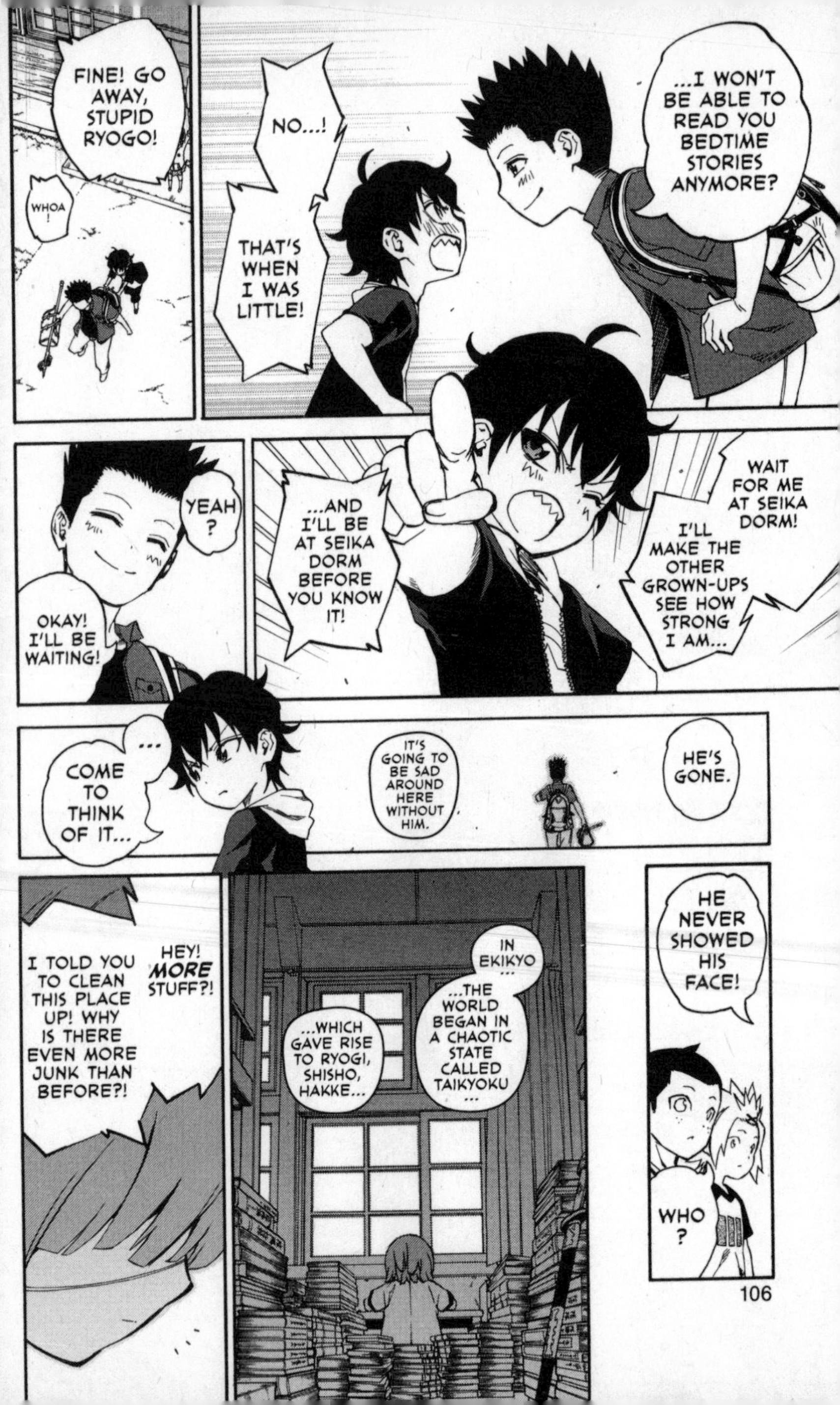
...I WON'T BE ABLE TO READ YOU BEDTIME STORIES ANYMORE?
NO...!
THAT'S WHEN I WAS LITTLE!
FINE! GO AWAY, STUPID RYOGO!
WHOA!
WAIT FOR ME AT SEIKA DORM!
I'LL MAKE THE OTHER GROWN-UPS SEE HOW STRONG I AM...
...AND I'LL BE AT SEIKA DORM BEFORE YOU KNOW IT!
YEAH?
OKAY! I'LL BE WAITING!
HE'S GONE.
IT'S GOING TO BE SAD AROUND HERE WITHOUT HIM.
...
COME TO THINK OF IT...
HE NEVER SHOWED HIS FACE!
WHO?
IN EKIKYO...
...THE WORLD BEGAN IN A CHAOTIC STATE CALLED TAIKYOKU...
...WHICH GAVE RISE TO RYOGI, SHISHO, HAKKE...
HEY! *MORE* STUFF?!
I TOLD YOU TO CLEAN THIS PLACE UP! WHY IS THERE EVEN MORE JUNK THAN BEFORE?!

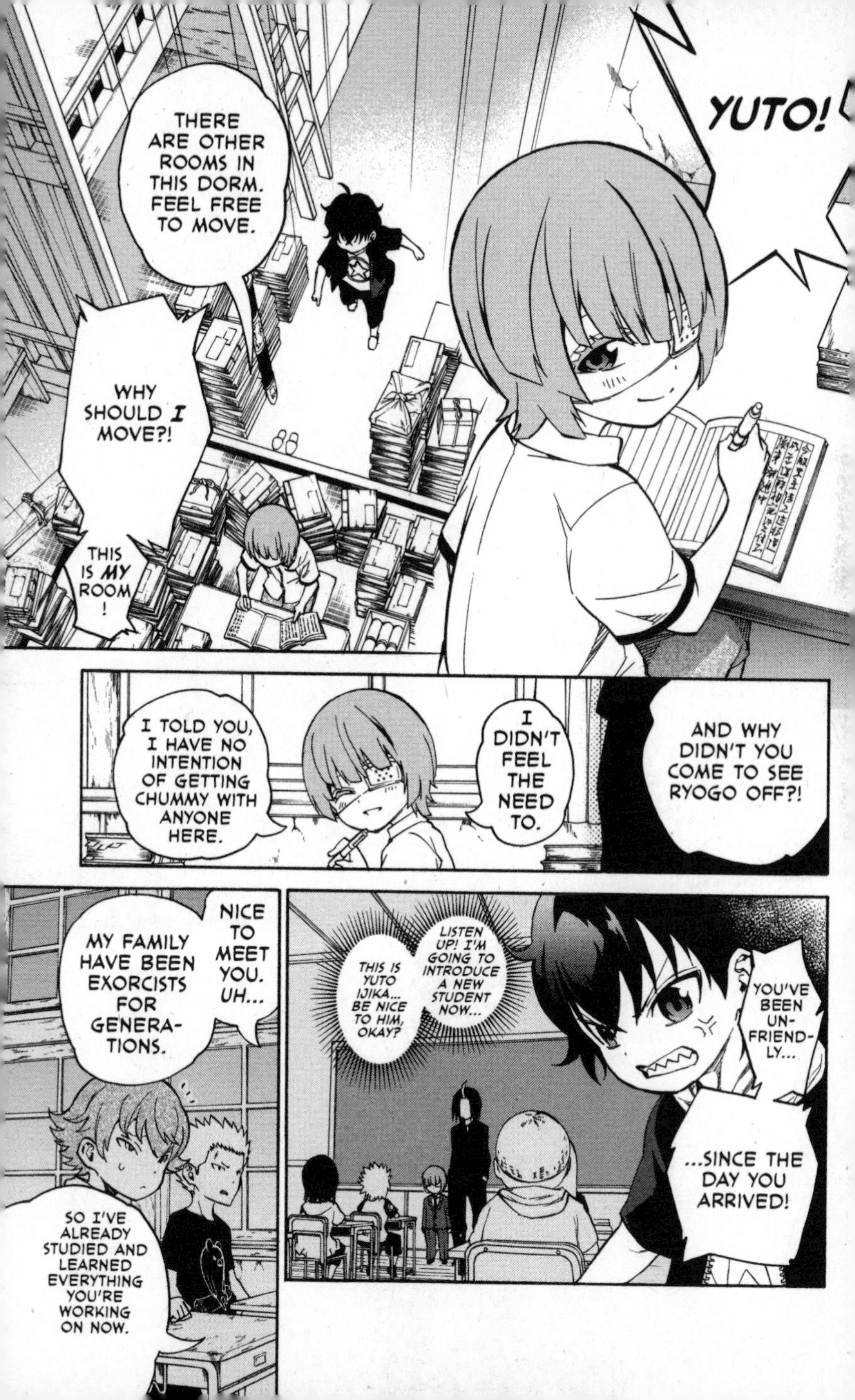
YUTO!
THERE ARE OTHER ROOMS IN THIS DORM. FEEL FREE TO MOVE.
WHY SHOULD I MOVE?!
THIS IS MY ROOM!
AND WHY DIDN'T YOU COME TO SEE RYOGO OFF?!
I DIDN'T FEEL THE NEED TO.
I TOLD YOU, I HAVE NO INTENTION OF GETTING CHUMMY WITH ANYONE HERE.
YOU'VE BEEN UN-FRIEND-LY...
...SINCE THE DAY YOU ARRIVED!
LISTEN UP! I'M GOING TO INTRODUCE A NEW STUDENT NOW...
THIS IS YUTO IJIKA... BE NICE TO HIM, OKAY?
NICE TO MEET YOU. UH...
MY FAMILY HAVE BEEN EXORCISTS FOR GENERATIONS.
SO I'VE ALREADY STUDIED AND LEARNED EVERYTHING YOU'RE WORKING ON NOW.

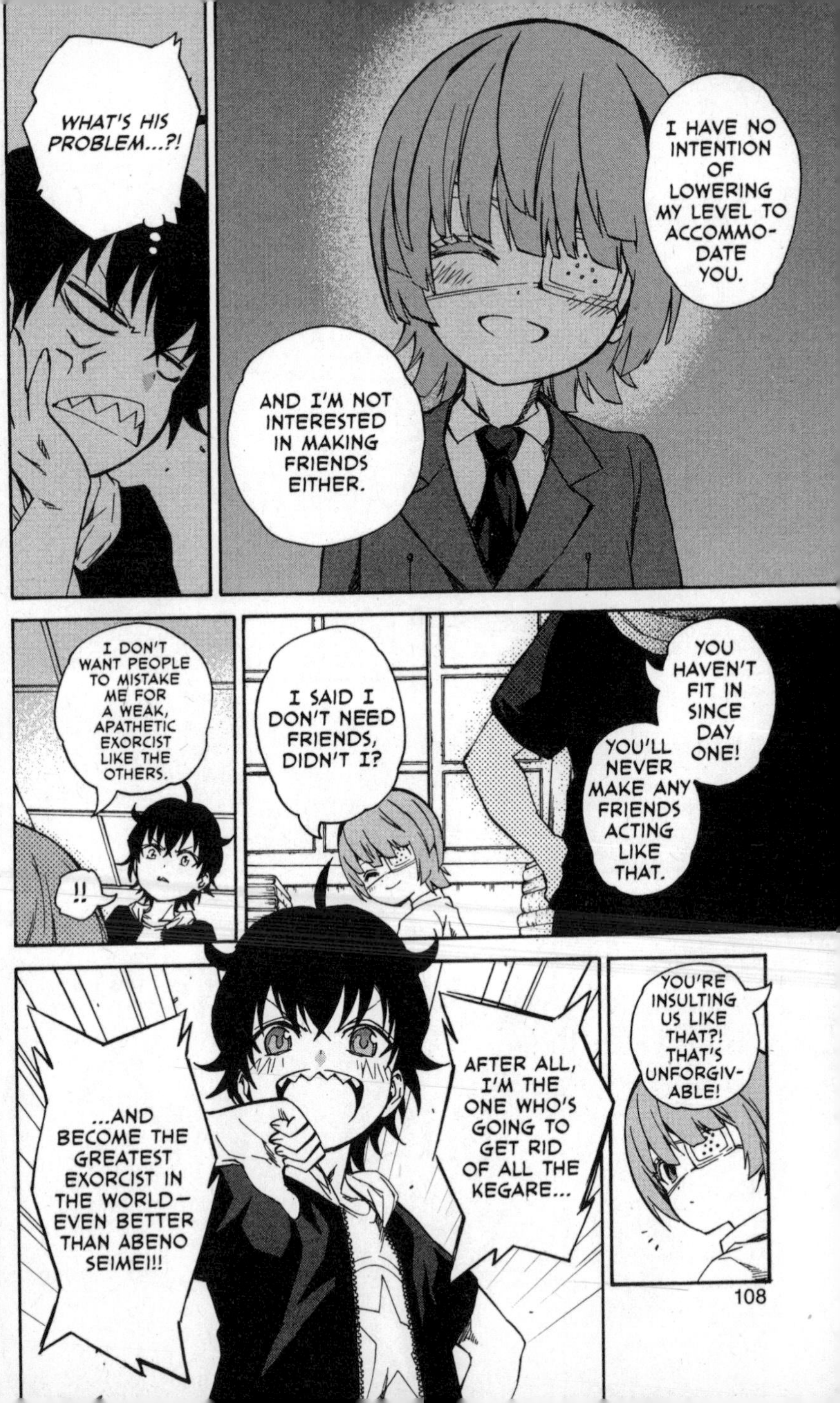
I HAVE NO INTENTION OF LOWERING MY LEVEL TO ACCOMMO-DATE YOU.
AND I'M NOT INTERESTED IN MAKING FRIENDS EITHER.
WHAT'S HIS PROBLEM...?!
YOU HAVEN'T FIT IN SINCE DAY ONE!
YOU'LL NEVER MAKE ANY FRIENDS ACTING LIKE THAT.
I SAID I DON'T NEED FRIENDS, DIDN'T I?
I DON'T WANT PEOPLE TO MISTAKE ME FOR A WEAK, APATHETIC EXORCIST LIKE THE OTHERS.
!!
YOU'RE INSULTING US LIKE THAT?! THAT'S UNFORGIV-ABLE!
AFTER ALL, I'M THE ONE WHO'S GOING TO GET RID OF ALL THE KEGARE...
...AND BECOME THE GREATEST EXORCIST IN THE WORLD—EVEN BETTER THAN ABENO SEIMEI!!!

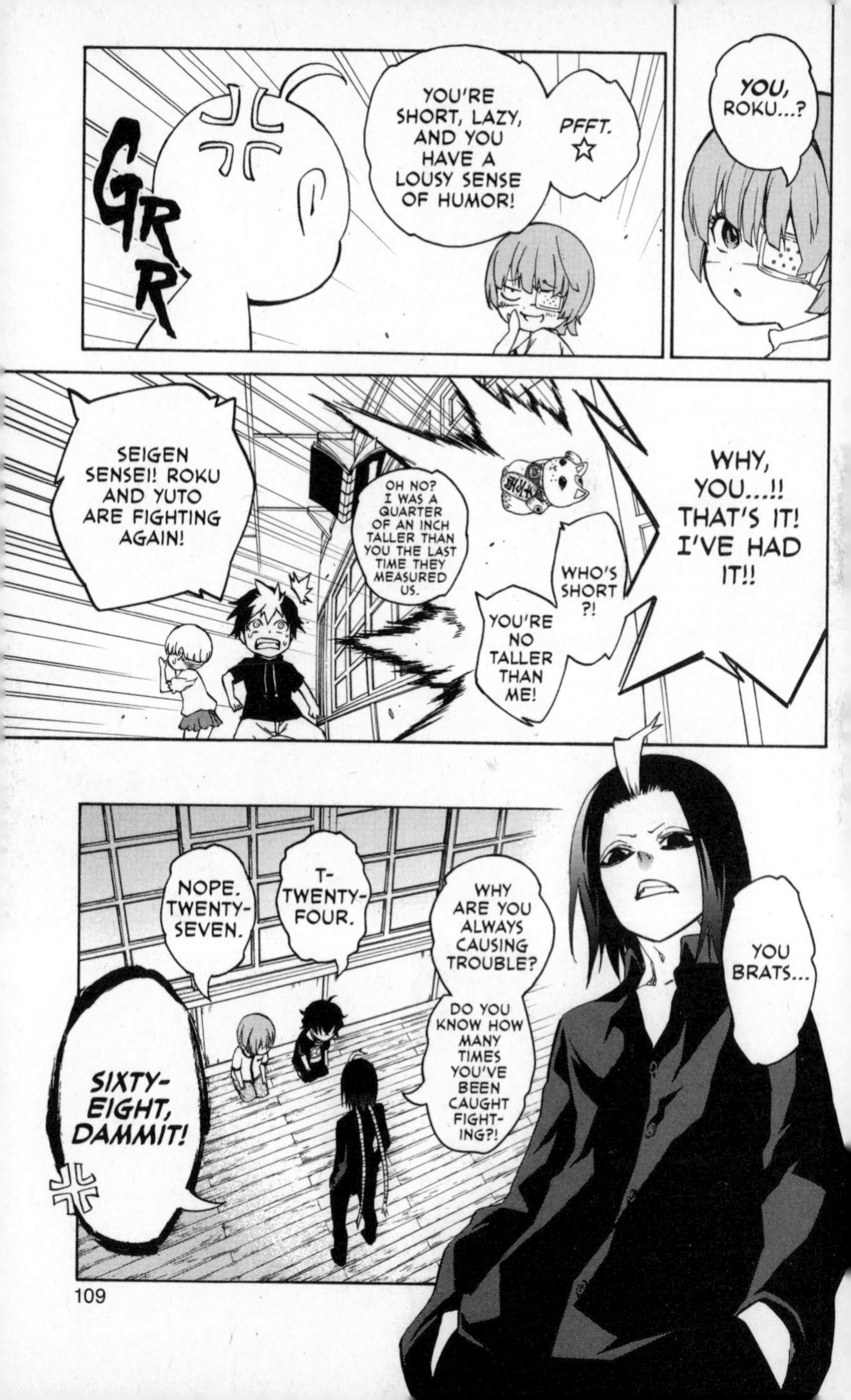
YOU, ROKU...?
YOU'RE SHORT, LAZY, AND YOU HAVE A LOUSY SENSE OF HUMOR!
PFFT. ☆
GRR
WHY, YOU...!! THAT'S IT! I'VE HAD IT!!
WHO'S SHORT ?!
YOU'RE NO TALLER THAN ME!
OH NO? I WAS A QUARTER OF AN INCH TALLER THAN YOU THE LAST TIME THEY MEASURED US.
SEIGEN SENSEI!! ROKU AND YUTO ARE FIGHTING AGAIN!
YOU BRATS...
WHY ARE YOU ALWAYS CAUSING TROUBLE?
DO YOU KNOW HOW MANY TIMES YOU'VE BEEN CAUGHT FIGHT-ING?!
T-TWENTY-FOUR.
NOPE. TWENTY-SEVEN.
SIXTY-EIGHT, DAMMIT!

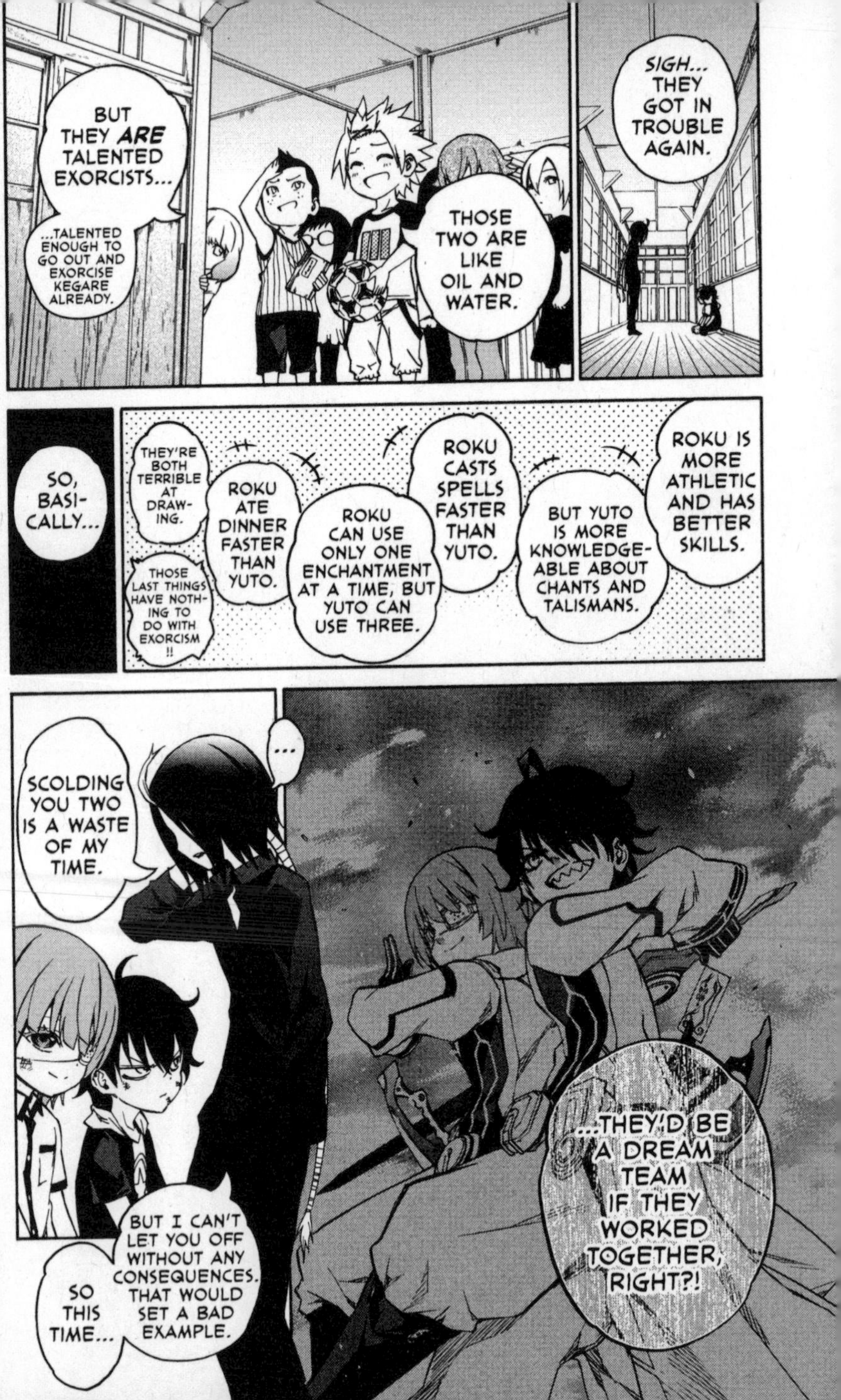
SIGH... THEY GOT IN TROUBLE AGAIN.
THOSE TWO ARE LIKE OIL AND WATER.
BUT THEY *ARE* TALENTED EXORCISTS...
...TALENTED ENOUGH TO GO OUT AND EXORCISE KEGARE ALREADY.
ROKU IS MORE ATHLETIC AND HAS BETTER SKILLS.
BUT YUTO IS MORE KNOWLEDGEABLE ABOUT CHANTS AND TALISMANS.
ROKU CASTS SPELLS FASTER THAN YUTO.
ROKU CAN USE ONLY ONE ENCHANTMENT AT A TIME, BUT YUTO CAN USE THREE.
ROKU ATE DINNER FASTER THAN YUTO.
THEY'RE BOTH TERRIBLE AT DRAWING.
THOSE LAST THINGS HAVE NOTHING TO DO WITH EXORCISM!!
SO, BASICALLY...
...THEY'D BE A DREAM TEAM IF THEY WORKED TOGETHER, RIGHT?!
...
SCOLDING YOU TWO IS A WASTE OF MY TIME.
BUT I CAN'T LET YOU OFF WITHOUT ANY CONSEQUENCES. THAT WOULD SET A BAD EXAMPLE.
SO THIS TIME...

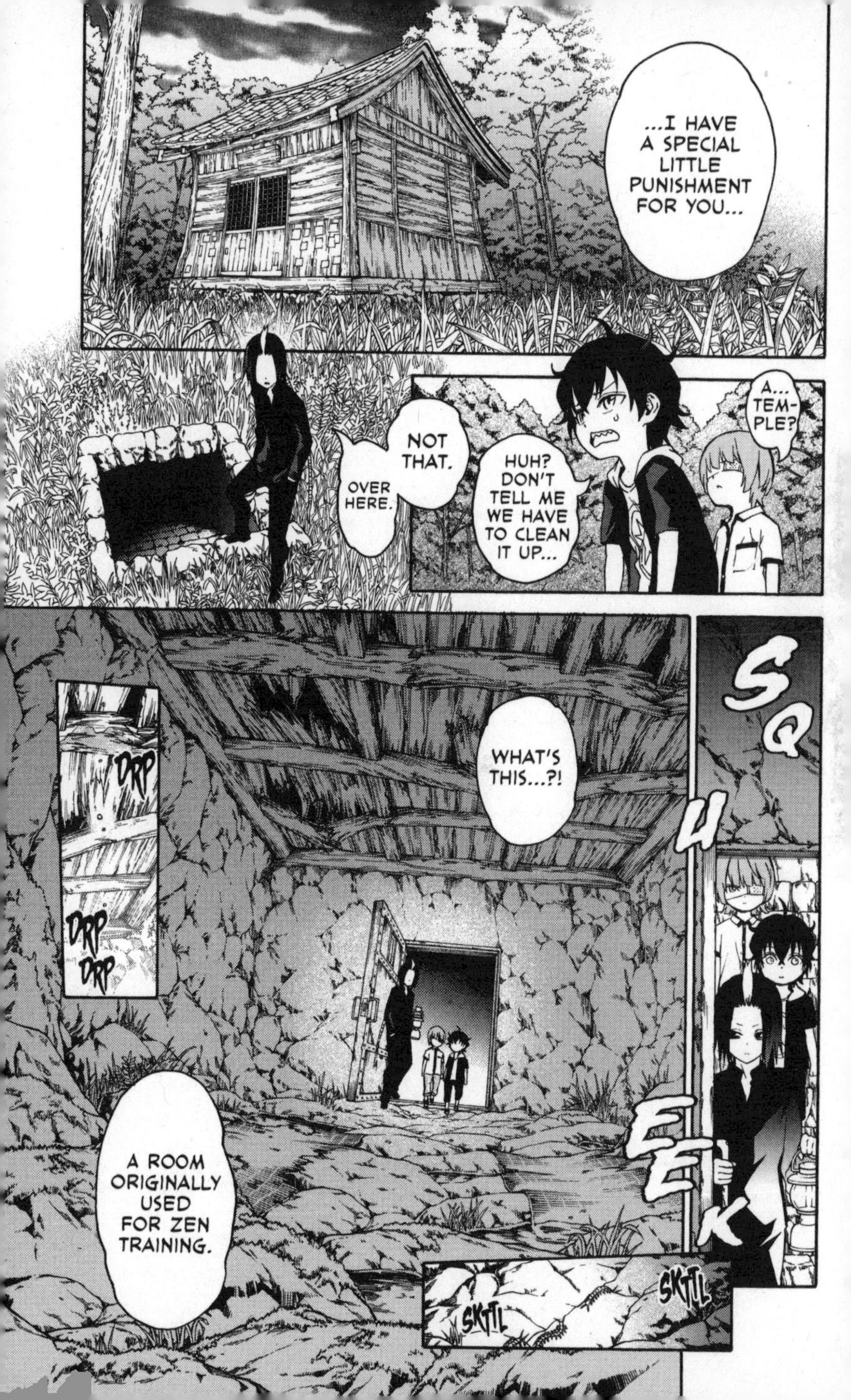
...I HAVE A SPECIAL LITTLE PUNISHMENT FOR YOU...
A... TEMPLE?
HUH? DON'T TELL ME WE HAVE TO CLEAN IT UP...
NOT THAT.
OVER HERE.
SQUEEK
WHAT'S THIS...?!
DRP
DRP DRP
A ROOM ORIGINALLY USED FOR ZEN TRAINING.
SKTTL
SKTTL

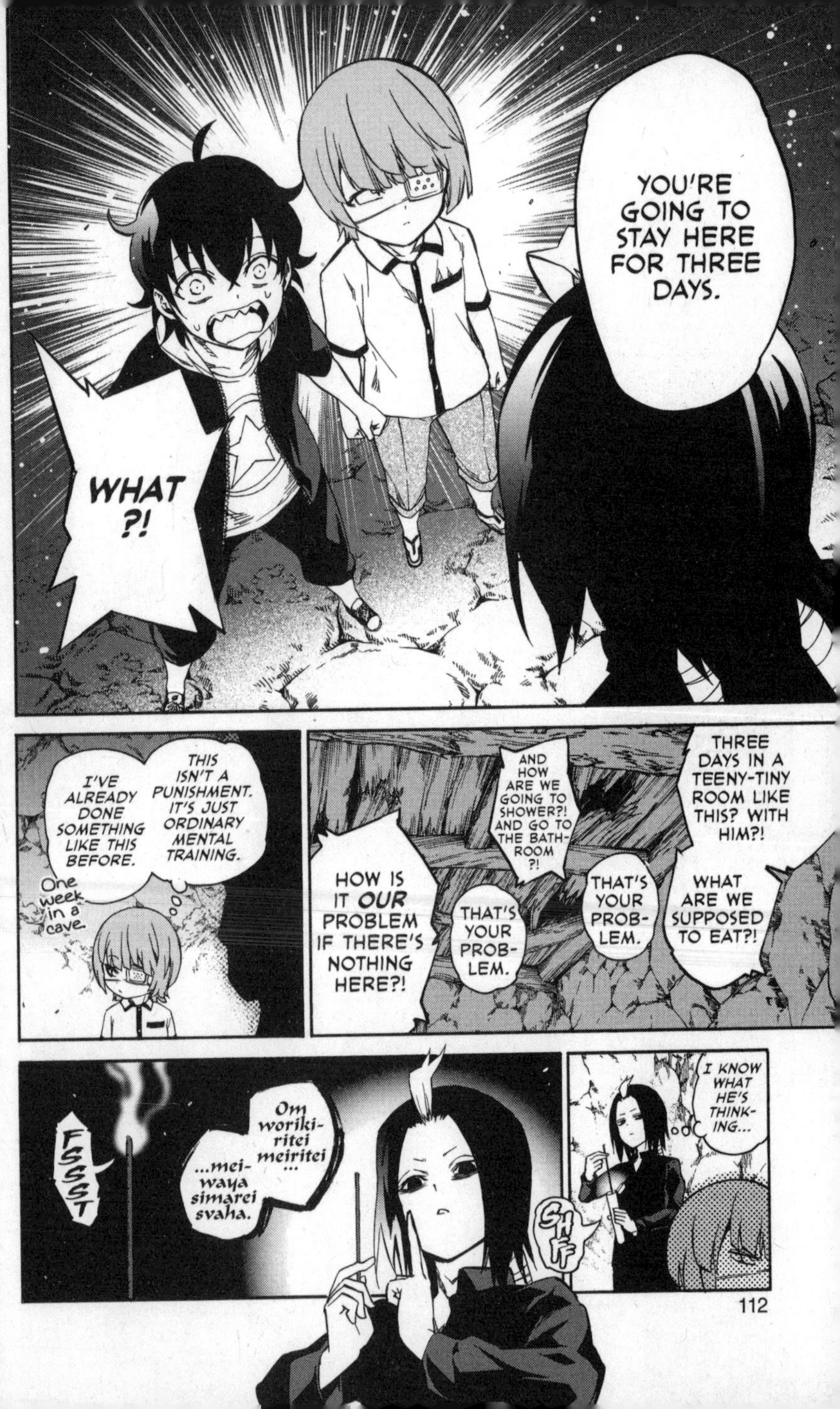
YOU'RE GOING TO STAY HERE FOR THREE DAYS.
WHAT?!
THREE DAYS IN A TEENY-TINY ROOM LIKE THIS? WITH HIM?!
WHAT ARE WE SUPPOSED TO EAT?!
THAT'S YOUR PROBLEM.
AND HOW ARE WE GOING TO SHOWER?! AND GO TO THE BATHROOM?!
THAT'S YOUR PROBLEM.
HOW IS IT OUR PROBLEM IF THERE'S NOTHING HERE?!
THIS ISN'T A PUNISHMENT. IT'S JUST ORDINARY MENTAL TRAINING.
I'VE ALREADY DONE SOMETHING LIKE THIS BEFORE.
One week in a cave.
I KNOW WHAT HE'S THINKING...
SHFF
Om worikiritei meiritei...
...meiwaya simarei svaha.
FSSST

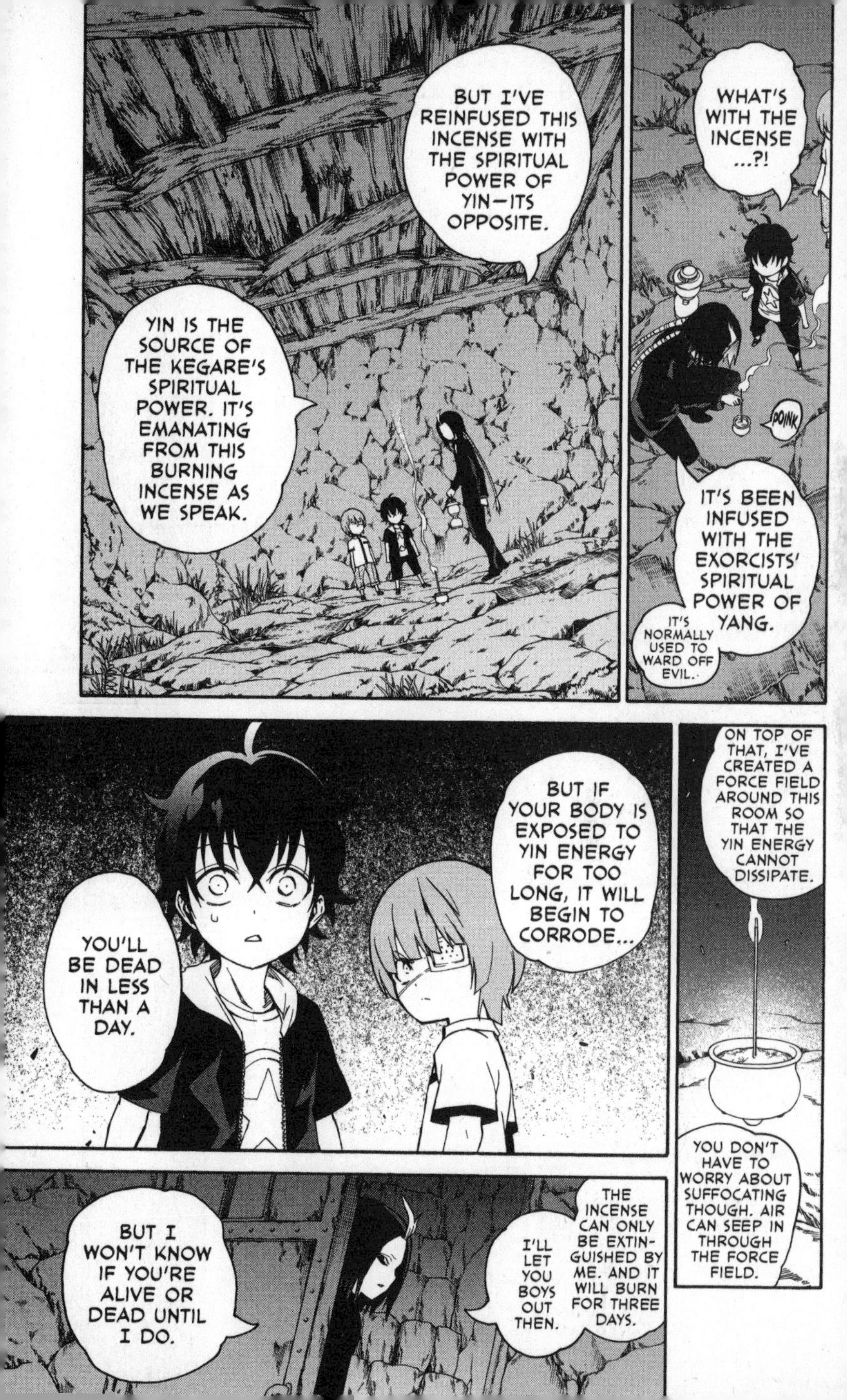
WHAT'S WITH THE INCENSE ...?!
POINK
IT'S BEEN INFUSED WITH THE EXORCISTS' SPIRITUAL POWER OF YANG.
IT'S NORMALLY USED TO WARD OFF EVIL.
BUT I'VE REINFUSED THIS INCENSE WITH THE SPIRITUAL POWER OF YIN—ITS OPPOSITE.
YIN IS THE SOURCE OF THE KEGARE'S SPIRITUAL POWER. IT'S EMANATING FROM THIS BURNING INCENSE AS WE SPEAK.
ON TOP OF THAT, I'VE CREATED A FORCE FIELD AROUND THIS ROOM SO THAT THE YIN ENERGY CANNOT DISSIPATE.
YOU DON'T HAVE TO WORRY ABOUT SUFFOCATING THOUGH. AIR CAN SEEP IN THROUGH THE FORCE FIELD.
BUT IF YOUR BODY IS EXPOSED TO YIN ENERGY FOR TOO LONG, IT WILL BEGIN TO CORRODE...
YOU'LL BE DEAD IN LESS THAN A DAY.
THE INCENSE CAN ONLY BE EXTIN-GUISHED BY ME. AND IT WILL BURN FOR THREE DAYS.
I'LL LET YOU BOYS OUT THEN.
BUT I WON'T KNOW IF YOU'RE ALIVE OR DEAD UNTIL I DO.

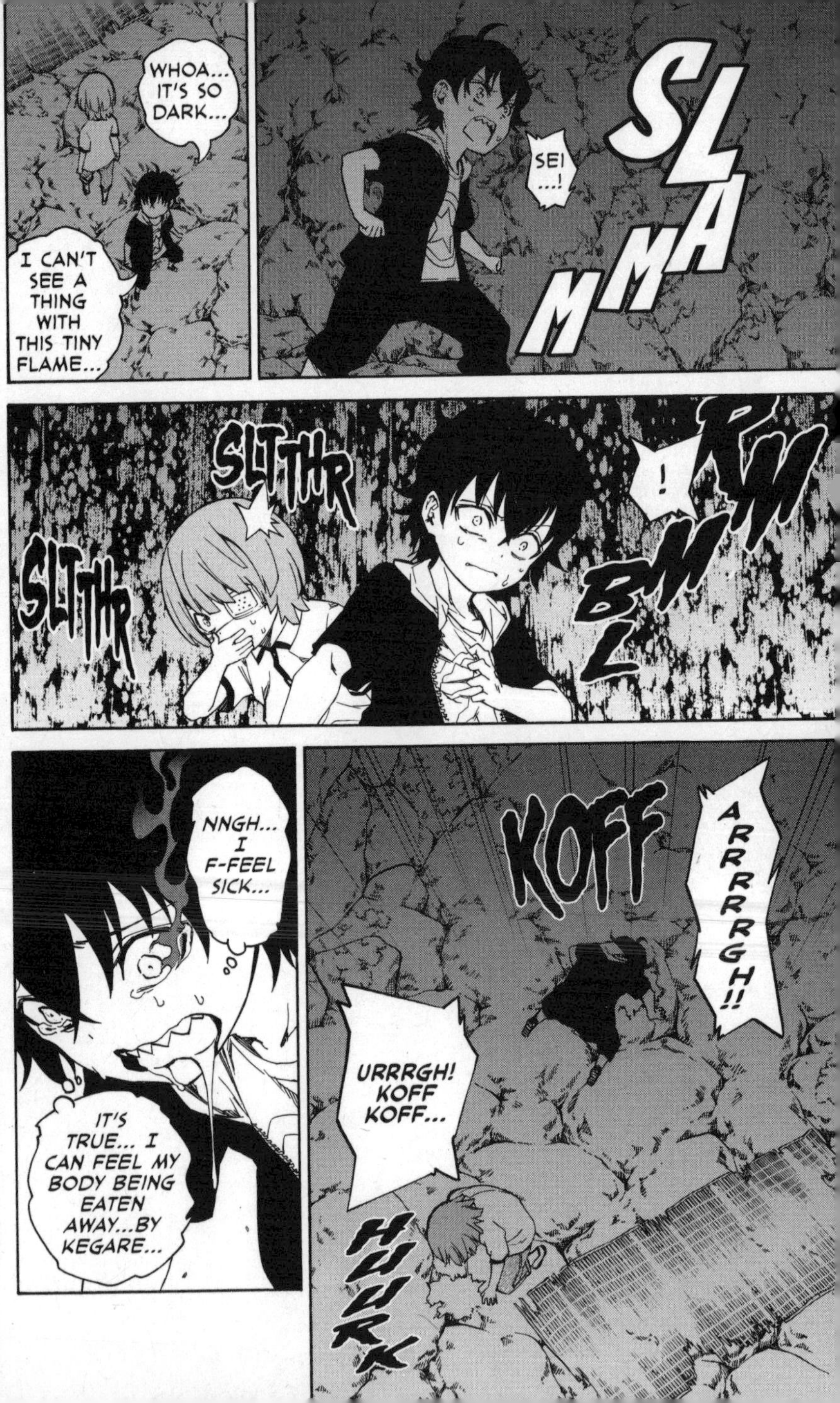
SLAMMM
SEI ...!
WHOA... IT'S SO DARK...
I CAN'T SEE A THING WITH THIS TINY FLAME...
!
SLITHR
SLITHR
ARRRRRGH!!
KOFF
URRRGH! KOFF KOFF...
HUURK
NNGH... I F-FEEL SICK...
IT'S TRUE... I CAN FEEL MY BODY BEING EATEN AWAY...BY KEGARE...

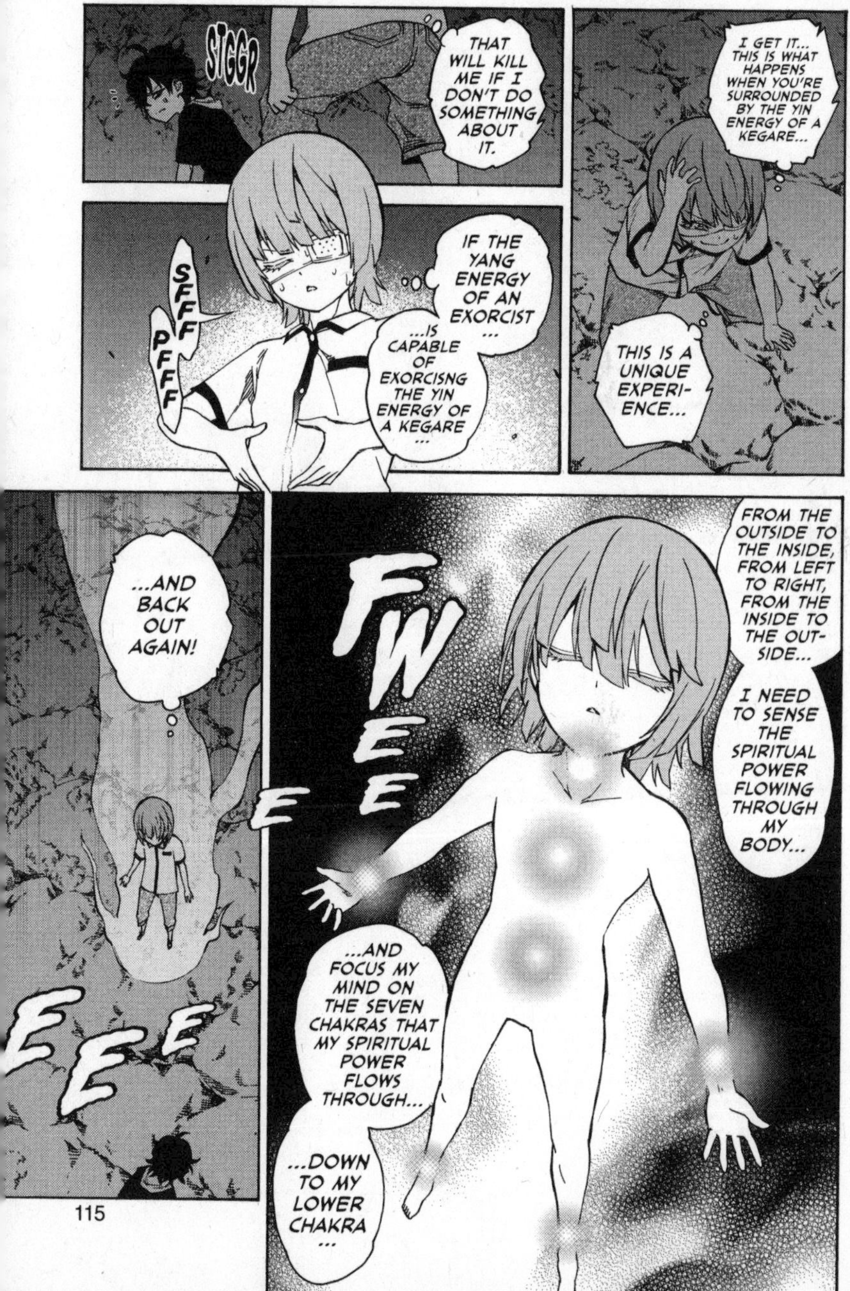
I GET IT... THIS IS WHAT HAPPENS WHEN YOU'RE SURROUNDED BY THE YIN ENERGY OF A KEGARE...
THIS IS A UNIQUE EXPERI-ENCE...
THAT WILL KILL ME IF I DON'T DO SOMETHING ABOUT IT.
SIGGR
IF THE YANG ENERGY OF AN EXORCIST...
...IS CAPABLE OF EXORCISNG THE YIN ENERGY OF A KEGARE...
SFFF PFFF
FROM THE OUTSIDE TO THE INSIDE, FROM LEFT TO RIGHT, FROM THE INSIDE TO THE OUT-SIDE...
I NEED TO SENSE THE SPIRITUAL POWER FLOWING THROUGH MY BODY...
FWEEE
...AND FOCUS MY MIND ON THE SEVEN CHAKRAS THAT MY SPIRITUAL POWER FLOWS THROUGH...
...DOWN TO MY LOWER CHAKRA...
...AND BACK OUT AGAIN!
EEE

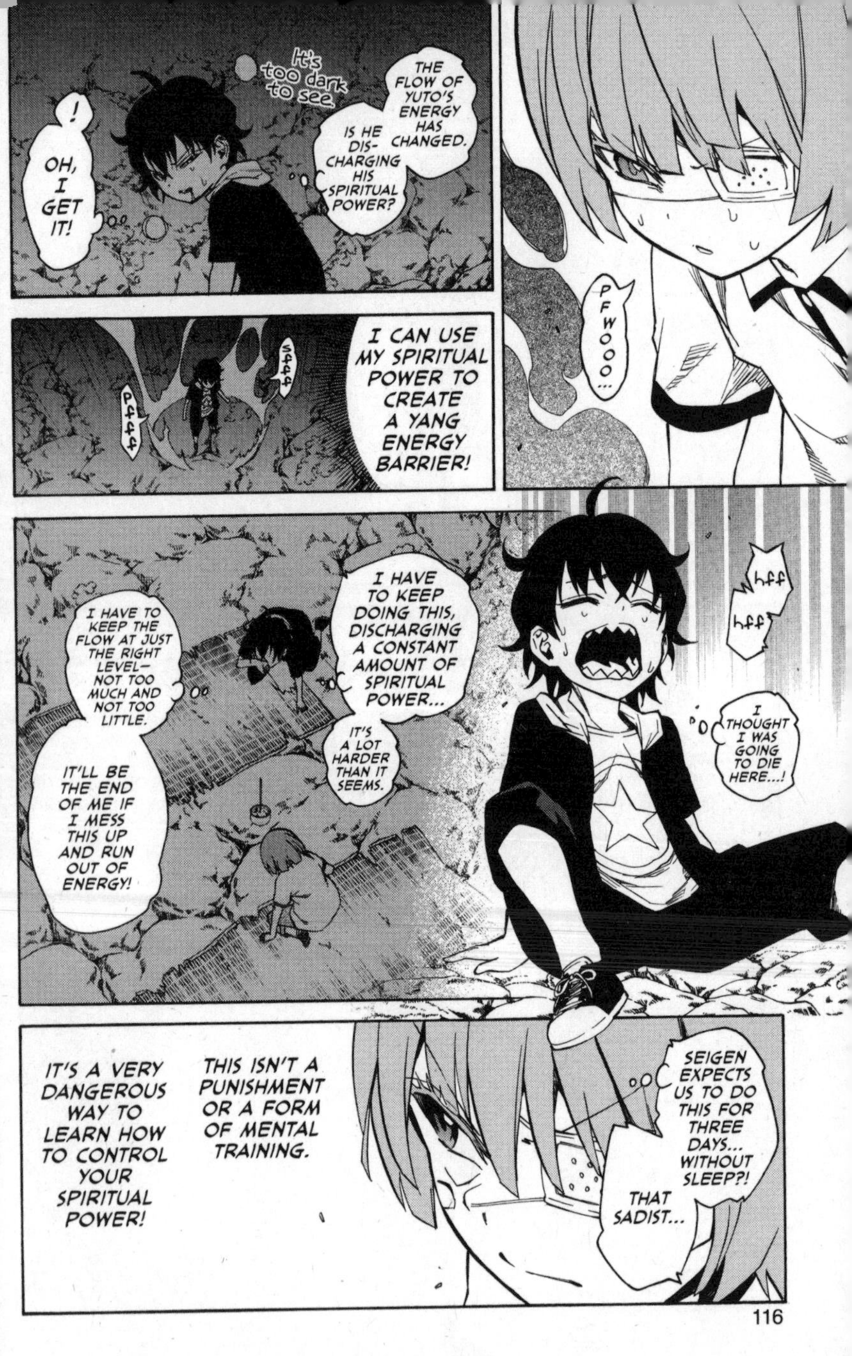
PFWOOO...
THE FLOW OF YUTO'S ENERGY HAS CHANGED.
IS HE DISCHARGING HIS SPIRITUAL POWER?
It's too dark to see.
!
OH, I GET IT!
I CAN USE MY SPIRITUAL POWER TO CREATE A YANG ENERGY BARRIER!
sfff
pfff
hff
hff
I THOUGHT I WAS GOING TO DIE HERE...!
I HAVE TO KEEP DOING THIS, DISCHARGING A CONSTANT AMOUNT OF SPIRITUAL POWER...
IT'S A LOT HARDER THAN IT SEEMS.
I HAVE TO KEEP THE FLOW AT JUST THE RIGHT LEVEL— NOT TOO MUCH AND NOT TOO LITTLE.
IT'LL BE THE END OF ME IF I MESS THIS UP AND RUN OUT OF ENERGY!
SEIGEN EXPECTS US TO DO THIS FOR THREE DAYS... WITHOUT SLEEP?!
THAT SADIST...
THIS ISN'T A PUNISHMENT OR A FORM OF MENTAL TRAINING.
IT'S A VERY DANGEROUS WAY TO LEARN HOW TO CONTROL YOUR SPIRITUAL POWER!

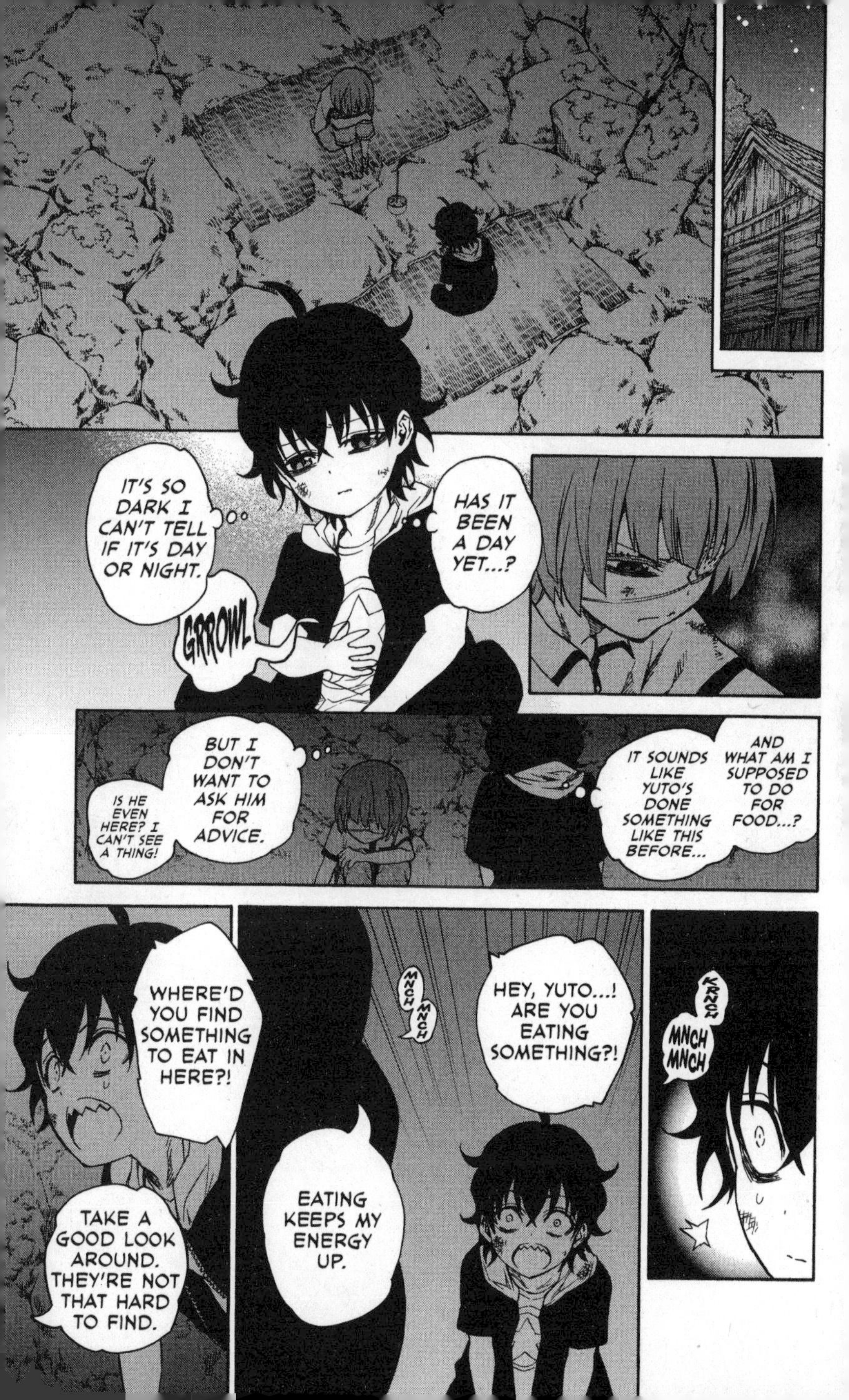
HAS IT BEEN A DAY YET...?
IT'S SO DARK I CAN'T TELL IF IT'S DAY OR NIGHT.
GRROWL
AND WHAT AM I SUPPOSED TO DO FOR FOOD...?
IT SOUNDS LIKE YUTO'S DONE SOMETHING LIKE THIS BEFORE...
BUT I DON'T WANT TO ASK HIM FOR ADVICE.
IS HE EVEN HERE? I CAN'T SEE A THING!
KRNCH
MNCH MNCH
HEY, YUTO...! ARE YOU EATING SOMETHING?!
MNCH MNCH
EATING KEEPS MY ENERGY UP.
WHERE'D YOU FIND SOMETHING TO EAT IN HERE?!
TAKE A GOOD LOOK AROUND. THEY'RE NOT THAT HARD TO FIND.

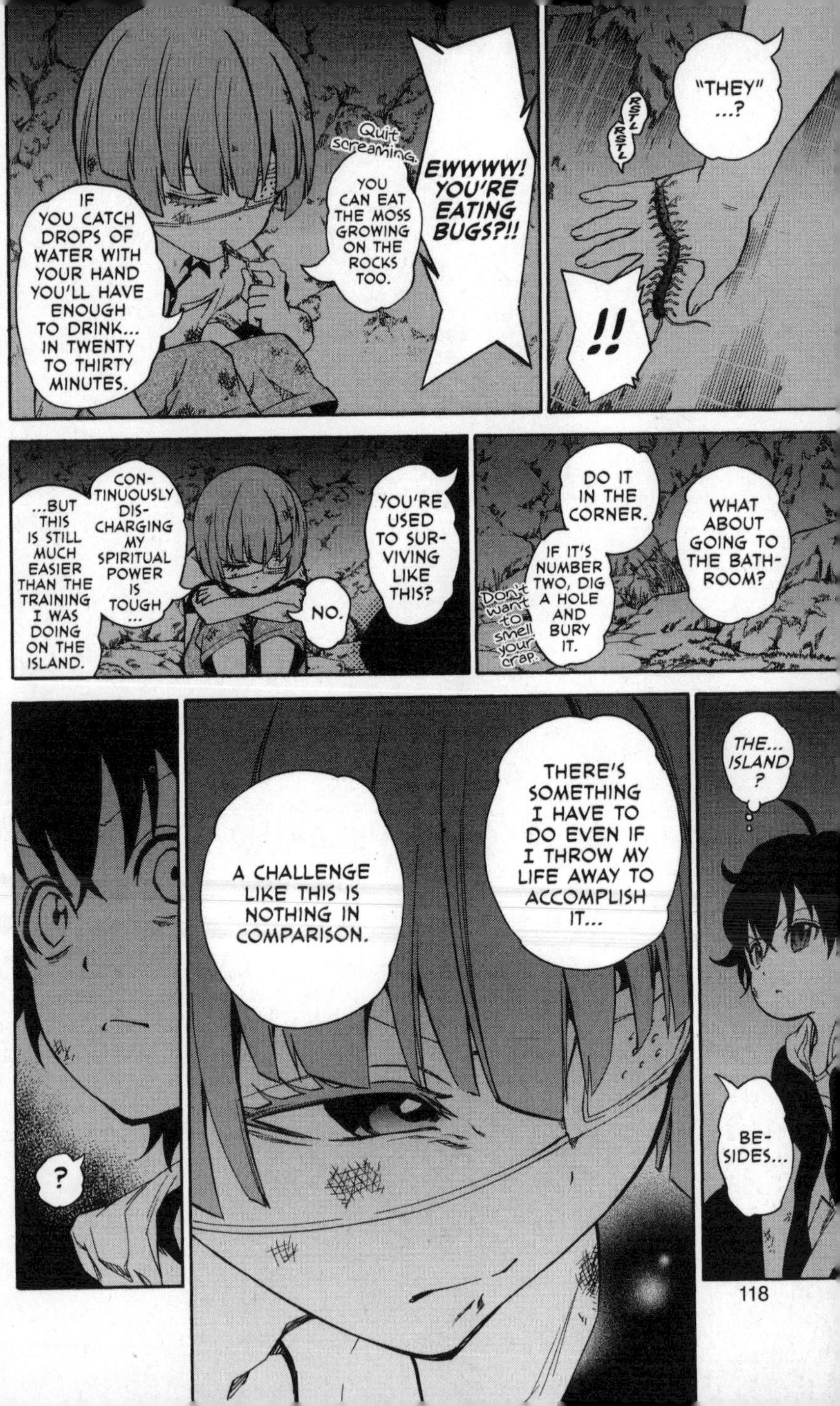
"THEY" ...?
RSTL RSTL
!!
EWWWW! YOU'RE EATING BUGS?!!
Quit screaming.
YOU CAN EAT THE MOSS GROWING ON THE ROCKS TOO.
IF YOU CATCH DROPS OF WATER WITH YOUR HAND YOU'LL HAVE ENOUGH TO DRINK... IN TWENTY TO THIRTY MINUTES.
WHAT ABOUT GOING TO THE BATH-ROOM?
DO IT IN THE CORNER.
IF IT'S NUMBER TWO, DIG A HOLE AND BURY IT.
Don't want to smell your crap.
YOU'RE USED TO SUR-VIVING LIKE THIS?
NO.
CON-TINUOUSLY DIS-CHARGING MY SPIRITUAL POWER IS TOUGH...
...BUT THIS IS STILL MUCH EASIER THAN THE TRAINING I WAS DOING ON THE ISLAND.
THE... ISLAND?
BE-SIDES...
THERE'S SOMETHING I HAVE TO DO EVEN IF I THROW MY LIFE AWAY TO ACCOMPLISH IT...
A CHALLENGE LIKE THIS IS NOTHING IN COMPARISON.
?

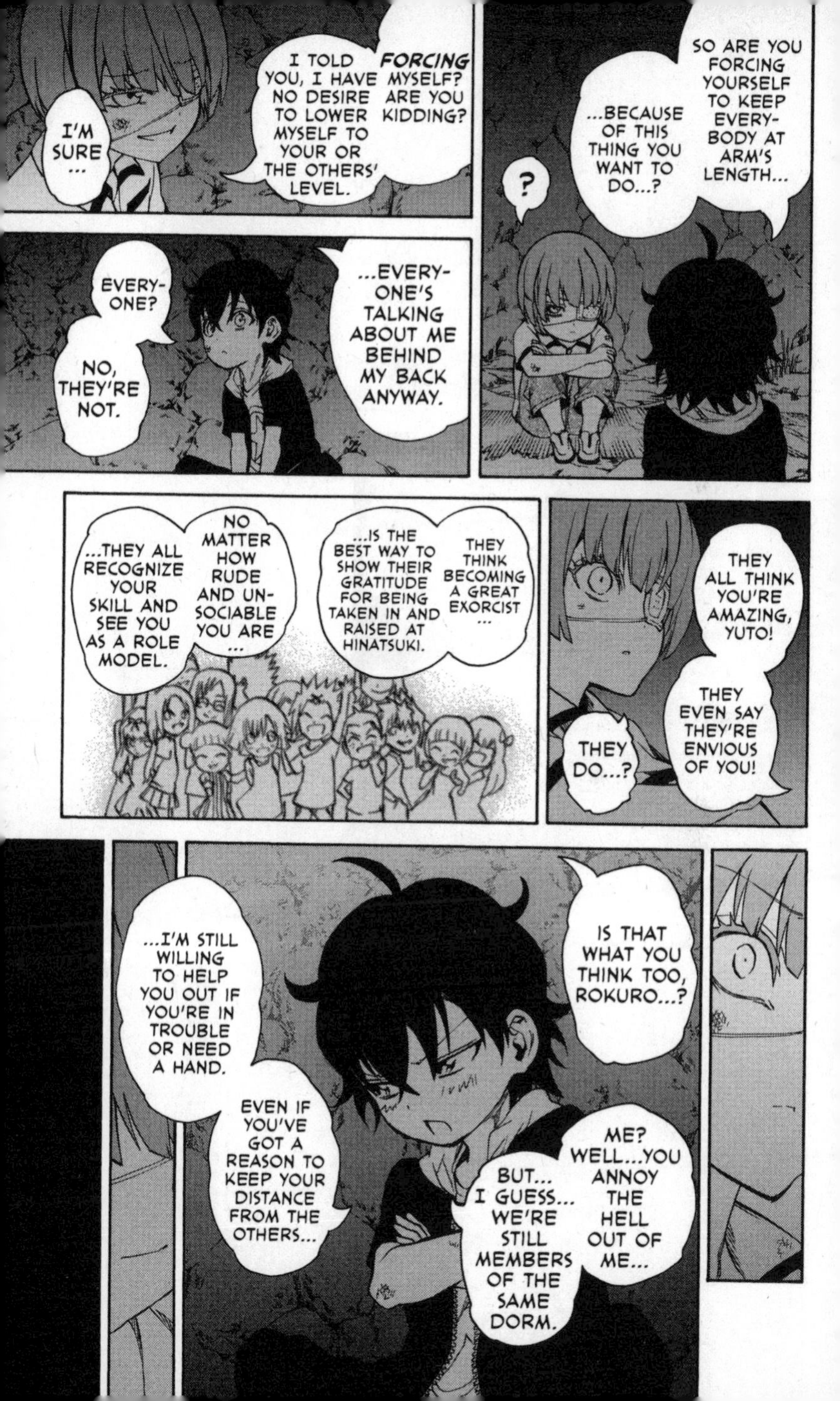

SO ARE YOU FORCING YOURSELF TO KEEP EVERYBODY AT ARM'S LENGTH...
...BECAUSE OF THIS THING YOU WANT TO DO...?
?
FORCING MYSELF? ARE YOU KIDDING?
I TOLD YOU, I HAVE NO DESIRE TO LOWER MYSELF TO YOUR OR THE OTHERS' LEVEL.
I'M SURE...
...EVERYONE'S TALKING ABOUT ME BEHIND MY BACK ANYWAY.
EVERYONE?
NO, THEY'RE NOT.
THEY ALL THINK YOU'RE AMAZING, YUTO!
THEY EVEN SAY THEY'RE ENVIOUS OF YOU!
THEY DO...?
THEY THINK BECOMING A GREAT EXORCIST...
...IS THE BEST WAY TO SHOW THEIR GRATITUDE FOR BEING TAKEN IN AND RAISED AT HINATSUKI.
NO MATTER HOW RUDE AND UNSOCIABLE YOU ARE...
...THEY ALL RECOGNIZE YOUR SKILL AND SEE YOU AS A ROLE MODEL.
IS THAT WHAT YOU THINK TOO, ROKURO...?
ME? WELL...YOU ANNOY THE HELL OUT OF ME...
BUT... I GUESS... WE'RE STILL MEMBERS OF THE SAME DORM.
EVEN IF YOU'VE GOT A REASON TO KEEP YOUR DISTANCE FROM THE OTHERS...
...I'M STILL WILLING TO HELP YOU OUT IF YOU'RE IN TROUBLE OR NEED A HAND.

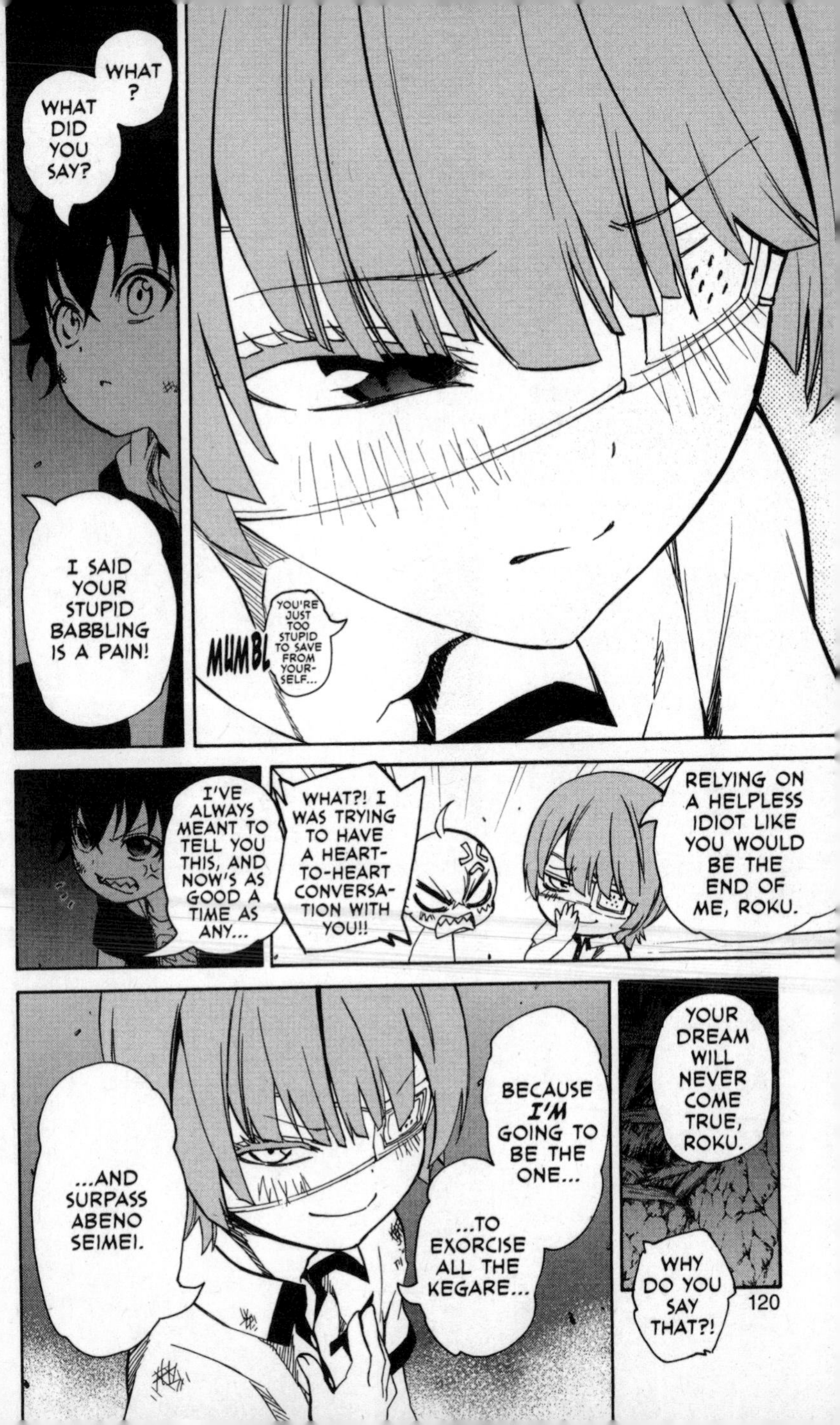
MUMBL
YOU'RE JUST TOO STUPID TO SAVE FROM YOUR-SELF...
WHAT? WHAT DID YOU SAY?
I SAID YOUR STUPID BABBLING IS A PAIN!
RELYING ON A HELPLESS IDIOT LIKE YOU WOULD BE THE END OF ME, ROKU.
WHAT?! I WAS TRYING TO HAVE A HEART-TO-HEART CONVERSA-TION WITH YOU!!
I'VE ALWAYS MEANT TO TELL YOU THIS, AND NOW'S AS GOOD A TIME AS ANY...
YOUR DREAM WILL NEVER COME TRUE, ROKU.
WHY DO YOU SAY THAT?!
BECAUSE *I'M* GOING TO BE THE ONE...
...TO EXORCISE ALL THE KEGARE...
...AND SURPASS ABENO SEIMEI.

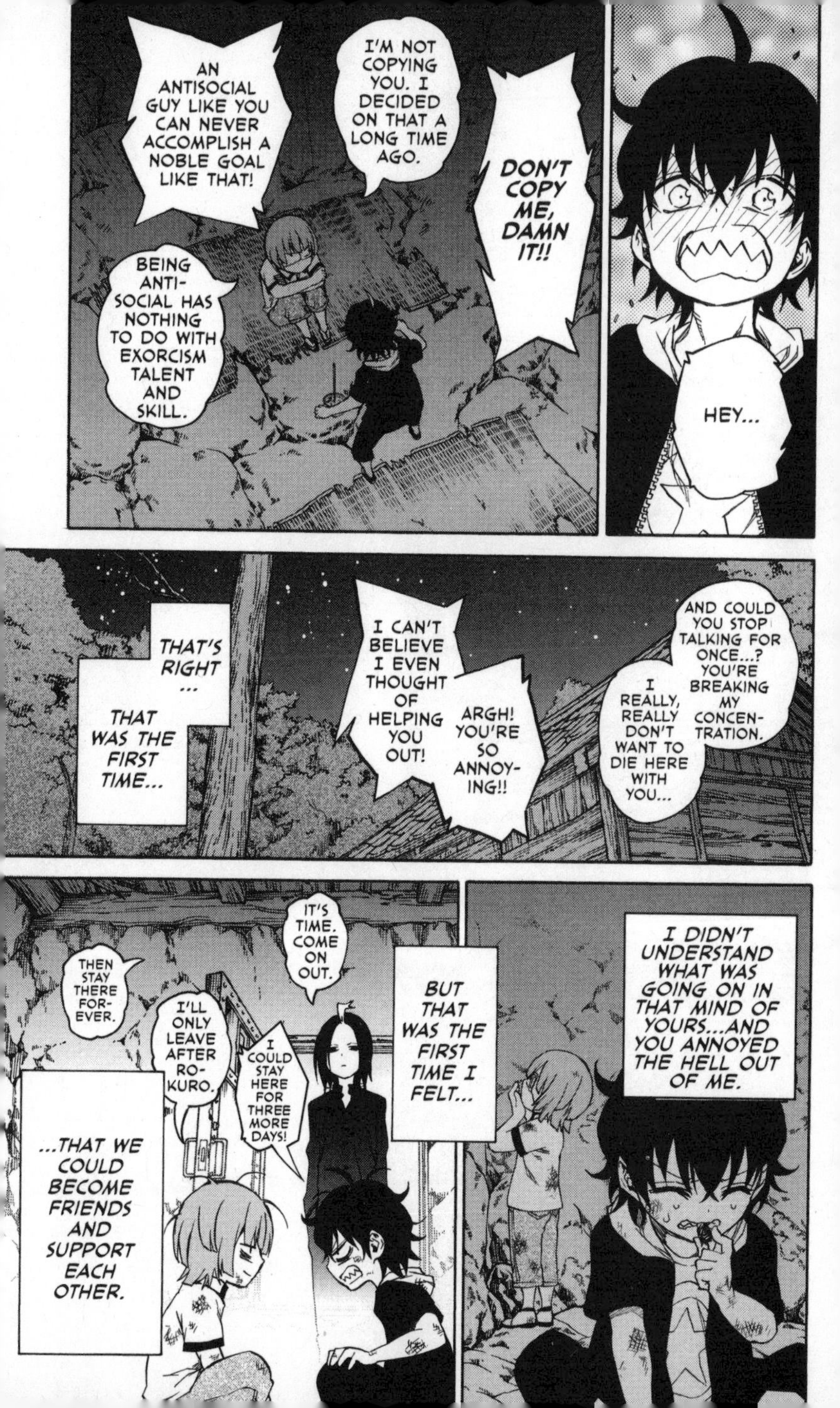
HEY...
DON'T COPY ME, DAMN IT!!
I'M NOT COPYING YOU. I DECIDED ON THAT A LONG TIME AGO.
AN ANTISOCIAL GUY LIKE YOU CAN NEVER ACCOMPLISH A NOBLE GOAL LIKE THAT!
BEING ANTI-SOCIAL HAS NOTHING TO DO WITH EXORCISM TALENT AND SKILL.
AND COULD YOU STOP TALKING FOR ONCE...? YOU'RE BREAKING MY CONCENTRATION.
I REALLY, REALLY DON'T WANT TO DIE HERE WITH YOU...
ARGH! YOU'RE SO ANNOYING!!
I CAN'T BELIEVE I EVEN THOUGHT OF HELPING YOU OUT!
THAT'S RIGHT... THAT WAS THE FIRST TIME...
I DIDN'T UNDERSTAND WHAT WAS GOING ON IN THAT MIND OF YOURS...AND YOU ANNOYED THE HELL OUT OF ME.
BUT THAT WAS THE FIRST TIME I FELT...
IT'S TIME. COME ON OUT.
I COULD STAY HERE FOR THREE MORE DAYS!
I'LL ONLY LEAVE AFTER ROKURO.
THEN STAY THERE FOREVER.
...THAT WE COULD BECOME FRIENDS AND SUPPORT EACH OTHER.

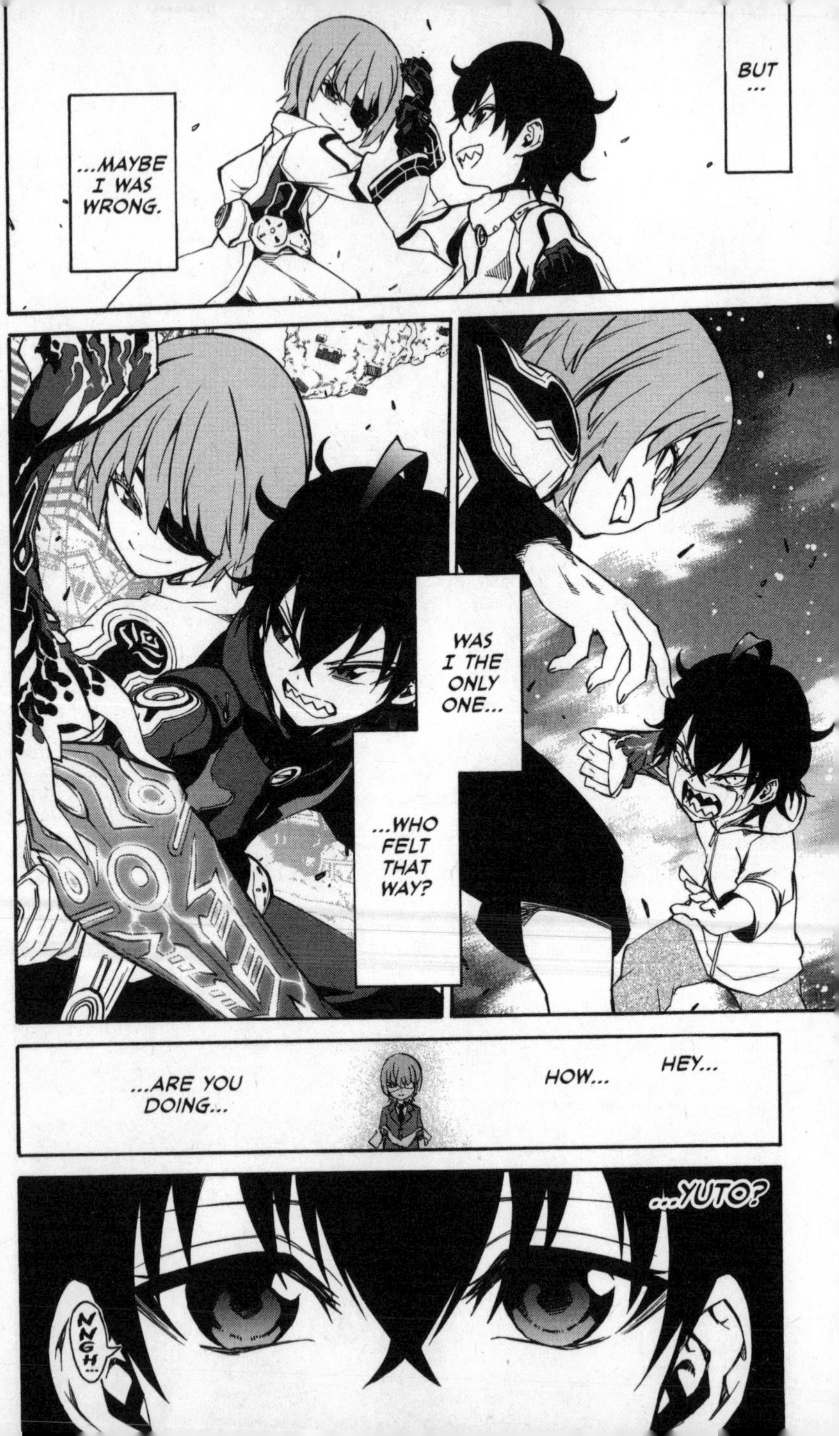
BUT ...
...MAYBE I WAS WRONG.
WAS I THE ONLY ONE...
...WHO FELT THAT WAY?
HEY...
HOW...
...ARE YOU DOING...
...YUTO?
NNGH...

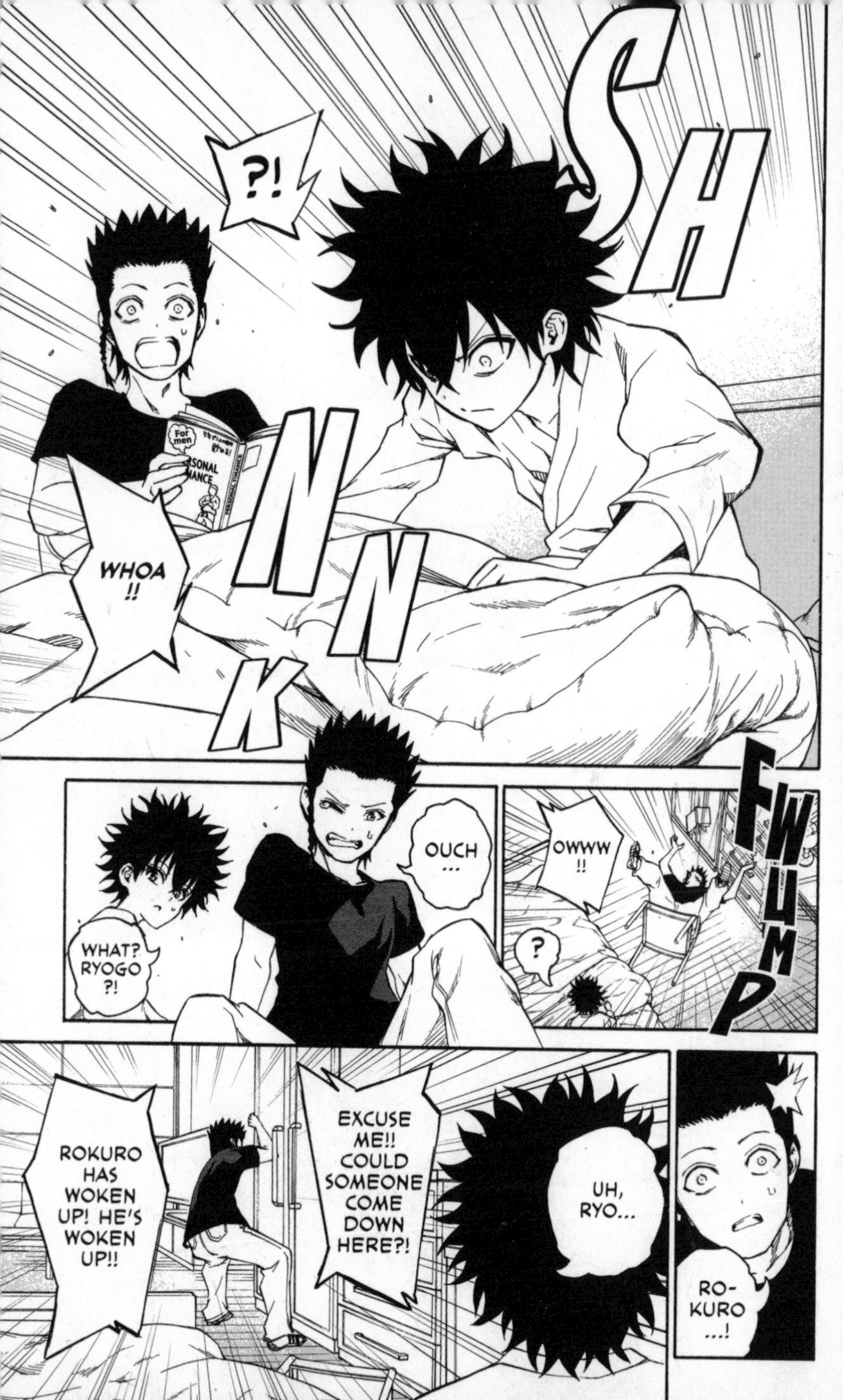
SHNNK
?!
For men
WHOA !!
FWUMP
OWWW !!
?
OUCH ...
WHAT? RYOGO ?!
RO-KURO ...!
UH, RYO...
EXCUSE ME!! COULD SOMEONE COME DOWN HERE?!
ROKURO HAS WOKEN UP! HE'S WOKEN UP!!

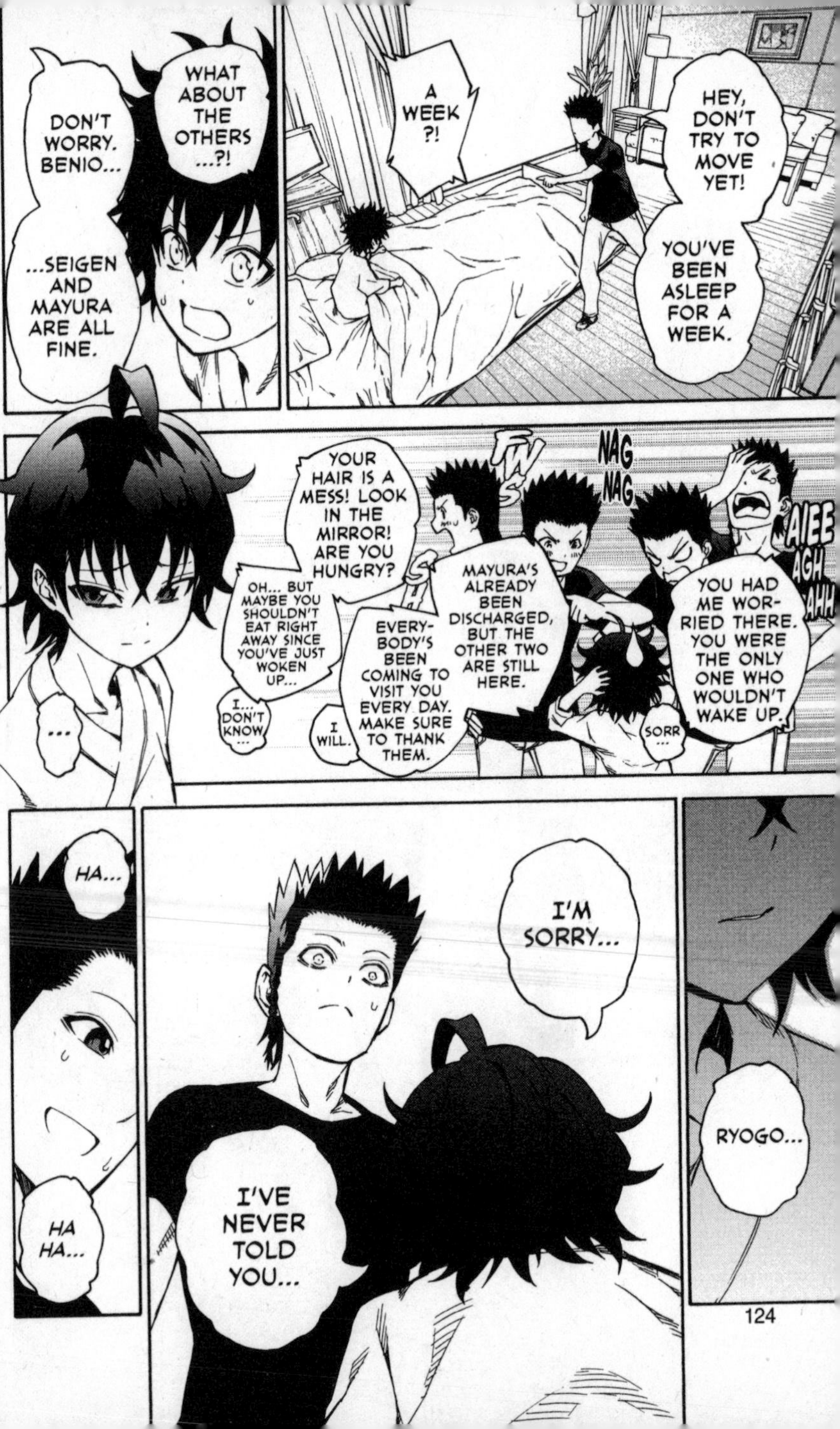

HEY, DON'T TRY TO MOVE YET!
YOU'VE BEEN ASLEEP FOR A WEEK.
A WEEK?!
WHAT ABOUT THE OTHERS...?!
DON'T WORRY. BENIO...
...SEIGEN AND MAYURA ARE ALL FINE.
AIEEAGHAHH
NAG NAG
YOU HAD ME WORRIED THERE. YOU WERE THE ONLY ONE WHO WOULDN'T WAKE UP.
SORR...
FWS
MAYURA'S ALREADY BEEN DISCHARGED, BUT THE OTHER TWO ARE STILL HERE.
YOUR HAIR IS A MESS! LOOK IN THE MIRROR! ARE YOU HUNGRY?
EVERYBODY'S BEEN COMING TO VISIT YOU EVERY DAY. MAKE SURE TO THANK THEM.
I WILL.
OH... BUT MAYBE YOU SHOULDN'T EAT RIGHT AWAY SINCE YOU'VE JUST WOKEN UP...
I... DON'T KNOW...
...
RYOGO...
I'M SORRY...
I'VE NEVER TOLD YOU...
HA...
HA HA...

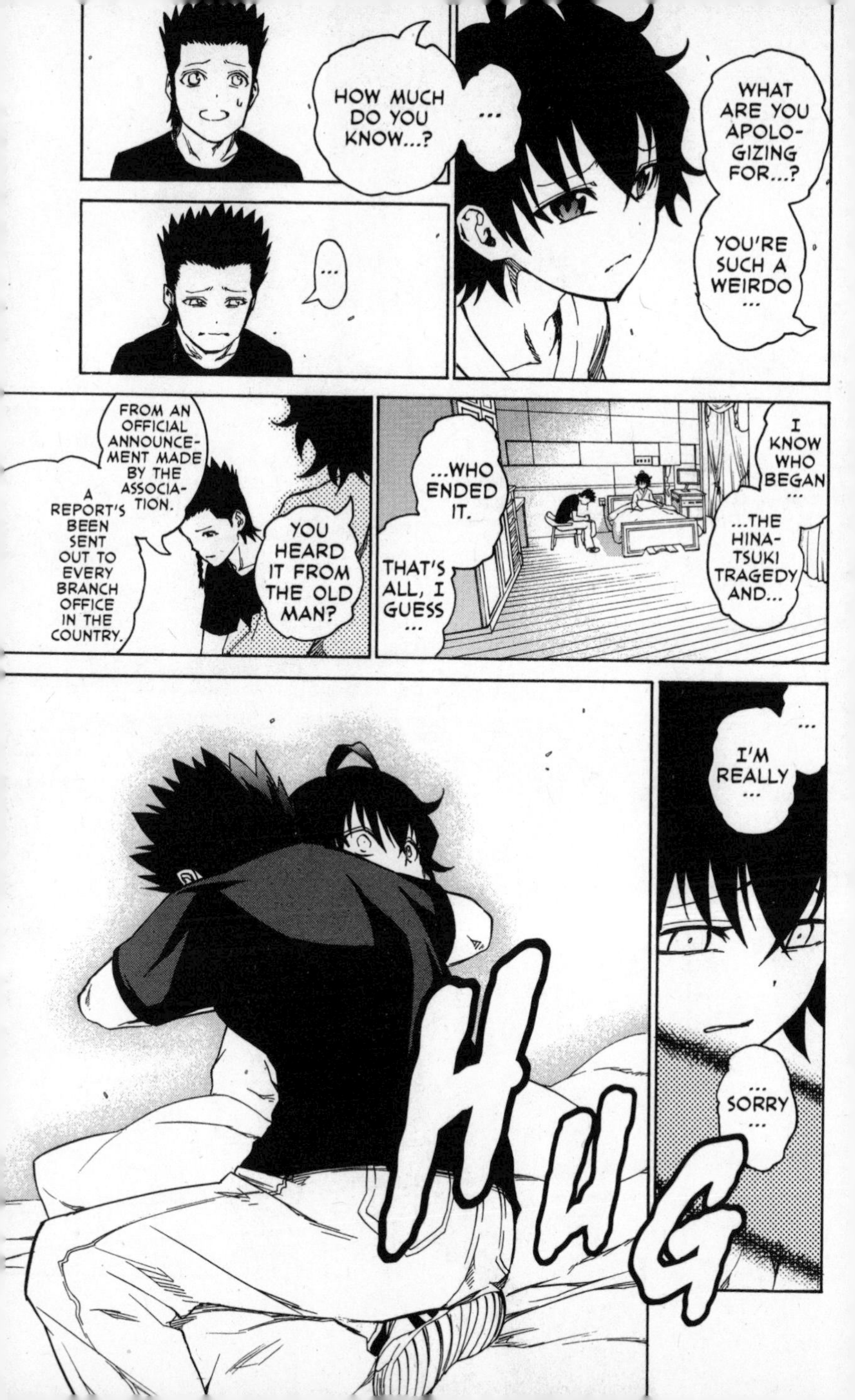
WHAT ARE YOU APOLOGIZING FOR...?
YOU'RE SUCH A WEIRDO...
...
HOW MUCH DO YOU KNOW...?
...
I KNOW WHO BEGAN... ...THE HINATSUKI TRAGEDY AND...
...WHO ENDED IT.
THAT'S ALL, I GUESS...
YOU HEARD IT FROM THE OLD MAN?
FROM AN OFFICIAL ANNOUNCEMENT MADE BY THE ASSOCIATION.
A REPORT'S BEEN SENT OUT TO EVERY BRANCH OFFICE IN THE COUNTRY.
... I'M REALLY...
...SORRY...
HUG

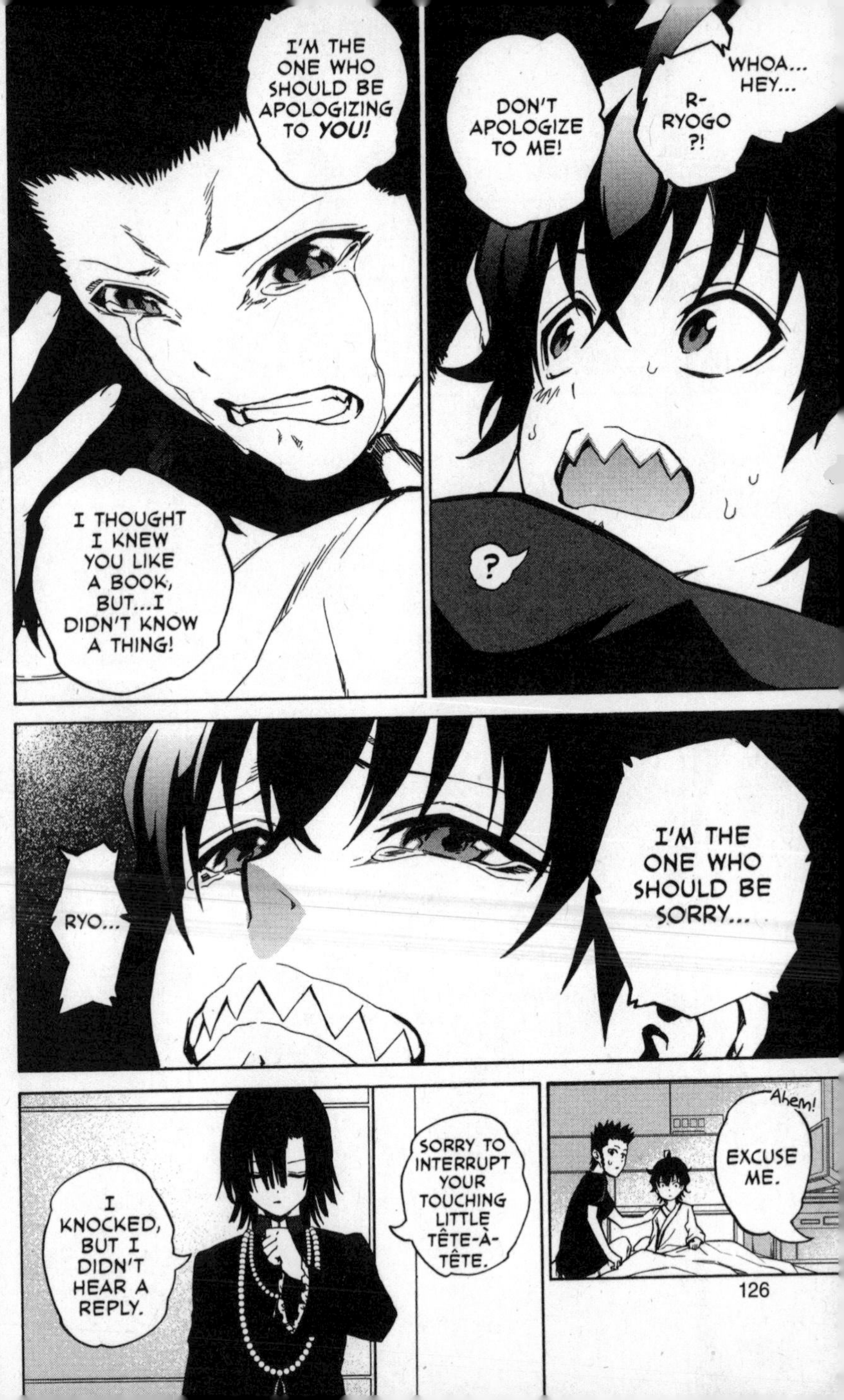
WHOA... HEY...
R-RYOGO?!
DON'T APOLOGIZE TO ME!
?
I'M THE ONE WHO SHOULD BE APOLOGIZING TO *YOU!*
I THOUGHT I KNEW YOU LIKE A BOOK, BUT...I DIDN'T KNOW A THING!
I'M THE ONE WHO SHOULD BE SORRY...
RYO...
Ahem!
EXCUSE ME.
SORRY TO INTERRUPT YOUR TOUCHING LITTLE TÊTE-À-TÊTE.
I KNOCKED, BUT I DIDN'T HEAR A REPLY.

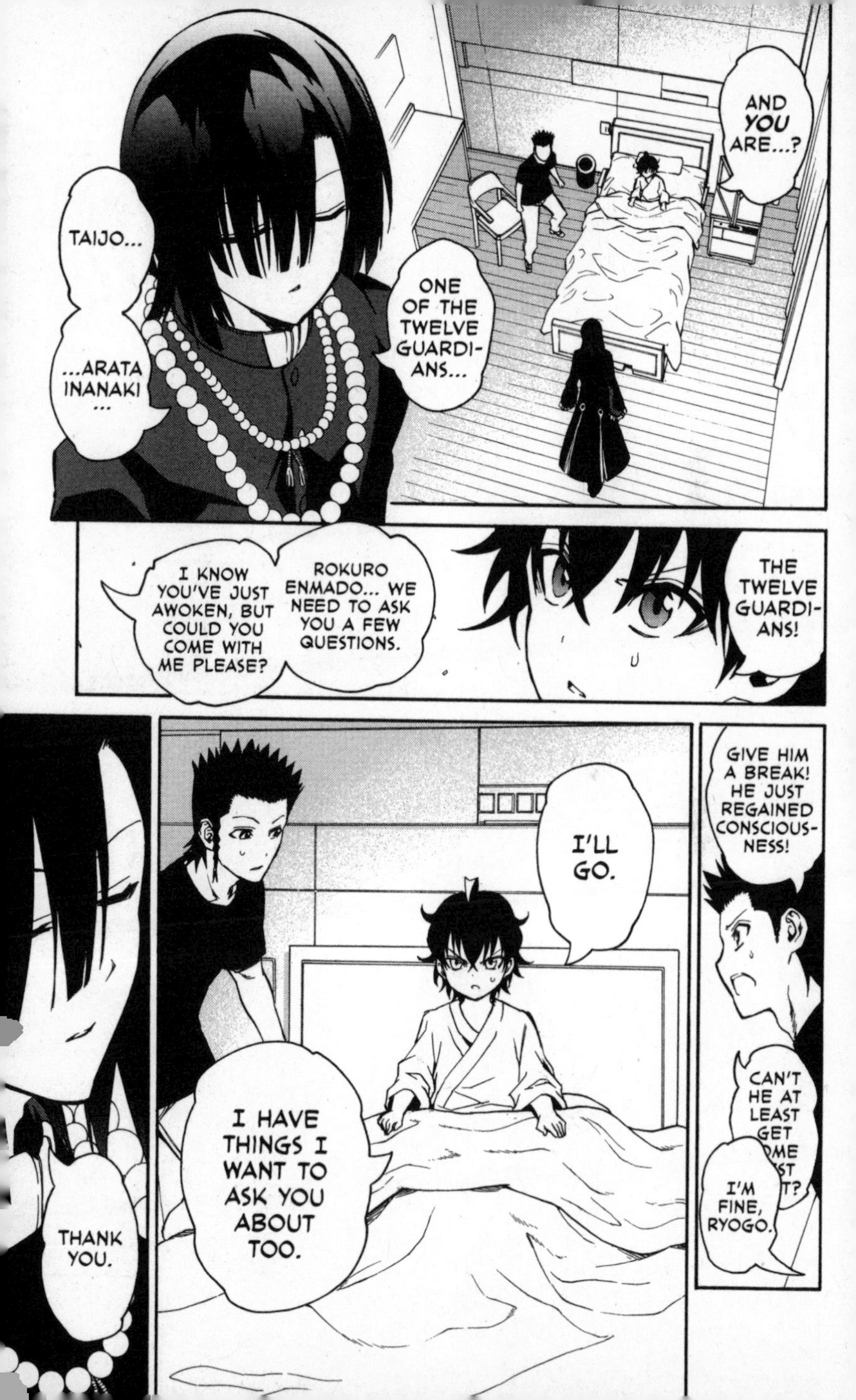
AND YOU ARE...?
TAIJO...
...ARATA INANAKI...
ONE OF THE TWELVE GUARDI-ANS...
THE TWELVE GUARDI-ANS!
ROKURO ENMADO... WE NEED TO ASK YOU A FEW QUESTIONS.
I KNOW YOU'VE JUST AWOKEN, BUT COULD YOU COME WITH ME PLEASE?
GIVE HIM A BREAK! HE JUST REGAINED CONSCIOUS-NESS!
CAN'T HE AT LEAST GET
I'M FINE, RYOGO.
I'LL GO.
I HAVE THINGS I WANT TO ASK YOU ABOUT TOO.
THANK YOU.

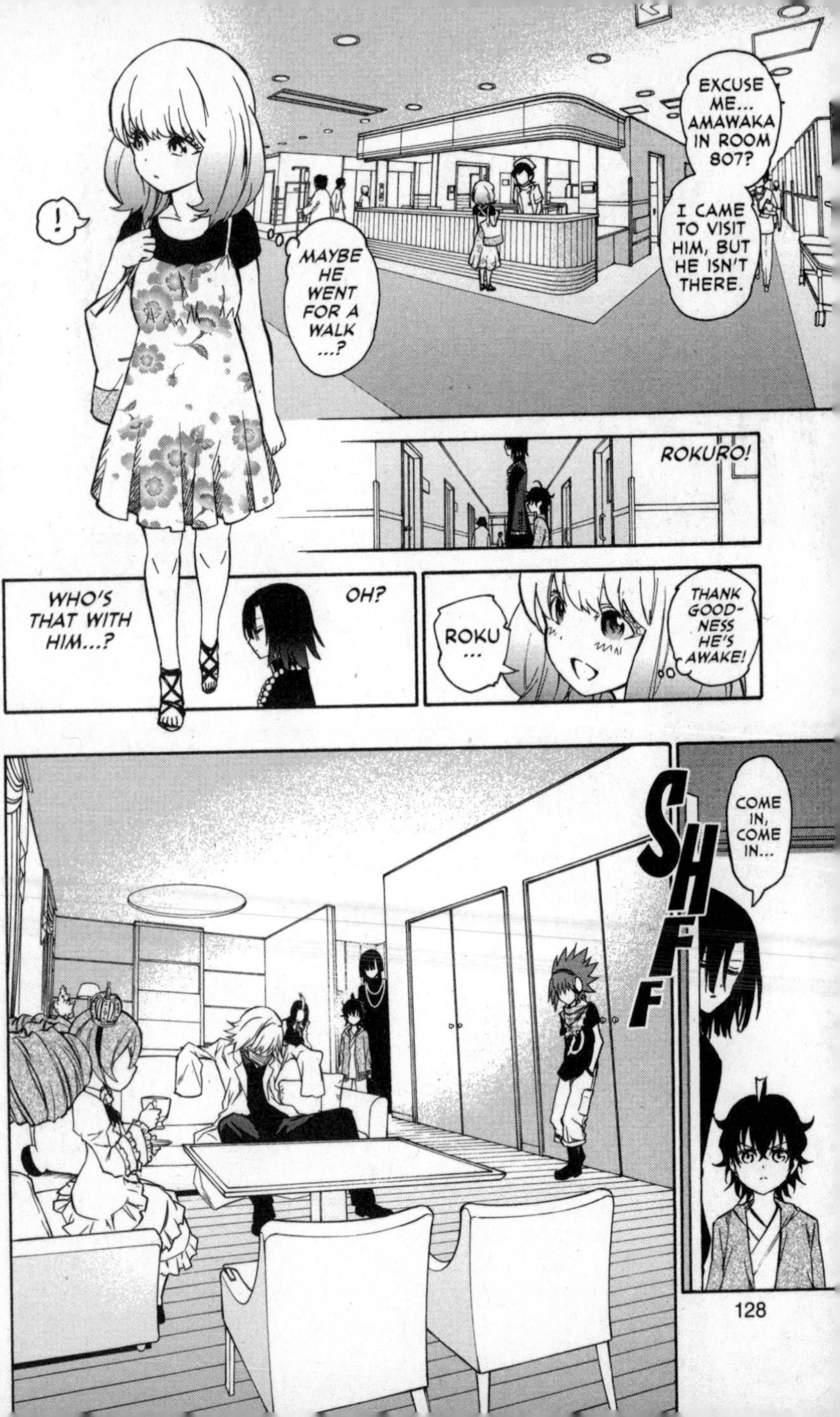
EXCUSE ME... AMAWAKA IN ROOM 807?
I CAME TO VISIT HIM, BUT HE ISN'T THERE.
MAYBE HE WENT FOR A WALK ...?
!
ROKURO!
THANK GOODNESS HE'S AWAKE!
ROKU ...
OH?
WHO'S THAT WITH HIM...?
COME IN, COME IN...
SHFF

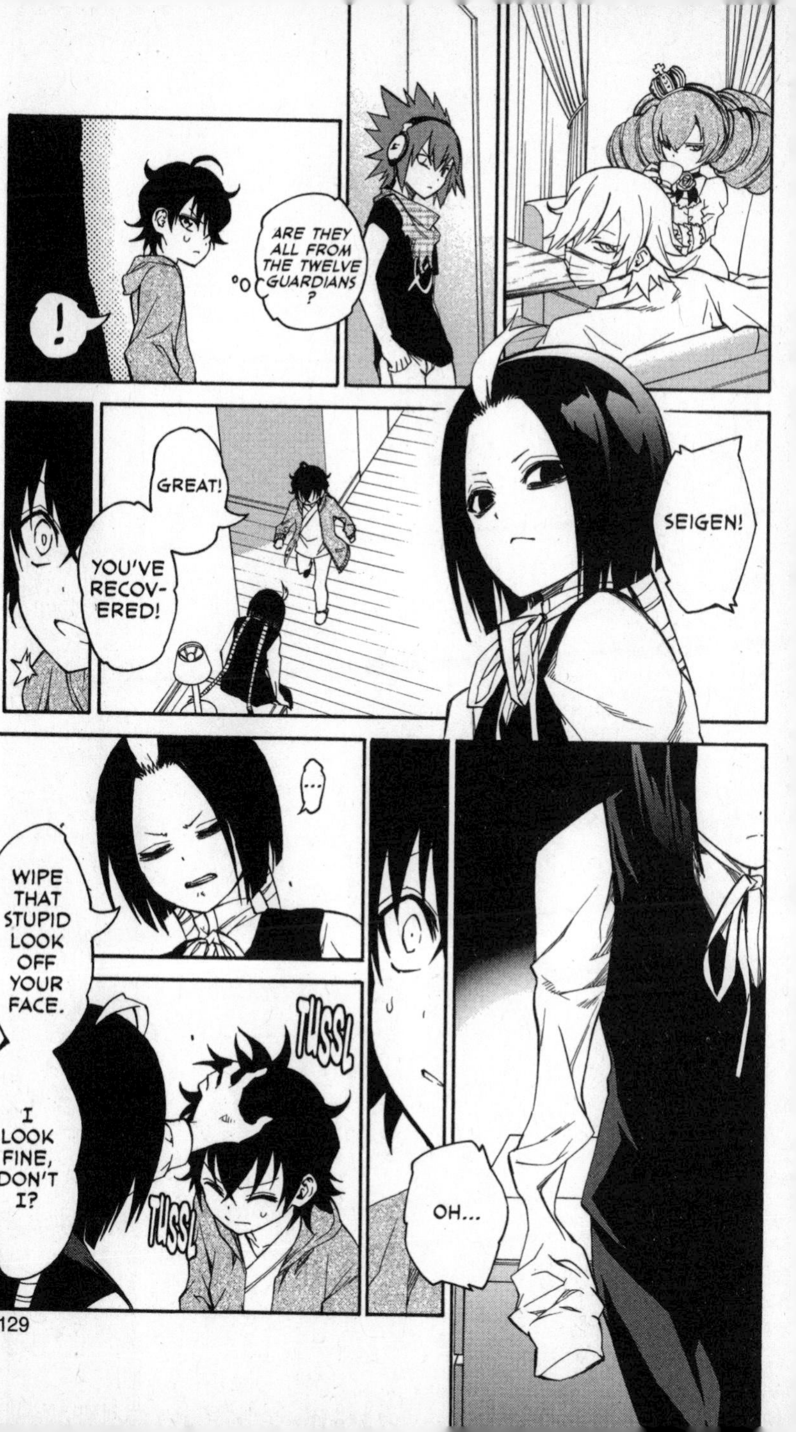
ARE THEY ALL FROM THE TWELVE GUARDIANS?
!
SEIGEN!
GREAT!
YOU'VE RECOVERED!
OH...
...
WIPE THAT STUPID LOOK OFF YOUR FACE.
TUSSL
I LOOK FINE, DON'T I?
TUSSL

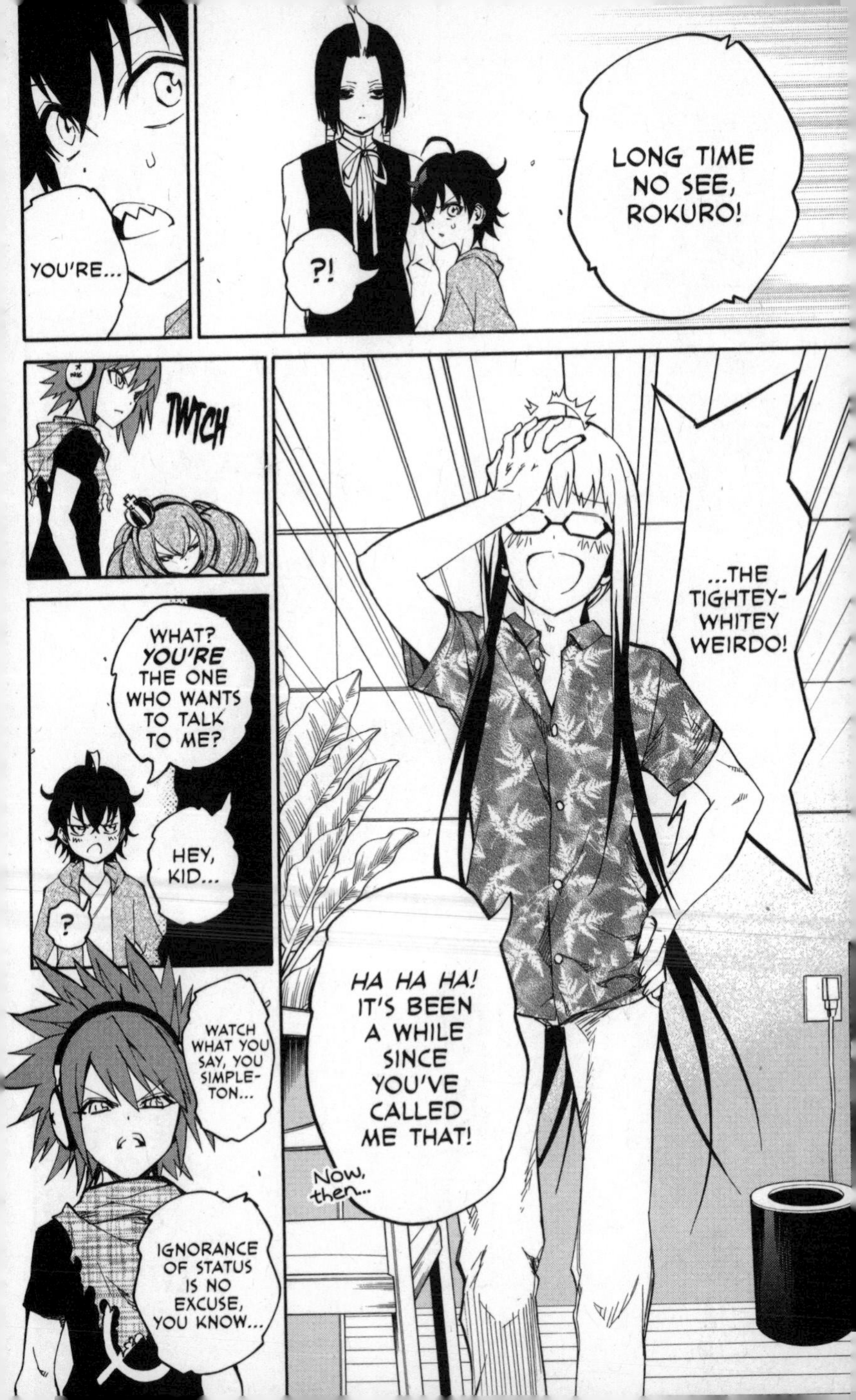
LONG TIME NO SEE, ROKURO!
?!
YOU'RE...
...THE TIGHTEY-WHITEY WEIRDO!
HA HA HA! IT'S BEEN A WHILE SINCE YOU'VE CALLED ME THAT!
Now, then...
TWITCH
WHAT? YOU'RE THE ONE WHO WANTS TO TALK TO ME?
HEY, KID...
?
WATCH WHAT YOU SAY, YOU SIMPLETON...
IGNORANCE OF STATUS IS NO EXCUSE, YOU KNOW...

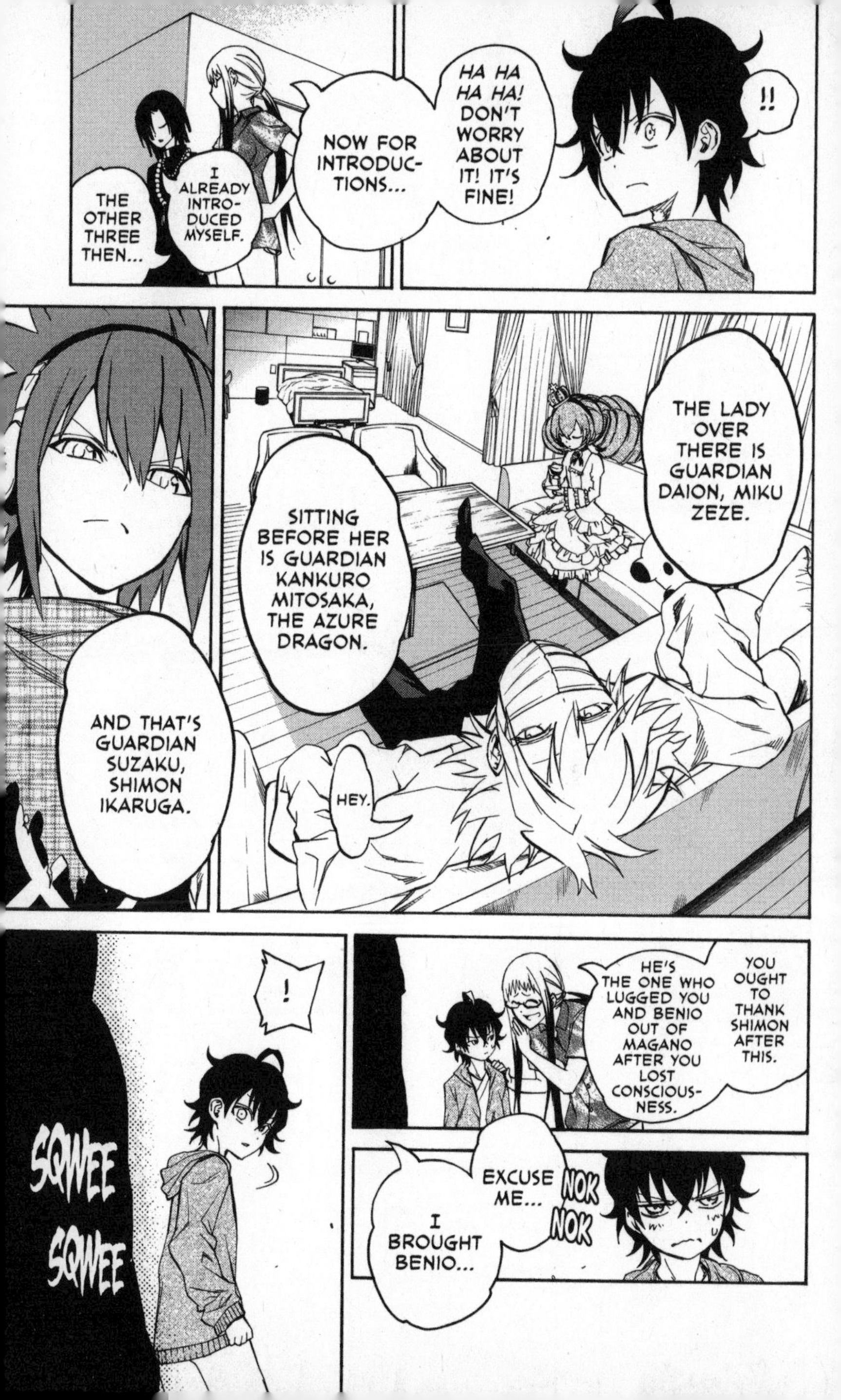
!!
HA HA HA HA! DON'T WORRY ABOUT IT! IT'S FINE!
NOW FOR INTRODUCTIONS...
I ALREADY INTRODUCED MYSELF.
THE OTHER THREE THEN...
THE LADY OVER THERE IS GUARDIAN DAION, MIKU ZEZE.
SITTING BEFORE HER IS GUARDIAN KANKURO MITOSAKA, THE AZURE DRAGON.
HEY.
AND THAT'S GUARDIAN SUZAKU, SHIMON IKARUGA.
YOU OUGHT TO THANK SHIMON AFTER THIS.
HE'S THE ONE WHO LUGGED YOU AND BENIO OUT OF MAGANO AFTER YOU LOST CONSCIOUSNESS.
NOK NOK
EXCUSE ME...
I BROUGHT BENIO...
!
SQWEE SQWEE

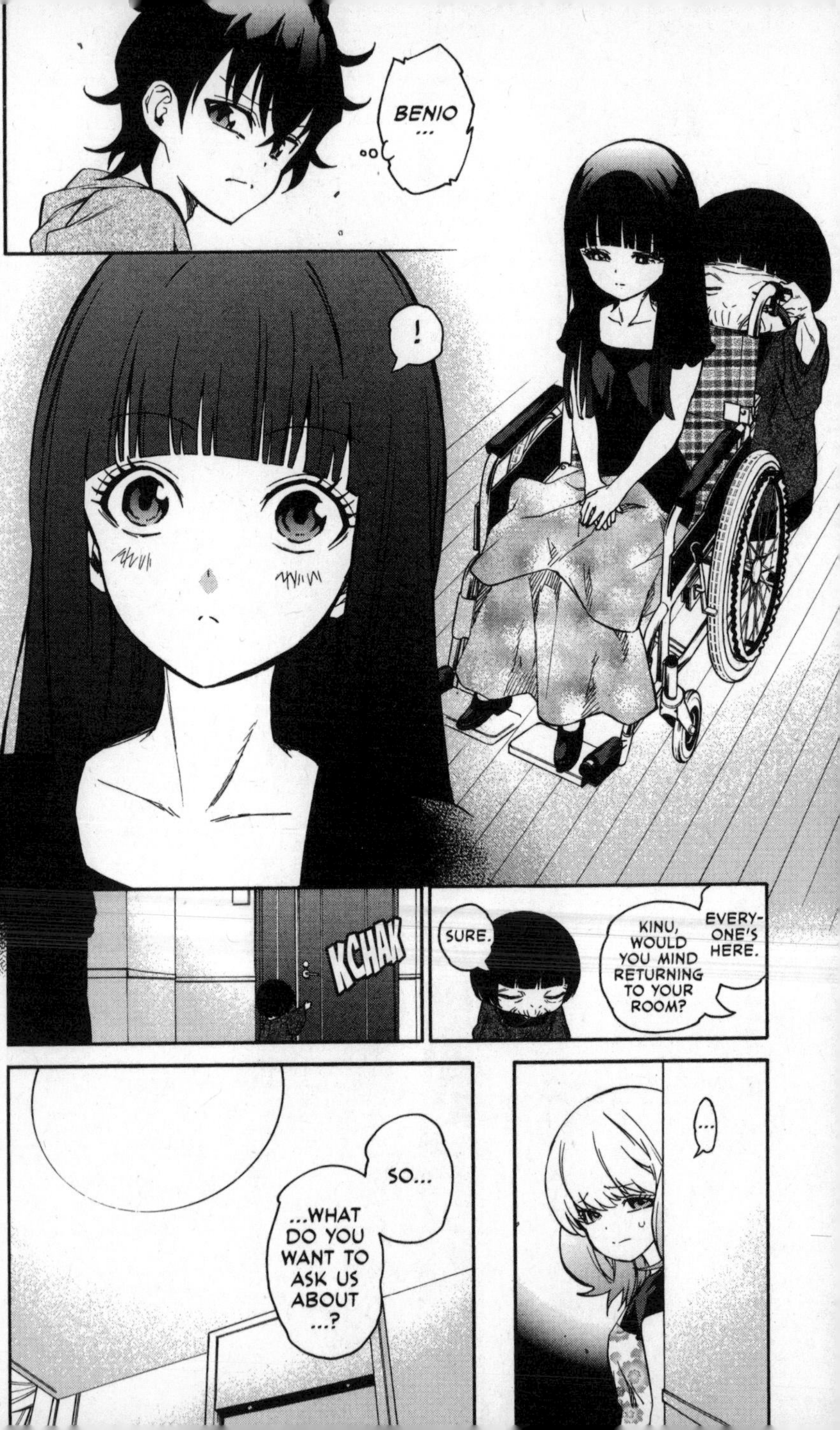
BENIO ...
!
EVERYONE'S HERE.
KINU, WOULD YOU MIND RETURNING TO YOUR ROOM?
SURE.
KCHAK
...
SO...
...WHAT DO YOU WANT TO ASK US ABOUT ...?

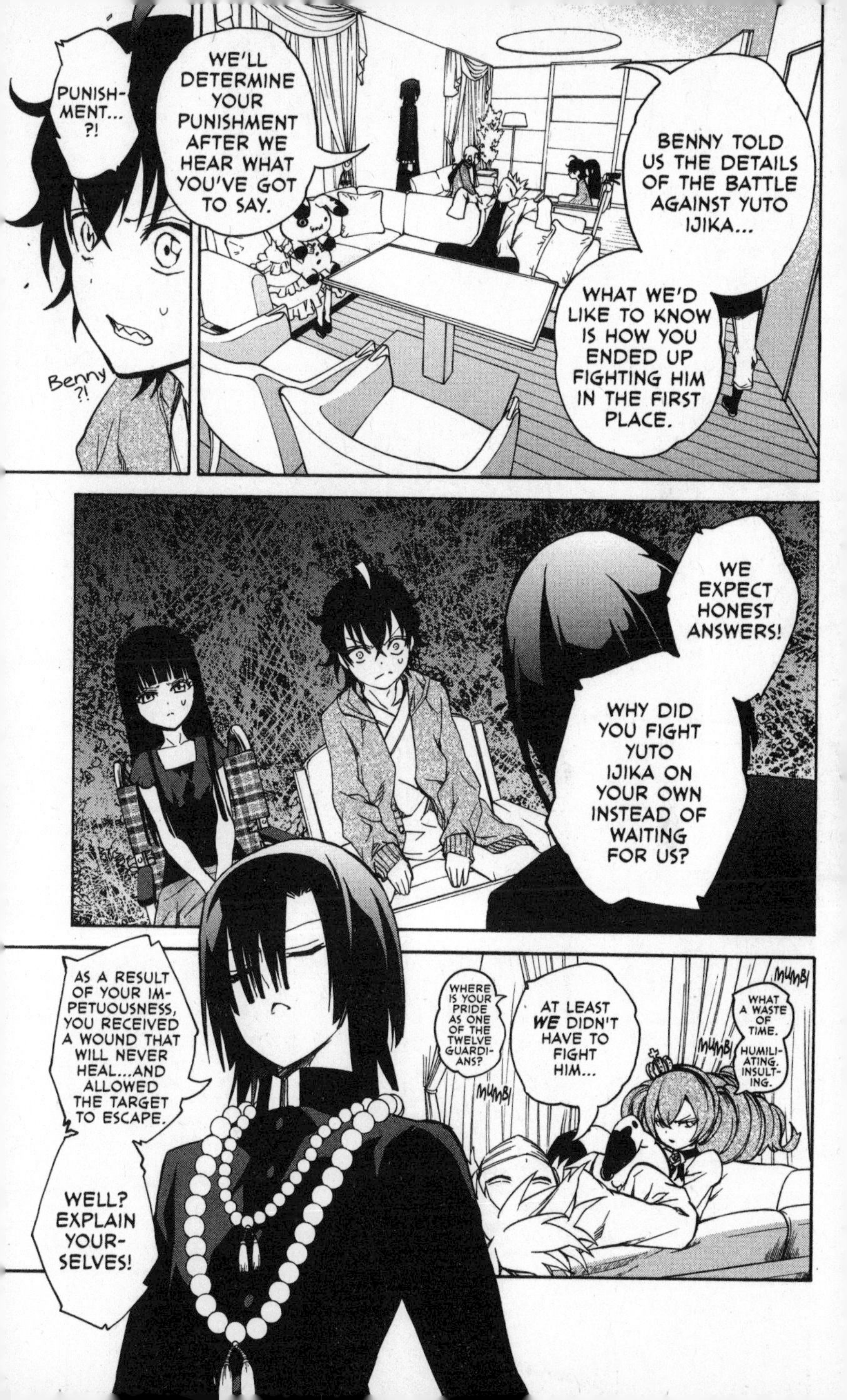
BENNY TOLD US THE DETAILS OF THE BATTLE AGAINST YUTO IJIKA...
WHAT WE'D LIKE TO KNOW IS HOW YOU ENDED UP FIGHTING HIM IN THE FIRST PLACE.
WE'LL DETERMINE YOUR PUNISHMENT AFTER WE HEAR WHAT YOU'VE GOT TO SAY.
PUNISHMENT...?!
Benny?!
WE EXPECT HONEST ANSWERS!
WHY DID YOU FIGHT YUTO IJIKA ON YOUR OWN INSTEAD OF WAITING FOR US?
MUMBI
WHAT A WASTE OF TIME.
HUMILIATING. INSULTING.
MUMBI
AT LEAST *WE* DIDN'T HAVE TO FIGHT HIM...
MUMBI
WHERE IS YOUR PRIDE AS ONE OF THE TWELVE GUARDIANS?
AS A RESULT OF YOUR IMPETUOUSNESS, YOU RECEIVED A WOUND THAT WILL NEVER HEAL...AND ALLOWED THE TARGET TO ESCAPE.
WELL? EXPLAIN YOURSELVES!

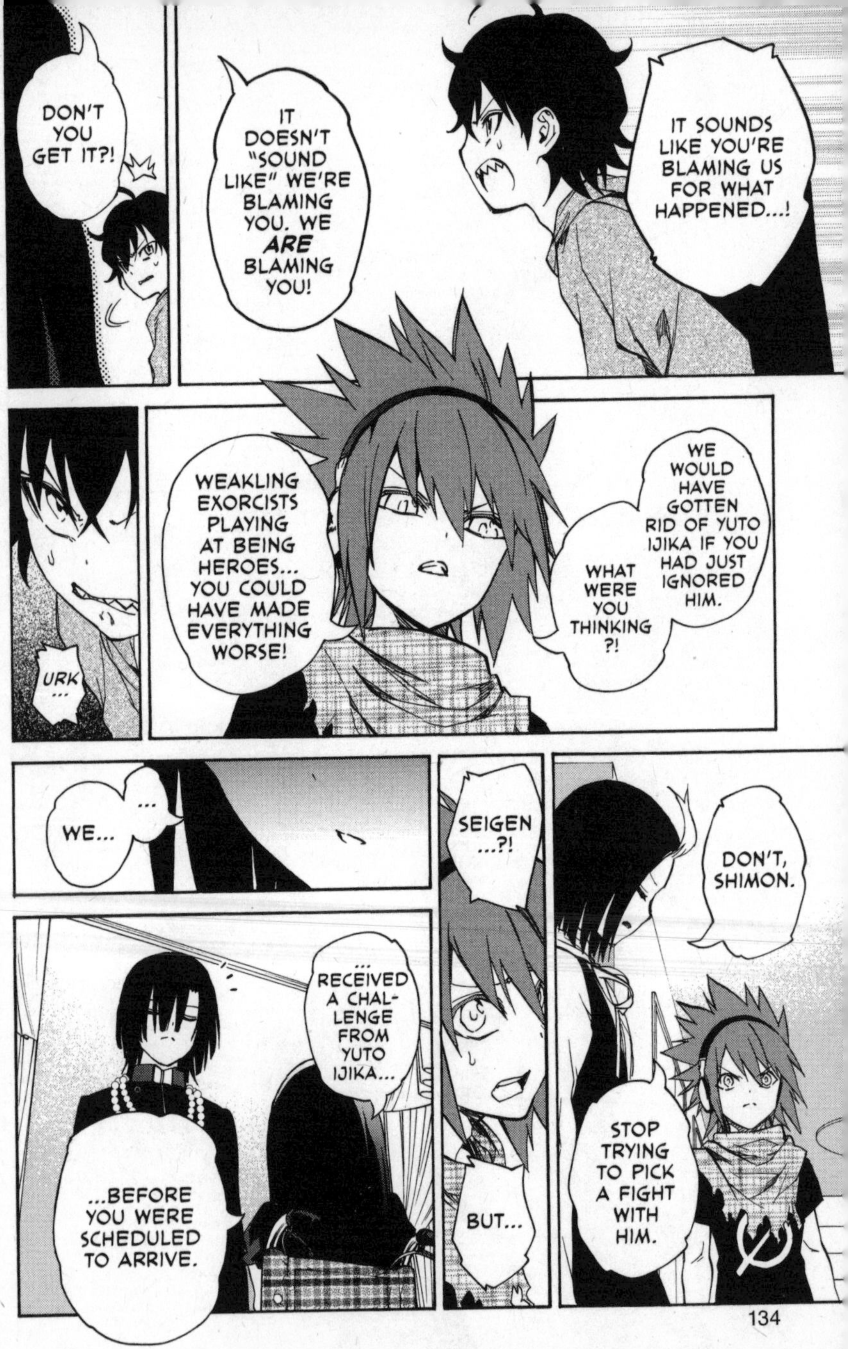
IT SOUNDS LIKE YOU'RE BLAMING US FOR WHAT HAPPENED...!
IT DOESN'T "SOUND LIKE" WE'RE BLAMING YOU. WE *ARE* BLAMING YOU!
DON'T YOU GET IT?!
WE WOULD HAVE GOTTEN RID OF YUTO IJIKA IF YOU HAD JUST IGNORED HIM.
WHAT WERE YOU THINKING ?!
WEAKLING EXORCISTS PLAYING AT BEING HEROES... YOU COULD HAVE MADE EVERYTHING WORSE!
URK ...
DON'T, SHIMON.
STOP TRYING TO PICK A FIGHT WITH HIM.
SEIGEN ...?!
BUT...
...
WE...
... RECEIVED A CHAL-LENGE FROM YUTO IJIKA...
...BEFORE YOU WERE SCHEDULED TO ARRIVE.

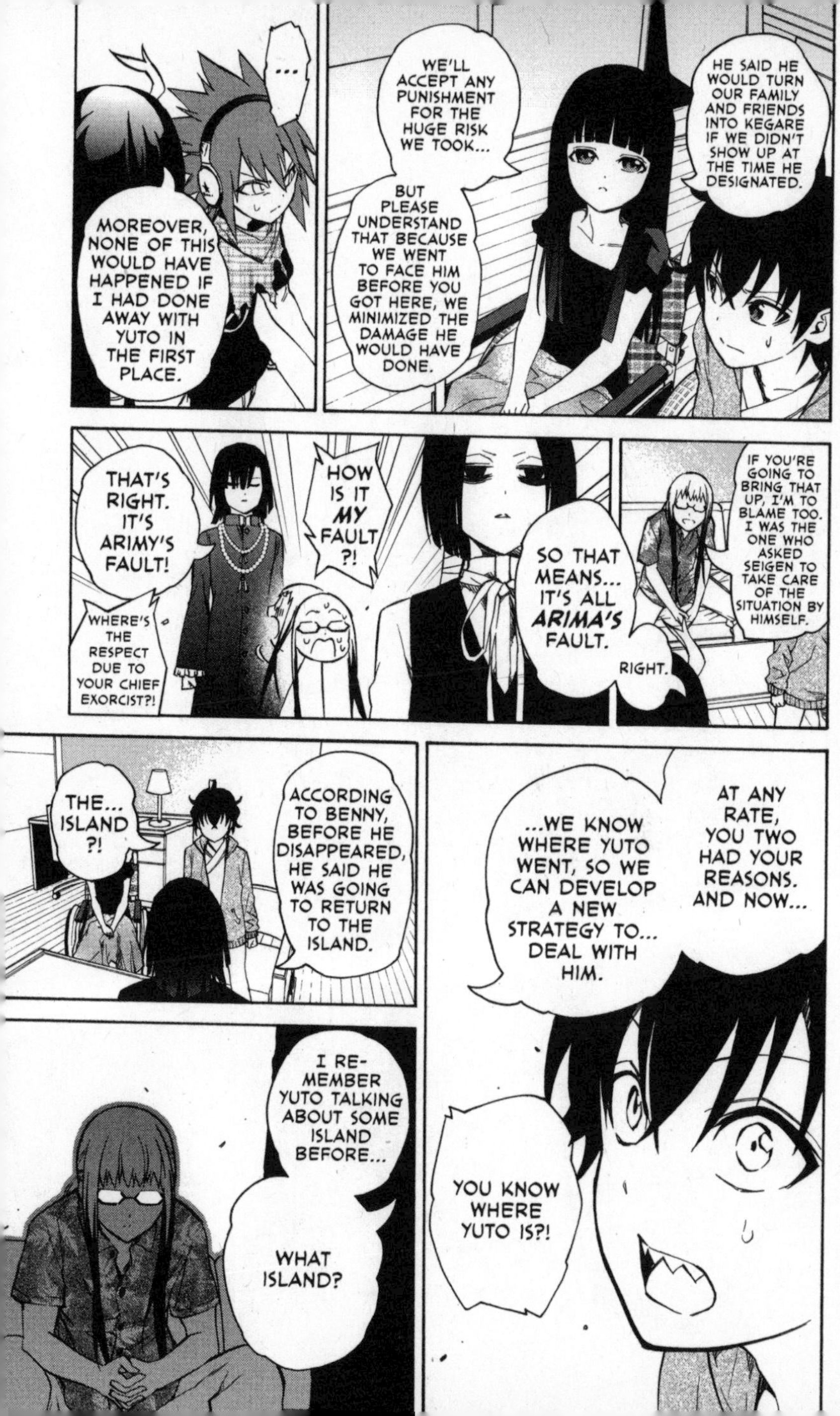
HE SAID HE WOULD TURN OUR FAMILY AND FRIENDS INTO KEGARE IF WE DIDN'T SHOW UP AT THE TIME HE DESIGNATED.
WE'LL ACCEPT ANY PUNISHMENT FOR THE HUGE RISK WE TOOK...
BUT PLEASE UNDERSTAND THAT BECAUSE WE WENT TO FACE HIM BEFORE YOU GOT HERE, WE MINIMIZED THE DAMAGE HE WOULD HAVE DONE.
...
MOREOVER, NONE OF THIS WOULD HAVE HAPPENED IF I HAD DONE AWAY WITH YUTO IN THE FIRST PLACE.
IF YOU'RE GOING TO BRING THAT UP, I'M TO BLAME TOO. I WAS THE ONE WHO ASKED SEIGEN TO TAKE CARE OF THE SITUATION BY HIMSELF.
SO THAT MEANS... IT'S ALL ARIMA'S FAULT.
RIGHT.
HOW IS IT MY FAULT?!
THAT'S RIGHT. IT'S ARIMY'S FAULT!
WHERE'S THE RESPECT DUE TO YOUR CHIEF EXORCIST?!
AT ANY RATE, YOU TWO HAD YOUR REASONS. AND NOW...
...WE KNOW WHERE YUTO WENT, SO WE CAN DEVELOP A NEW STRATEGY TO... DEAL WITH HIM.
YOU KNOW WHERE YUTO IS?!
ACCORDING TO BENNY, BEFORE HE DISAPPEARED, HE SAID HE WAS GOING TO RETURN TO THE ISLAND.
THE... ISLAND?!
I RE-MEMBER YUTO TALKING ABOUT SOME ISLAND BEFORE...
WHAT ISLAND?

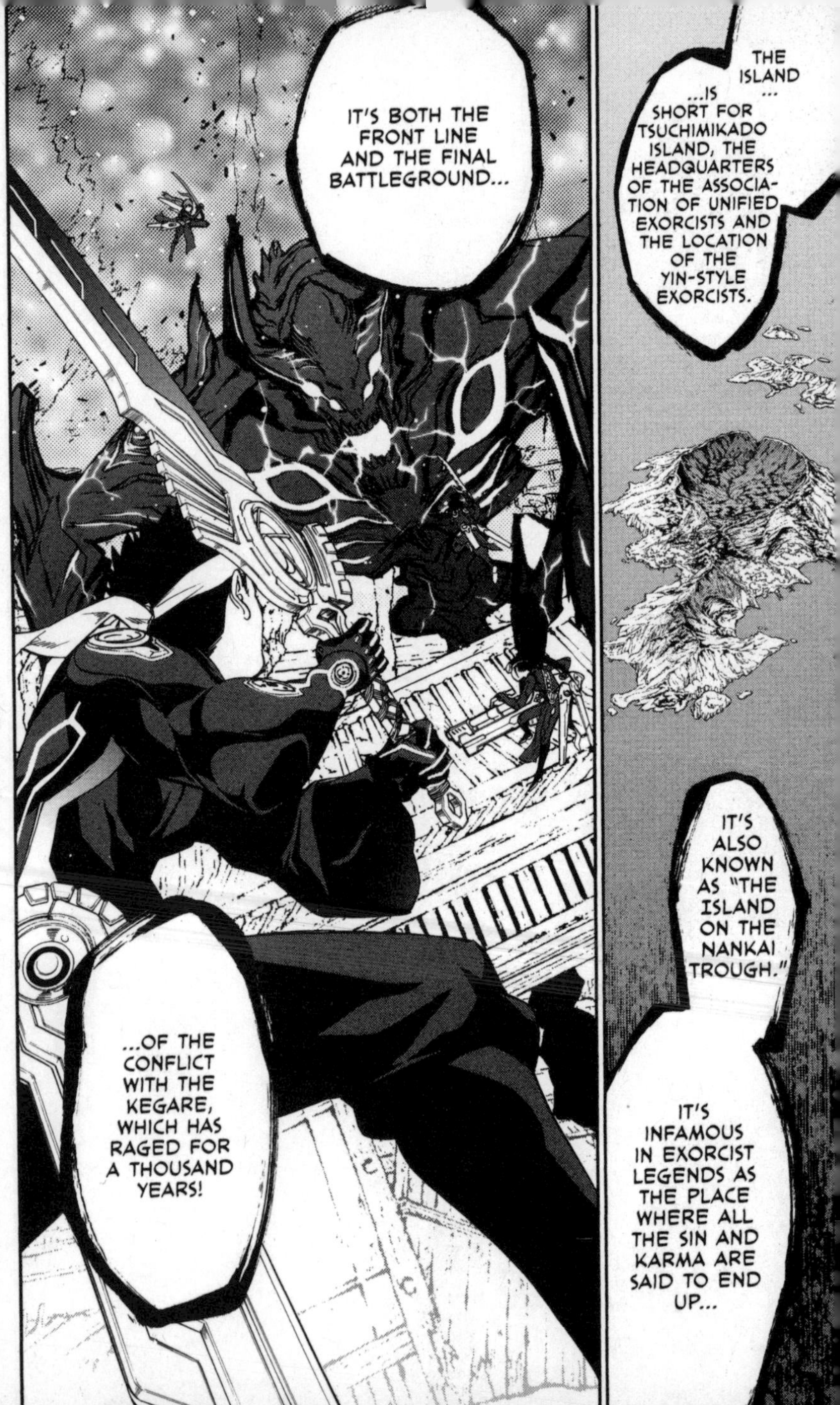
THE ISLAND...
...IS SHORT FOR TSUCHIMIKADO ISLAND, THE HEADQUARTERS OF THE ASSOCIATION OF UNIFIED EXORCISTS AND THE LOCATION OF THE YIN-STYLE EXORCISTS.
IT'S ALSO KNOWN AS "THE ISLAND ON THE NANKAI TROUGH."
IT'S INFAMOUS IN EXORCIST LEGENDS AS THE PLACE WHERE ALL THE SIN AND KARMA ARE SAID TO END UP...
IT'S BOTH THE FRONT LINE AND THE FINAL BATTLEGROUND...
...OF THE CONFLICT WITH THE KEGARE, WHICH HAS RAGED FOR A THOUSAND YEARS!

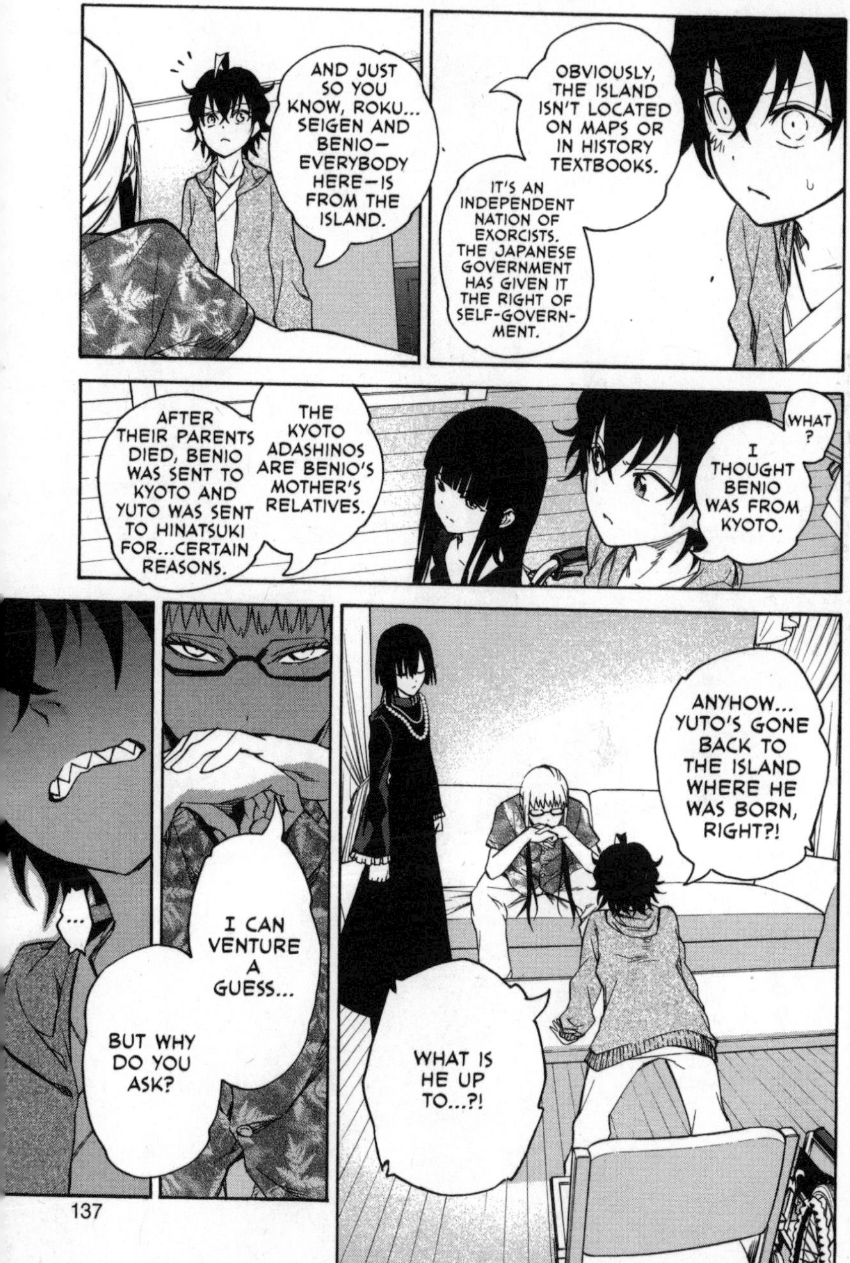
OBVIOUSLY, THE ISLAND ISN'T LOCATED ON MAPS OR IN HISTORY TEXTBOOKS.
IT'S AN INDEPENDENT NATION OF EXORCISTS. THE JAPANESE GOVERNMENT HAS GIVEN IT THE RIGHT OF SELF-GOVERNMENT.
AND JUST SO YOU KNOW, ROKU... SEIGEN AND BENIO—EVERYBODY HERE—IS FROM THE ISLAND.
WHAT?
I THOUGHT BENIO WAS FROM KYOTO.
THE KYOTO ADASHINOS ARE BENIO'S MOTHER'S RELATIVES.
AFTER THEIR PARENTS DIED, BENIO WAS SENT TO KYOTO AND YUTO WAS SENT TO HINATSUKI FOR...CERTAIN REASONS.
ANYHOW... YUTO'S GONE BACK TO THE ISLAND WHERE HE WAS BORN, RIGHT?!
WHAT IS HE UP TO...?!
I CAN VENTURE A GUESS...
BUT WHY DO YOU ASK?
...

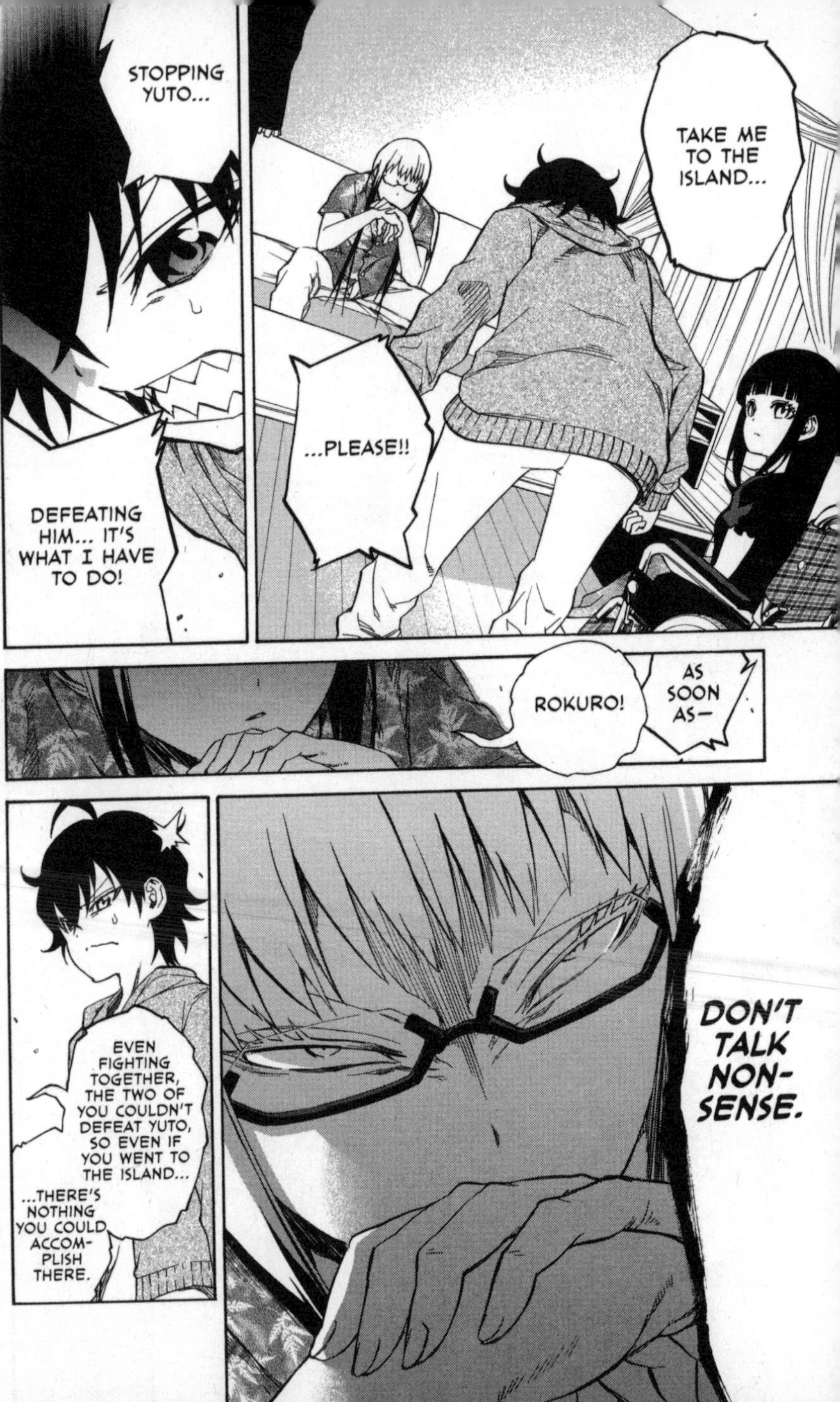
TAKE ME TO THE ISLAND...
...PLEASE!!
STOPPING YUTO...
DEFEATING HIM... IT'S WHAT I HAVE TO DO!
AS SOON AS—
ROKURO!
DON'T TALK NON-SENSE.
EVEN FIGHTING TOGETHER, THE TWO OF YOU COULDN'T DEFEAT YUTO, SO EVEN IF YOU WENT TO THE ISLAND...
...THERE'S NOTHING YOU COULD ACCOM-PLISH THERE.

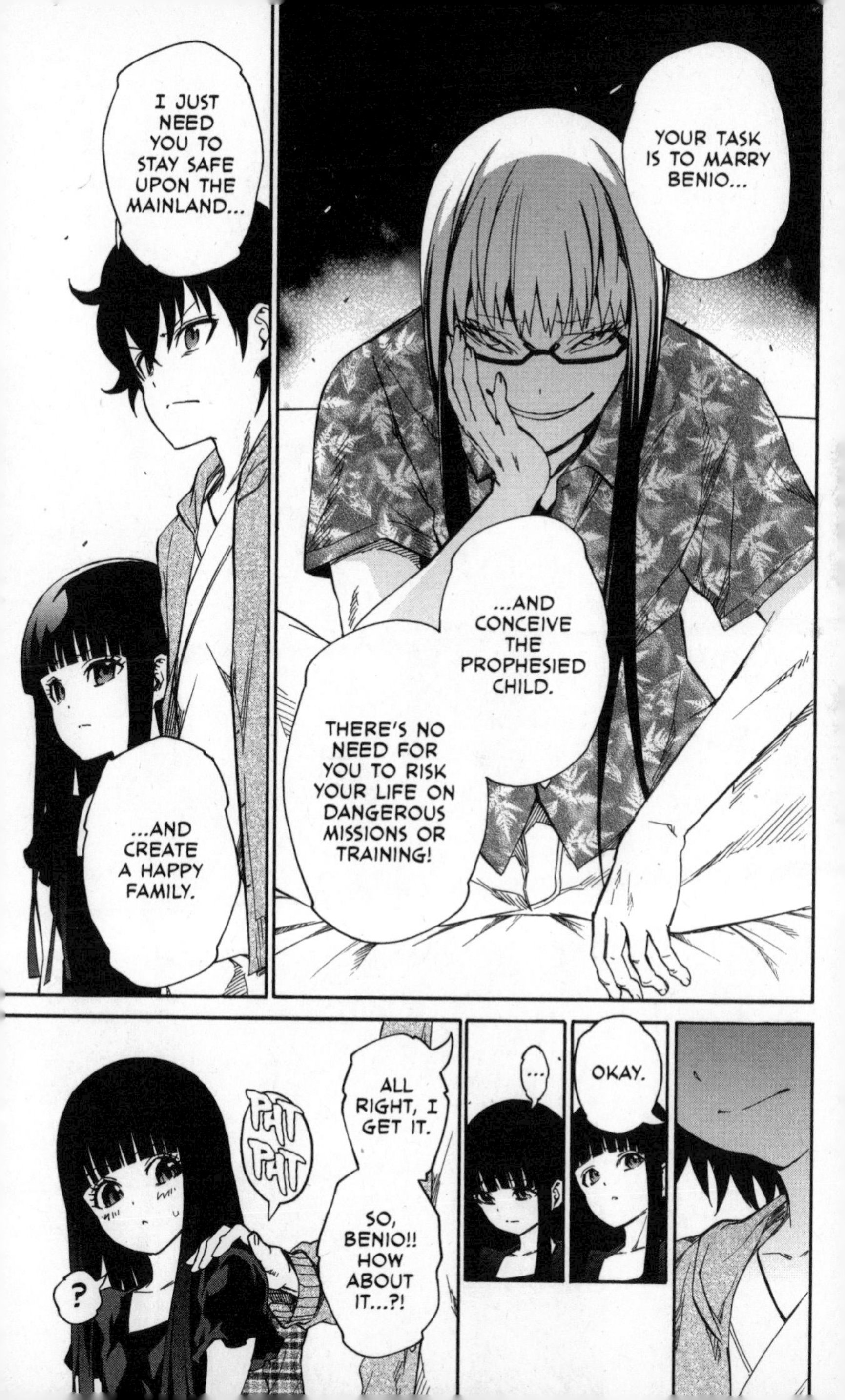
YOUR TASK IS TO MARRY BENIO...
...AND CONCEIVE THE PROPHESIED CHILD.
THERE'S NO NEED FOR YOU TO RISK YOUR LIFE ON DANGEROUS MISSIONS OR TRAINING!
I JUST NEED YOU TO STAY SAFE UPON THE MAINLAND...
...AND CREATE A HAPPY FAMILY.
OKAY.
...
ALL RIGHT, I GET IT.
PAT PAT
SO, BENIO!! HOW ABOUT IT...?!
?

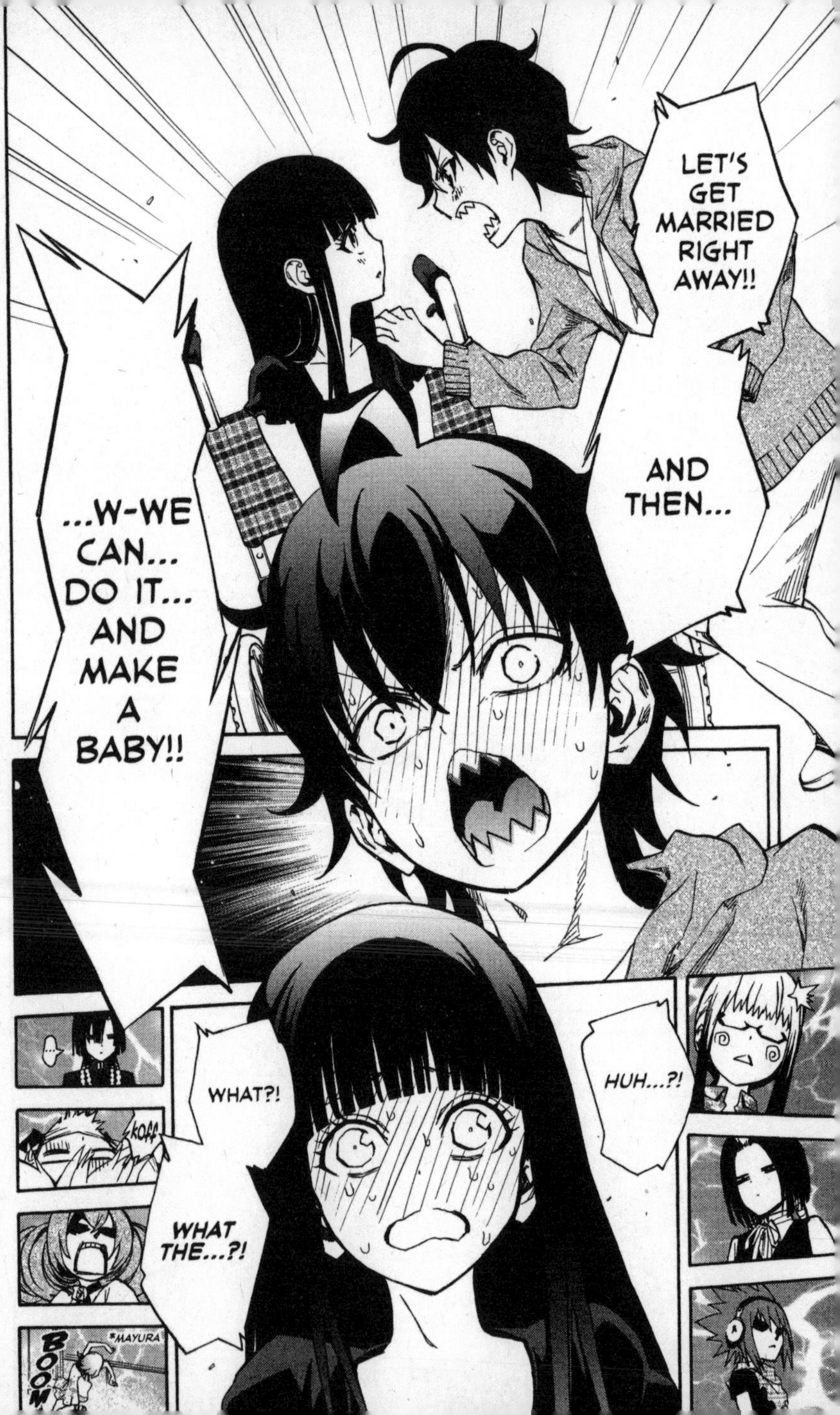
LET'S GET MARRIED RIGHT AWAY!!
AND THEN...
...W-WE CAN... DO IT... AND MAKE A BABY!!
HUH...?!
WHAT?!
WHAT THE...?!
...
KOFF
BOOM
*MAYURA

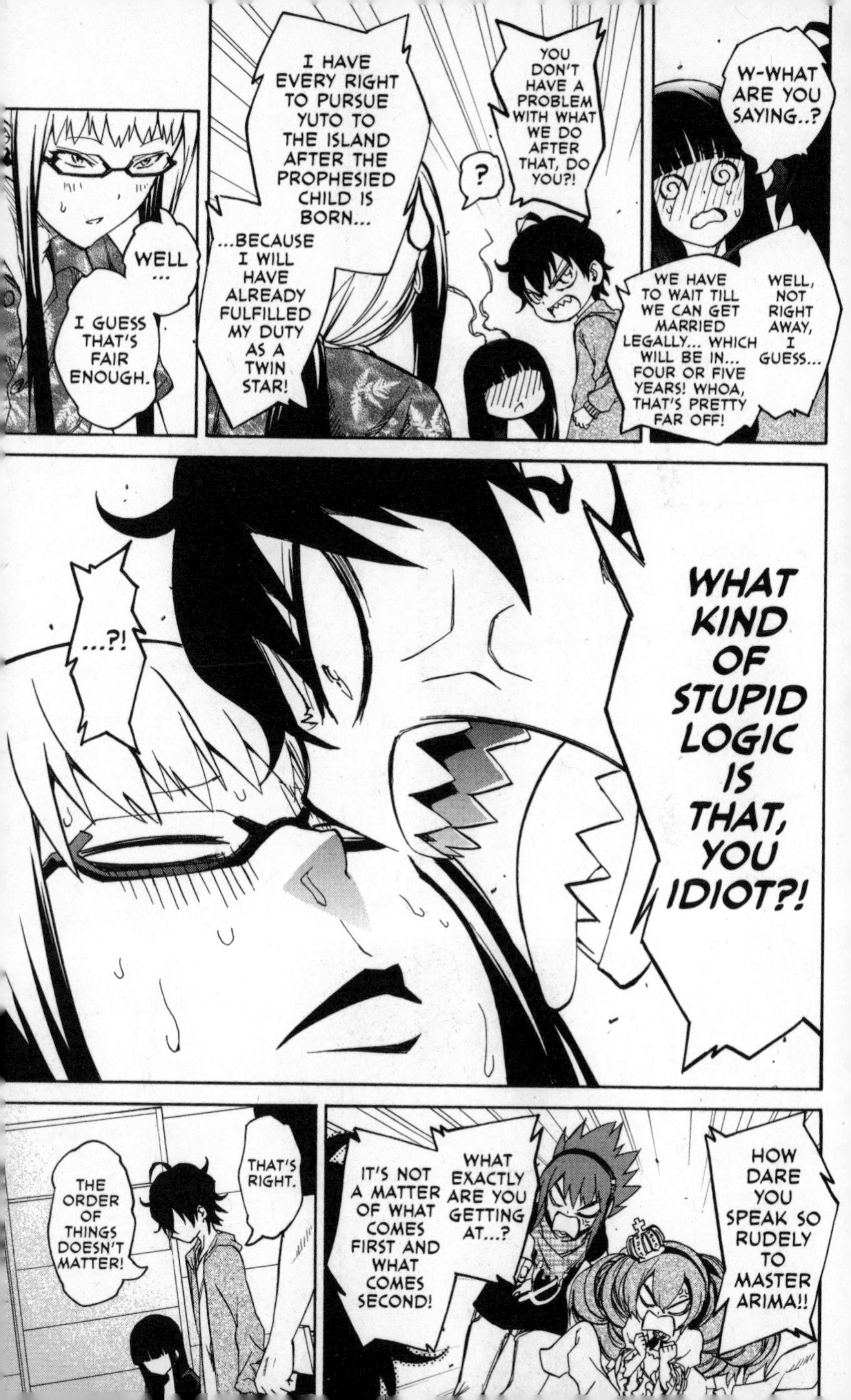
W-WHAT ARE YOU SAYING..?
WELL, NOT RIGHT AWAY, I GUESS...
WE HAVE TO WAIT TILL WE CAN GET MARRIED LEGALLY... WHICH WILL BE IN... FOUR OR FIVE YEARS! WHOA, THAT'S PRETTY FAR OFF!
YOU DON'T HAVE A PROBLEM WITH WHAT WE DO AFTER THAT, DO YOU?!
?
I HAVE EVERY RIGHT TO PURSUE YUTO TO THE ISLAND AFTER THE PROPHESIED CHILD IS BORN...
...BECAUSE I WILL HAVE ALREADY FULFILLED MY DUTY AS A TWIN STAR!
WELL...
I GUESS THAT'S FAIR ENOUGH.
WHAT KIND OF STUPID LOGIC IS THAT, YOU IDIOT?!
...?!
HOW DARE YOU SPEAK SO RUDELY TO MASTER ARIMA!!
WHAT EXACTLY ARE YOU GETTING AT...?
IT'S NOT A MATTER OF WHAT COMES FIRST AND WHAT COMES SECOND!
THAT'S RIGHT.
THE ORDER OF THINGS DOESN'T MATTER!

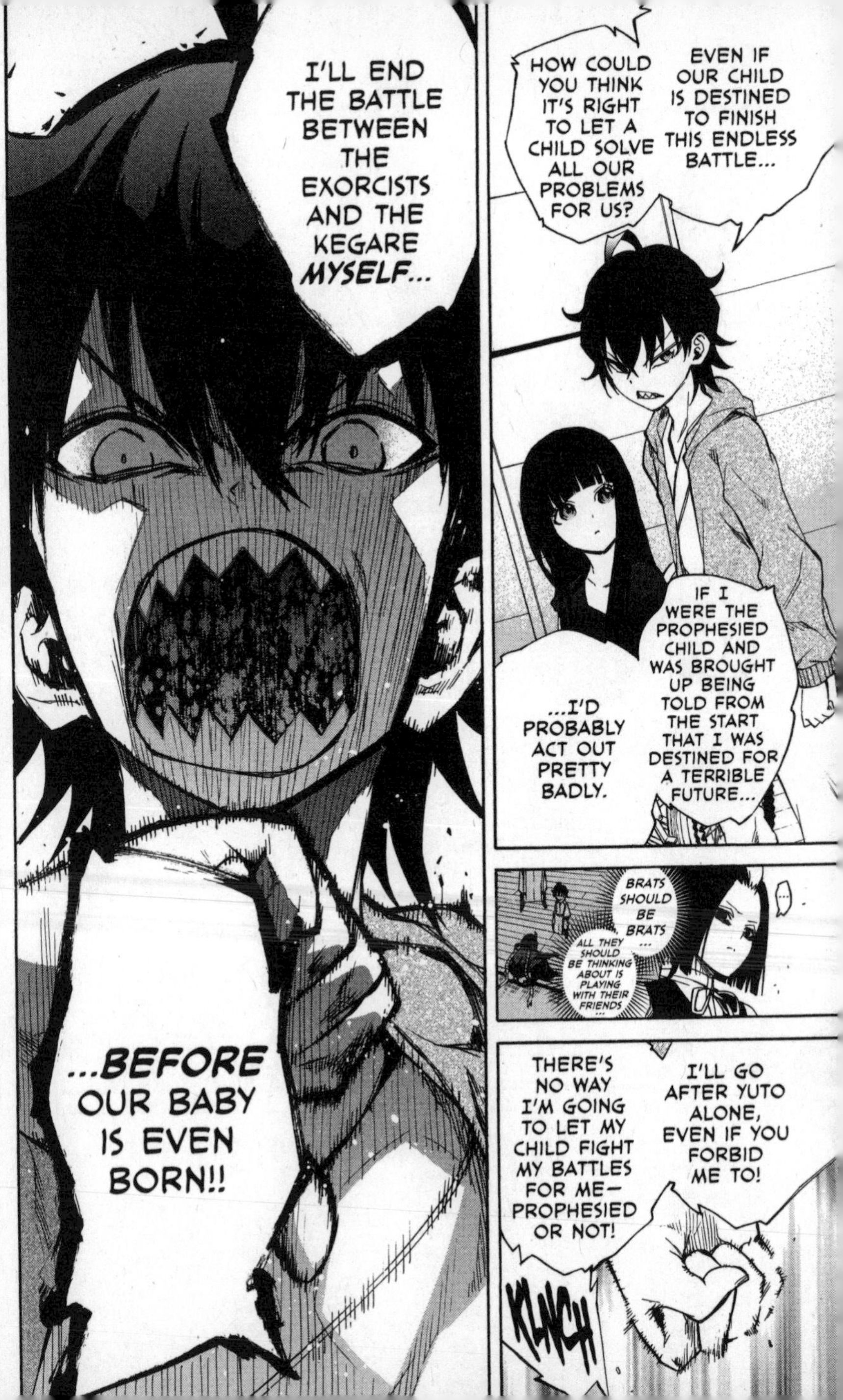
EVEN IF OUR CHILD IS DESTINED TO FINISH THIS ENDLESS BATTLE...
HOW COULD YOU THINK IT'S RIGHT TO LET A CHILD SOLVE ALL OUR PROBLEMS FOR US?
IF I WERE THE PROPHESIED CHILD AND WAS BROUGHT UP BEING TOLD FROM THE START THAT I WAS DESTINED FOR A TERRIBLE FUTURE...
...I'D PROBABLY ACT OUT PRETTY BADLY.
...
BRATS SHOULD BE BRATS...
ALL THEY SHOULD BE THINKING ABOUT IS PLAYING WITH THEIR FRIENDS...
I'LL GO AFTER YUTO ALONE, EVEN IF YOU FORBID ME TO!
THERE'S NO WAY I'M GOING TO LET MY CHILD FIGHT MY BATTLES FOR ME—PROPHESIED OR NOT!
KLINCH
I'LL END THE BATTLE BETWEEN THE EXORCISTS AND THE KEGARE *MYSELF*...
...*BEFORE* OUR BABY IS EVEN BORN!!

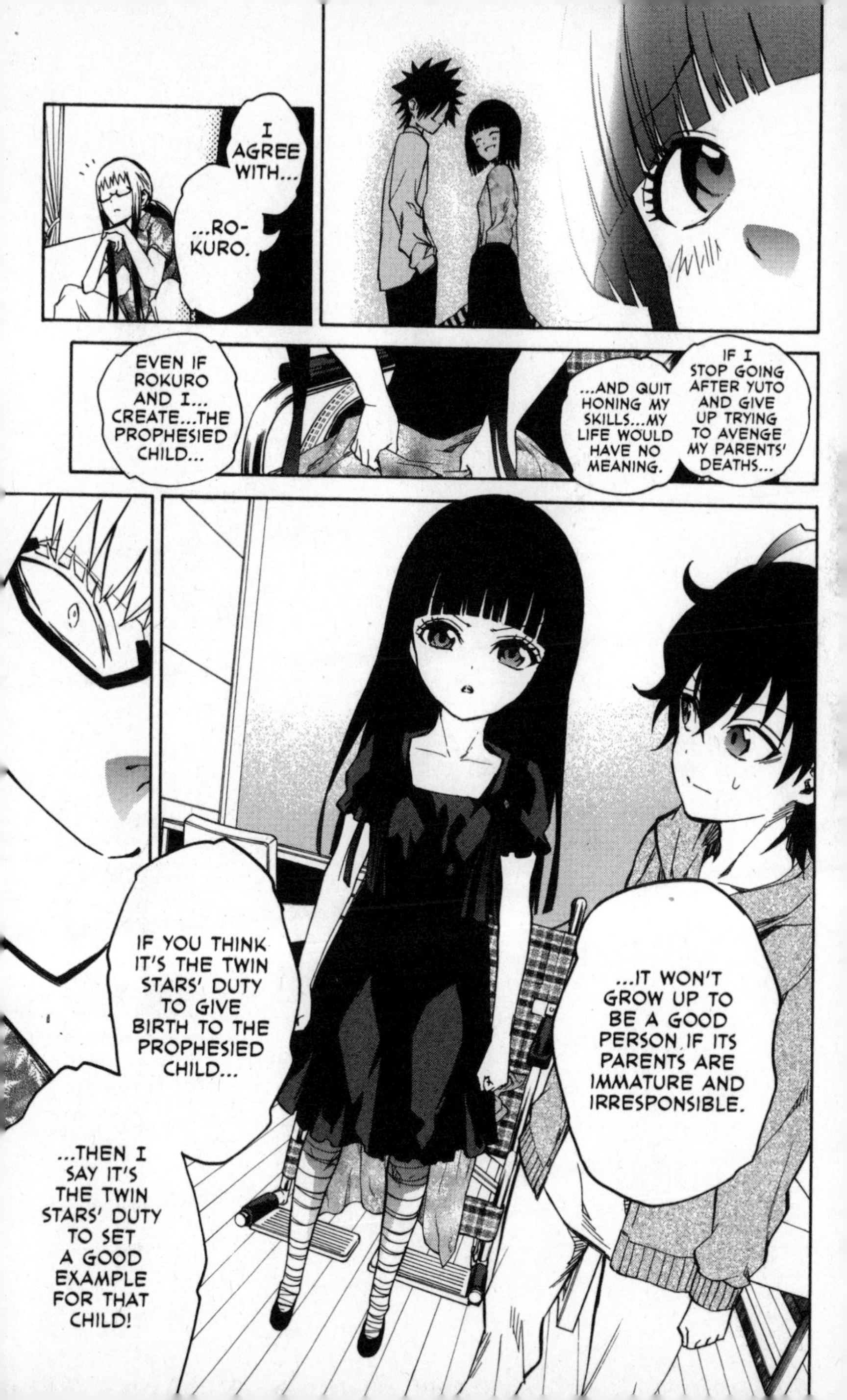
I AGREE WITH...
...RO-KURO.
IF I STOP GOING AFTER YUTO AND GIVE UP TRYING TO AVENGE MY PARENTS' DEATHS...
...AND QUIT HONING MY SKILLS...MY LIFE WOULD HAVE NO MEANING.
EVEN IF ROKURO AND I... CREATE...THE PROPHESIED CHILD...
...IT WON'T GROW UP TO BE A GOOD PERSON IF ITS PARENTS ARE IMMATURE AND IRRESPONSIBLE.
IF YOU THINK IT'S THE TWIN STARS' DUTY TO GIVE BIRTH TO THE PROPHESIED CHILD...
...THEN I SAY IT'S THE TWIN STARS' DUTY TO SET A GOOD EXAMPLE FOR THAT CHILD!

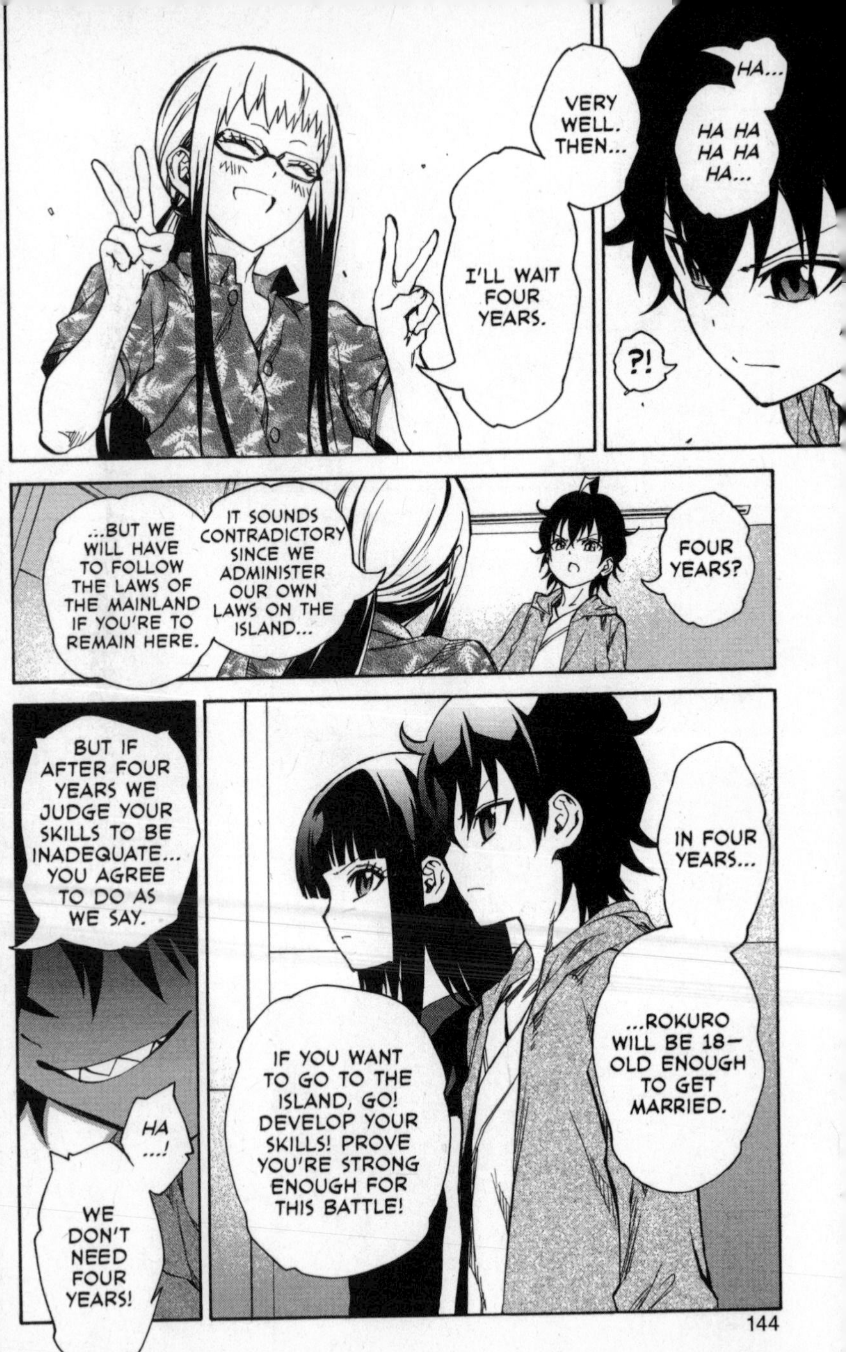
HA...
HA HA HA HA HA...
?!
VERY WELL. THEN...
I'LL WAIT FOUR YEARS.
FOUR YEARS?
IT SOUNDS CONTRADICTORY SINCE WE ADMINISTER OUR OWN LAWS ON THE ISLAND...
...BUT WE WILL HAVE TO FOLLOW THE LAWS OF THE MAINLAND IF YOU'RE TO REMAIN HERE.
IN FOUR YEARS...
...ROKURO WILL BE 18—OLD ENOUGH TO GET MARRIED.
IF YOU WANT TO GO TO THE ISLAND, GO! DEVELOP YOUR SKILLS! PROVE YOU'RE STRONG ENOUGH FOR THIS BATTLE!
BUT IF AFTER FOUR YEARS WE JUDGE YOUR SKILLS TO BE INADEQUATE... YOU AGREE TO DO AS WE SAY.
HA ...!
WE DON'T NEED FOUR YEARS!

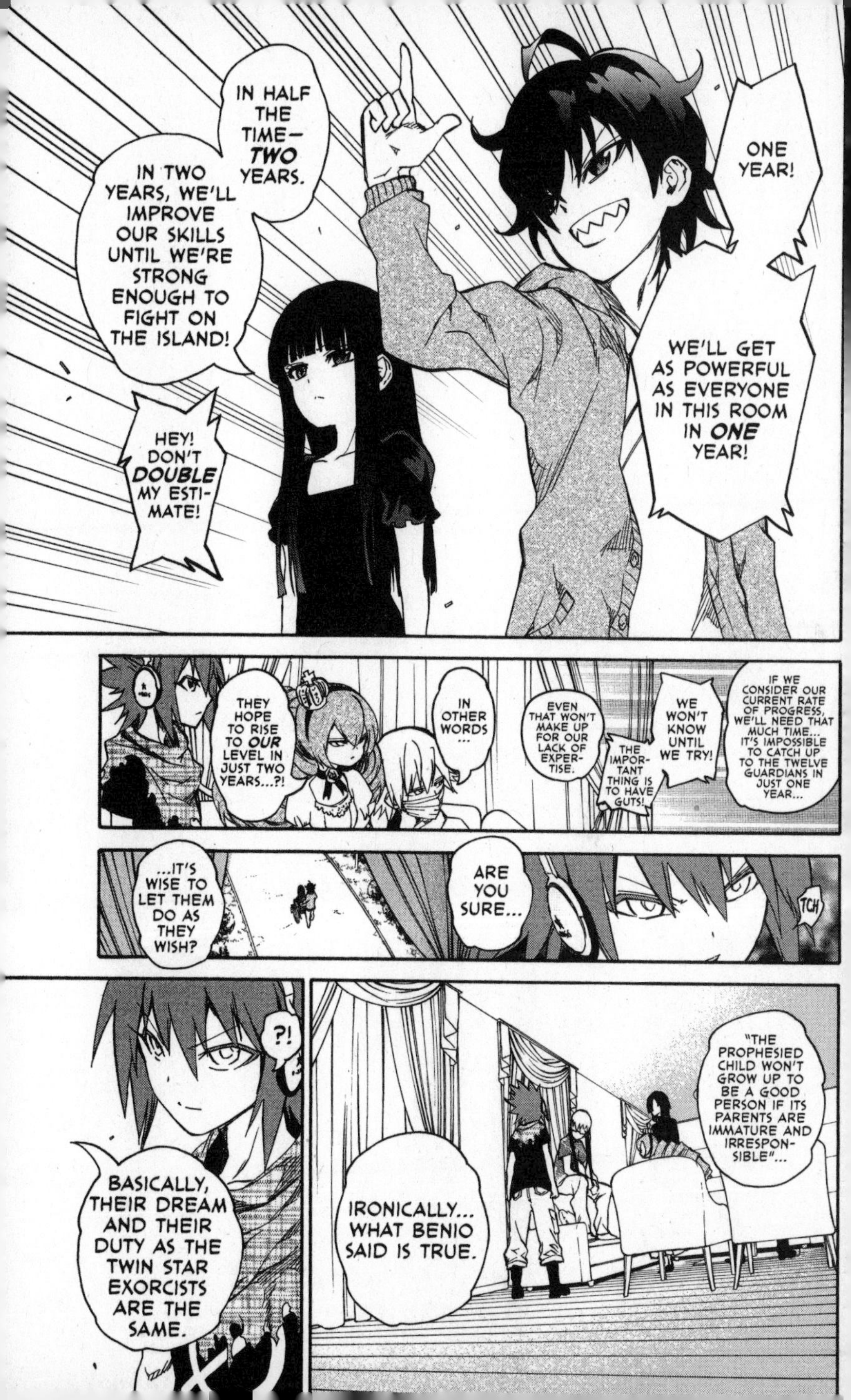
ONE YEAR!
WE'LL GET AS POWERFUL AS EVERYONE IN THIS ROOM IN *ONE* YEAR!
IN HALF THE TIME— *TWO* YEARS.
IN TWO YEARS, WE'LL IMPROVE OUR SKILLS UNTIL WE'RE STRONG ENOUGH TO FIGHT ON THE ISLAND!
HEY! DON'T *DOUBLE* MY ESTI-MATE!
IF WE CONSIDER OUR CURRENT RATE OF PROGRESS, WE'LL NEED THAT MUCH TIME... IT'S IMPOSSIBLE TO CATCH UP TO THE TWELVE GUARDIANS IN JUST ONE YEAR...
WE WON'T KNOW UNTIL WE TRY!
THE IMPOR-TANT THING IS TO HAVE GUTS!
EVEN THAT WON'T MAKE UP FOR OUR LACK OF EXPER-TISE.
IN OTHER WORDS ...
THEY HOPE TO RISE TO *OUR* LEVEL IN JUST TWO YEARS...?!
TCH
ARE YOU SURE...
...IT'S WISE TO LET THEM DO AS THEY WISH?
"THE PROPHESIED CHILD WON'T GROW UP TO BE A GOOD PERSON IF ITS PARENTS ARE IMMATURE AND IRRESPON-SIBLE"...
IRONICALLY... WHAT BENIO SAID IS TRUE.
?!
BASICALLY, THEIR DREAM AND THEIR DUTY AS THE TWIN STAR EXORCISTS ARE THE SAME.

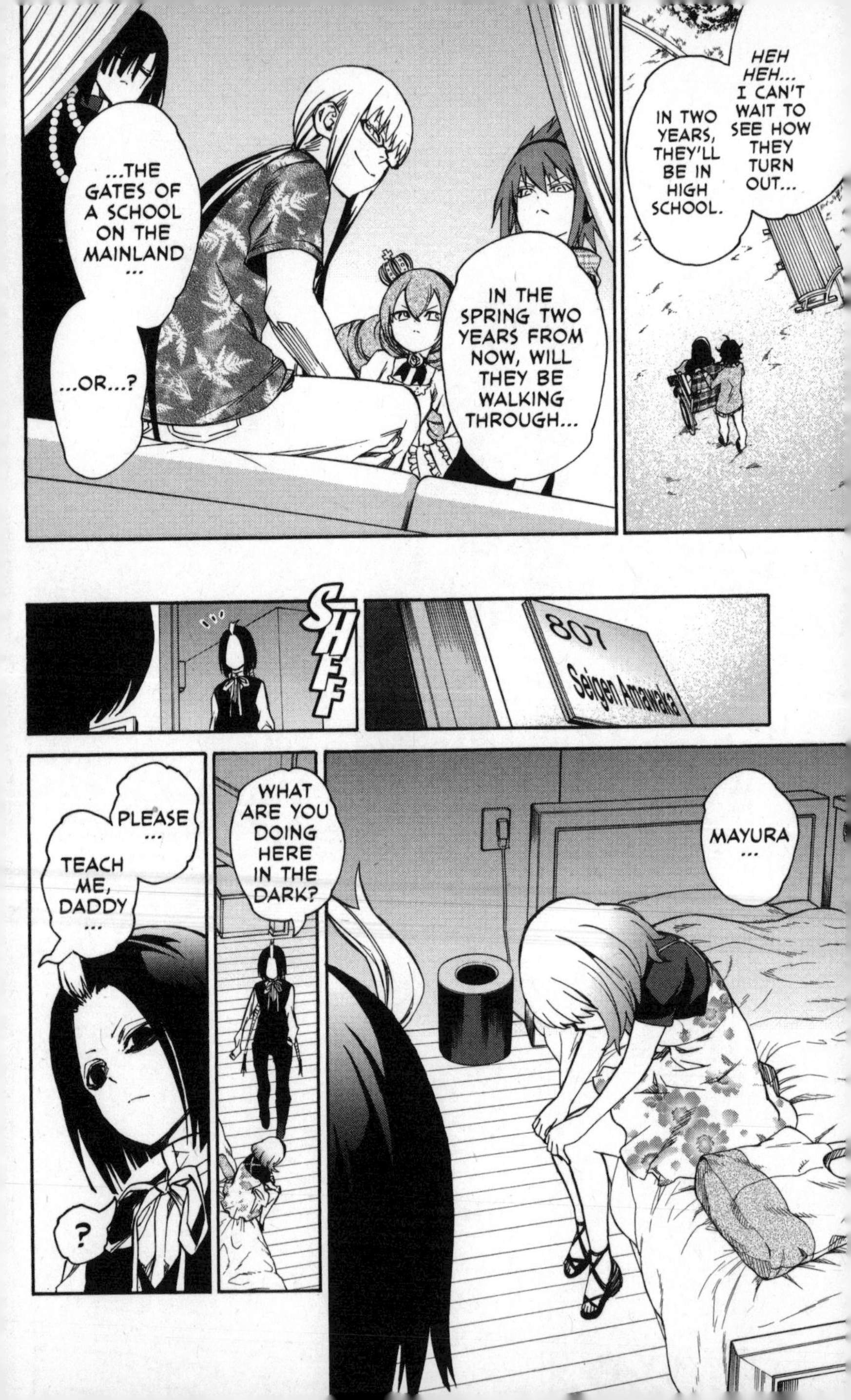
HEH HEH... I CAN'T WAIT TO SEE HOW THEY TURN OUT...
IN TWO YEARS, THEY'LL BE IN HIGH SCHOOL.
IN THE SPRING TWO YEARS FROM NOW, WILL THEY BE WALKING THROUGH...
...THE GATES OF A SCHOOL ON THE MAINLAND...
...OR...?
807
Seigen Amawaka
SHFF
MAYURA...
WHAT ARE YOU DOING HERE IN THE DARK?
PLEASE...
TEACH ME, DADDY...
?

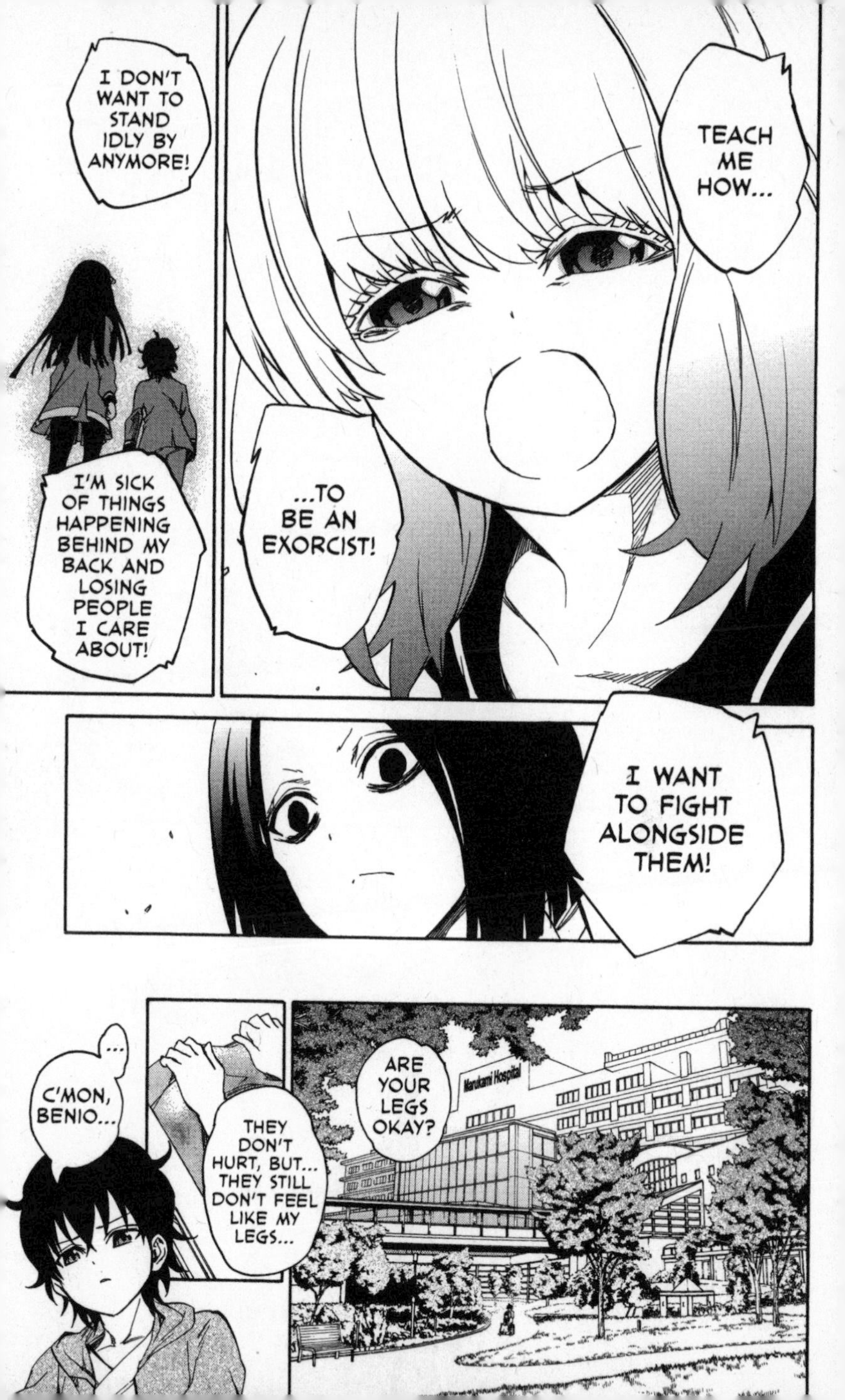
TEACH ME HOW...
...TO BE AN EXORCIST!
I DON'T WANT TO STAND IDLY BY ANYMORE!
I'M SICK OF THINGS HAPPENING BEHIND MY BACK AND LOSING PEOPLE I CARE ABOUT!
I WANT TO FIGHT ALONGSIDE THEM!
Marukami Hospital
ARE YOUR LEGS OKAY?
THEY DON'T HURT, BUT... THEY STILL DON'T FEEL LIKE MY LEGS...
...
C'MON, BENIO...

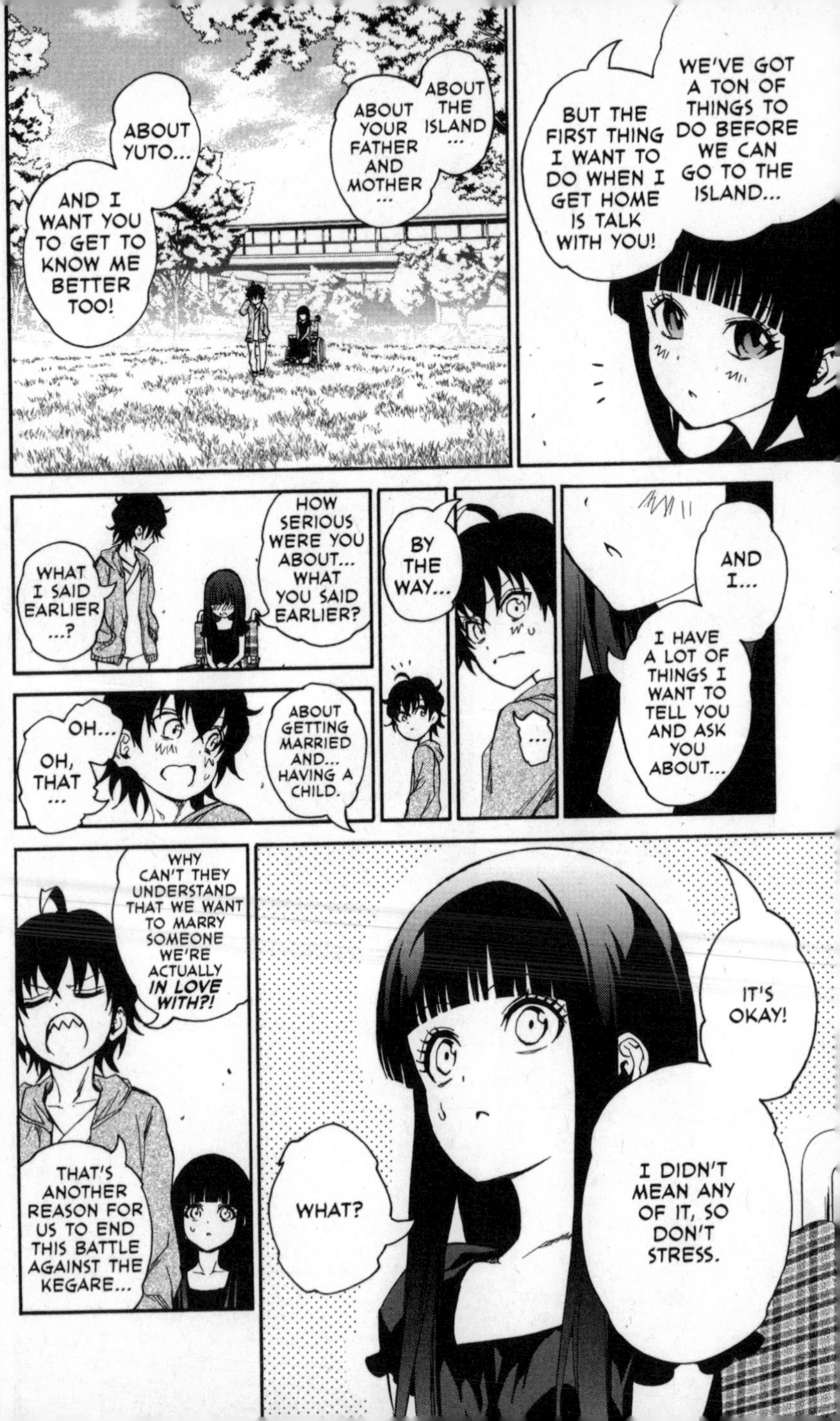
WE'VE GOT A TON OF THINGS TO DO BEFORE WE CAN GO TO THE ISLAND...
BUT THE FIRST THING I WANT TO DO WHEN I GET HOME IS TALK WITH YOU!
ABOUT THE ISLAND...
ABOUT YOUR FATHER AND MOTHER...
ABOUT YUTO...
AND I WANT YOU TO GET TO KNOW ME BETTER TOO!
AND I...
I HAVE A LOT OF THINGS I WANT TO TELL YOU AND ASK YOU ABOUT...
...
BY THE WAY...
HOW SERIOUS WERE YOU ABOUT... WHAT YOU SAID EARLIER?
WHAT I SAID EARLIER...?
ABOUT GETTING MARRIED AND... HAVING A CHILD.
OH...
OH, THAT...
IT'S OKAY!
I DIDN'T MEAN ANY OF IT, SO DON'T STRESS.
WHAT?
WHY CAN'T THEY UNDERSTAND THAT WE WANT TO MARRY SOMEONE WE'RE ACTUALLY *IN LOVE WITH?!*
THAT'S ANOTHER REASON FOR US TO END THIS BATTLE AGAINST THE KEGARE...

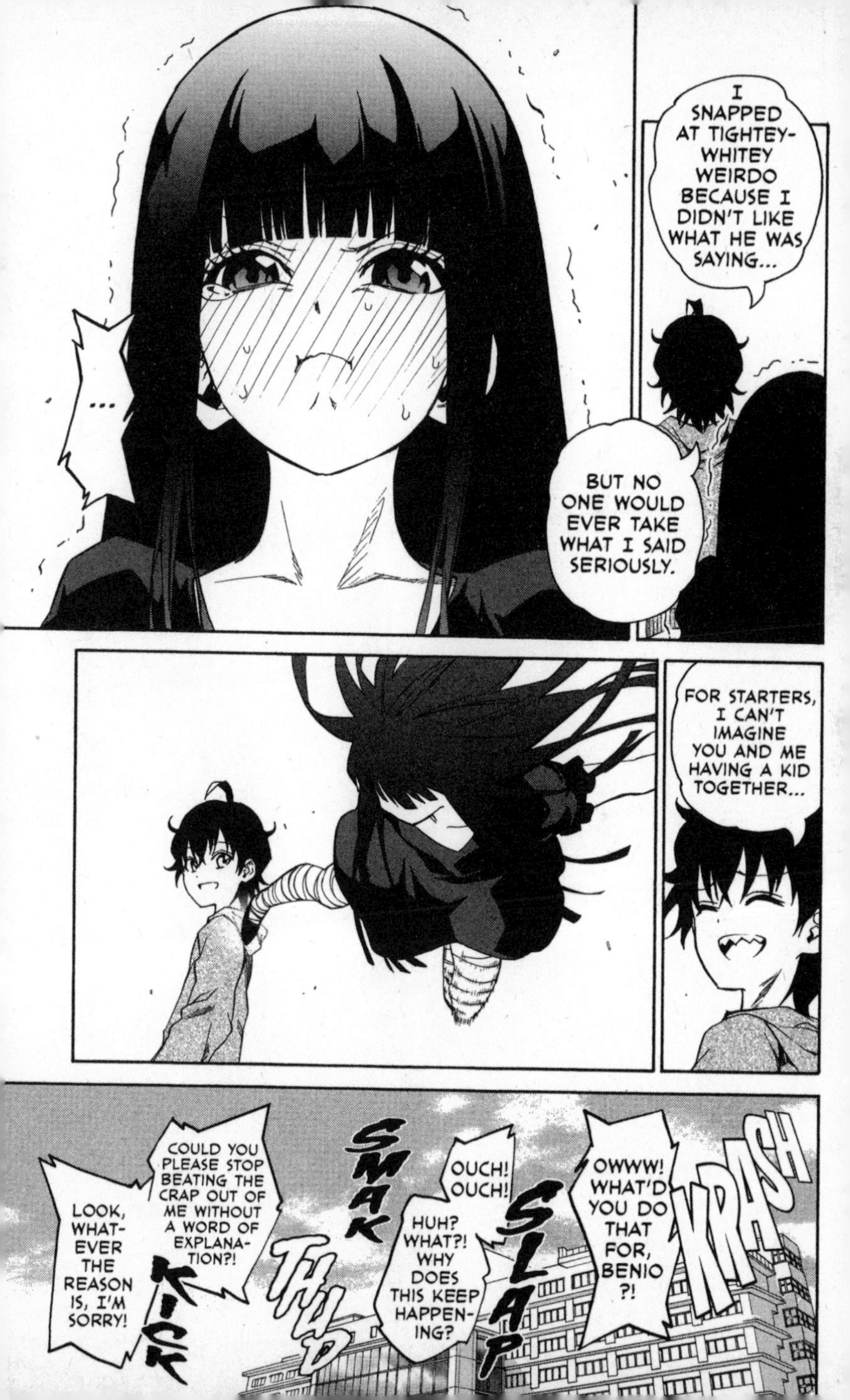
I SNAPPED AT TIGHTEY-WHITEY WEIRDO BECAUSE I DIDN'T LIKE WHAT HE WAS SAYING...
BUT NO ONE WOULD EVER TAKE WHAT I SAID SERIOUSLY.
...
FOR STARTERS, I CAN'T IMAGINE YOU AND ME HAVING A KID TOGETHER...
KRASH
OWWW! WHAT'D YOU DO THAT FOR, BENIO?!
SLAP
OUCH! OUCH!
HUH? WHAT?! WHY DOES THIS KEEP HAPPEN-ING?
SMAK
THUD
COULD YOU PLEASE STOP BEATING THE CRAP OUT OF ME WITHOUT A WORD OF EXPLANA-TION?!
KICK
LOOK, WHAT-EVER THE REASON IS, I'M SORRY!

# Column ⑫

## The Five Elements - Sojo & Sokoku

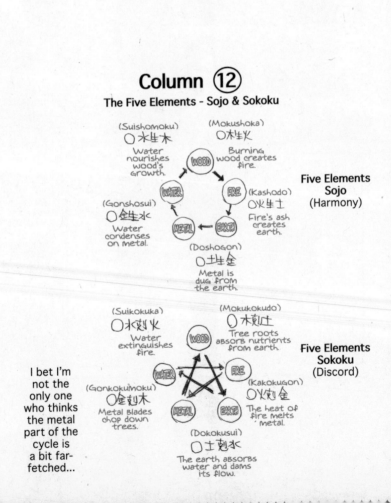

(Suishomoku)
○水生木
Water nourishes wood's growth.
(Mokushoka)
○木生火
Burning wood creates fire.
WOOD
FIRE
WATER
METAL
EARTH
(Kashodo)
○火生土
Fire's ash creates earth.
(Gonshosui)
○金生水
Water condenses on metal.
(Doshogon)
○土生金
Metal is dug from the earth.


**Five Elements Sojo**
(Harmony)

(Suikokuka)
○水剋火
Water extinguishes fire.
(Mokukokudo)
○木剋土
Tree roots absorb nutrients from earth.
WOOD
FIRE
WATER
METAL
EARTH
(Gonkokumoku)
○金剋木
Metal blades chop down trees.
(Kakokugon)
○火剋金
The heat of fire melts metal.
(Dokokusui)
○土剋水
The earth absorbs water and dams its flow.


**Five Elements Sokoku**
(Discord)

I bet I'm not the only one who thinks the metal part of the cycle is a bit far-fetched...

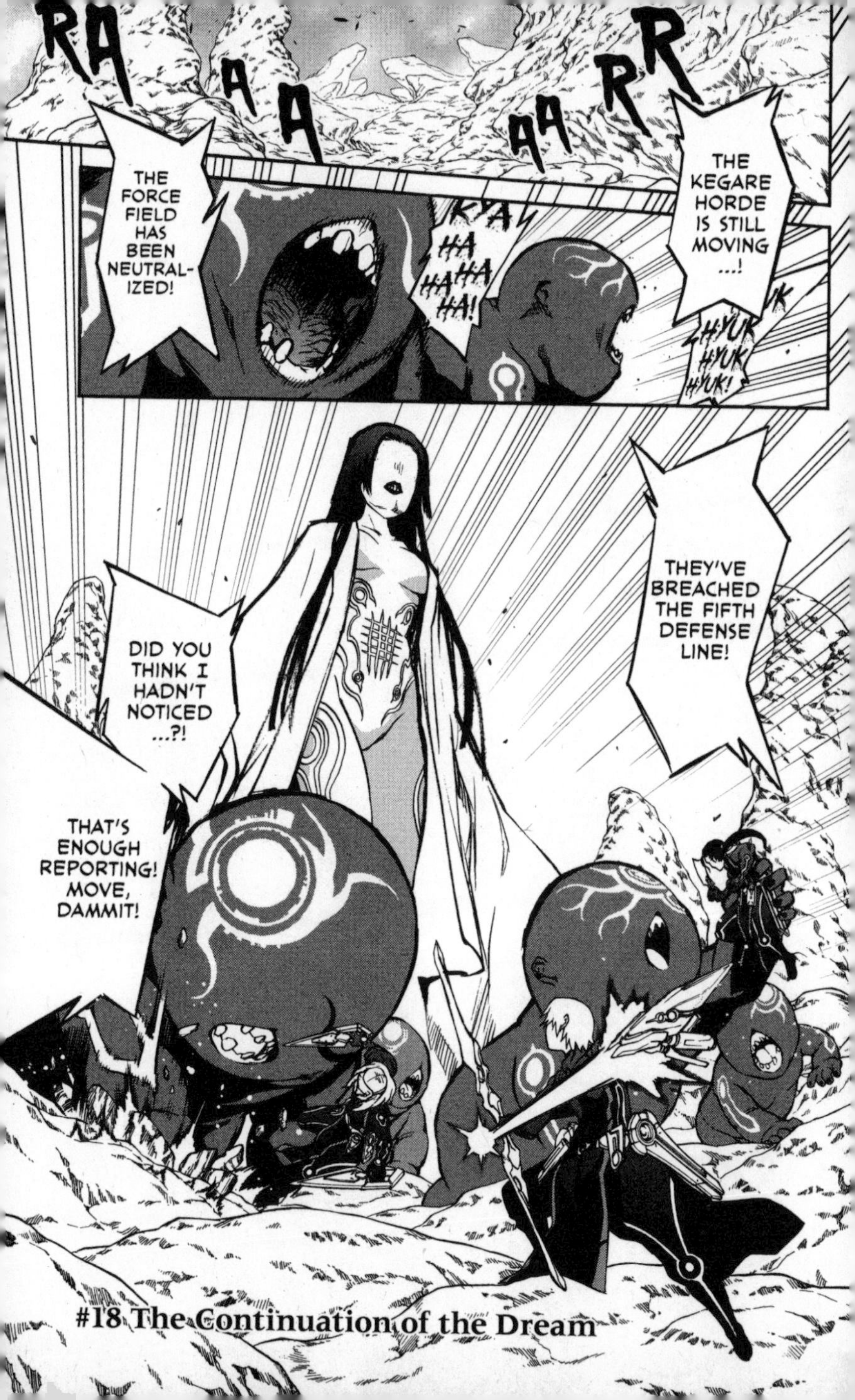
RAAAARRR
THE KEGARE HORDE IS STILL MOVING ...!
HYUK HYUK HYUK HYUK!
KYA HA HA HA HA!
THE FORCE FIELD HAS BEEN NEUTRAL-IZED!
THEY'VE BREACHED THE FIFTH DEFENSE LINE!
DID YOU THINK I HADN'T NOTICED ...?!
THAT'S ENOUGH REPORTING! MOVE, DAMMIT!

# #18 The Continuation of the Dream

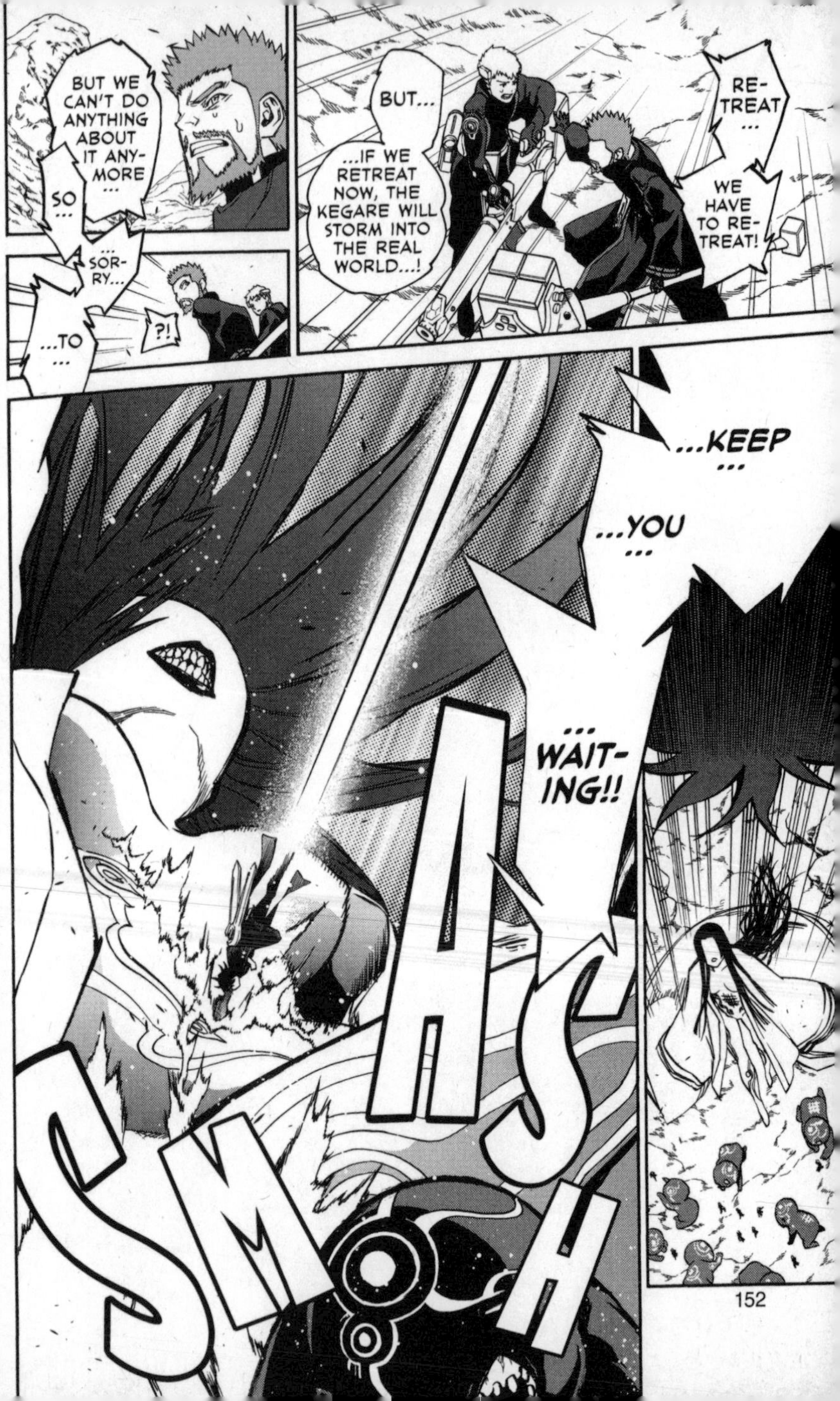
RE-TREAT...
WE HAVE TO RE-TREAT!
BUT...
...IF WE RETREAT NOW, THE KEGARE WILL STORM INTO THE REAL WORLD...!
BUT WE CAN'T DO ANYTHING ABOUT IT ANY-MORE...
SO...
...SOR-RY...
?!
...TO...
...KEEP...
...YOU...
...WAIT-ING!!
SMASH

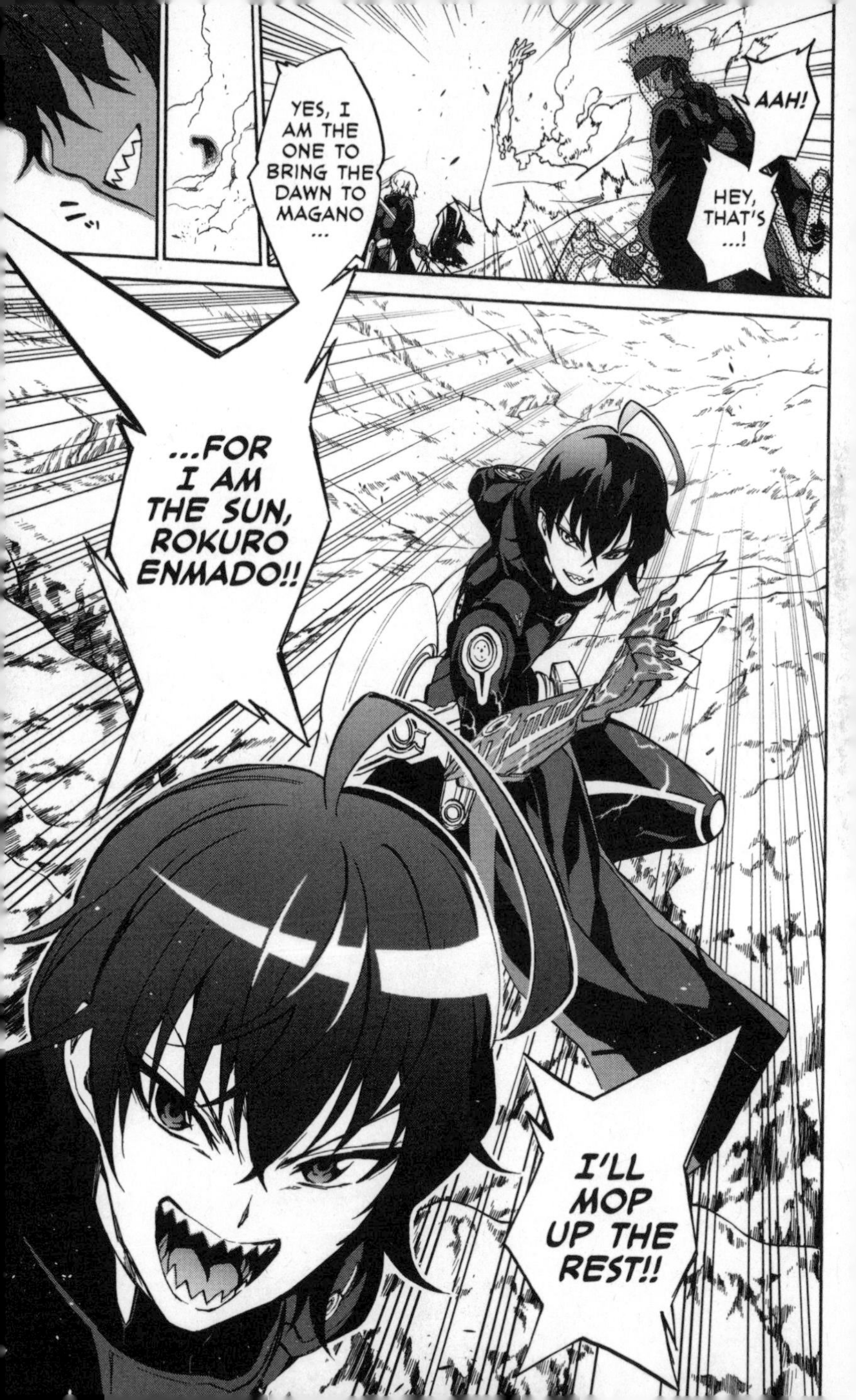
AAH!
HEY, THAT'S ...!
YES, I AM THE ONE TO BRING THE DAWN TO MAGANO ...
...FOR I AM THE SUN, ROKURO ENMADO!!
I'LL MOP UP THE REST!!

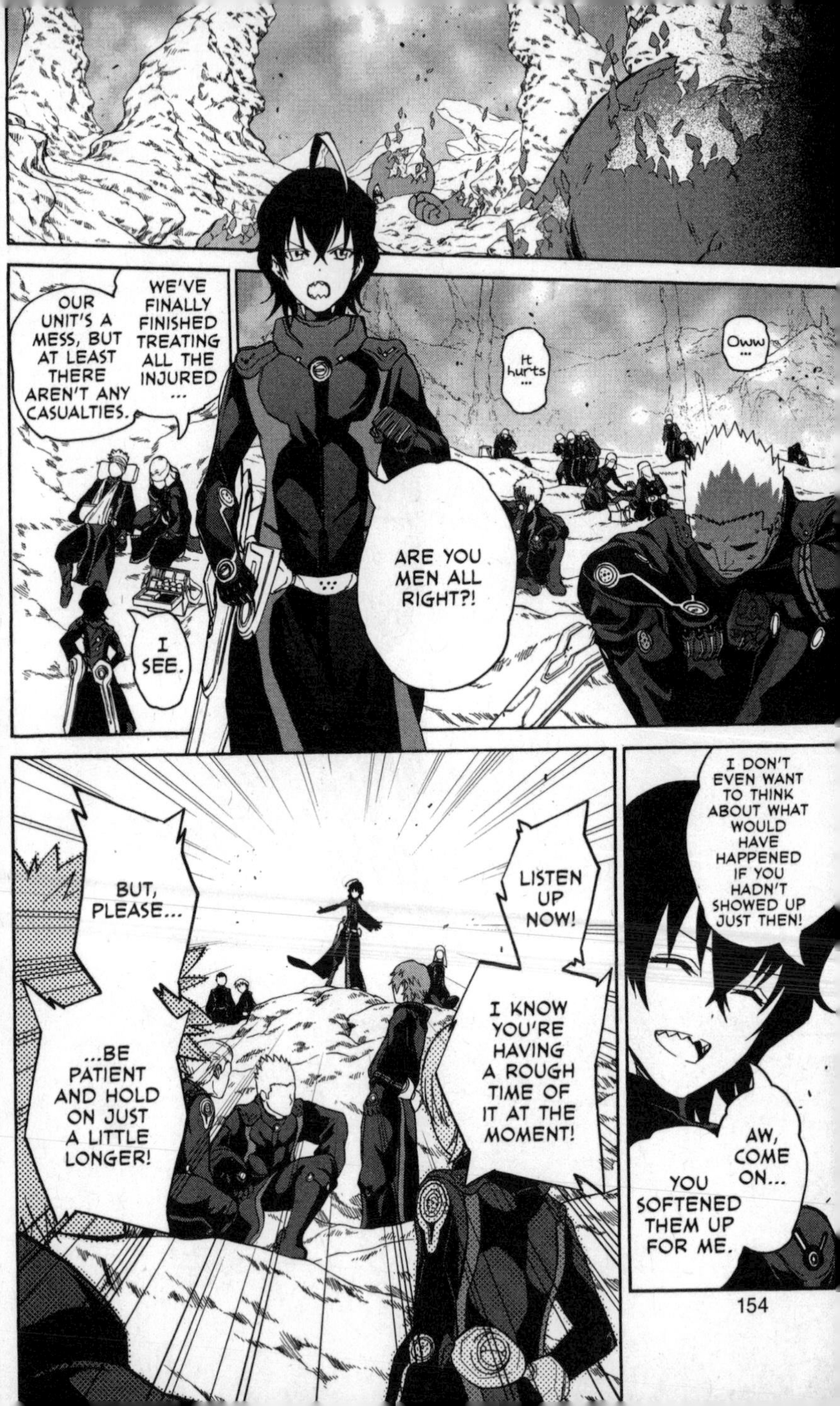
Oww...
It hurts...
ARE YOU MEN ALL RIGHT?!
WE'VE FINALLY FINISHED TREATING ALL THE INJURED...
OUR UNIT'S A MESS, BUT AT LEAST THERE AREN'T ANY CASUALTIES.
I SEE.
I DON'T EVEN WANT TO THINK ABOUT WHAT WOULD HAVE HAPPENED IF YOU HADN'T SHOWED UP JUST THEN!
AW, COME ON...
YOU SOFTENED THEM UP FOR ME.
LISTEN UP NOW!
I KNOW YOU'RE HAVING A ROUGH TIME OF IT AT THE MOMENT!
BUT, PLEASE...
...BE PATIENT AND HOLD ON JUST A LITTLE LONGER!

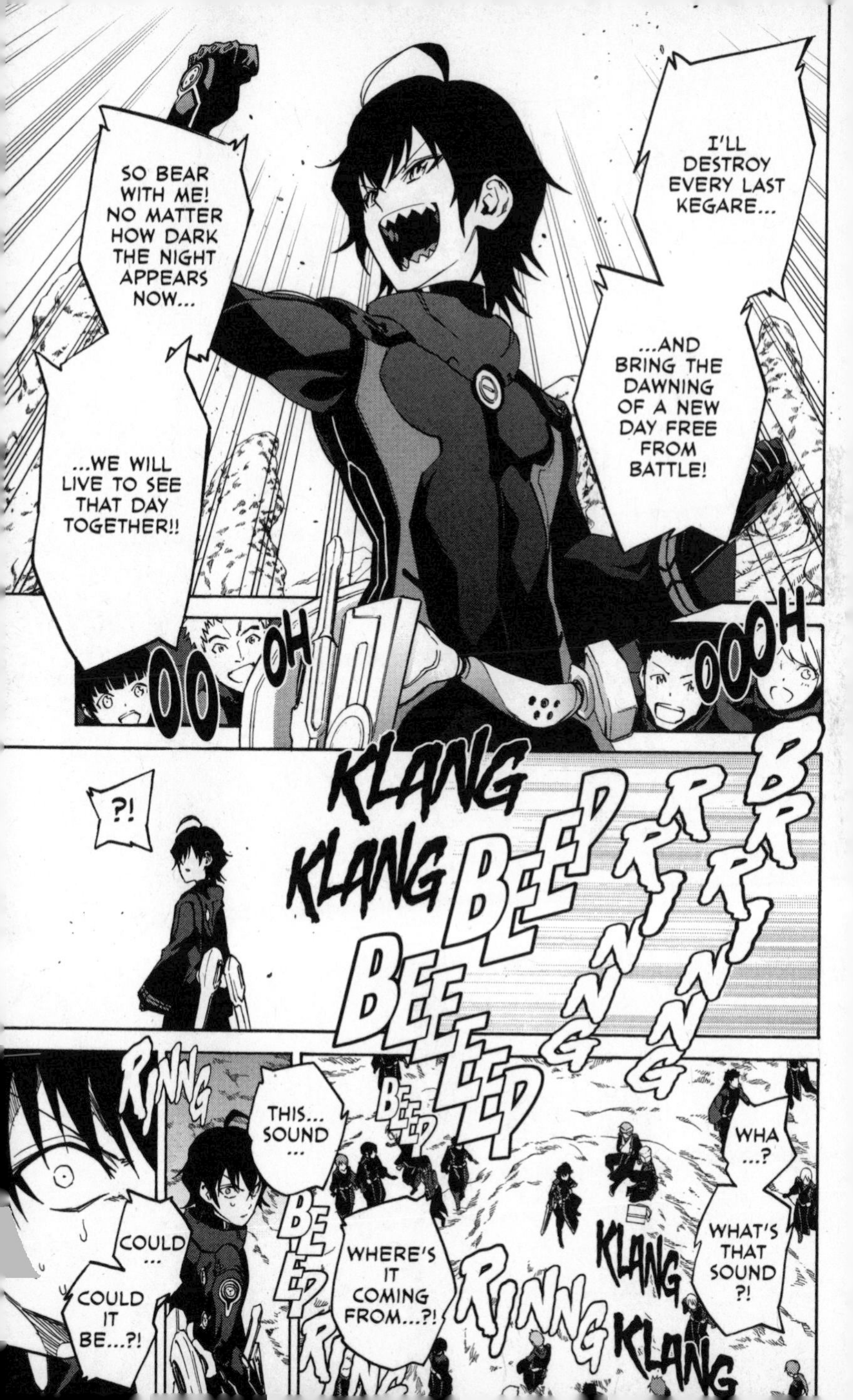
I'LL DESTROY EVERY LAST KEGARE...
...AND BRING THE DAWNING OF A NEW DAY FREE FROM BATTLE!
SO BEAR WITH ME! NO MATTER HOW DARK THE NIGHT APPEARS NOW...
...WE WILL LIVE TO SEE THAT DAY TOGETHER!!
OOOH
OOOH
BRRIIING
RRINNG
BEEP
BEEEEP
KLANG
KLANG
?!
WHA ...?
WHAT'S THAT SOUND ?!
KLANG
KLANG
RINNG
BEEP
WHERE'S IT COMING FROM...?!
BEEP
THIS... SOUND ...
RINNG
COULD ...
COULD IT BE...?!

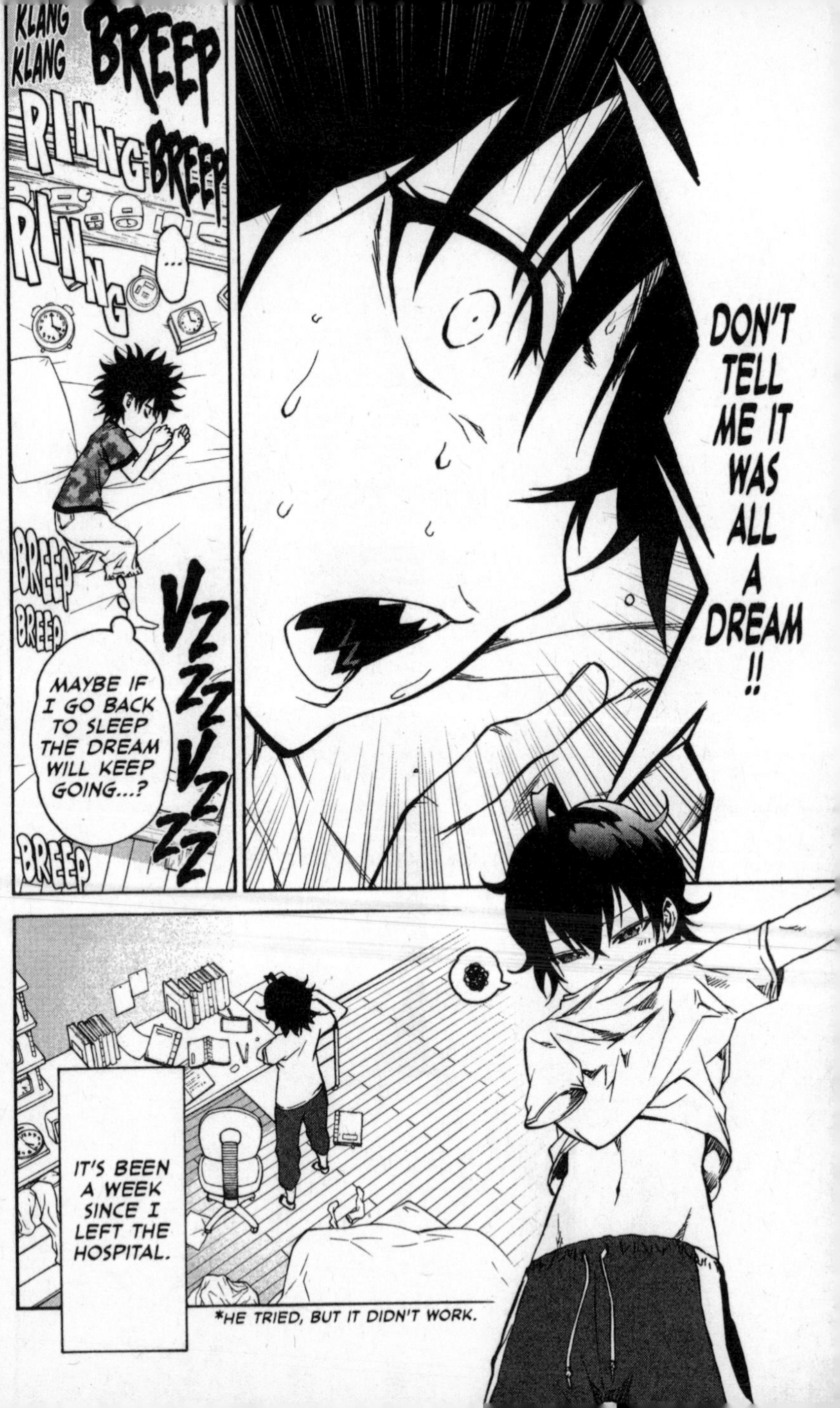
DON'T TELL ME IT WAS ALL A DREAM!!
KLANG KLANG
BREEP
RINNG
BREEP
RINNG
...
BREEP
BREEP
VZZZ VZZZ
MAYBE IF I GO BACK TO SLEEP THE DREAM WILL KEEP GOING...?
BREEP
IT'S BEEN A WEEK SINCE I LEFT THE HOSPITAL.
*HE TRIED, BUT IT DIDN'T WORK.

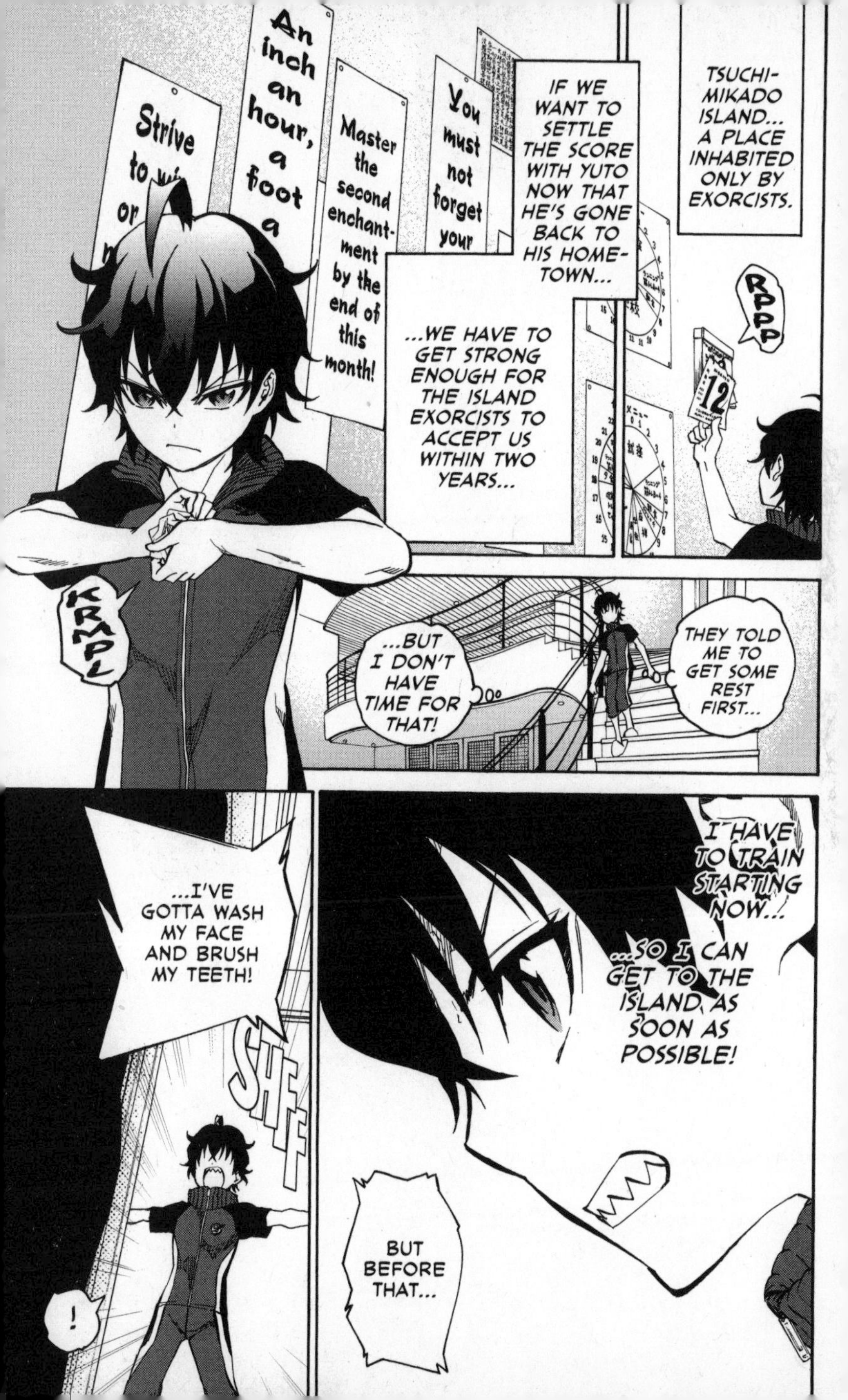
TSUCHIMIKADO ISLAND... A PLACE INHABITED ONLY BY EXORCISTS.
RPPP
IF WE WANT TO SETTLE THE SCORE WITH YUTO NOW THAT HE'S GONE BACK TO HIS HOMETOWN...
...WE HAVE TO GET STRONG ENOUGH FOR THE ISLAND EXORCISTS TO ACCEPT US WITHIN TWO YEARS...
You must not forget your
Master the second enchantment by the end of this month!
An inch an hour, a foot a
Strive
KRMPL
THEY TOLD ME TO GET SOME REST FIRST...
...BUT I DON'T HAVE TIME FOR THAT!
I HAVE TO TRAIN STARTING NOW...
...SO I CAN GET TO THE ISLAND AS SOON AS POSSIBLE!
BUT BEFORE THAT...
...I'VE GOTTA WASH MY FACE AND BRUSH MY TEETH!
SHFF
!

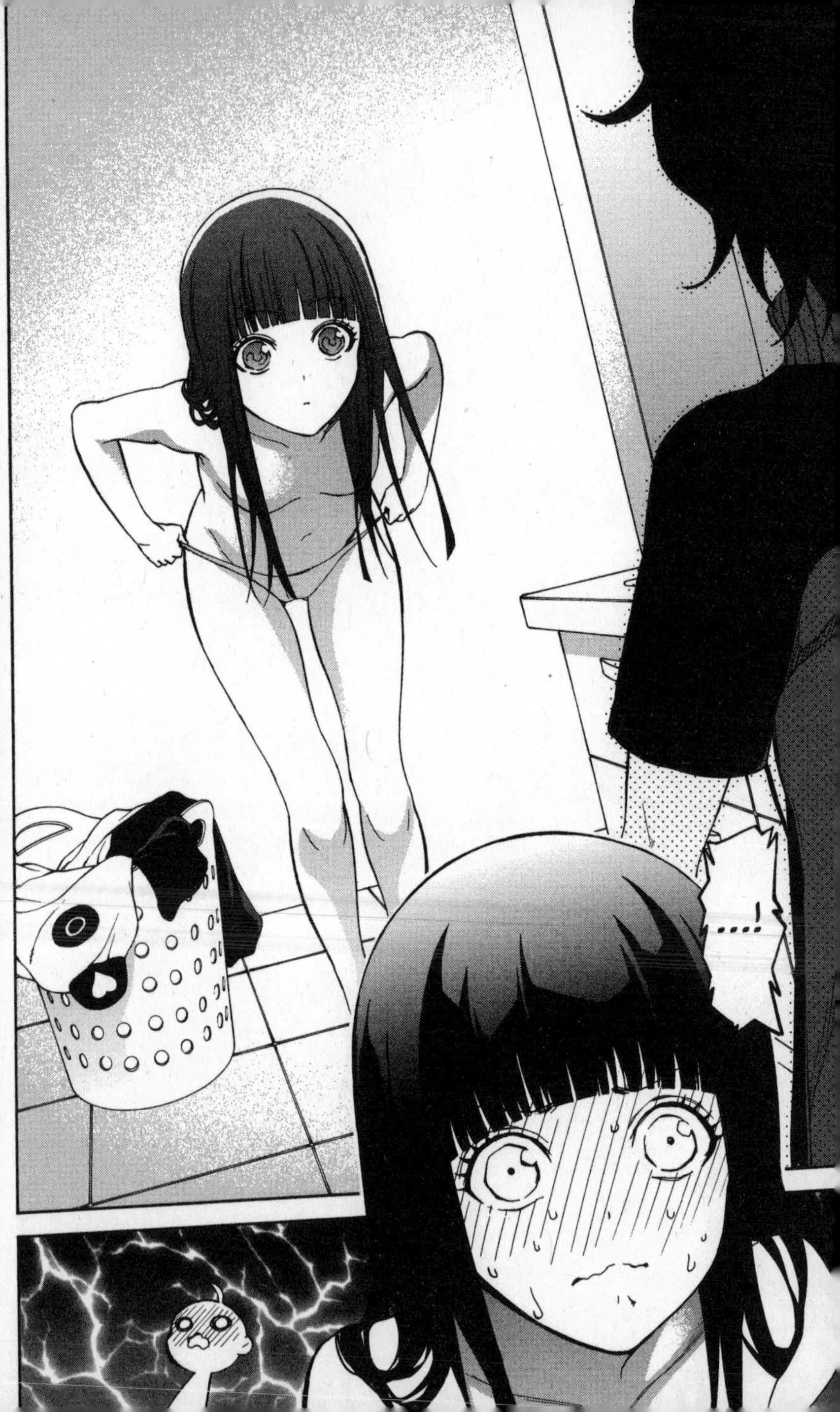
...!

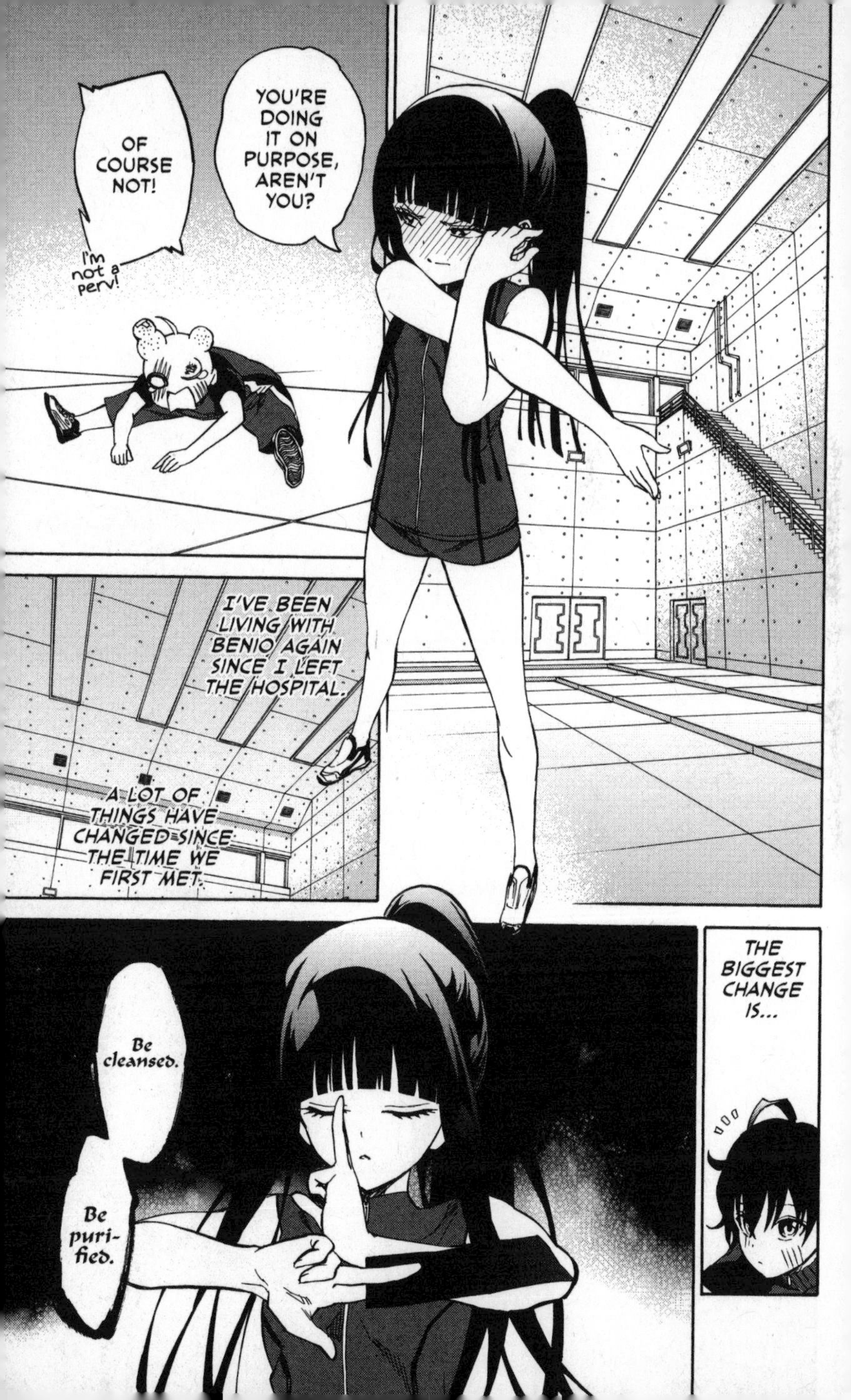
YOU'RE DOING IT ON PURPOSE, AREN'T YOU?
OF COURSE NOT!
I'm not a perv!
I'VE BEEN LIVING WITH BENIO AGAIN SINCE I LEFT THE HOSPITAL.
A LOT OF THINGS HAVE CHANGED SINCE THE TIME WE FIRST MET.
THE BIGGEST CHANGE IS...
Be cleansed.
Be puri-fied.

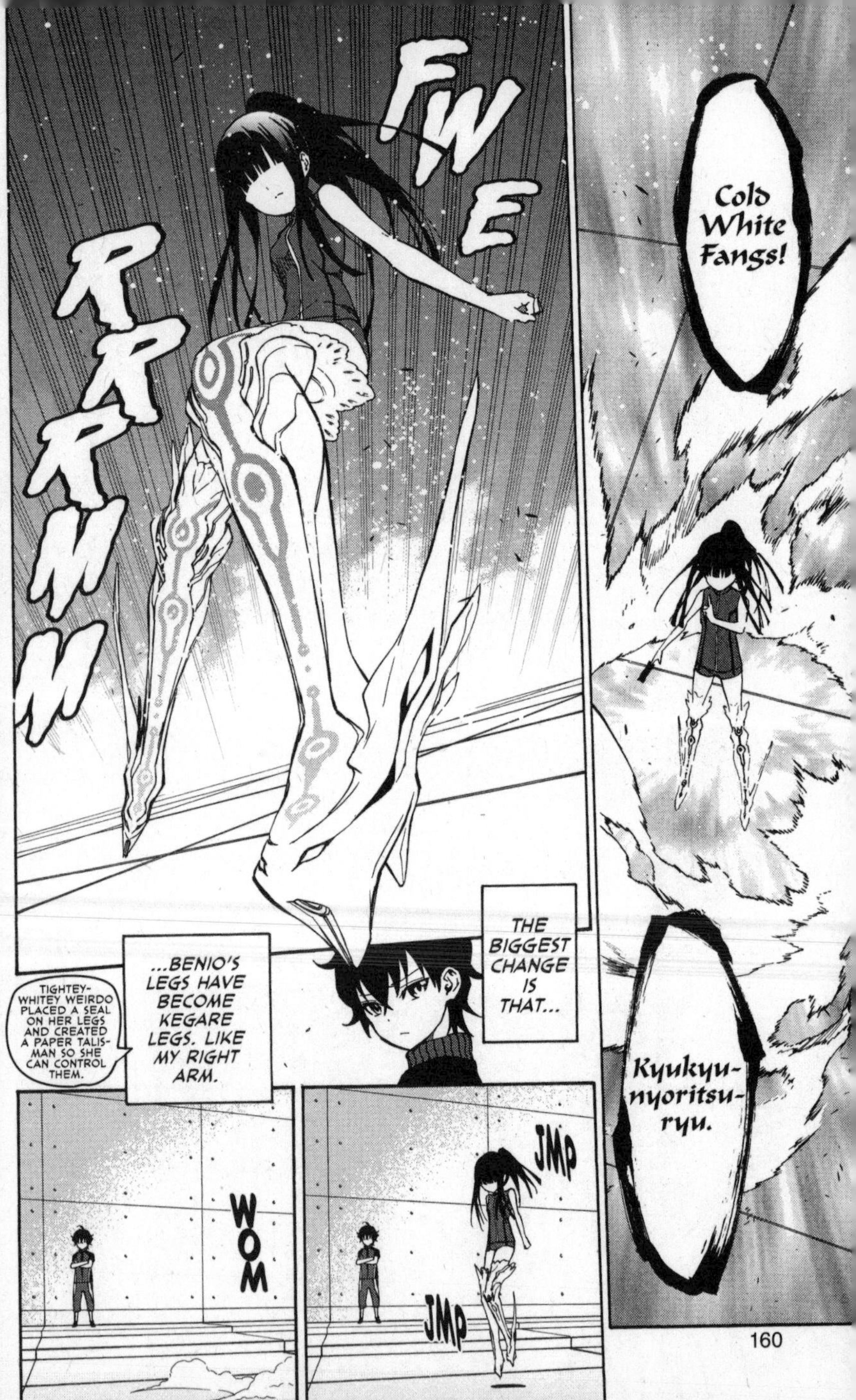
Cold White Fangs!
Kyukyu-nyoritsu-ryu.
FWE
RRRMM
THE BIGGEST CHANGE IS THAT...
...BENIO'S LEGS HAVE BECOME KEGARE LEGS. LIKE MY RIGHT ARM.
TIGHTEY-WHITEY WEIRDO PLACED A SEAL ON HER LEGS AND CREATED A PAPER TALISMAN SO SHE CAN CONTROL THEM.
JMP
JMP
WOM

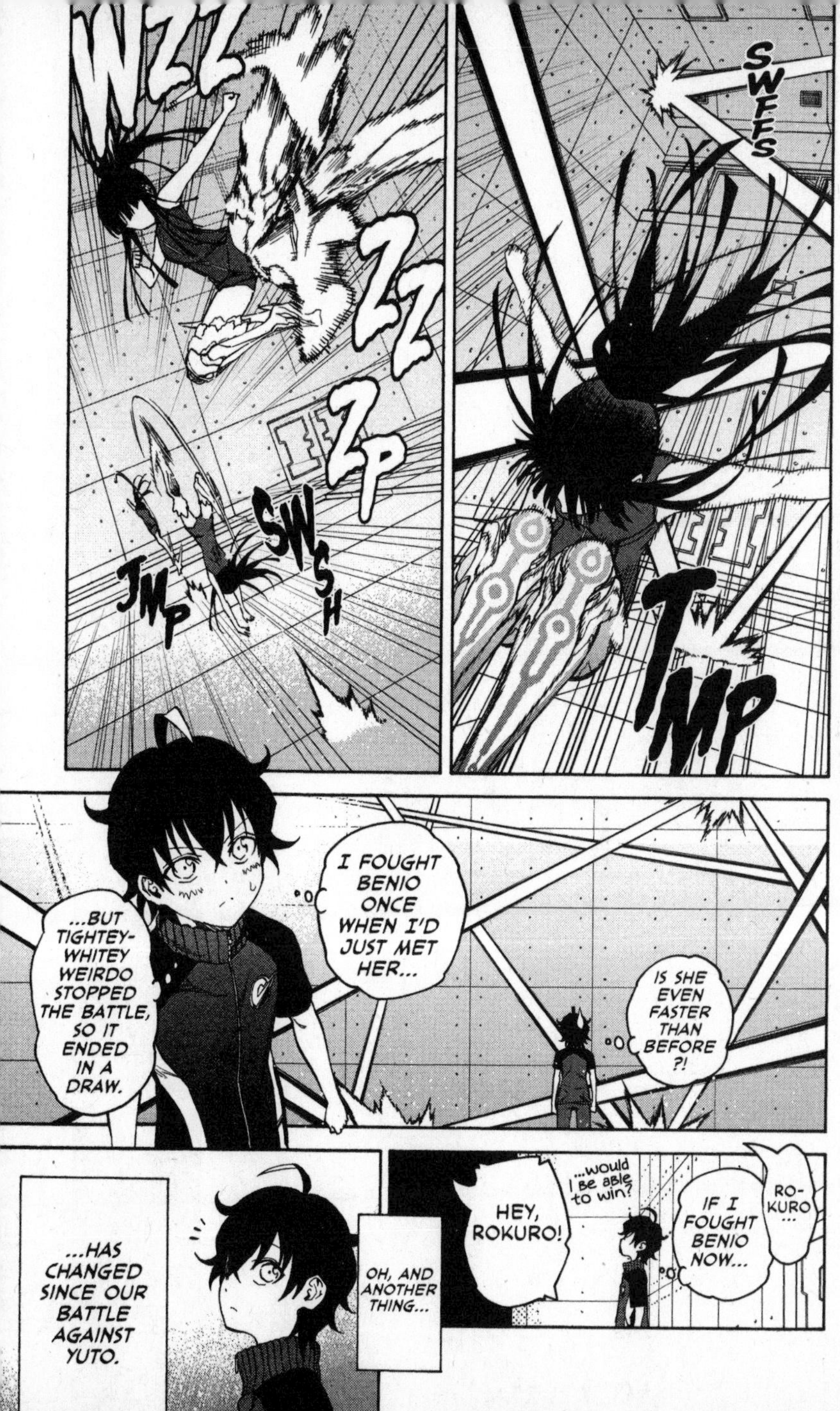
SWFFS
TMP
WZZ
ZZZP
SWSH
JMP
IS SHE EVEN FASTER THAN BEFORE?!
I FOUGHT BENIO ONCE WHEN I'D JUST MET HER...
...BUT TIGHTEY-WHITEY WEIRDO STOPPED THE BATTLE, SO IT ENDED IN A DRAW.
ROKURO...
IF I FOUGHT BENIO NOW...
...would I be able to win?
HEY, ROKURO!
OH, AND ANOTHER THING...
...HAS CHANGED SINCE OUR BATTLE AGAINST YUTO.

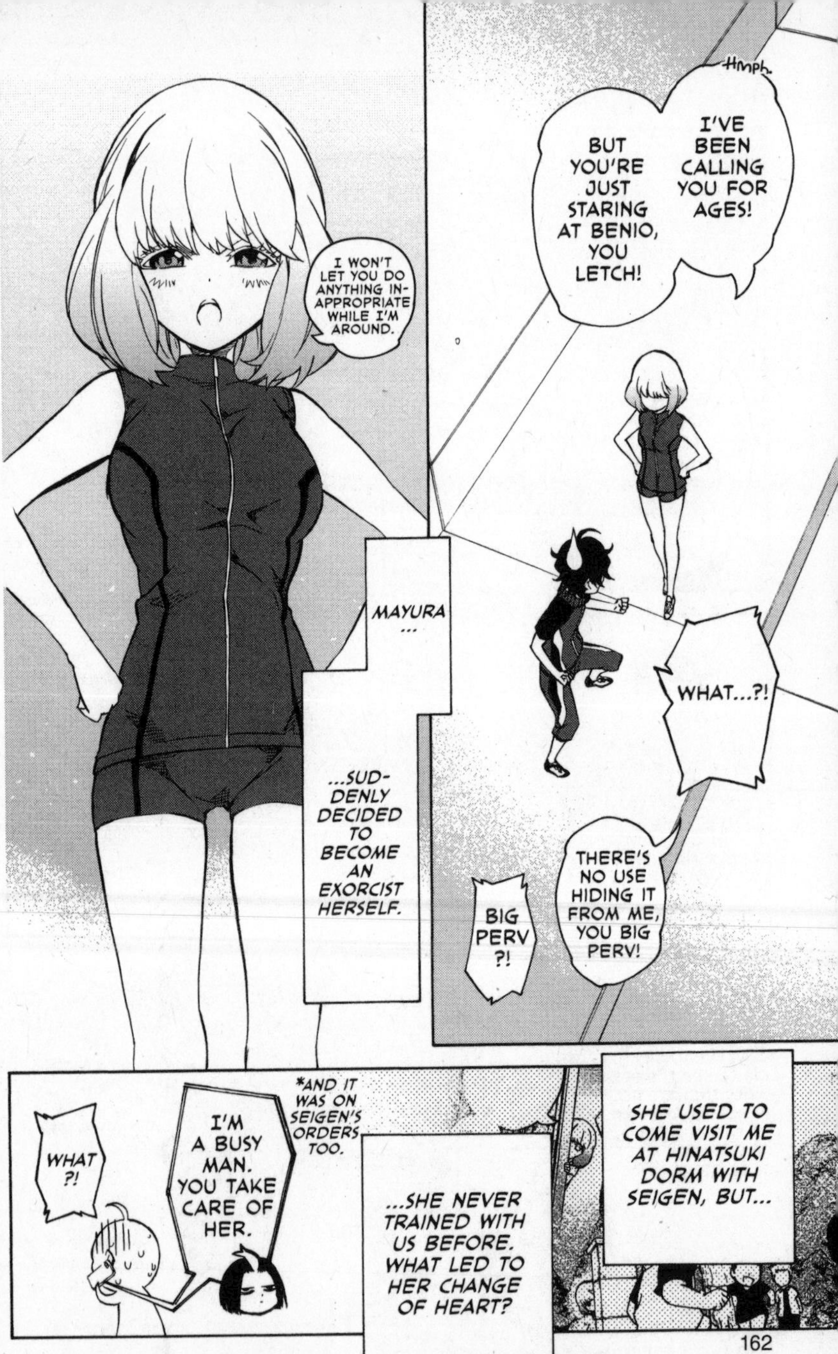
Hmph.
I'VE BEEN CALLING YOU FOR AGES!
BUT YOU'RE JUST STARING AT BENIO, YOU LETCH!
WHAT...?!
THERE'S NO USE HIDING IT FROM ME, YOU BIG PERV!
BIG PERV?!
I WON'T LET YOU DO ANYTHING IN-APPROPRIATE WHILE I'M AROUND.
MAYURA...
...SUD-DENLY DECIDED TO BECOME AN EXORCIST HERSELF.
SHE USED TO COME VISIT ME AT HINATSUKI DORM WITH SEIGEN, BUT...
...SHE NEVER TRAINED WITH US BEFORE. WHAT LED TO HER CHANGE OF HEART?
*AND IT WAS ON SEIGEN'S ORDERS TOO.
I'M A BUSY MAN. YOU TAKE CARE OF HER.
WHAT?!

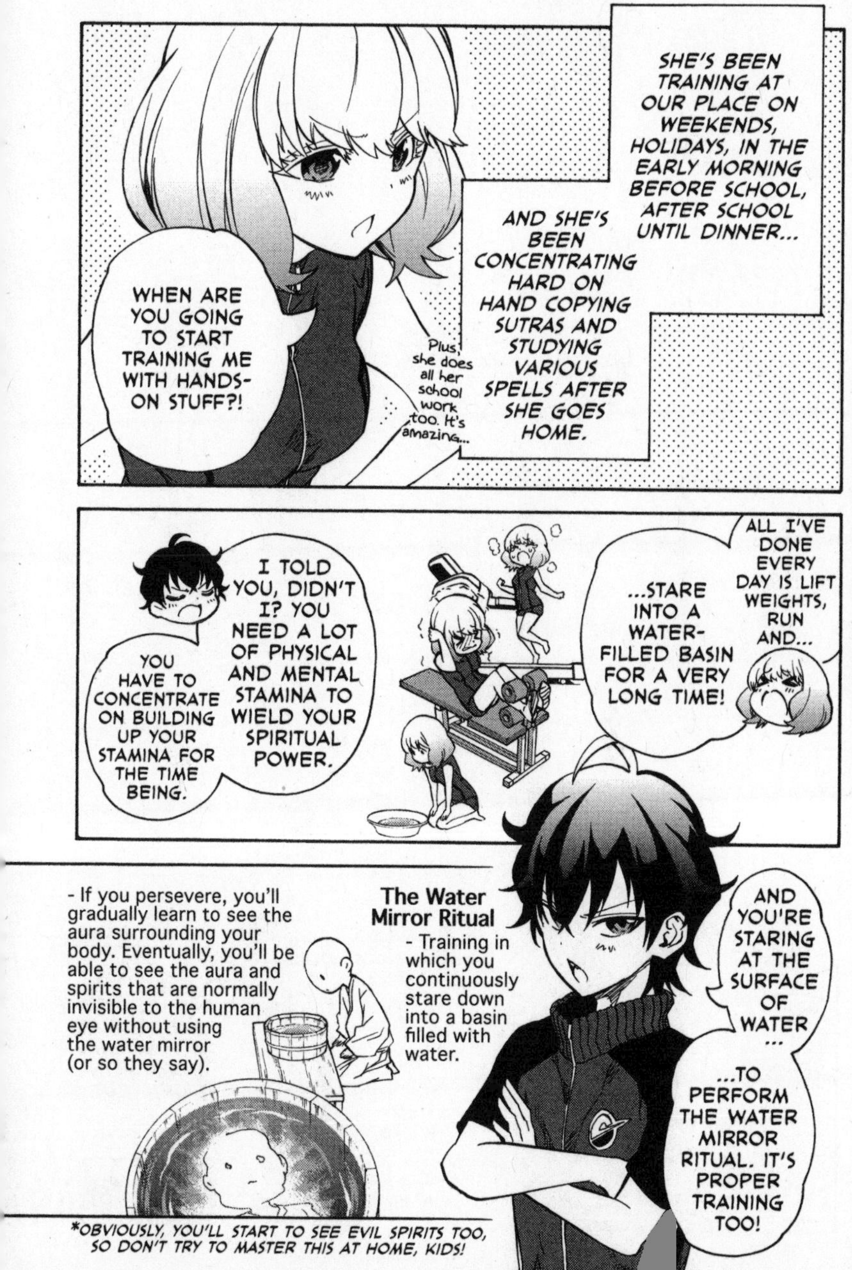
SHE'S BEEN TRAINING AT OUR PLACE ON WEEKENDS, HOLIDAYS, IN THE EARLY MORNING BEFORE SCHOOL, AFTER SCHOOL UNTIL DINNER...
AND SHE'S BEEN CONCENTRATING HARD ON HAND COPYING SUTRAS AND STUDYING VARIOUS SPELLS AFTER SHE GOES HOME.
Plus, she does all her school work too. It's amazing...
WHEN ARE YOU GOING TO START TRAINING ME WITH HANDS-ON STUFF?!
ALL I'VE DONE EVERY DAY IS LIFT WEIGHTS, RUN AND...
...STARE INTO A WATER-FILLED BASIN FOR A VERY LONG TIME!
I TOLD YOU, DIDN'T I? YOU NEED A LOT OF PHYSICAL AND MENTAL STAMINA TO WIELD YOUR SPIRITUAL POWER.
YOU HAVE TO CONCENTRATE ON BUILDING UP YOUR STAMINA FOR THE TIME BEING.
AND YOU'RE STARING AT THE SURFACE OF WATER...
...TO PERFORM THE WATER MIRROR RITUAL. IT'S PROPER TRAINING TOO!
The Water Mirror Ritual
- Training in which you continuously stare down into a basin filled with water.
- If you persevere, you'll gradually learn to see the aura surrounding your body. Eventually, you'll be able to see the aura and spirits that are normally invisible to the human eye without using the water mirror (or so they say).
*OBVIOUSLY, YOU'LL START TO SEE EVIL SPIRITS TOO, SO DON'T TRY TO MASTER THIS AT HOME, KIDS!

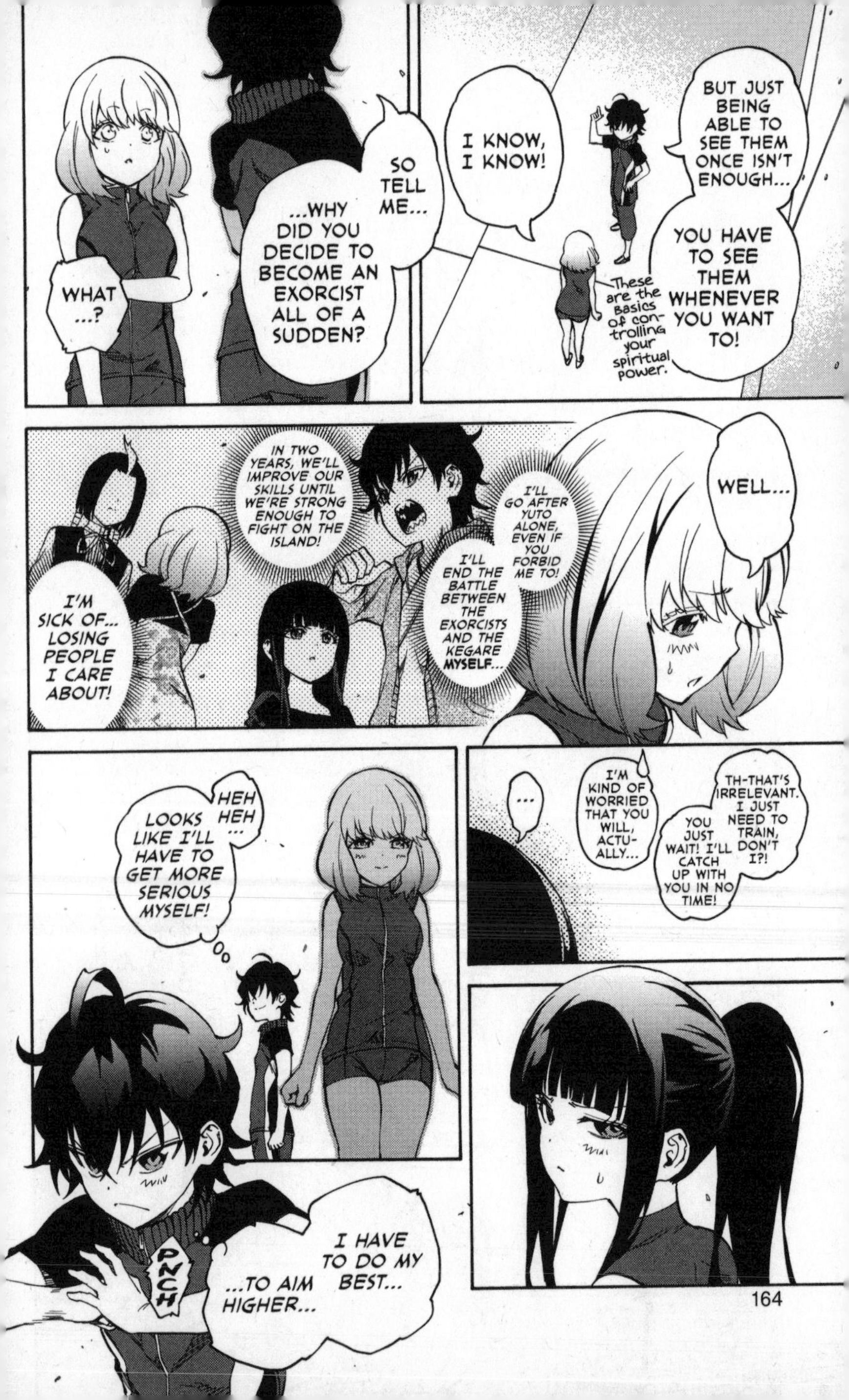
BUT JUST BEING ABLE TO SEE THEM ONCE ISN'T ENOUGH...
YOU HAVE TO SEE THEM WHENEVER YOU WANT TO!
These are the Basics of controlling your spiritual power.
I KNOW, I KNOW!
SO TELL ME...
...WHY DID YOU DECIDE TO BECOME AN EXORCIST ALL OF A SUDDEN?
WHAT ...?
WELL...
I'LL GO AFTER YUTO ALONE, EVEN IF YOU FORBID ME TO!
I'LL END THE BATTLE BETWEEN THE EXORCISTS AND THE KEGARE MYSELF...
IN TWO YEARS, WE'LL IMPROVE OUR SKILLS UNTIL WE'RE STRONG ENOUGH TO FIGHT ON THE ISLAND!
I'M SICK OF... LOSING PEOPLE I CARE ABOUT!
TH-THAT'S IRRELEVANT. I JUST NEED TO TRAIN, DON'T I?!
YOU JUST WAIT! I'LL CATCH UP WITH YOU IN NO TIME!
I'M KIND OF WORRIED THAT YOU WILL, ACTU-ALLY...
...
HEH HEH ...
LOOKS LIKE I'LL HAVE TO GET MORE SERIOUS MYSELF!
I HAVE TO DO MY BEST...
...TO AIM HIGHER...
PNCH

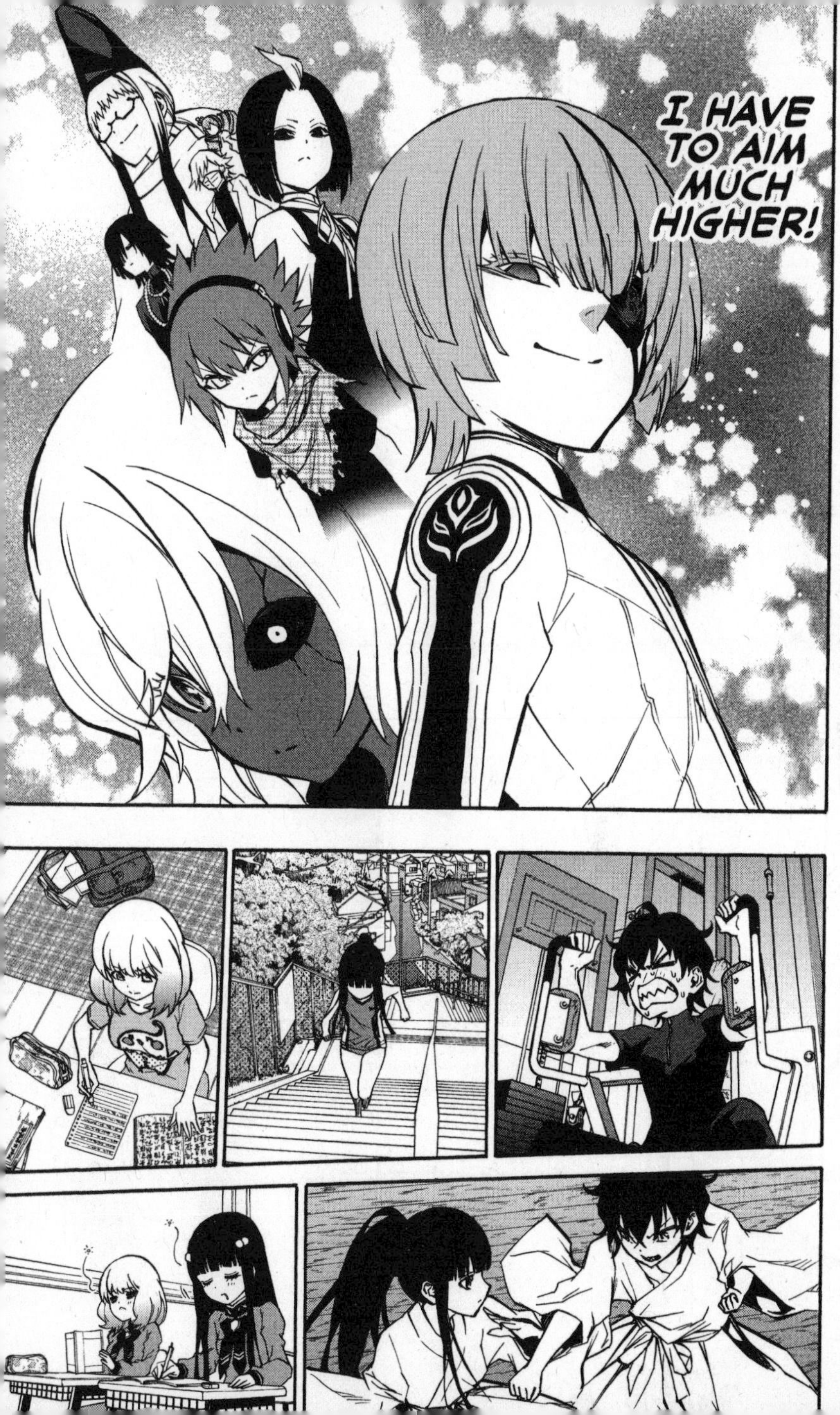
I HAVE TO AIM MUCH HIGHER!

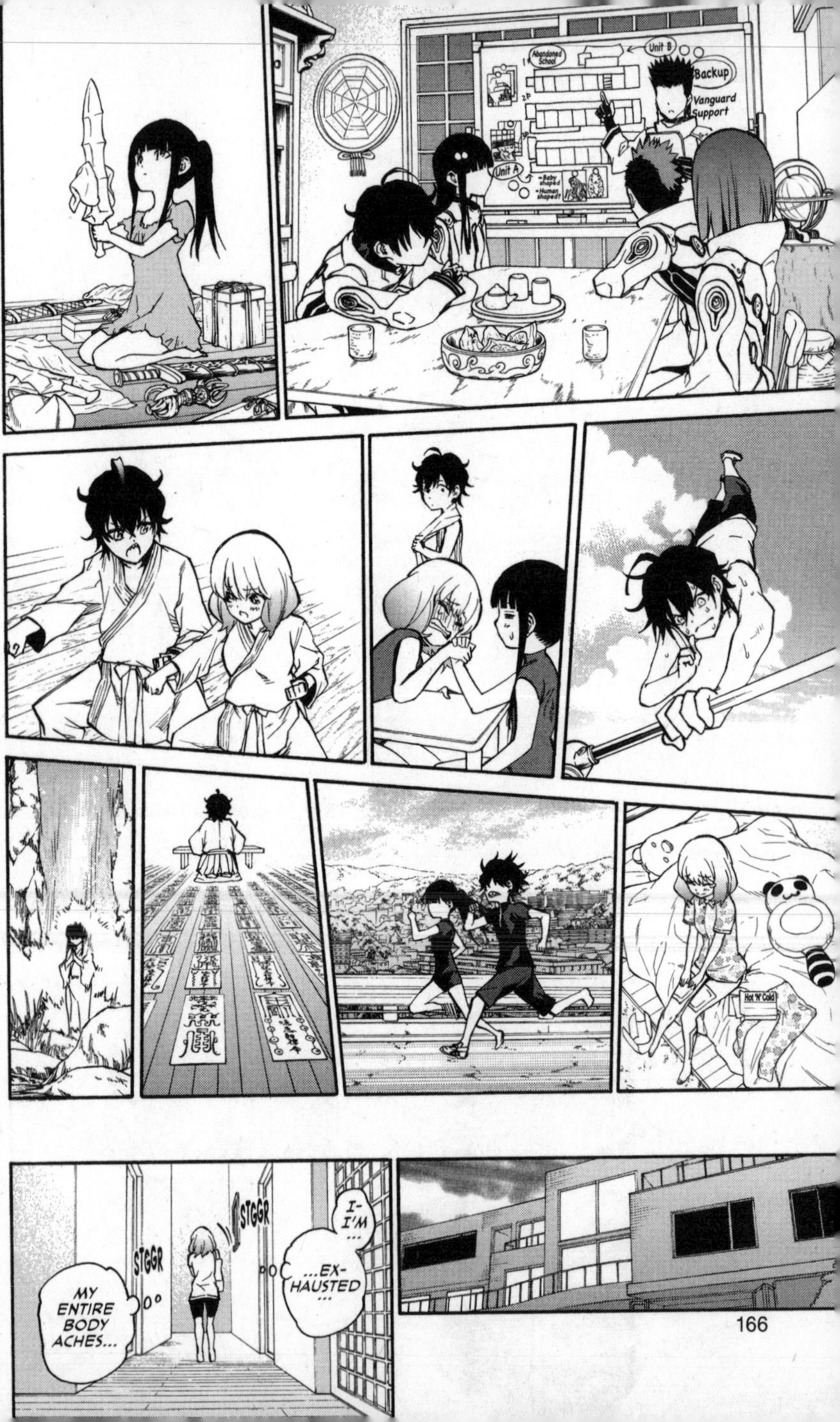
Abandoned School
Unit B
Backup
Vanguard
Support
Unit A
-Baby shaped
-Human shaped?
Hot 'N' Cold
I- I'M...
STGGR
...EX- HAUSTED...
STGGR
MY ENTIRE BODY ACHES...

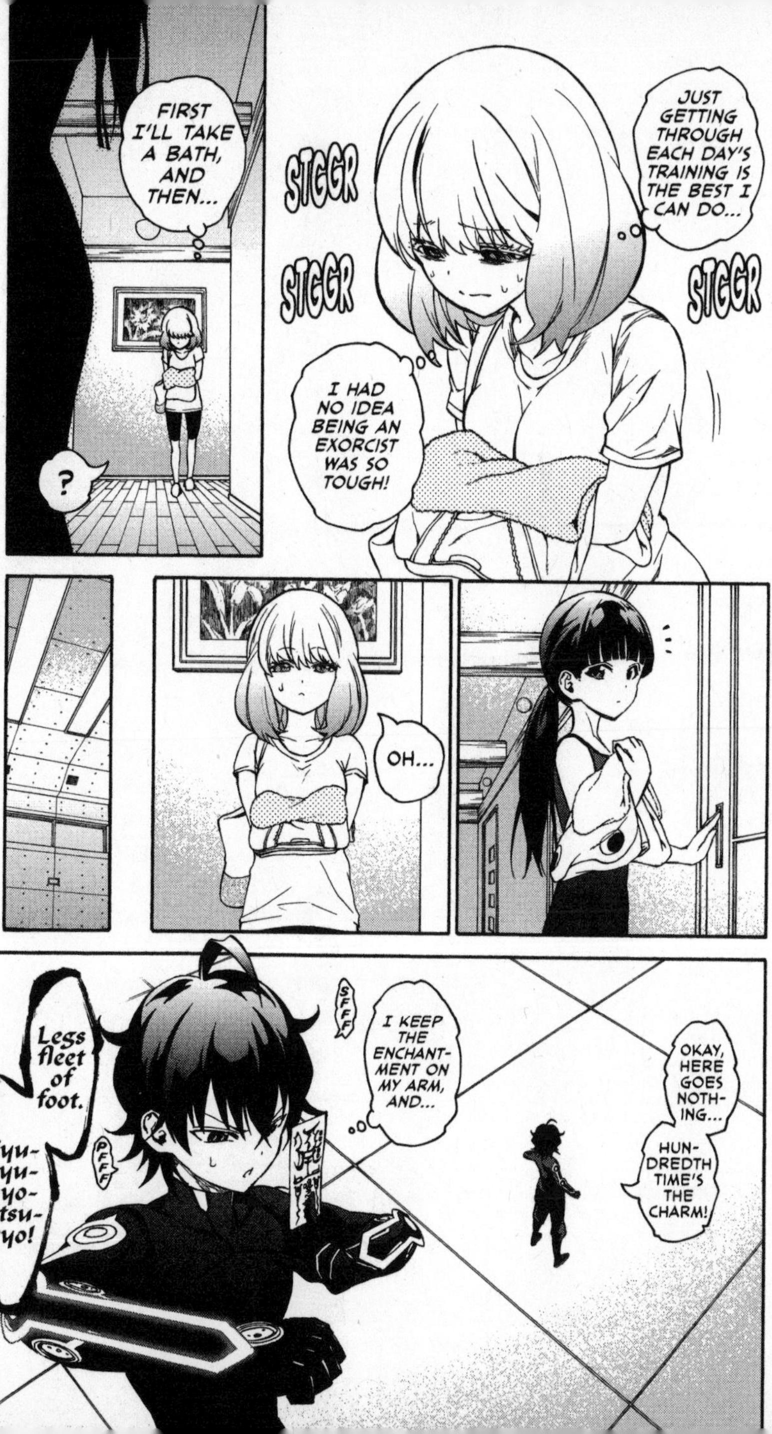
JUST GETTING THROUGH EACH DAY'S TRAINING IS THE BEST I CAN DO...
STGGR
STGGR
STGGR
I HAD NO IDEA BEING AN EXORCIST WAS SO TOUGH!
FIRST I'LL TAKE A BATH, AND THEN...
?
OH...
OKAY, HERE GOES NOTHING...
HUNDREDTH TIME'S THE CHARM!
I KEEP THE ENCHANTMENT ON MY ARM, AND...
SFFF
PFFF
Legs fleet of foot.
Kyukyunyoritsuryo!

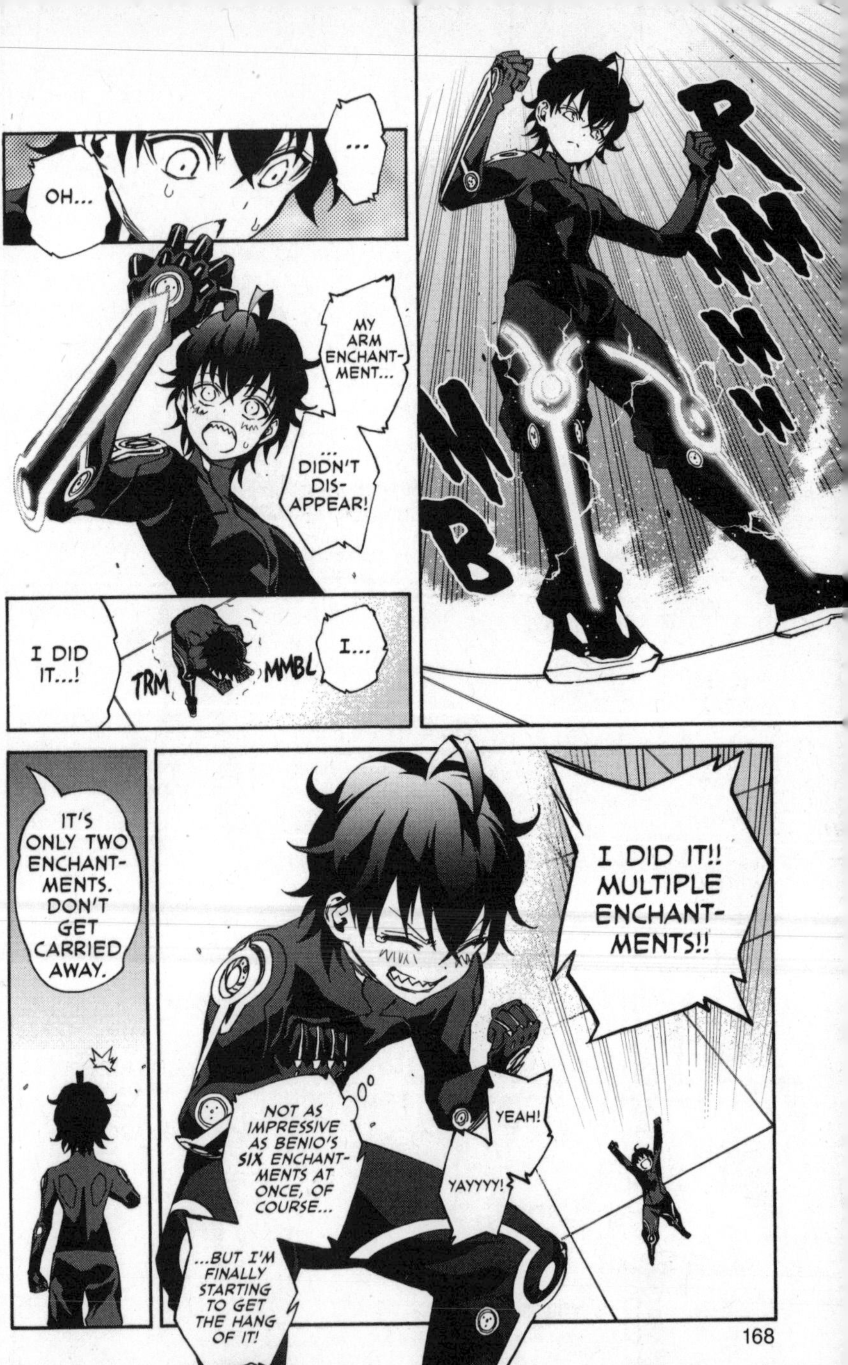
RMMMM
MMB
...
OH...
MY ARM ENCHANTMENT...
...DIDN'T DISAPPEAR!
I...
MMBL
TRM
I DID IT...!
I DID IT!! MULTIPLE ENCHANTMENTS!!
YEAH!
YAYYYY!
NOT AS IMPRESSIVE AS BENIO'S **SIX** ENCHANTMENTS AT ONCE, OF COURSE...
...BUT I'M FINALLY STARTING TO GET THE HANG OF IT!
IT'S ONLY TWO ENCHANTMENTS. DON'T GET CARRIED AWAY.

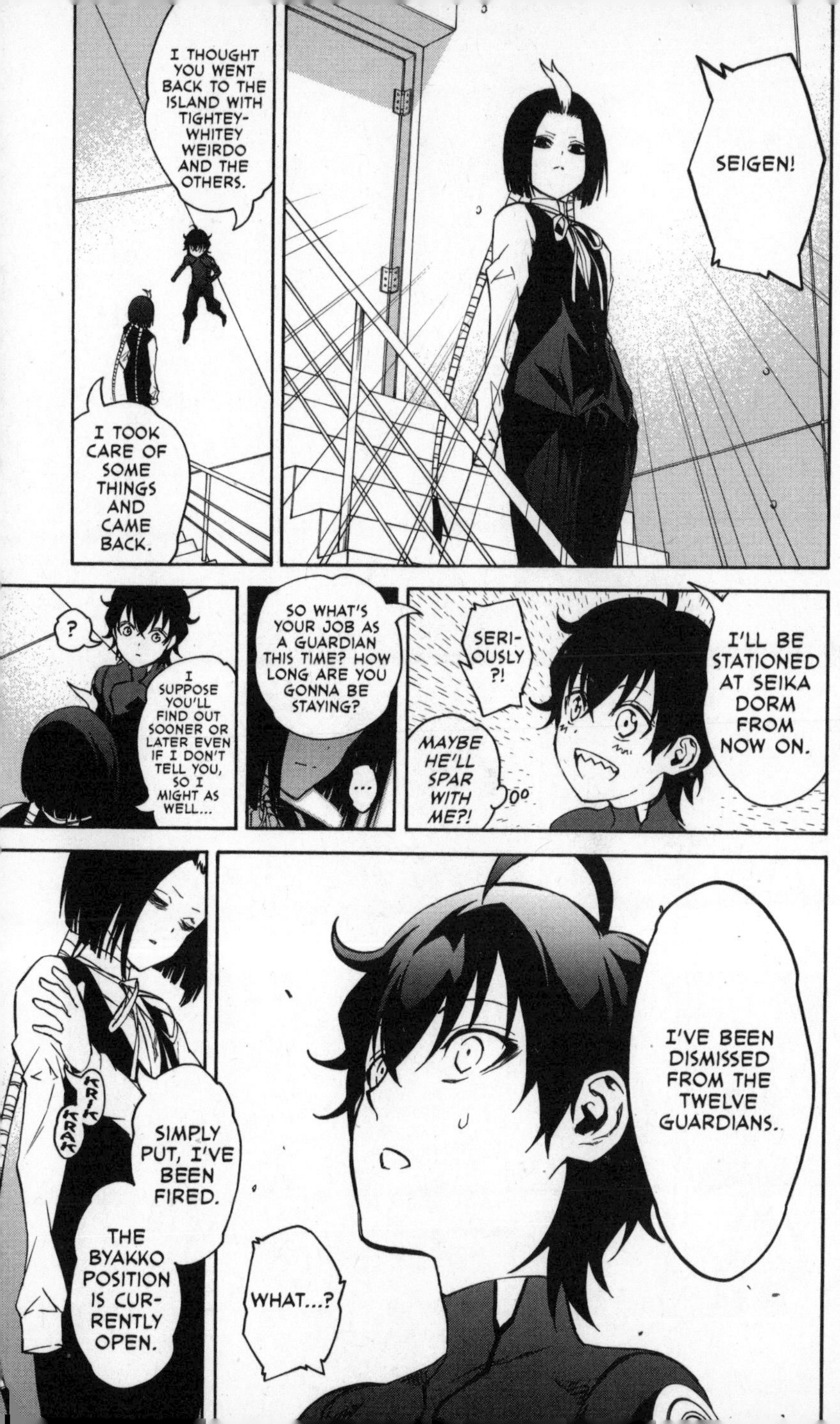
SEIGEN!
I THOUGHT YOU WENT BACK TO THE ISLAND WITH TIGHTEY-WHITEY WEIRDO AND THE OTHERS.
I TOOK CARE OF SOME THINGS AND CAME BACK.
I'LL BE STATIONED AT SEIKA DORM FROM NOW ON.
SERIOUSLY?!
MAYBE HE'LL SPAR WITH ME?!
SO WHAT'S YOUR JOB AS A GUARDIAN THIS TIME? HOW LONG ARE YOU GONNA BE STAYING?
...
?
I SUPPOSE YOU'LL FIND OUT SOONER OR LATER EVEN IF I DON'T TELL YOU, SO I MIGHT AS WELL...
I'VE BEEN DISMISSED FROM THE TWELVE GUARDIANS.
WHAT...?
KRIK
KRAK
SIMPLY PUT, I'VE BEEN FIRED.
THE BYAKKO POSITION IS CURRENTLY OPEN.

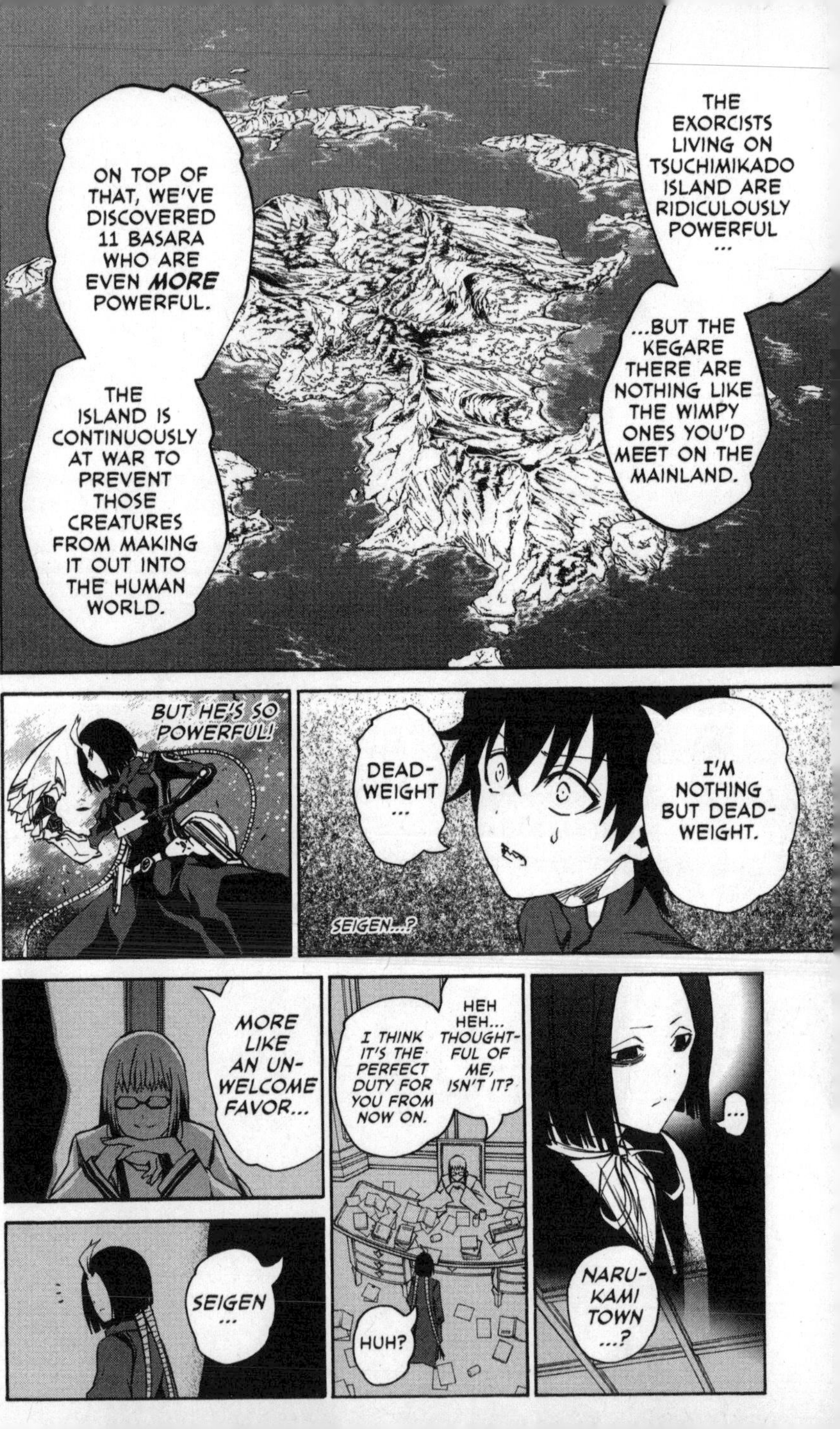
THE EXORCISTS LIVING ON TSUCHIMIKADO ISLAND ARE RIDICULOUSLY POWERFUL ...
...BUT THE KEGARE THERE ARE NOTHING LIKE THE WIMPY ONES YOU'D MEET ON THE MAINLAND.
ON TOP OF THAT, WE'VE DISCOVERED 11 BASARA WHO ARE EVEN *MORE* POWERFUL.
THE ISLAND IS CONTINUOUSLY AT WAR TO PREVENT THOSE CREATURES FROM MAKING IT OUT INTO THE HUMAN WORLD.
I'M NOTHING BUT DEAD-WEIGHT.
DEAD-WEIGHT ...
SEIGEN...?
BUT HE'S SO POWERFUL!
...
NARU-KAMI TOWN ...?
HEH HEH... THOUGHT-FUL OF ME, ISN'T IT?
I THINK IT'S THE PERFECT DUTY FOR YOU FROM NOW ON.
HUH?
MORE LIKE AN UN-WELCOME FAVOR...
SEIGEN ...

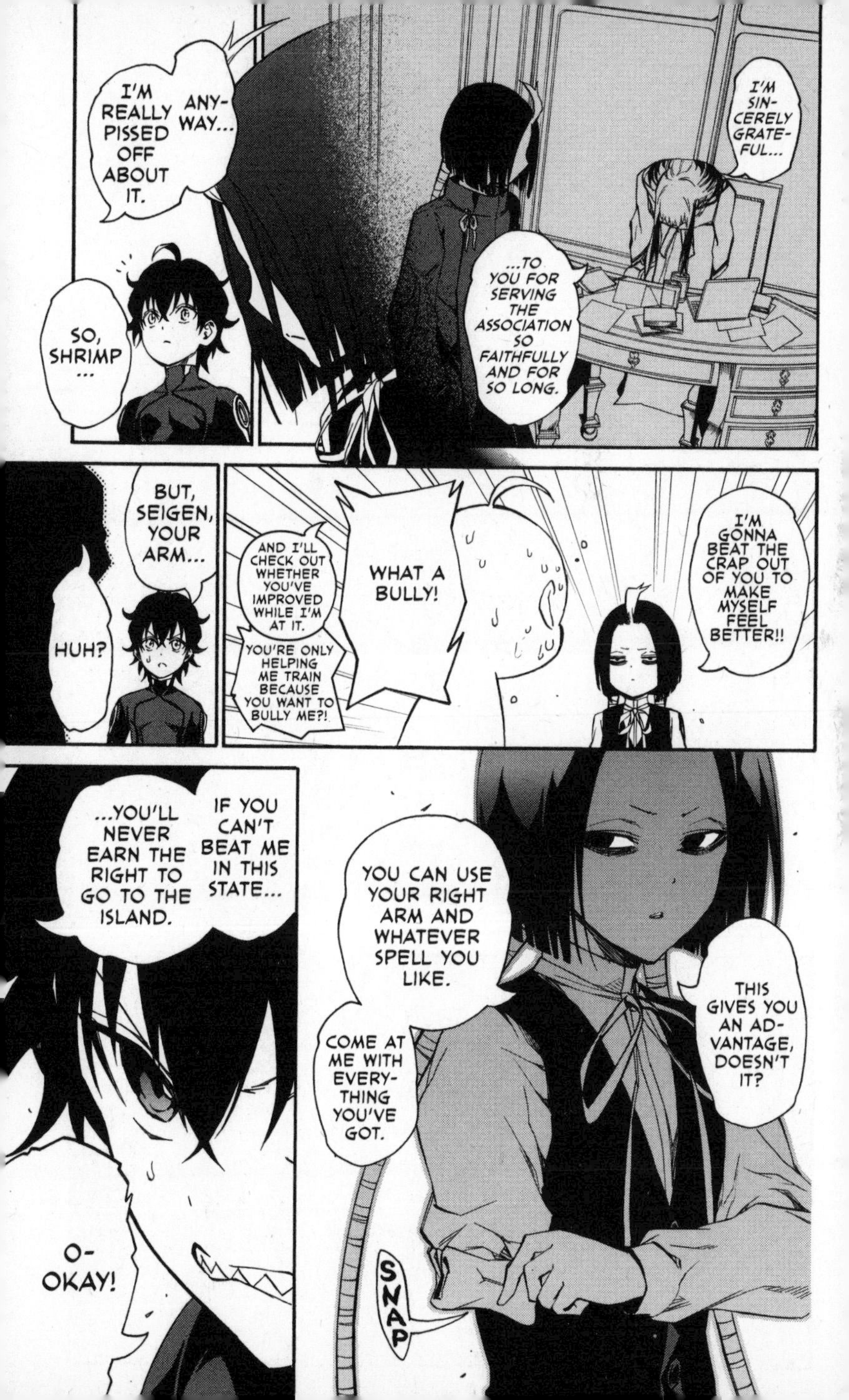

I'M SINCERELY GRATEFUL...
...TO YOU FOR SERVING THE ASSOCIATION SO FAITHFULLY AND FOR SO LONG.
ANYWAY...
I'M REALLY PISSED OFF ABOUT IT.
SO, SHRIMP...
I'M GONNA BEAT THE CRAP OUT OF YOU TO MAKE MYSELF FEEL BETTER!!
WHAT A BULLY!
YOU'RE ONLY HELPING ME TRAIN BECAUSE YOU WANT TO BULLY ME?!
AND I'LL CHECK OUT WHETHER YOU'VE IMPROVED WHILE I'M AT IT.
BUT, SEIGEN, YOUR ARM...
HUH?
THIS GIVES YOU AN ADVANTAGE, DOESN'T IT?
YOU CAN USE YOUR RIGHT ARM AND WHATEVER SPELL YOU LIKE.
COME AT ME WITH EVERYTHING YOU'VE GOT.
SNAP
IF YOU CAN'T BEAT ME IN THIS STATE...
...YOU'LL NEVER EARN THE RIGHT TO GO TO THE ISLAND.
O-OKAY!

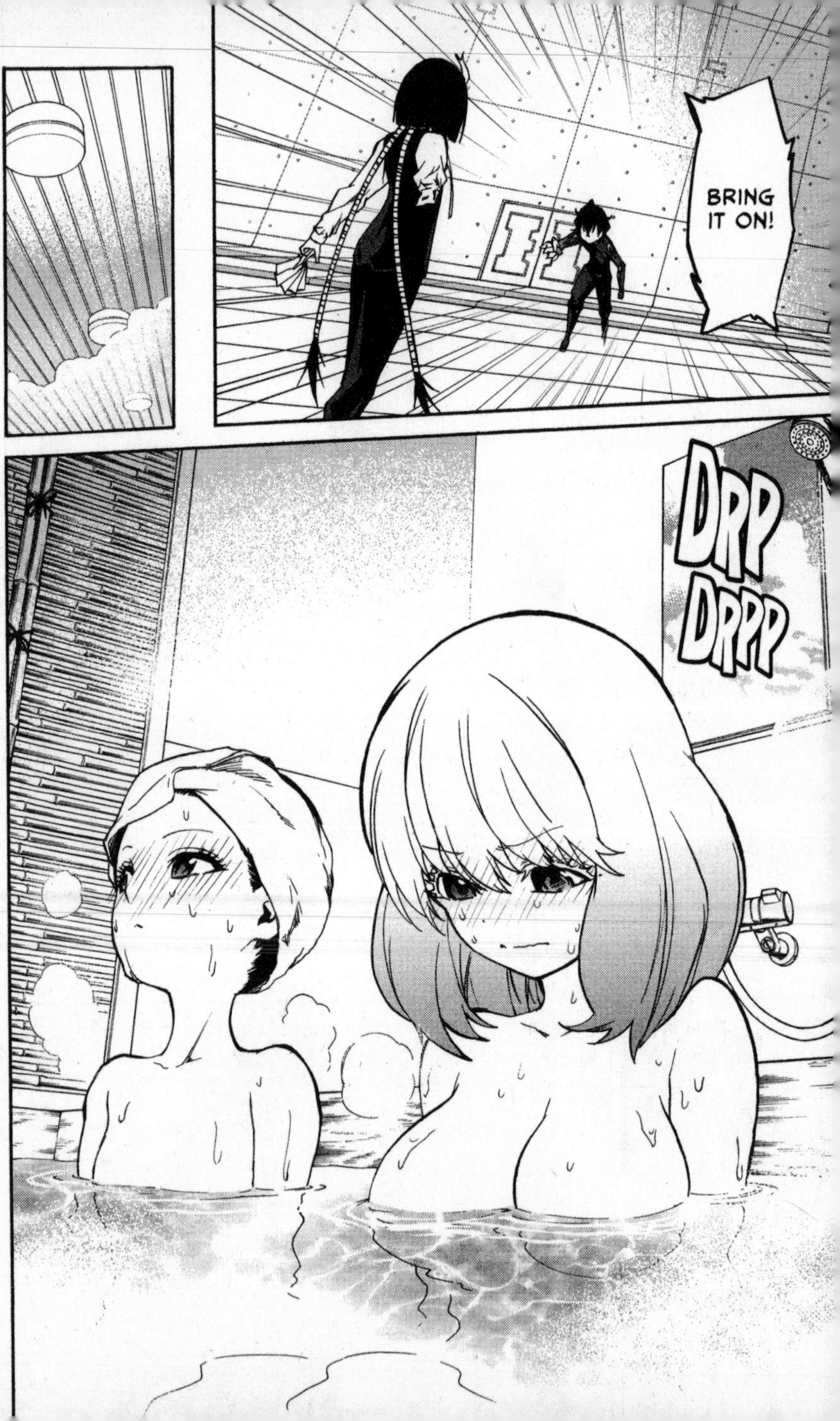
BRING IT ON!
DRP DRPP

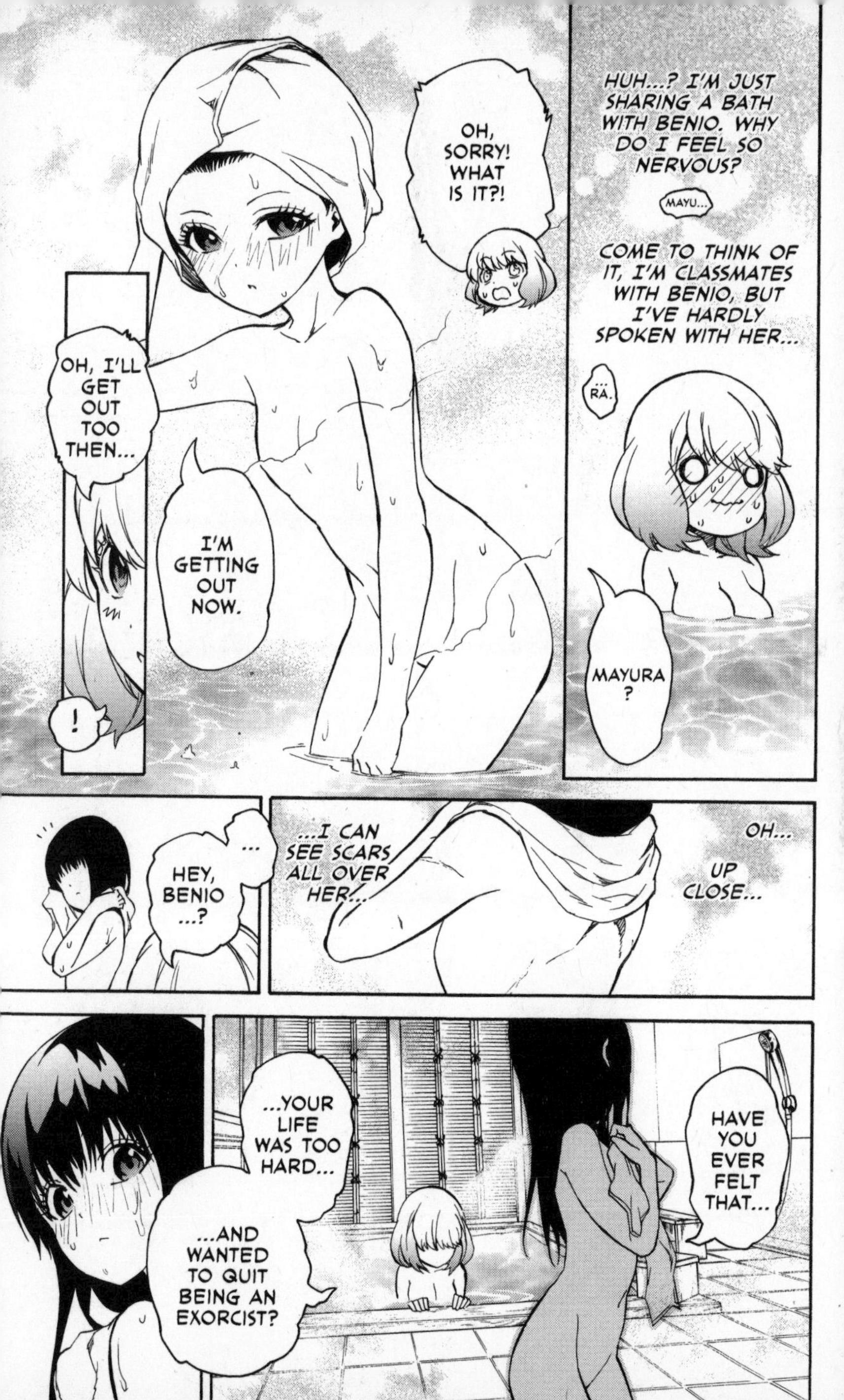
HUH...? I'M JUST SHARING A BATH WITH BENIO. WHY DO I FEEL SO NERVOUS?
MAYU...
COME TO THINK OF IT, I'M CLASSMATES WITH BENIO, BUT I'VE HARDLY SPOKEN WITH HER...
...RA.
MAYURA?
OH, SORRY! WHAT IS IT?!
I'M GETTING OUT NOW.
OH, I'LL GET OUT TOO THEN...
!
OH... UP CLOSE...
...I CAN SEE SCARS ALL OVER HER...
...
HEY, BENIO...?
HAVE YOU EVER FELT THAT...
...YOUR LIFE WAS TOO HARD...
...AND WANTED TO QUIT BEING AN EXORCIST?

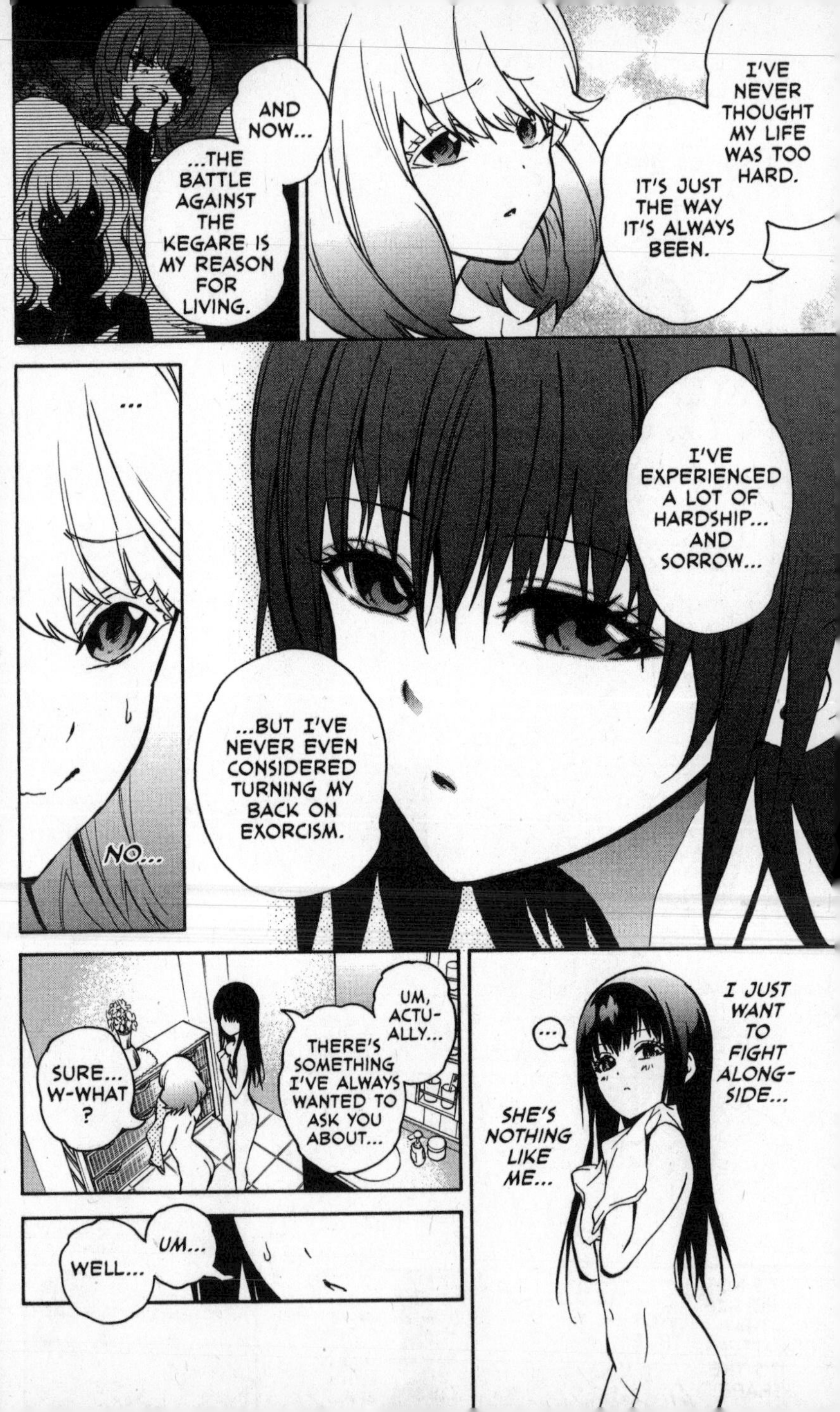
I'VE NEVER THOUGHT MY LIFE WAS TOO HARD.
IT'S JUST THE WAY IT'S ALWAYS BEEN.
AND NOW...
...THE BATTLE AGAINST THE KEGARE IS MY REASON FOR LIVING.
I'VE EXPERIENCED A LOT OF HARDSHIP... AND SORROW...
...BUT I'VE NEVER EVEN CONSIDERED TURNING MY BACK ON EXORCISM.
...
NO...
I JUST WANT TO FIGHT ALONG-SIDE...
...
SHE'S NOTHING LIKE ME...
UM, ACTU-ALLY...
THERE'S SOMETHING I'VE ALWAYS WANTED TO ASK YOU ABOUT...
SURE... W-WHAT?
UM...
WELL...

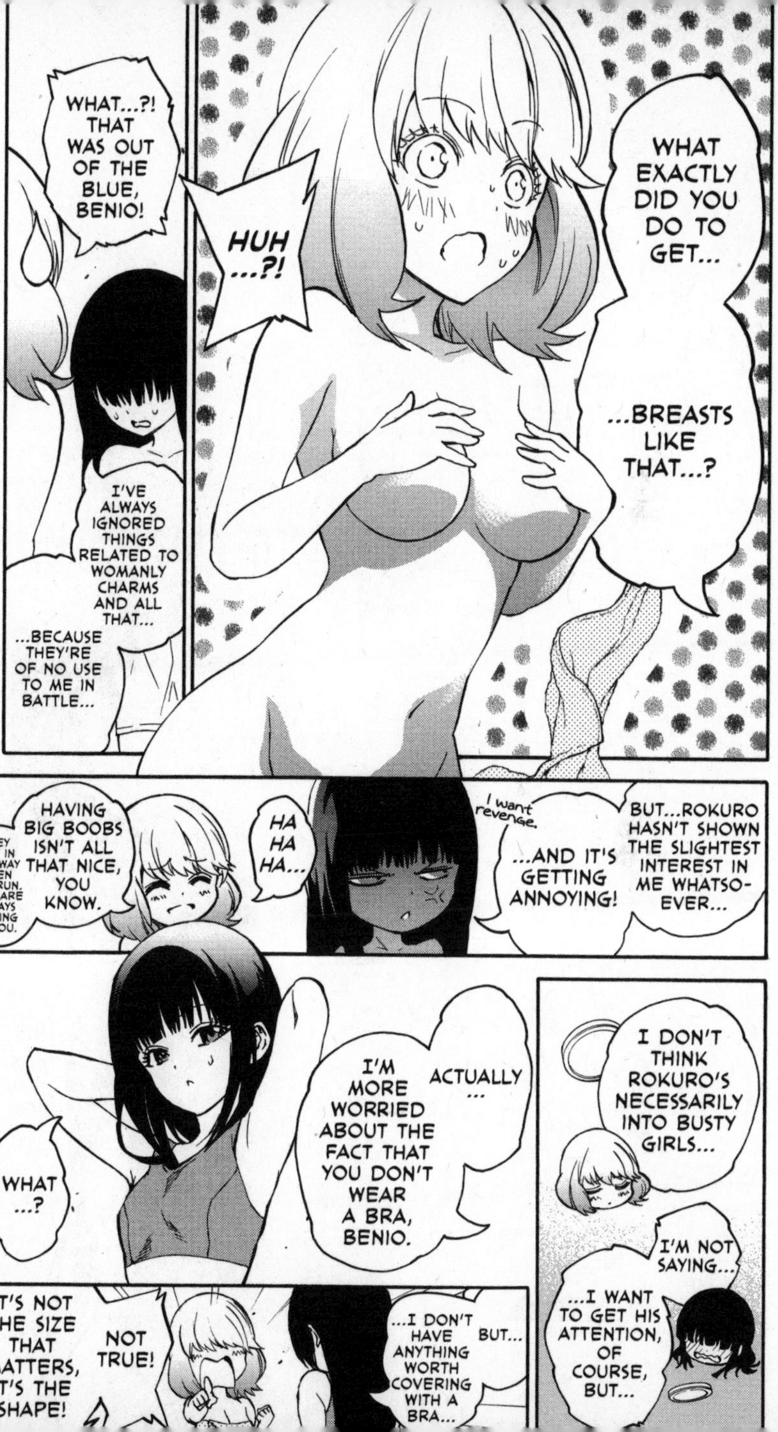
WHAT EXACTLY DID YOU DO TO GET...
...BREASTS LIKE THAT...?
HUH ...?!
WHAT...?! THAT WAS OUT OF THE BLUE, BENIO!
I'VE ALWAYS IGNORED THINGS RELATED TO WOMANLY CHARMS AND ALL THAT...
...BECAUSE THEY'RE OF NO USE TO ME IN BATTLE...
BUT...ROKURO HASN'T SHOWN THE SLIGHTEST INTEREST IN ME WHATSO-EVER...
I want revenge.
...AND IT'S GETTING ANNOYING!
HA HA HA...
HAVING BIG BOOBS ISN'T ALL THAT NICE, YOU KNOW.
THEY GET IN THE WAY WHEN YOU RUN. BOYS ARE ALWAYS STARING AT YOU.
I DON'T THINK ROKURO'S NECESSARILY INTO BUSTY GIRLS...
I'M NOT SAYING...
...I WANT TO GET HIS ATTENTION, OF COURSE, BUT...
ACTUALLY...
I'M MORE WORRIED ABOUT THE FACT THAT YOU DON'T WEAR A BRA, BENIO.
WHAT ...?
BUT...
...I DON'T HAVE ANYTHING WORTH COVERING WITH A BRA...
NOT TRUE!
IT'S NOT THE SIZE THAT MATTERS, IT'S THE SHAPE!

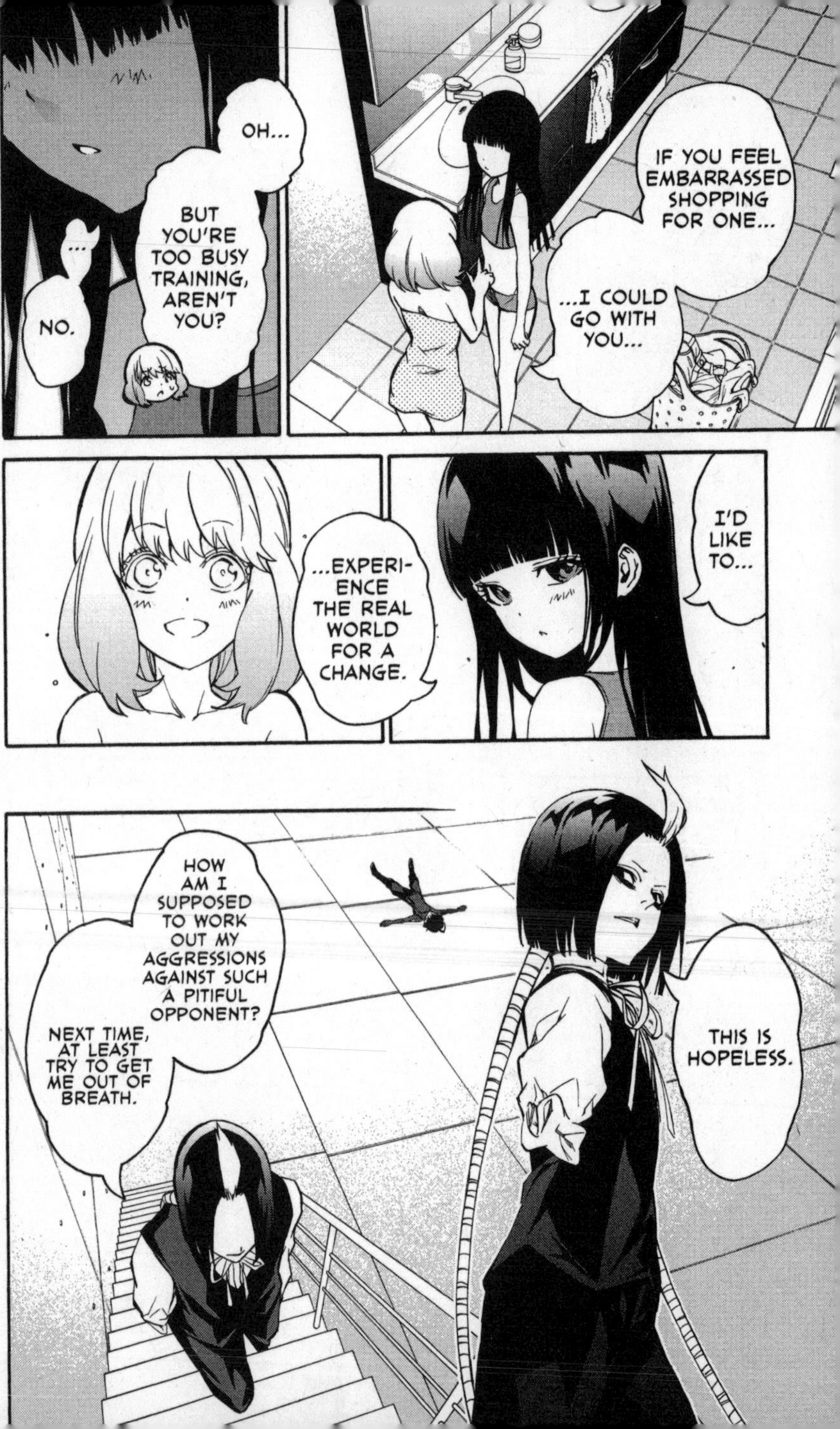
IF YOU FEEL EMBARRASSED SHOPPING FOR ONE...
...I COULD GO WITH YOU...
OH...
BUT YOU'RE TOO BUSY TRAINING, AREN'T YOU?
...
NO.
I'D LIKE TO...
...EXPERIENCE THE REAL WORLD FOR A CHANGE.
THIS IS HOPELESS.
HOW AM I SUPPOSED TO WORK OUT MY AGGRESSIONS AGAINST SUCH A PITIFUL OPPONENT?
NEXT TIME, AT LEAST TRY TO GET ME OUT OF BREATH.

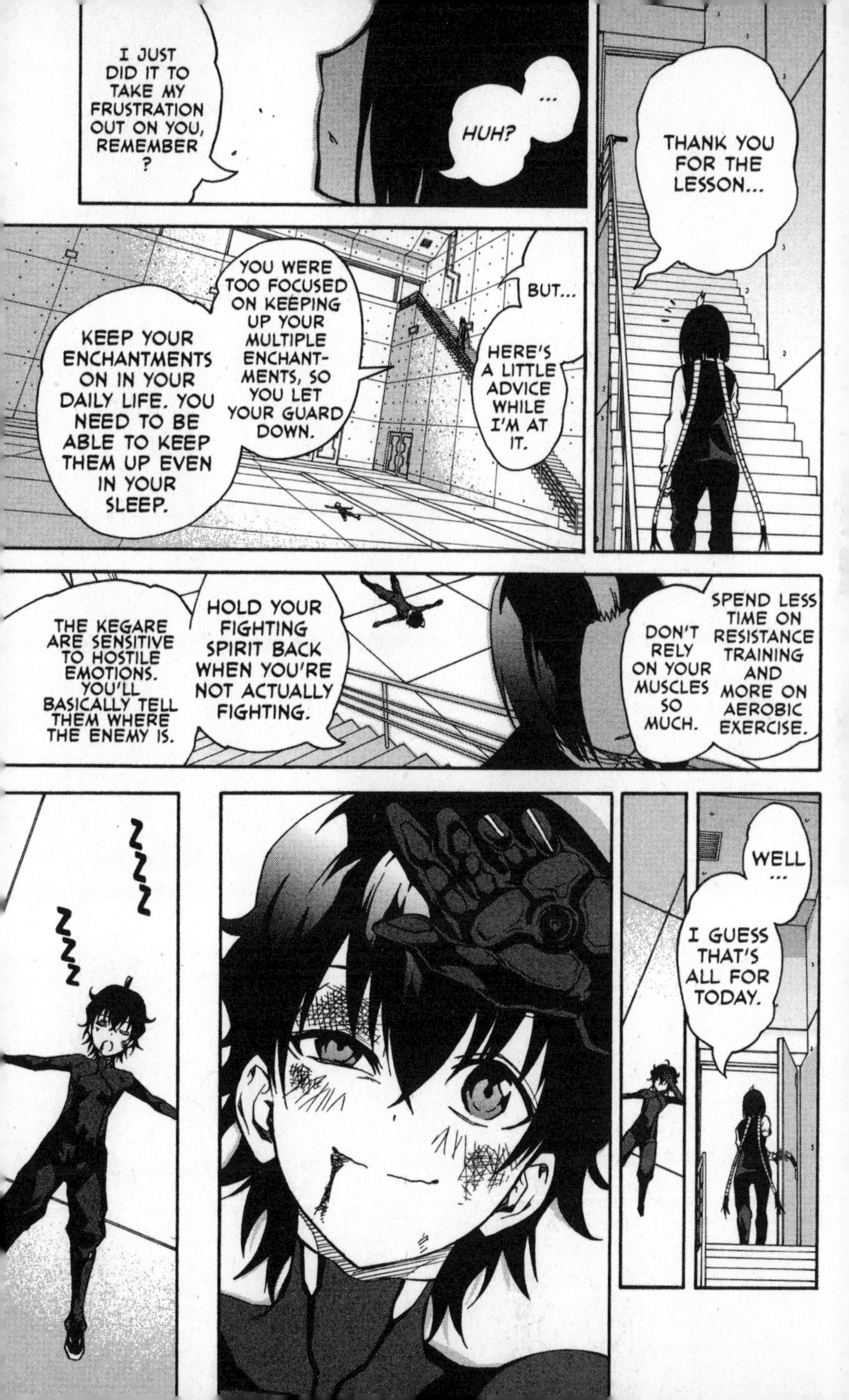
THANK YOU FOR THE LESSON...
...
HUH?
I JUST DID IT TO TAKE MY FRUSTRATION OUT ON YOU, REMEMBER?
BUT...
HERE'S A LITTLE ADVICE WHILE I'M AT IT.
YOU WERE TOO FOCUSED ON KEEPING UP YOUR MULTIPLE ENCHANT-MENTS, SO YOU LET YOUR GUARD DOWN.
KEEP YOUR ENCHANTMENTS ON IN YOUR DAILY LIFE. YOU NEED TO BE ABLE TO KEEP THEM UP EVEN IN YOUR SLEEP.
SPEND LESS TIME ON RESISTANCE TRAINING AND MORE ON AEROBIC EXERCISE.
DON'T RELY ON YOUR MUSCLES SO MUCH.
HOLD YOUR FIGHTING SPIRIT BACK WHEN YOU'RE NOT ACTUALLY FIGHTING.
THE KEGARE ARE SENSITIVE TO HOSTILE EMOTIONS. YOU'LL BASICALLY TELL THEM WHERE THE ENEMY IS.
WELL...
I GUESS THAT'S ALL FOR TODAY.
ZZZ
ZZZ

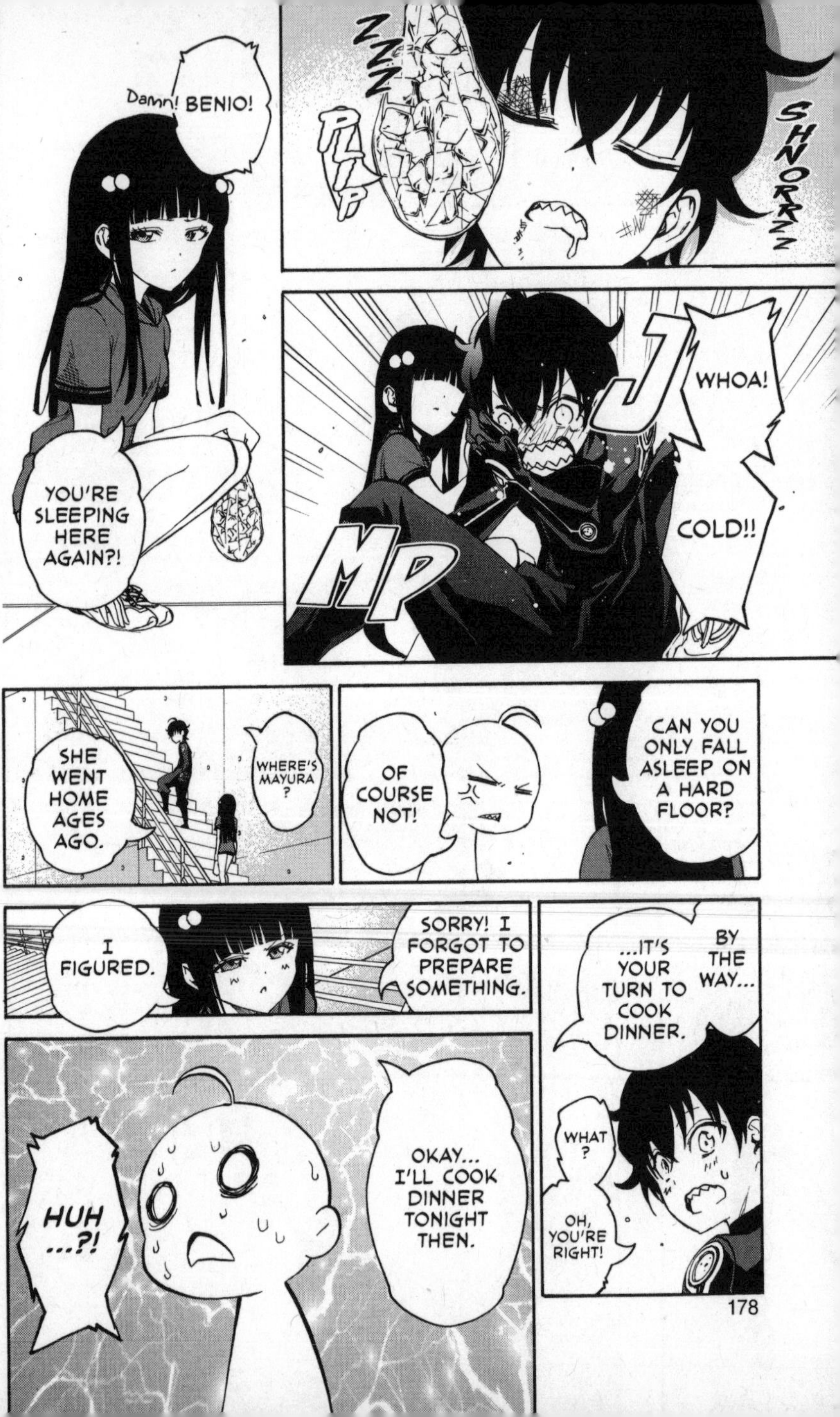
SHNORRZZ
ZZZ
PLIP
WHOA!
COLD!!
J
MP
Damn! BENIO!
YOU'RE SLEEPING HERE AGAIN?!
CAN YOU ONLY FALL ASLEEP ON A HARD FLOOR?
OF COURSE NOT!
WHERE'S MAYURA?
SHE WENT HOME AGES AGO.
BY THE WAY...
...IT'S YOUR TURN TO COOK DINNER.
WHAT?
OH, YOU'RE RIGHT!
SORRY! I FORGOT TO PREPARE SOMETHING.
I FIGURED.
OKAY... I'LL COOK DINNER TONIGHT THEN.
HUH...?!

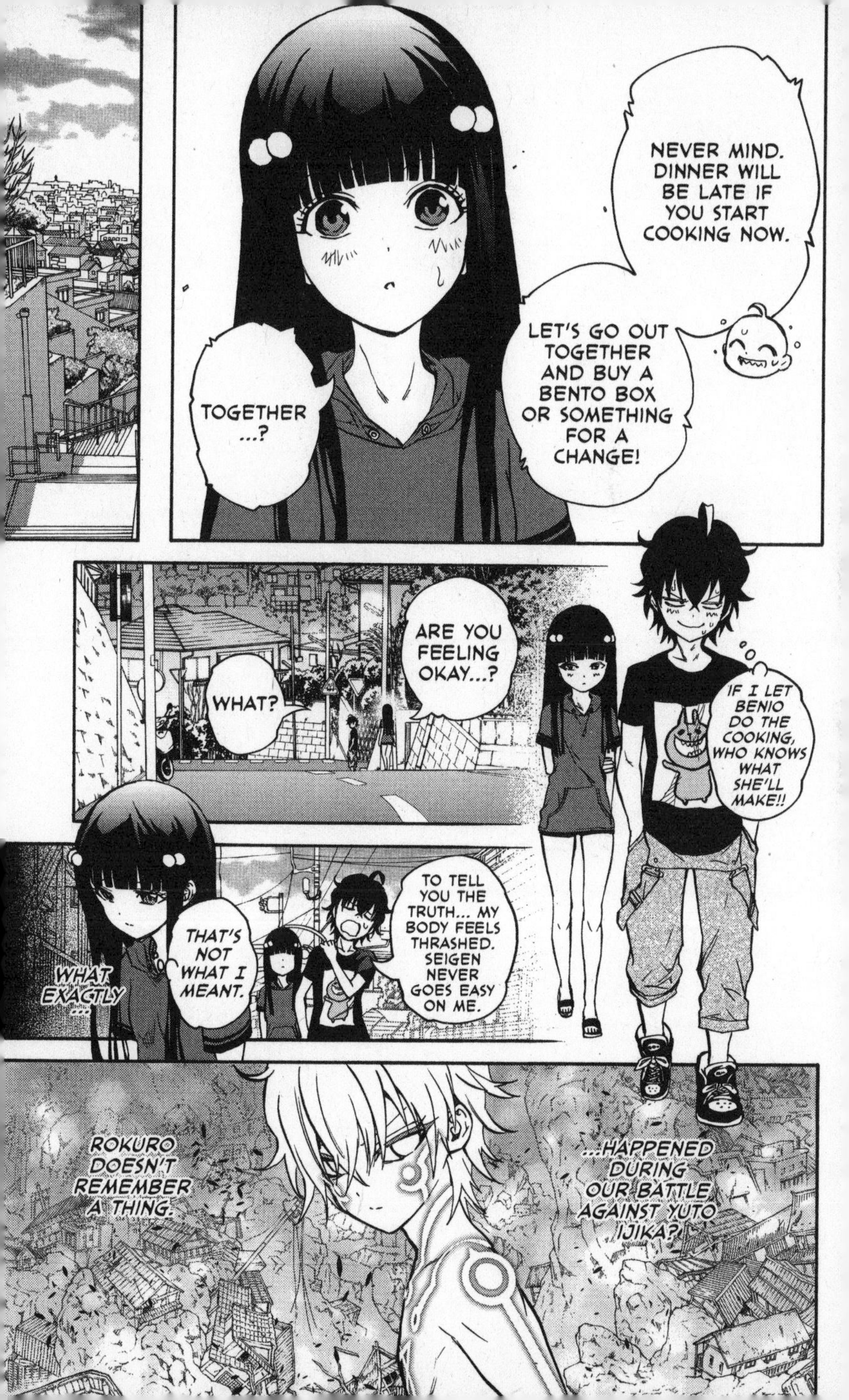
NEVER MIND. DINNER WILL BE LATE IF YOU START COOKING NOW.
LET'S GO OUT TOGETHER AND BUY A BENTO BOX OR SOMETHING FOR A CHANGE!
TOGETHER ...?
IF I LET BENIO DO THE COOKING, WHO KNOWS WHAT SHE'LL MAKE!!
ARE YOU FEELING OKAY...?
WHAT?
TO TELL YOU THE TRUTH... MY BODY FEELS THRASHED. SEIGEN NEVER GOES EASY ON ME.
THAT'S NOT WHAT I MEANT.
WHAT EXACTLY ...
...HAPPENED DURING OUR BATTLE AGAINST YUTO IJIKA?
ROKURO DOESN'T REMEMBER A THING.

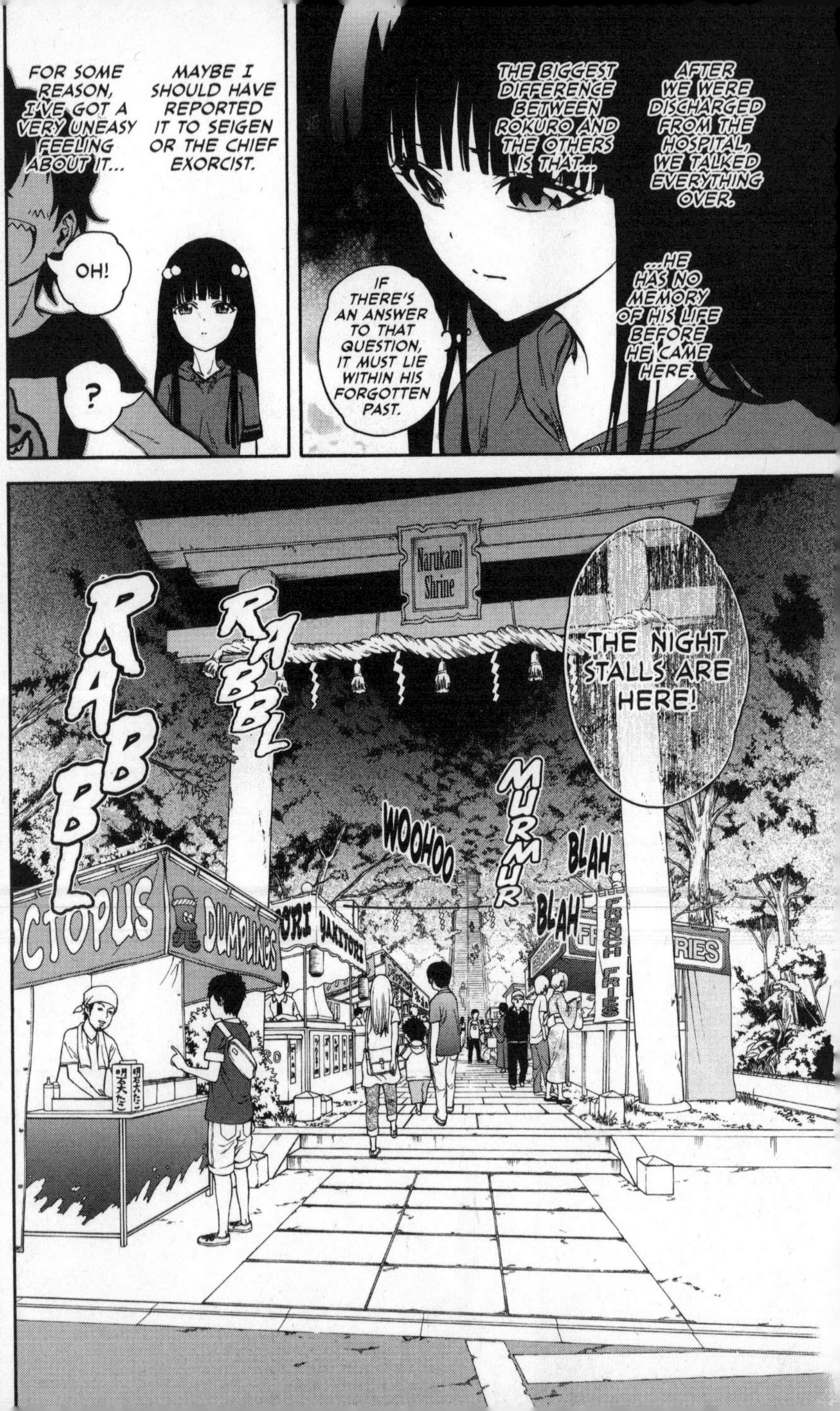
AFTER WE WERE DISCHARGED FROM THE HOSPITAL, WE TALKED EVERYTHING OVER.
THE BIGGEST DIFFERENCE BETWEEN ROKURO AND THE OTHERS IS THAT...
...HE HAS NO MEMORY OF HIS LIFE BEFORE HE CAME HERE.
IF THERE'S AN ANSWER TO THAT QUESTION, IT MUST LIE WITHIN HIS FORGOTTEN PAST.
MAYBE I SHOULD HAVE REPORTED IT TO SEIGEN OR THE CHIEF EXORCIST.
FOR SOME REASON, I'VE GOT A VERY UNEASY FEELING ABOUT IT...
OH!
?
Narukami Shrine
THE NIGHT STALLS ARE HERE!
RABBL
RABBL
MURMUR
WOOHOO
BLAH
BLAH
FRENCH FRIES
YAKITORI
OCTOPUS
DUMPLINGS

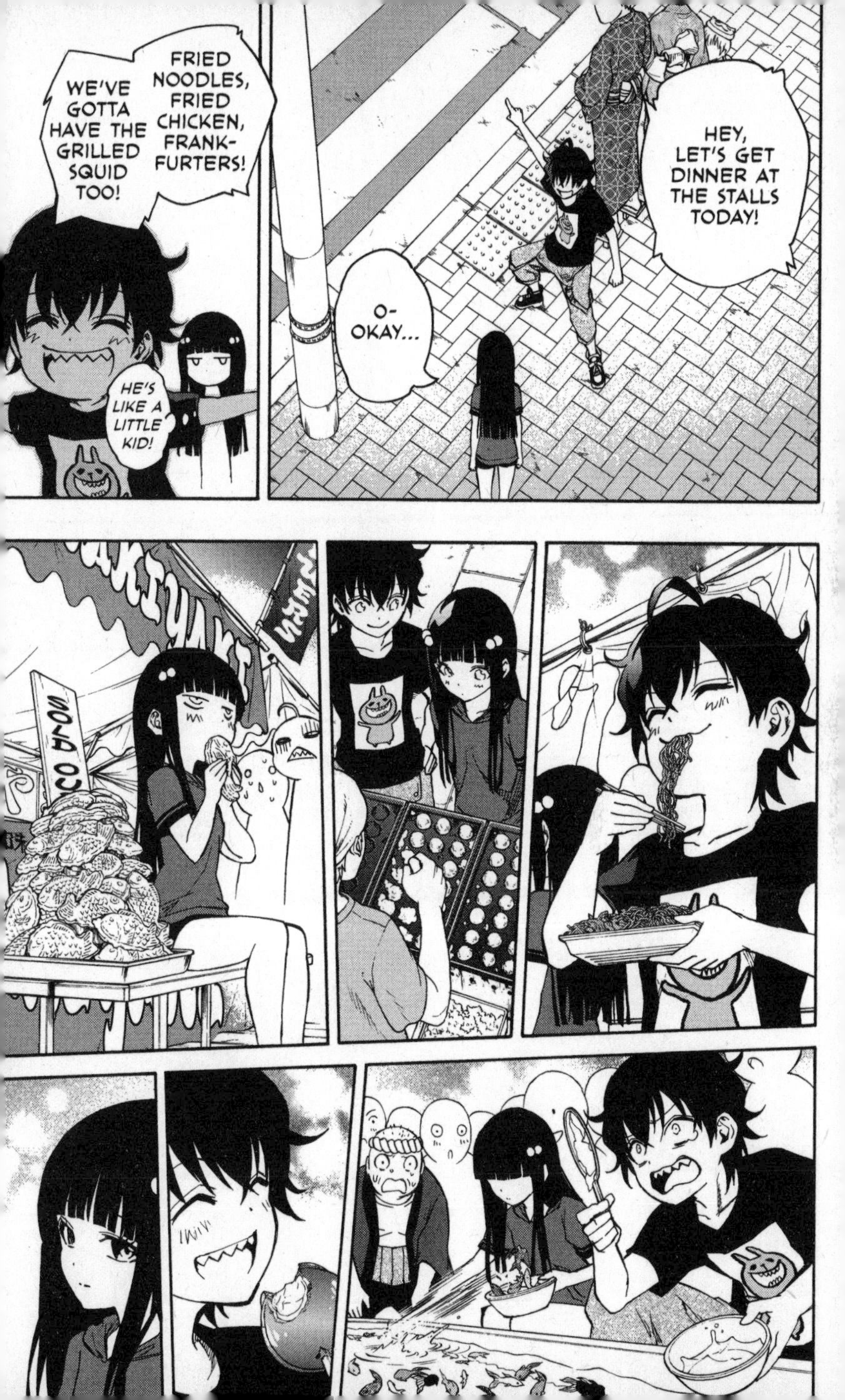
HEY, LET'S GET DINNER AT THE STALLS TODAY!
O-OKAY...
FRIED NOODLES, FRIED CHICKEN, FRANK-FURTERS!
WE'VE GOTTA HAVE THE GRILLED SQUID TOO!
HE'S LIKE A LITTLE KID!

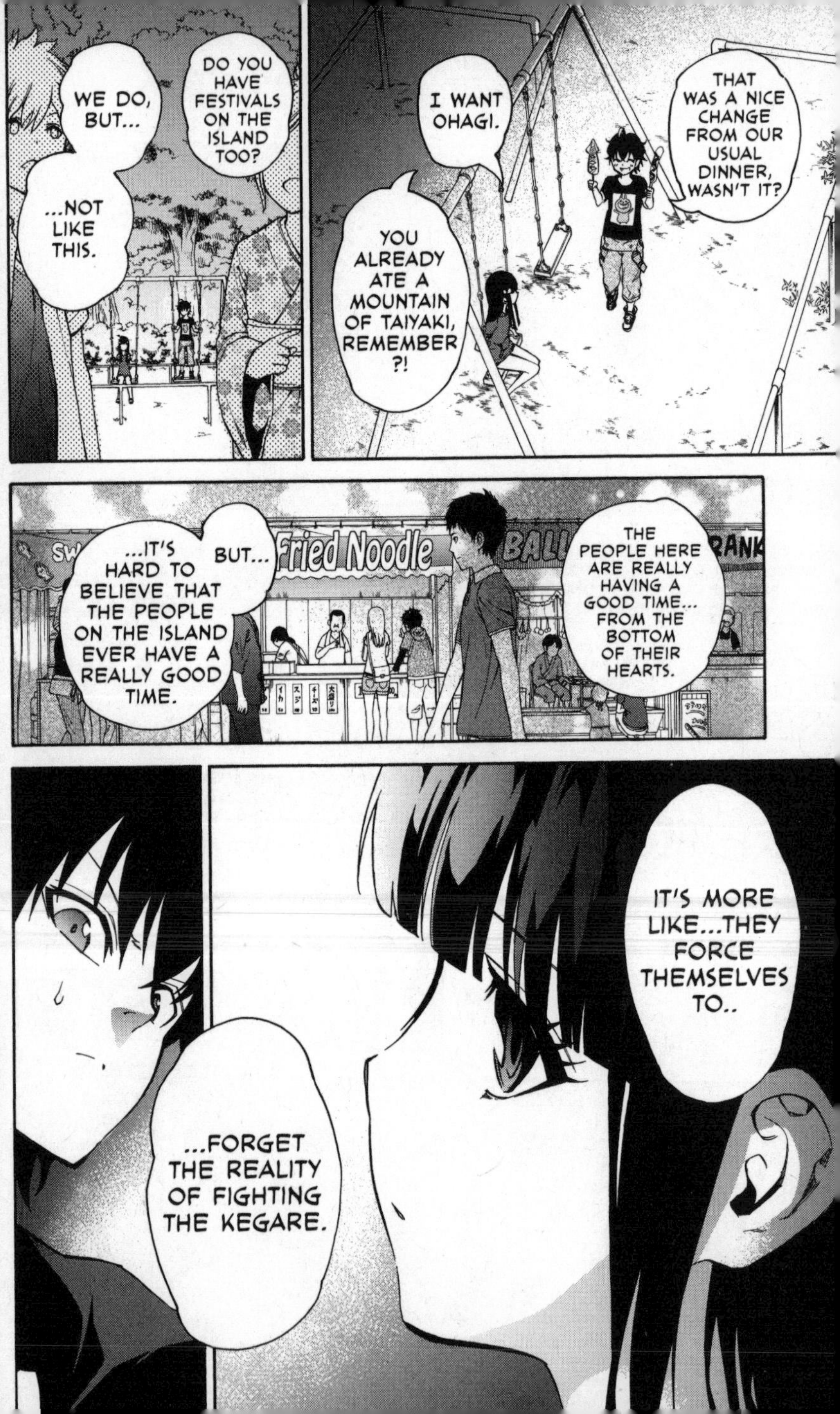
THAT WAS A NICE CHANGE FROM OUR USUAL DINNER, WASN'T IT?
I WANT OHAGI.
YOU ALREADY ATE A MOUNTAIN OF TAIYAKI, REMEMBER?!
DO YOU HAVE FESTIVALS ON THE ISLAND TOO?
WE DO, BUT...
...NOT LIKE THIS.
THE PEOPLE HERE ARE REALLY HAVING A GOOD TIME... FROM THE BOTTOM OF THEIR HEARTS.
Fried Noodle
BUT...
...IT'S HARD TO BELIEVE THAT THE PEOPLE ON THE ISLAND EVER HAVE A REALLY GOOD TIME.
IT'S MORE LIKE...THEY FORCE THEMSELVES TO..
...FORGET THE REALITY OF FIGHTING THE KEGARE.

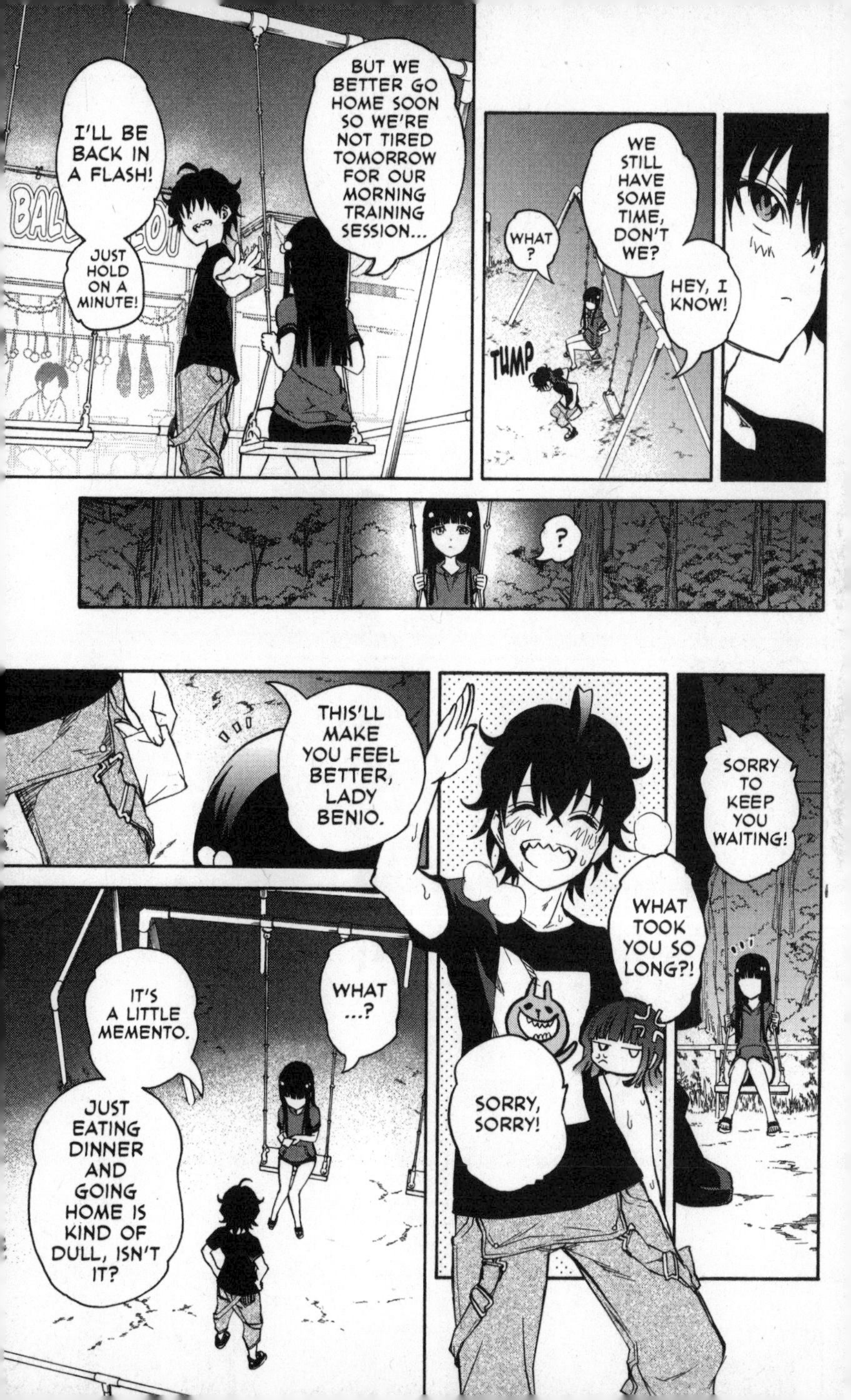
WE STILL HAVE SOME TIME, DON'T WE?
HEY, I KNOW!
WHAT?
TUMP
BUT WE BETTER GO HOME SOON SO WE'RE NOT TIRED TOMORROW FOR OUR MORNING TRAINING SESSION...
I'LL BE BACK IN A FLASH!
JUST HOLD ON A MINUTE!
?
SORRY TO KEEP YOU WAITING!
WHAT TOOK YOU SO LONG?!
SORRY, SORRY!
THIS'LL MAKE YOU FEEL BETTER, LADY BENIO.
WHAT ...?
IT'S A LITTLE MEMENTO.
JUST EATING DINNER AND GOING HOME IS KIND OF DULL, ISN'T IT?

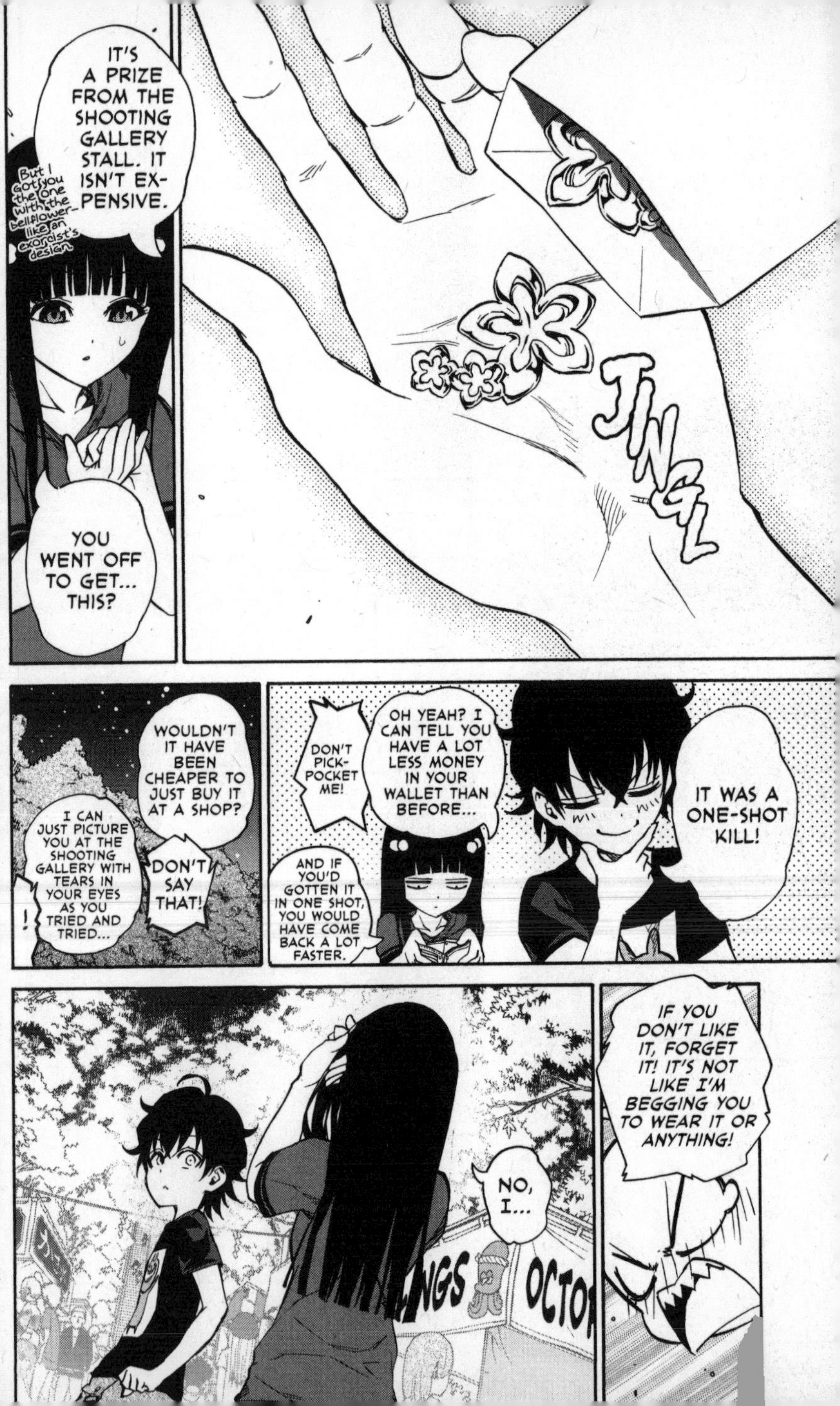
JINGL
YOU WENT OFF TO GET... THIS?
IT'S A PRIZE FROM THE SHOOTING GALLERY STALL. IT ISN'T EX-PENSIVE.
But I got you the one with the bellflower-like an exorcist's design
IT WAS A ONE-SHOT KILL!
OH YEAH? I CAN TELL YOU HAVE A LOT LESS MONEY IN YOUR WALLET THAN BEFORE...
DON'T PICK-POCKET ME!
AND IF YOU'D GOTTEN IT IN ONE SHOT, YOU WOULD HAVE COME BACK A LOT FASTER.
WOULDN'T IT HAVE BEEN CHEAPER TO JUST BUY IT AT A SHOP?
I CAN JUST PICTURE YOU AT THE SHOOTING GALLERY WITH TEARS IN YOUR EYES AS YOU TRIED AND TRIED...
DON'T SAY THAT!
!
IF YOU DON'T LIKE IT, FORGET IT! IT'S NOT LIKE I'M BEGGING YOU TO WEAR IT OR ANYTHING!
NO, I...
NGS
OCTO

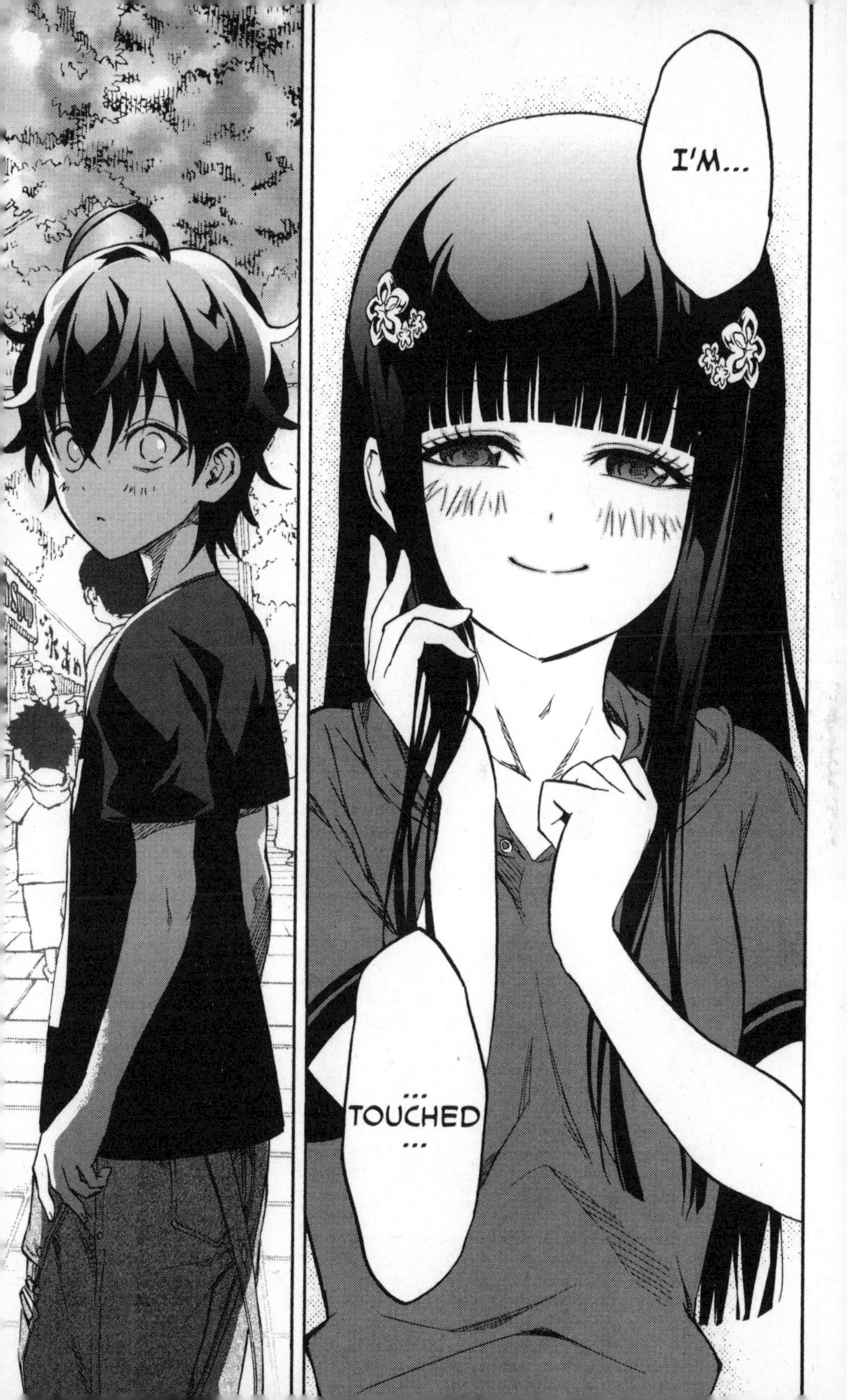
I'M...
...TOUCHED...

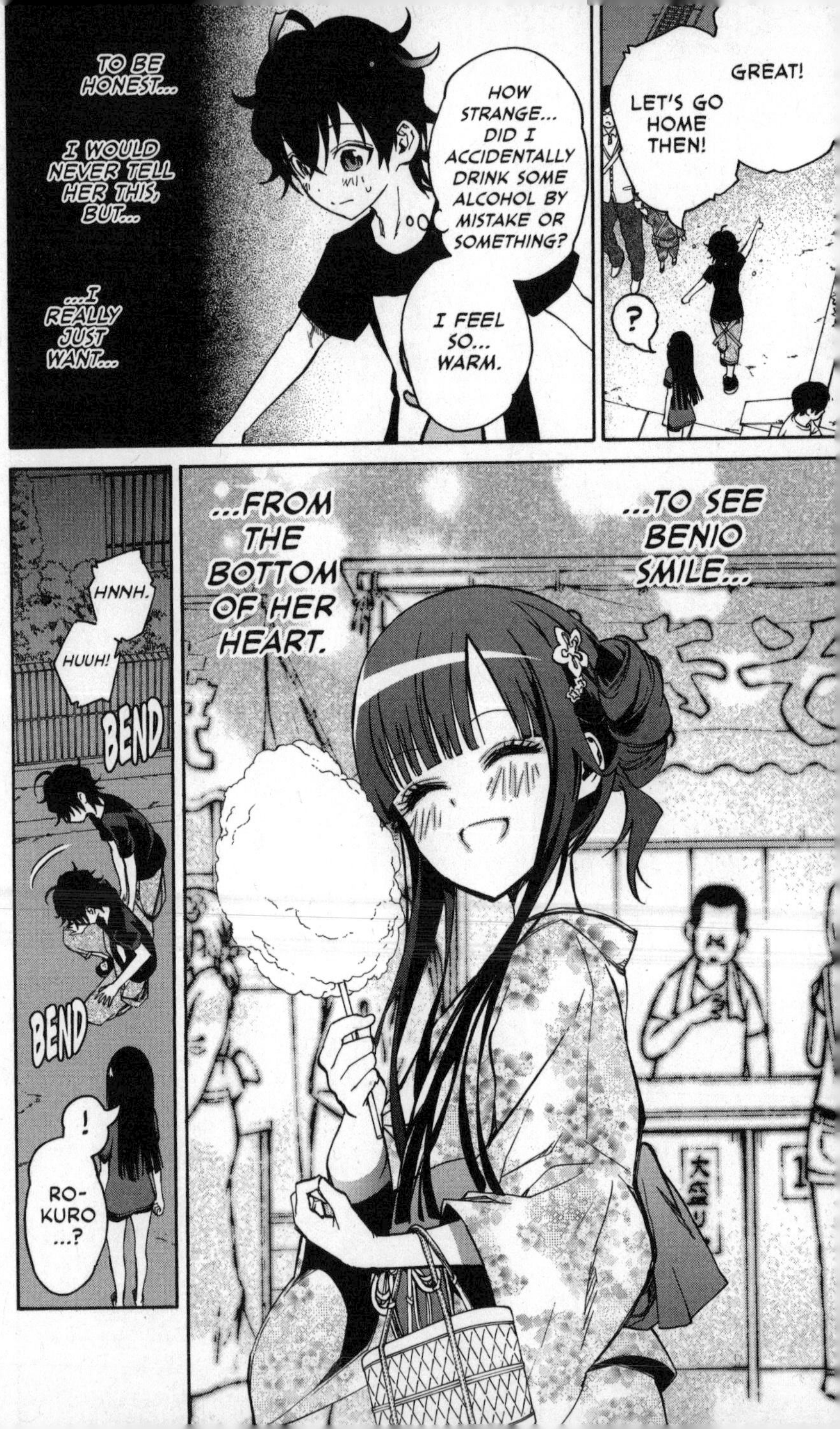
GREAT!
LET'S GO HOME THEN!
?
HOW STRANGE... DID I ACCIDENTALLY DRINK SOME ALCOHOL BY MISTAKE OR SOMETHING?
I FEEL SO... WARM.
TO BE HONEST...
I WOULD NEVER TELL HER THIS, BUT...
...I REALLY JUST WANT...
...TO SEE BENIO SMILE...
...FROM THE BOTTOM OF HER HEART.
HNNH.
HUUH!
BEND
BEND
!
RO-KURO ...?

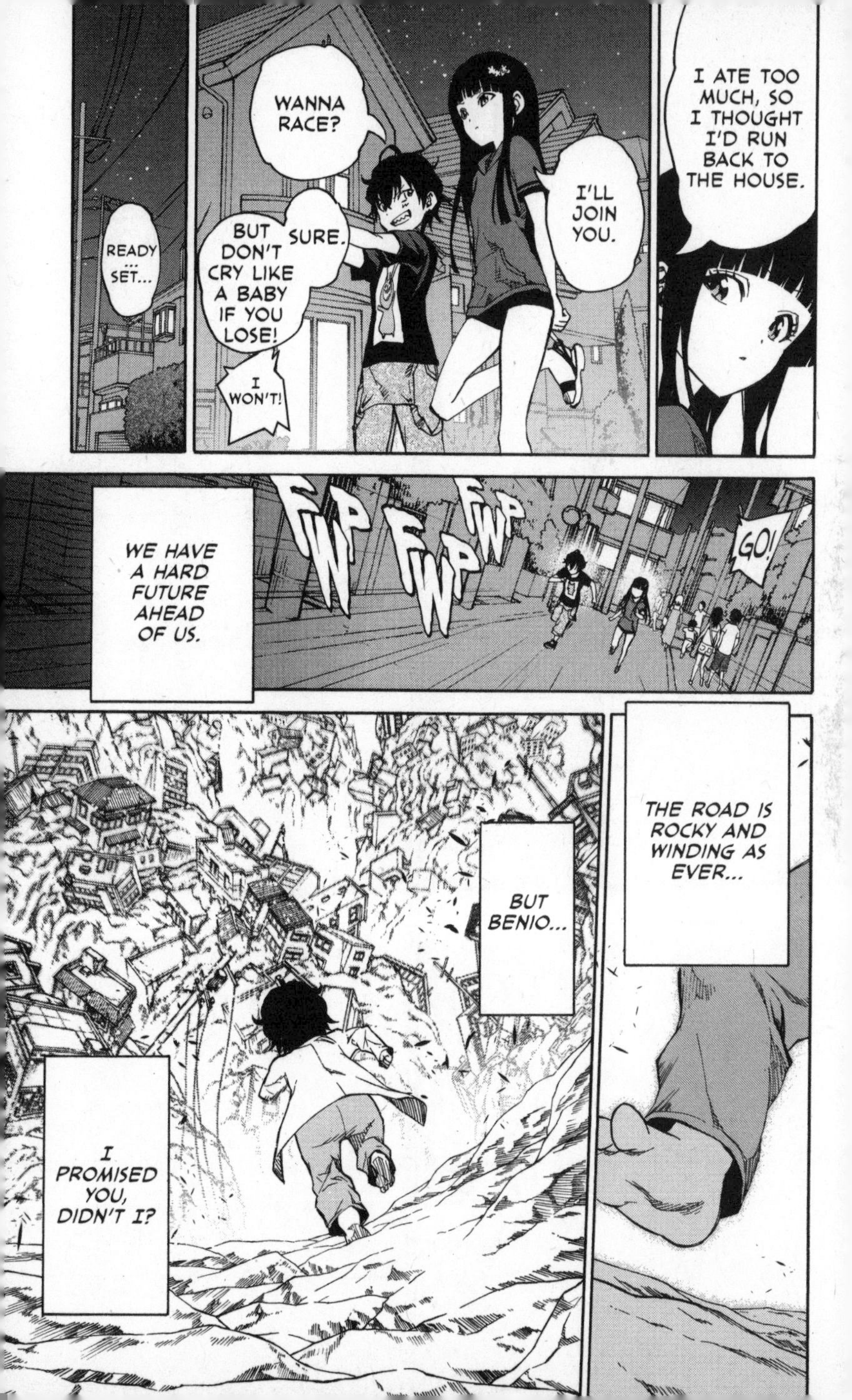
I ATE TOO MUCH, SO I THOUGHT I'D RUN BACK TO THE HOUSE.
I'LL JOIN YOU.
WANNA RACE?
SURE.
BUT DON'T CRY LIKE A BABY IF YOU LOSE!
I WON'T!
READY ... SET...
GO!
FWP FWP FWP FWP
WE HAVE A HARD FUTURE AHEAD OF US.
THE ROAD IS ROCKY AND WINDING AS EVER...
BUT BENIO...
I PROMISED YOU, DIDN'T I?

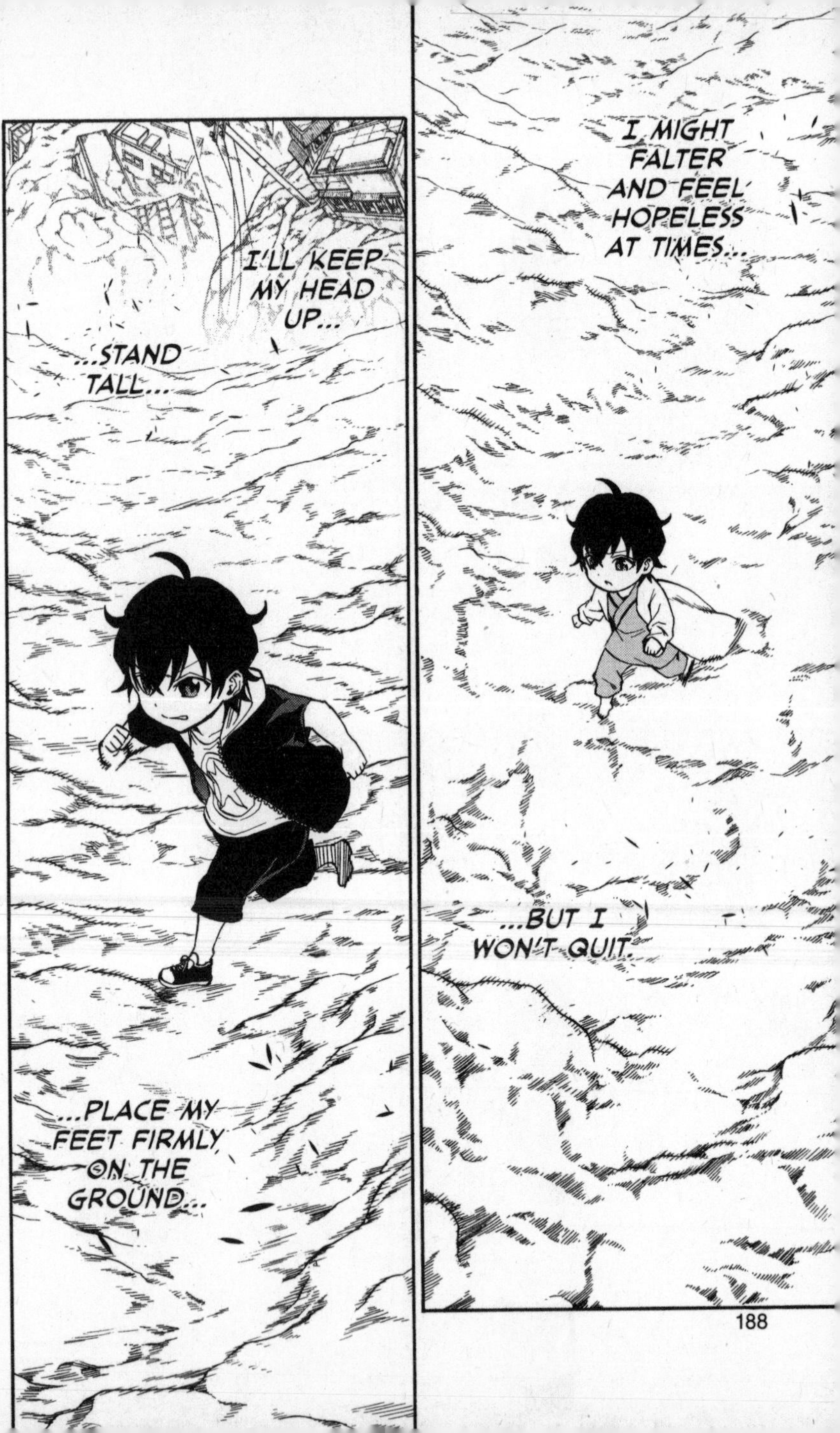
I MIGHT FALTER AND FEEL HOPELESS AT TIMES...
...BUT I WON'T QUIT.
I'LL KEEP MY HEAD UP...
...STAND TALL...
...PLACE MY FEET FIRMLY ON THE GROUND...

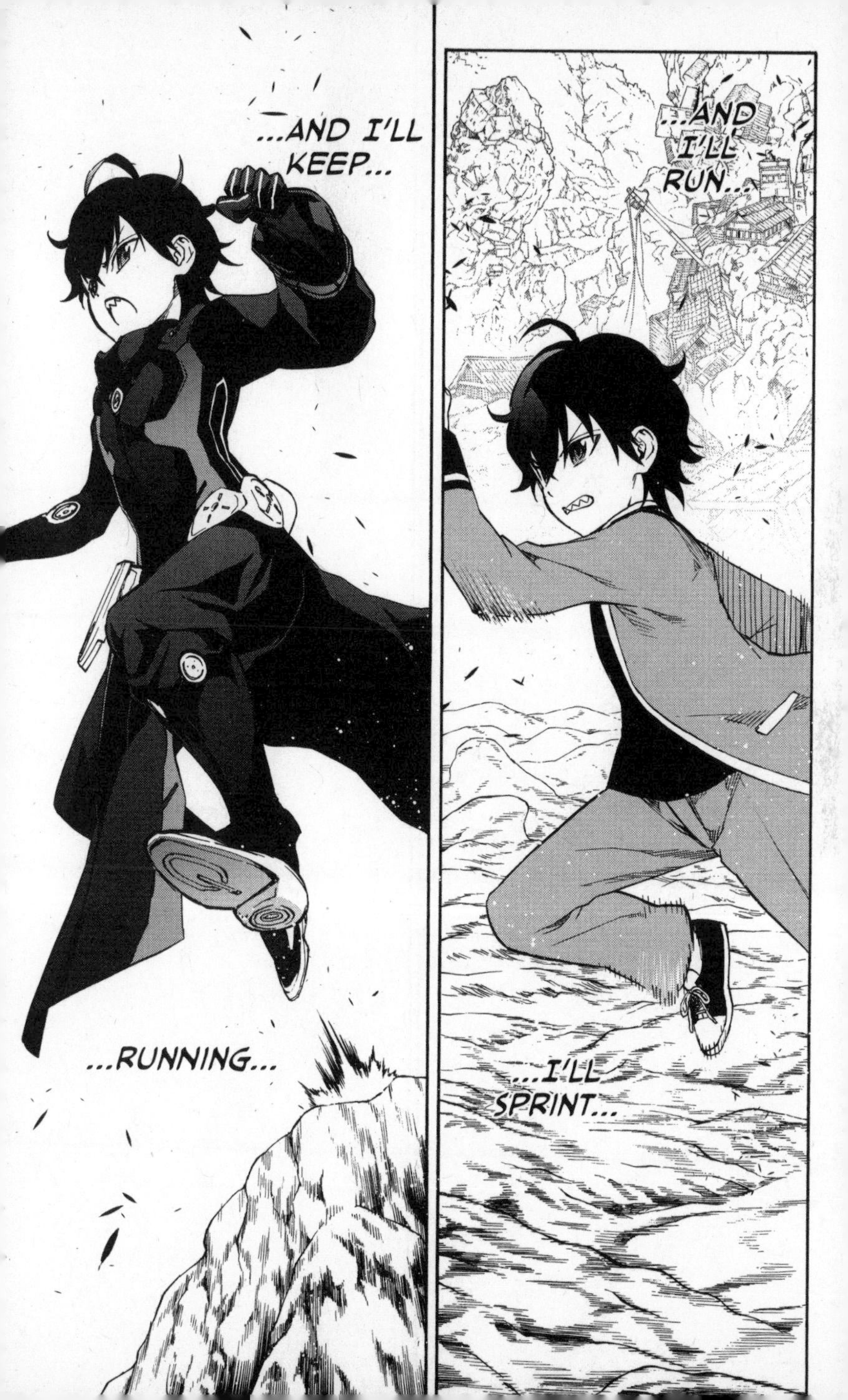
...AND I'LL RUN...
...I'LL SPRINT...
...AND I'LL KEEP...
...RUNNING...

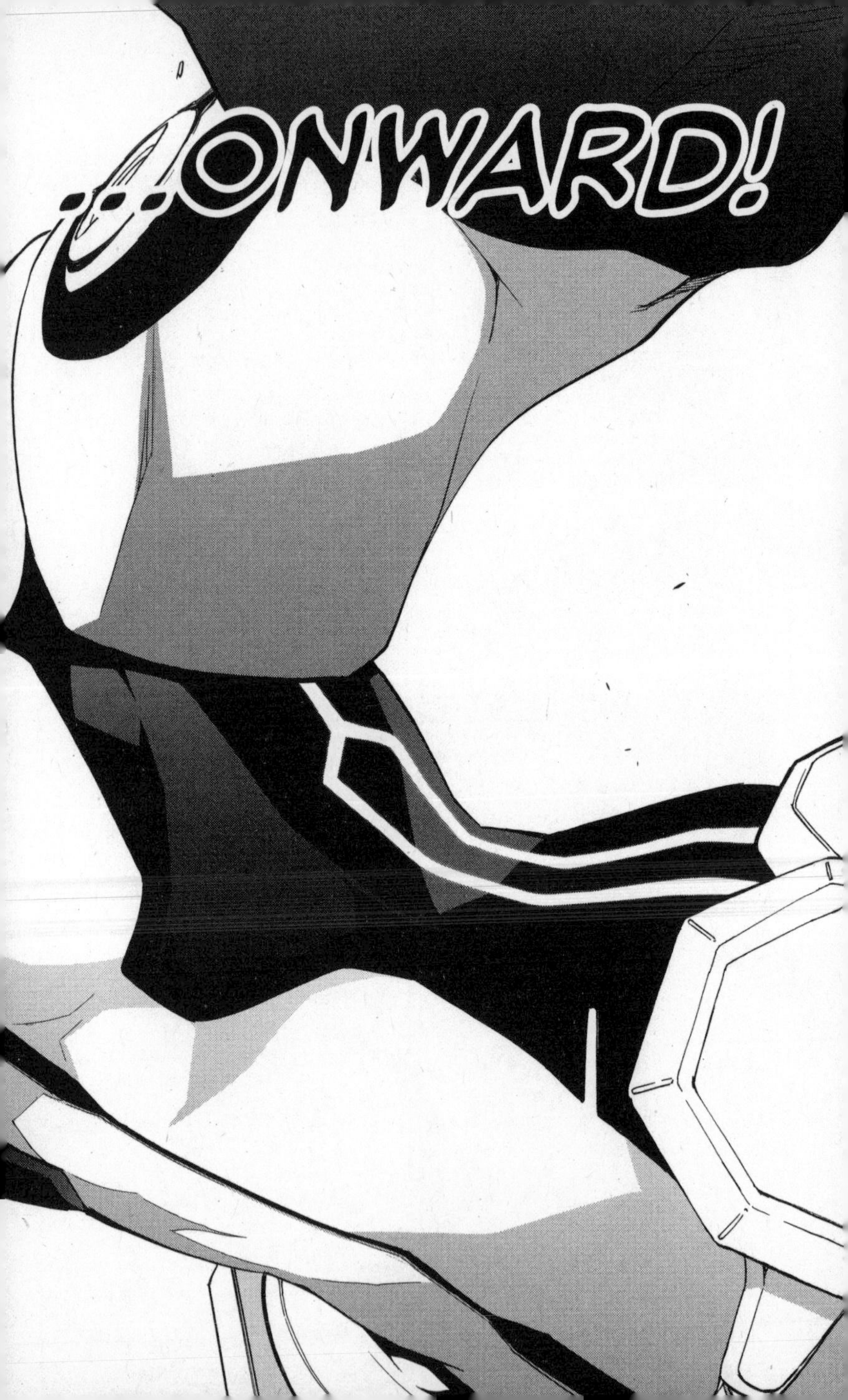
...ONWARD!

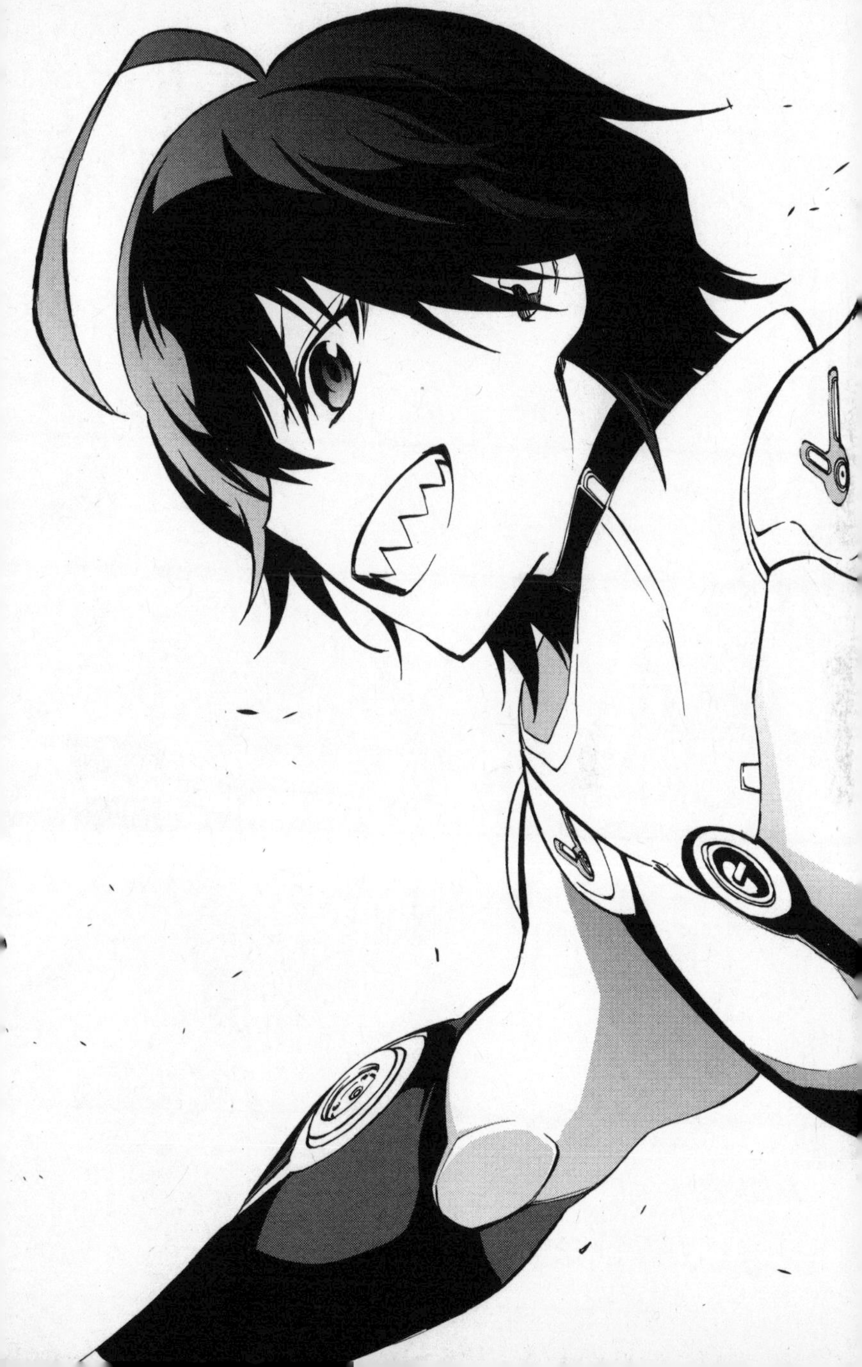

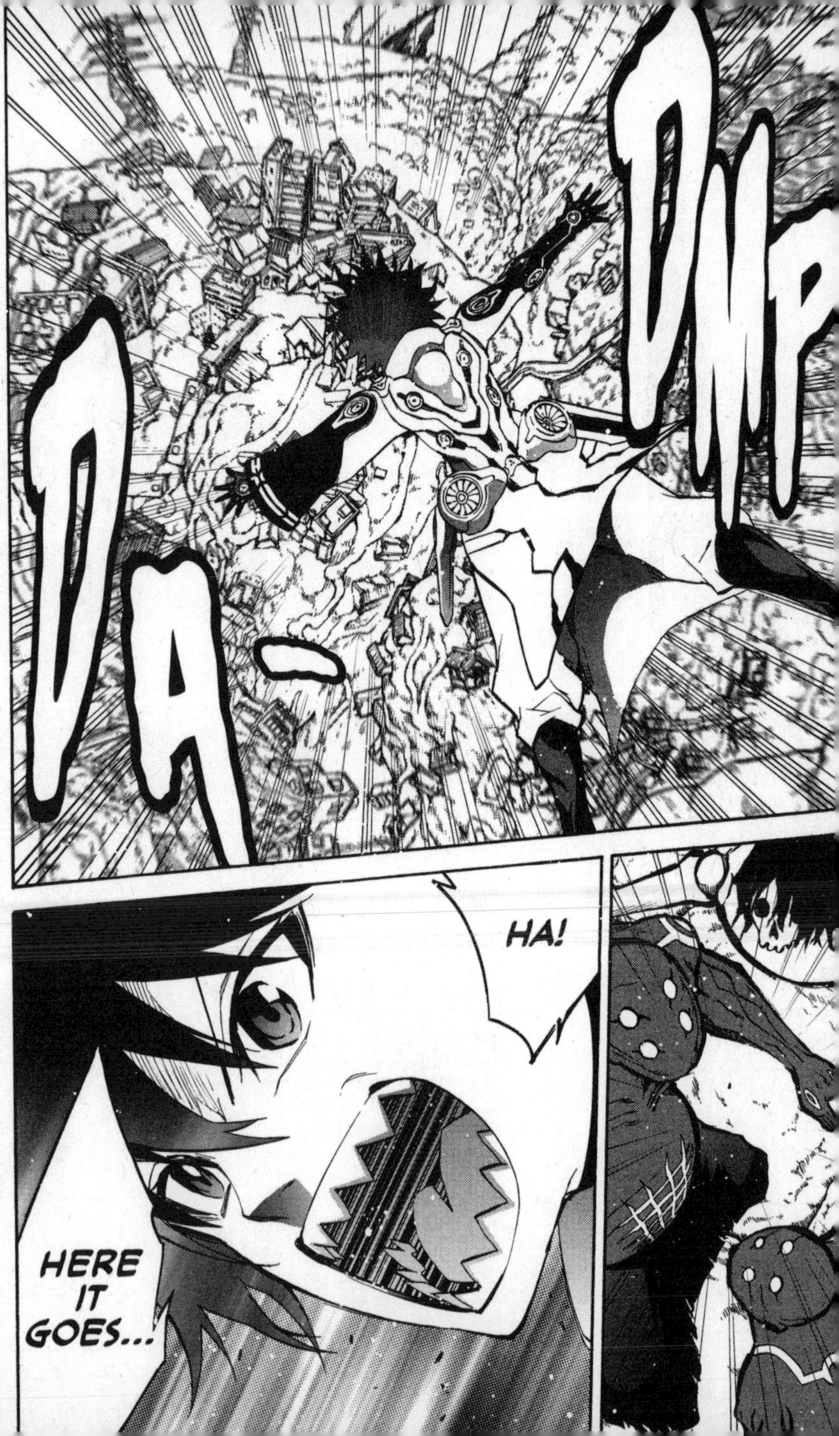
DA-
DUMP
HA!
HERE IT GOES...

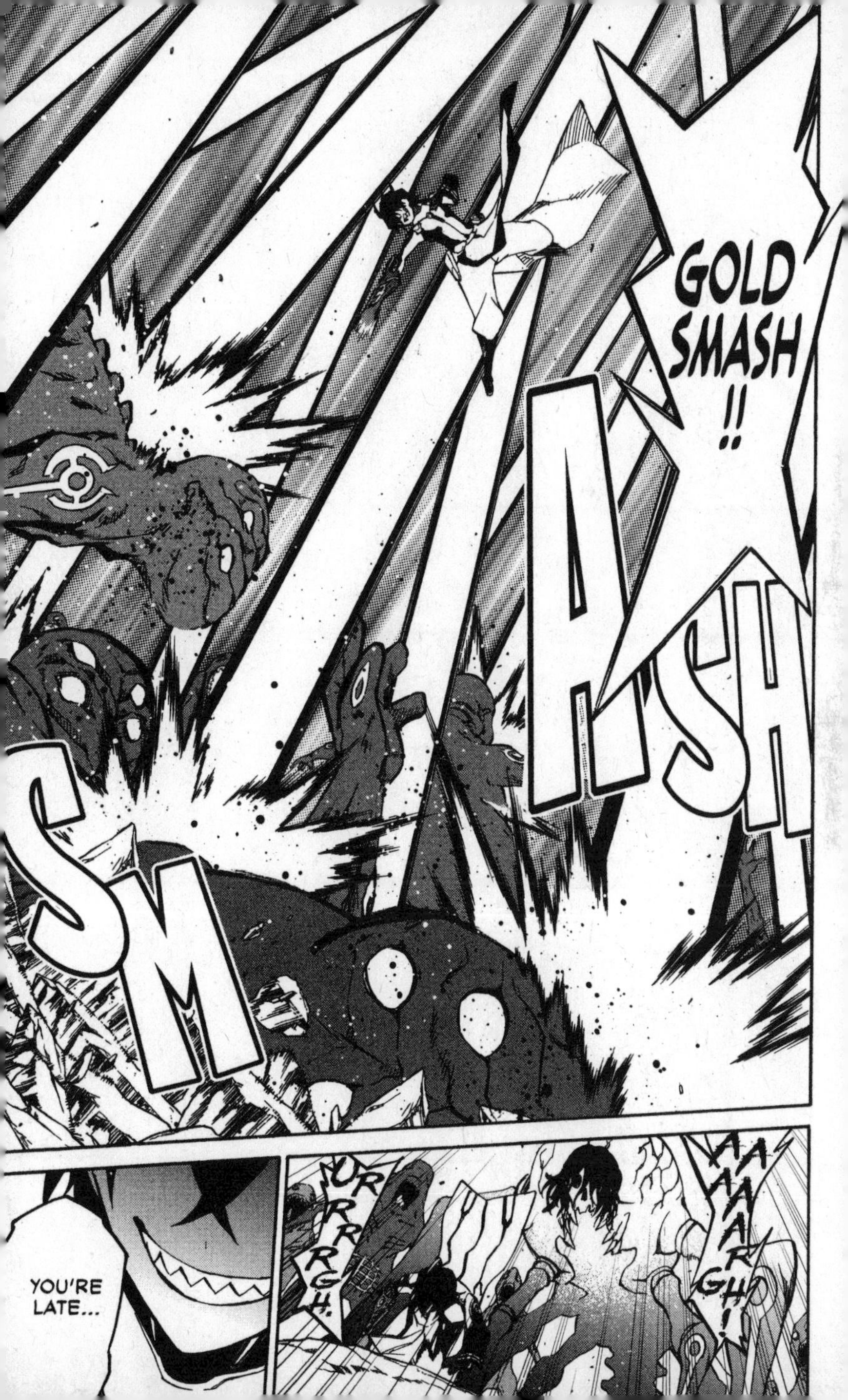
GOLD SMASH!!
SMASH
AAAAARGH!
URRRRGH!
YOU'RE LATE...

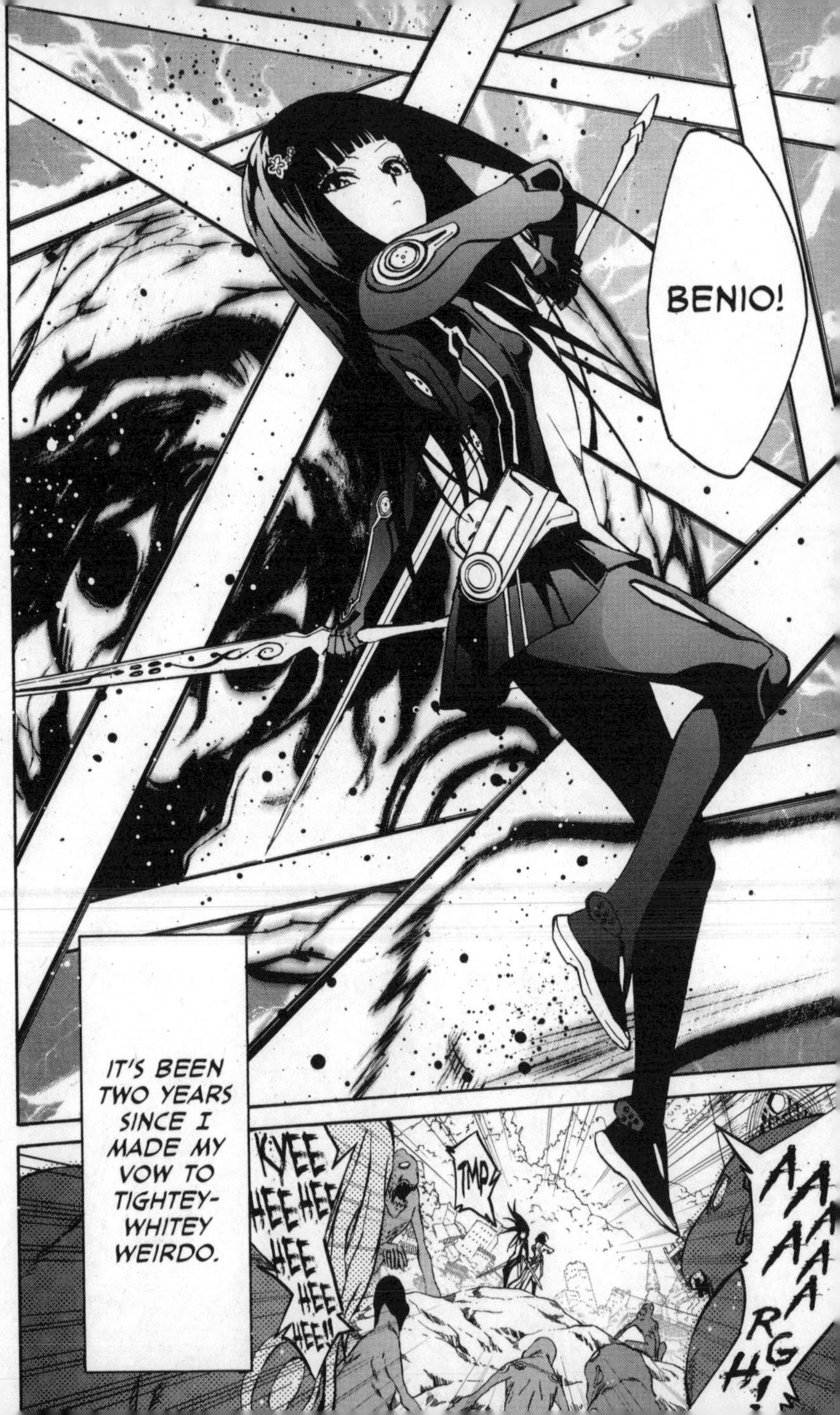
BENIO!
AAAAAARGH!
TMP
K-YEE HEE HEE HEE HEE HEE!!
IT'S BEEN TWO YEARS SINCE I MADE MY VOW TO TIGHTEY-WHITEY WEIRDO.

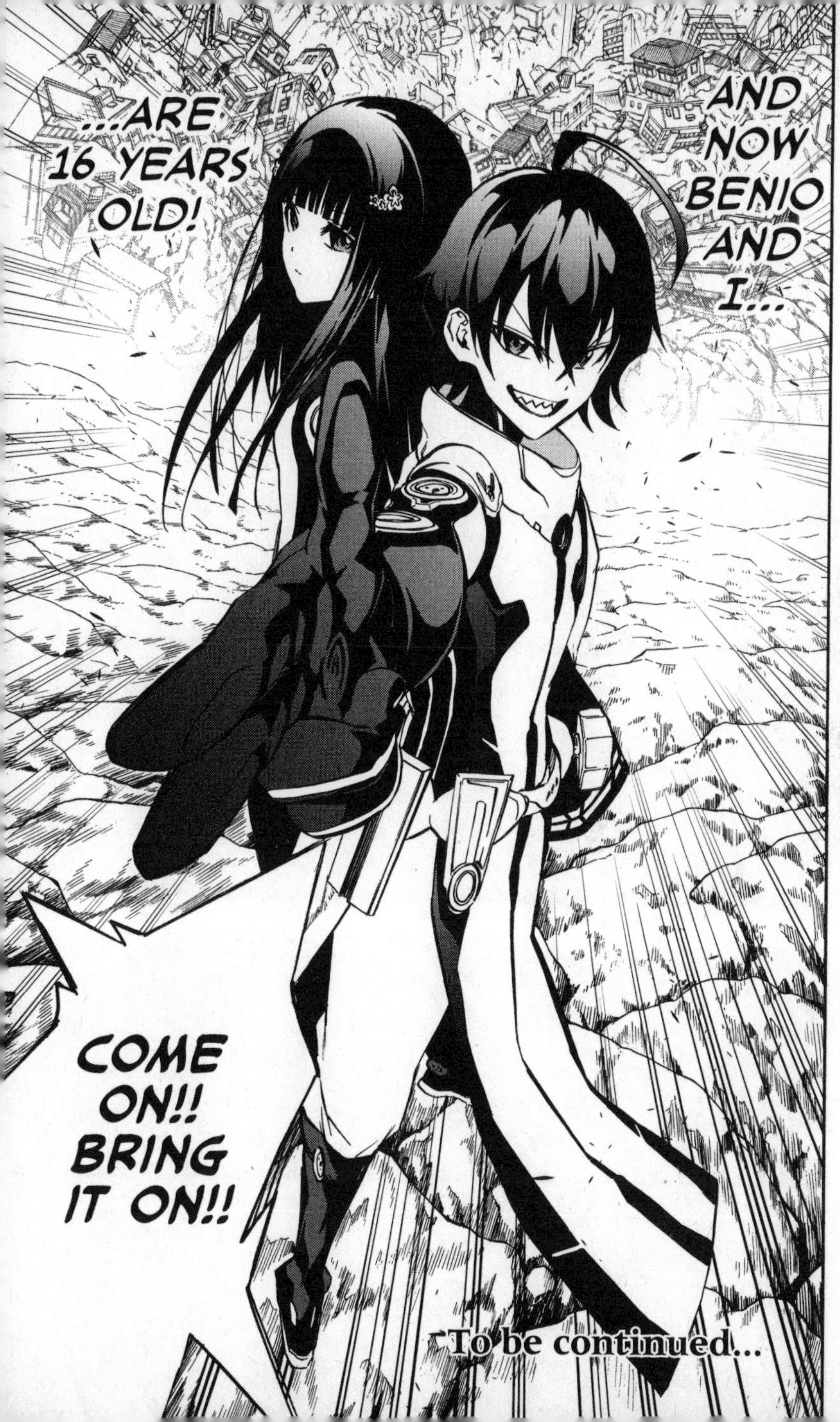
AND NOW BENIO AND I...
...ARE 16 YEARS OLD!
COME ON!! BRING IT ON!!
To be continued...

Twin Star Exorcists
ONMYOJI

#17, EN ROUTE TO ARIMA'S ROOM

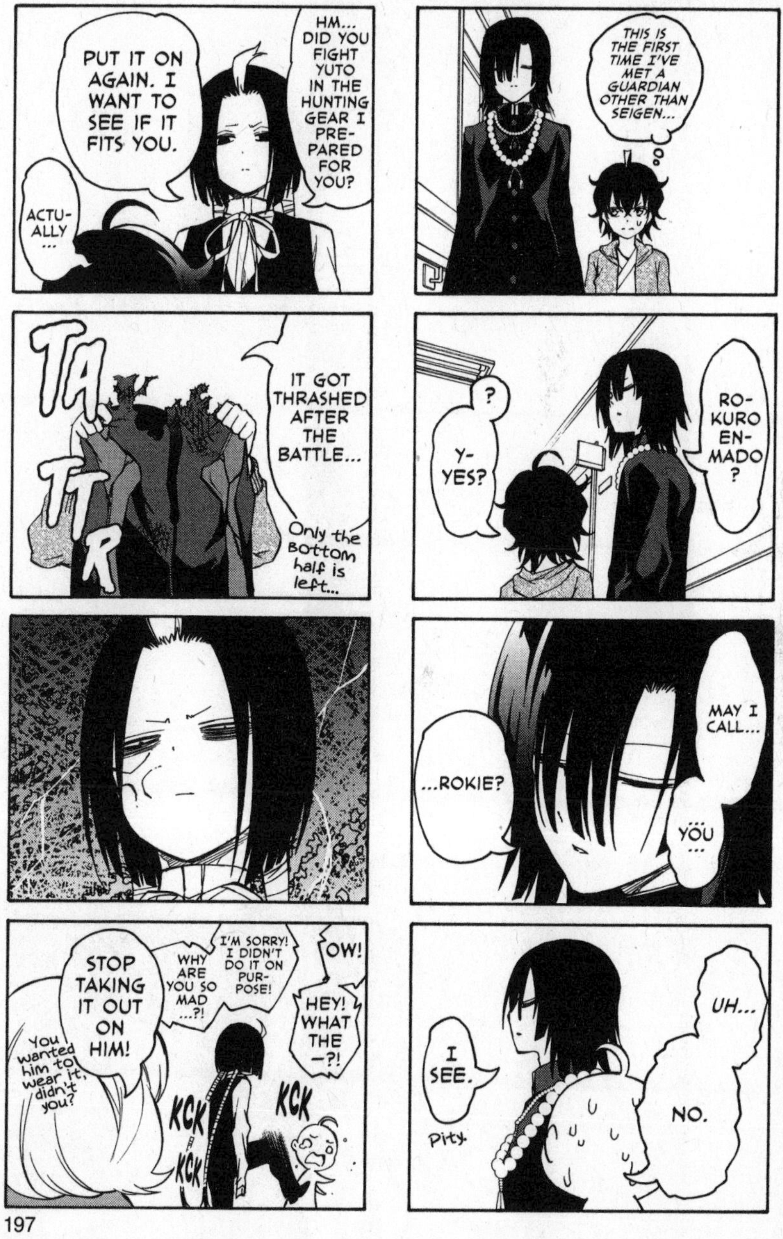
THIS IS THE FIRST TIME I'VE MET A GUARDIAN OTHER THAN SEIGEN...
RO-KURO EN-MADO?
?
Y-YES?
MAY I CALL...
...YOU...
...ROKIE?
UH...
NO.
I SEE.
Pity.
HM... DID YOU FIGHT YUTO IN THE HUNTING GEAR I PRE-PARED FOR YOU?
PUT IT ON AGAIN. I WANT TO SEE IF IT FITS YOU.
ACTU-ALLY...
IT GOT THRASHED AFTER THE BATTLE...
TATTR
Only the bottom half is left...
OW!
HEY! WHAT THE —?!
I'M SORRY! I DIDN'T DO IT ON PUR-POSE!
WHY ARE YOU SO MAD...?!
STOP TAKING IT OUT ON HIM!
You wanted him to wear it, didn't you?
KCK
KCK
KCK

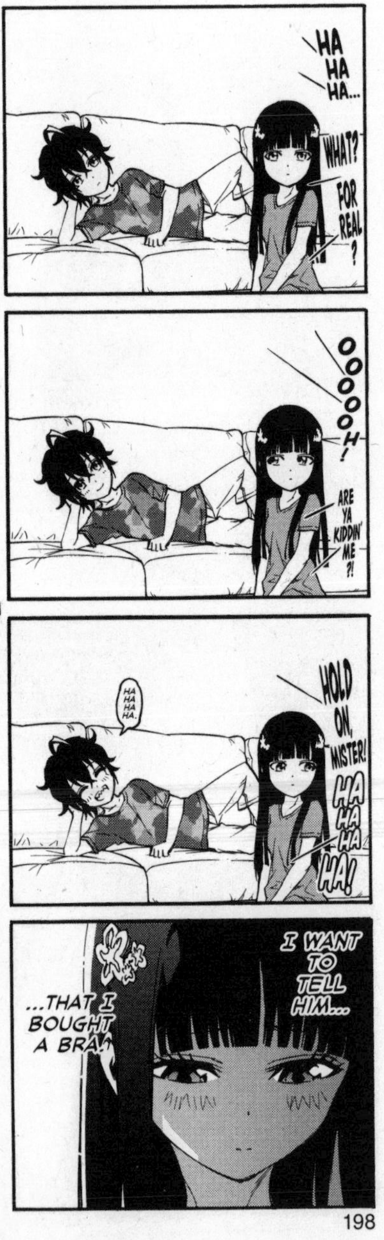
HA HA HA...
WHAT? FOR REAL?
OOOOOH!
ARE YA KIDDIN' ME?!
HOLD ON, MISTER!
HA HA HA HA!
HA HA HA HA.
I WANT TO TELL HIM...
...THAT I BOUGHT A BRA.

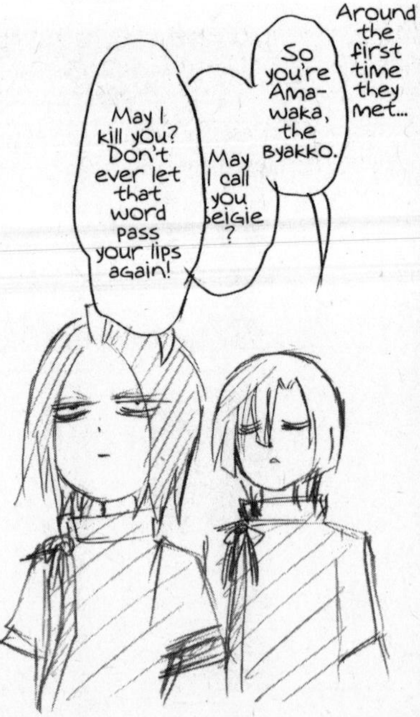
Around the first time they met...
So you're Amawaka, the Byakko.
May I call you Seigie?
May I kill you? Don't ever let that word pass your lips again!

★ Artwork ★

Kota Tokutsu
Tetsuro Kakiuchi
Kosuke Ono
Takumi Kikuta
Hiroshi Tsujiura
Tomohiro Fukuoka
Takahiro Fukumoto
Shu Kageyama
Yoshiaki Sukeno

★ Editor ★
Junichi Tamada

★ Graphic Novel Editor ★
Hiroshi Ikishima

★ Graphic Novel Design ★
Tatsuo Ishino (Freiheit)

In the previous volume, there's a scene in which Benio recalls her childhood and someone says, "The Adashino family is from the Earth family line." That was a total mistake on my part! It was meant to be "Fire," not "Earth"!

[Ed. note: This was already corrected in the English version.]

That might end up having nothing to do with the main story in the end, and I'm sure some of you might be thinking, "What difference does it make?" Nevertheless, I'd like to apologize and correct it. I'll have that part fixed in the reprints. I'm so sorry!

Image of the Prophesied Child (Rokuro's)

Yo Dad! Gimme some cash! I wanna score some ofuda dumplings!

YOSHIAKI SUKENO was born July 23, 1981, in Wakayama, Japan. He graduated from Kyoto Seika University, where he studied manga. In 2006, he won the Tezuka Award for Best Newcomer Shonen Manga Artist. In 2008, he began his previous work, the supernatural comedy *Binbougami ga!*, which was adapted into the anime *Good Luck Girl!* in 2012.

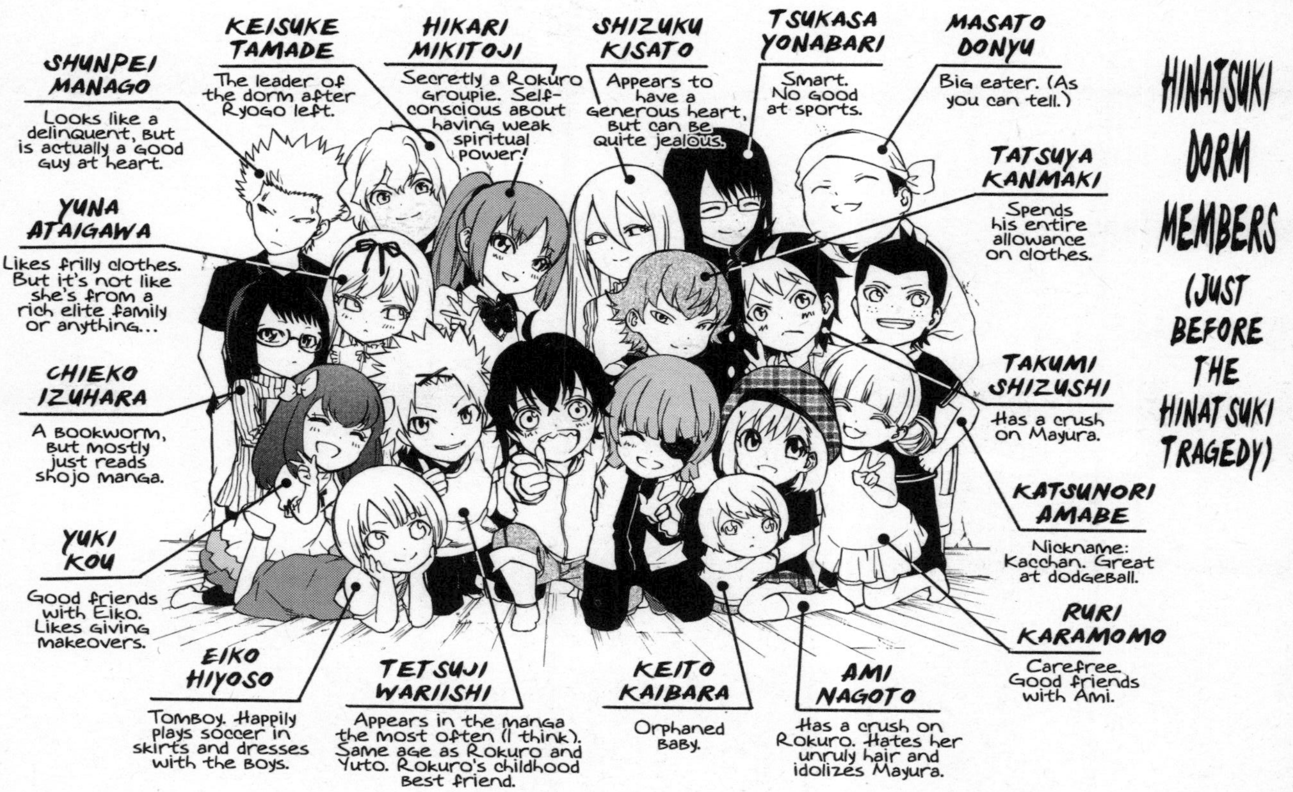
HINATSUKI DORM MEMBERS (JUST BEFORE THE HINATSUKI TRAGEDY)
MASATO DONYU
Big eater. (As you can tell.)
TSUKASA YONABARI
Smart. No good at sports.
SHIZUKU KISATO
Appears to have a generous heart, but can be quite jealous.
HIKARI MIKITOJI
Secretly a Rokuro groupie. Self-conscious about having weak spiritual power!
KEISUKE TAMADE
The leader of the dorm after Ryogo left.
SHUNPEI MANAGO
Looks like a delinquent, but is actually a good guy at heart.
TATSUYA KANMAKI
Spends his entire allowance on clothes.
YUNA ATAIGAWA
Likes frilly clothes. But it's not like she's from a rich elite family or anything...
TAKUMI SHIZUSHI
Has a crush on Mayura.
CHIEKO IZUHARA
A bookworm, but mostly just reads shojo manga.
KATSUNORI AMABE
Nickname: Kacchan. Great at dodgeball.
YUKI KOU
Good friends with Eiko. Likes giving makeovers.
RURI KARAMOMO
Carefree. Good friends with Ami.
AMI NAGOTO
Has a crush on Rokuro. Hates her unruly hair and idolizes Mayura.
KEITO KAIBARA
Orphaned baby.
TETSUJI WARIISHI
Appears in the manga the most often (I think). Same age as Rokuro and Yuto. Rokuro's childhood best friend.
EIKO HIYOSO
Tomboy. Happily plays soccer in skirts and dresses with the boys.

Scrapped cover sketch

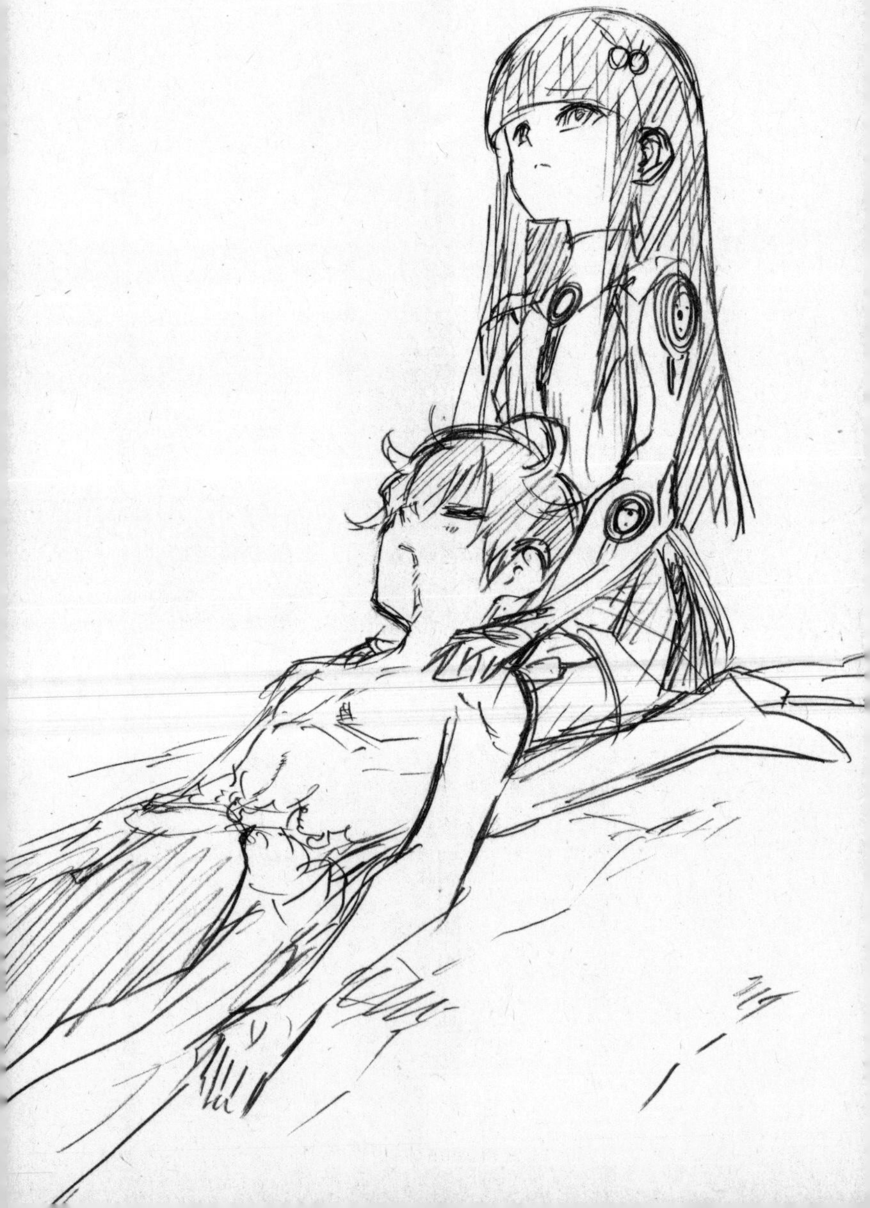

—SHONEN JUMP Manga Edition—

STORY & ART **Yoshiaki Sukeno**

TRANSLATION **Tetsuichiro Miyaki**
ENGLISH ADAPTATION **Bryant Turnage**
TOUCH-UP ART & LETTERING **Stephen Dutro**
DESIGN **Shawn Carrico**
EDITOR **Annette Roman**

SOUSEI NO ONMYOJI © 2013 by Yoshiaki Sukeno
All rights reserved.
First published in Japan in 2013 by SHUEISHA Inc., Tokyo.
English translation rights arranged by SHUEISHA Inc.

The stories, characters and incidents mentioned in this
publication are entirely fictional.

Printed in the U.S.A.

Published by VIZ Media, LLC
P.O. Box 77010
San Francisco, CA 94107

10 9 8 7 6 5 4 3 2 1
First printing, July 2016

www.viz.com

PARENTAL ADVISORY
TWIN STAR EXORCISTS is rated T for Teen
and is recommended for ages 13 and up.
This volume contains fantasy violence.
ratings.viz.com

www.shonenjump.com

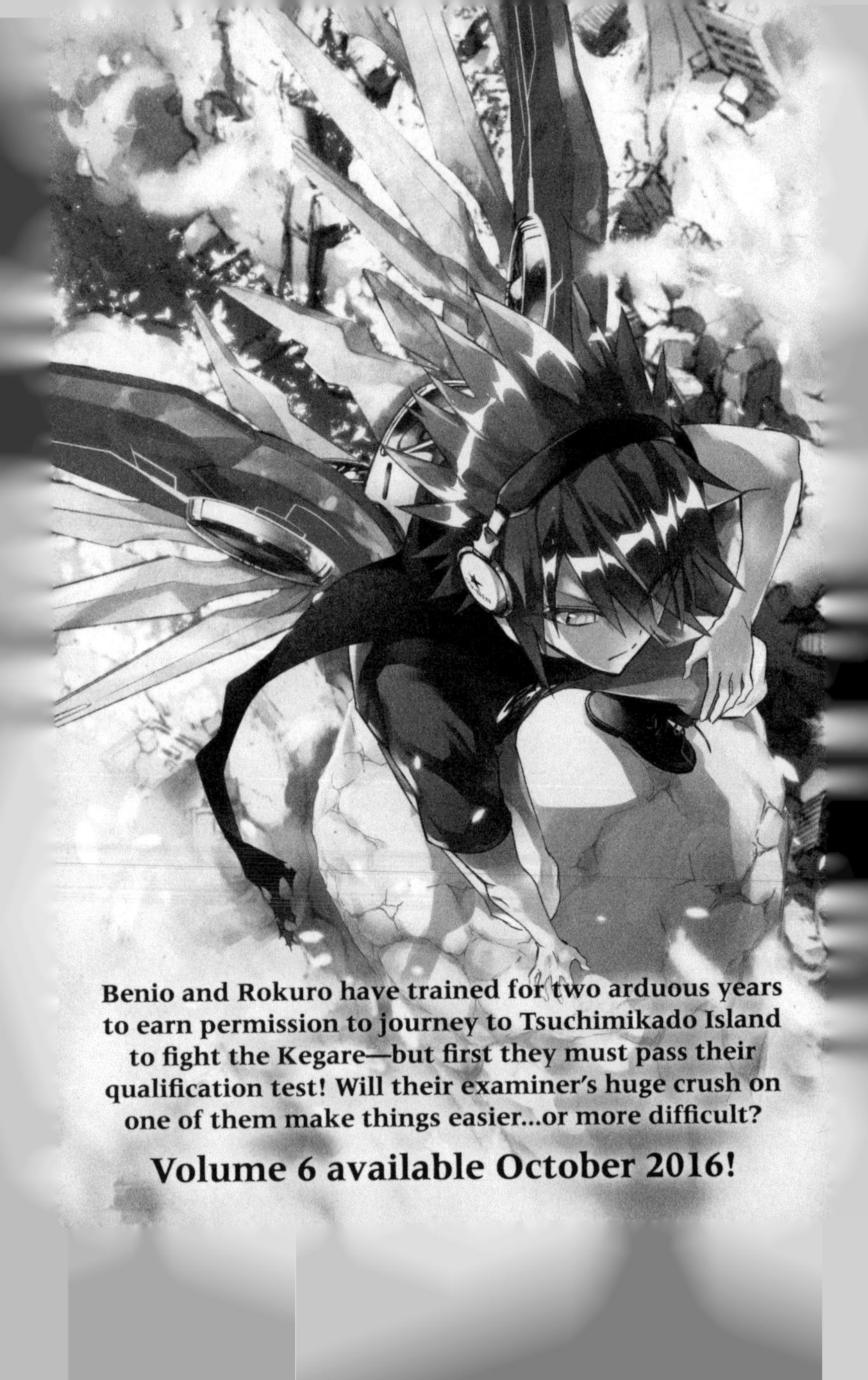

Benio and Rokuro have trained for two arduous years to earn permission to journey to Tsuchimikado Island to fight the Kegare—but first they must pass their qualification test! Will their examiner's huge crush on one of them make things easier...or more difficult?

**Volume 6 available October 2016!**

YOU'RE READING THE

# WRONG WAY!

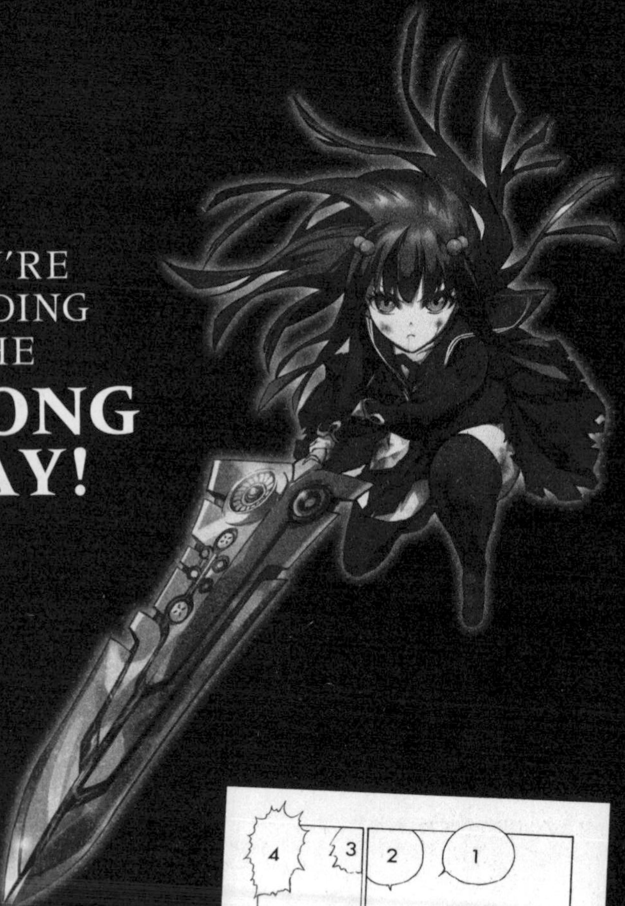

*Twin Star Exorcists* reads from right to left, starting n the upper-right corner. panese is read from right eft, meaning that action, und effects and word- on order are completely rsed from English order.

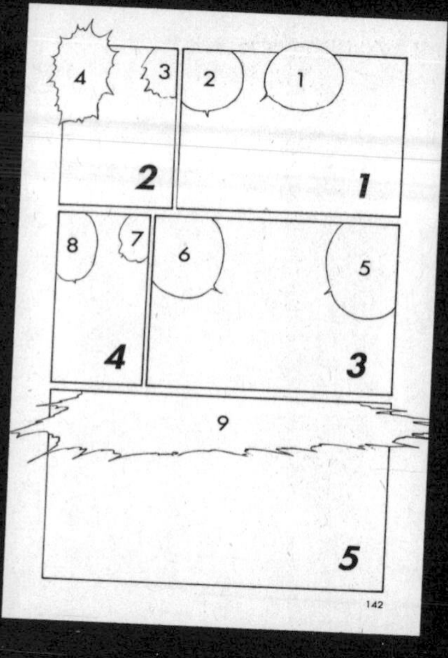

1
2
3
4
1
2
5
6
7
8
3
4
9
5
142